D1637198

GREAT GRAMMA ANN'S

SCRAP BOOK

GREAT GRAMMA
ANN'S
SCRAP BOOK

CONSISTING *of* RECIPES,
REMEDIES, CURES
(among other things)

AS THEY WERE
IN THE MID-1800s

compiled by
LYNDON KELLY

Outskirts Press, Inc.
Denver, Colorado

Outskirts Press, Inc.
http://www.outskirtspress.com

ISBN: 978-1-4327-4750-3
ISBN: 978-1-4327-4920-0

Library of Congress Control Number: 2009934034

Outskirts Press and the "OP" logo are trademarks belonging to Outskirts Press, Inc.

PRINTED IN THE UNITED STATES OF AMERICA

Table of Contents? There is none! You make your own as you read through this book. Many of the items you will have no use for, such as the remedy for Small Pox. And if you do decide to use some of the remedies and cures within these pages, I highly suggest that you consult your physician or druggist first. The recipes? Well, try some – they make for some good old fashioned eating.

Preface

GREAT GRAMMA ANN *and her collection of recipes, remedies and cures (among many other things) as they were in the mid 1800s...*

A dedication supposedly lends a bit of class to a book, especially if you're able to dedicate it to someone who has a bit of class herself. Now I don't know how classy my Great Gramma Ann was, seeing as how she kicked off way back in '69...that's 1869, I mean. I didn't have an opportunity to sample her cures or culinary skills first hand as I wasn't born until the late 20s...1927, that is. But let's just dedicate it to her, as she really did most of the work. I just copied it from her scrap book which was an old history book, "Willson's United States, Illustrated", published in the early 1800s and evidently was no longer being read.

All these items came out of periodicals published in newspapers, monthly magazines or annuals, i.e., almanacs etc. Great Gramma Ann would cut out these articles, cures, recipes, or any other article of interest to her and probably used flour paste (see "Scrap-Book Paste") to paste them in her scrap book. By reading her scrap book, you could almost tell what she would feed you for supper, and if it didn't set too well, the subsequent cure she would use to make you feel better...even to the point of preparing you for your funeral, if necessary.

In her scrap book she used all available space on the page by only gluing the edges of the clippings. This allowed her to tuck like items behind those glued in. She had many loose items saved in this manner. With no rhyme or reason, the clippings on some pages were mixed up with cures and recipes on the same page. Maybe that's in case the recipe didn't set well, she had a cure handy. I bet she knew just where to find what she was looking for.

Great Gramma Ann's' kitchen was unlike yours or mine today. Water was obtained by an old hand pump, an outside well, or by spring water piped into a reservoir with an overflow pipe, usually located in the kitchen for dipping.

In the summer their cellar was their refrigerator as it was always cooler than the house. In the winter time the pantry was used, just by closing the door, or leaving it cracked a little so things wouldn't freeze during those below zero temperatures that Vermont is so famous for.

Work space was usually a large table, and if you were affluent enough you just might have a fancy sideboard that would have a bin that would hold 25 lbs. of flour, plus another bin for corn meal or such, shelves to hold your spices and a drawer or two to hold all your kitchen utensils. Now that was a real uptown country kitchen! But what about the kitchen stove?

That big old cast iron stove would cook many a fine meal. The wood fire would be started early by the men before they left to do the chores so that when Great Gramma Ann got up for the day, and get their breakfast, the stove and oven would be up and ready to go and cook up their breakfast. Breakfast was always a big meal with bacon, sausage, eggs, mush, potatoes, home-made bread toast or biscuits, left-over's etc. The men rose early to get the milking done and the cattle fed, cleaning the barn and just plain working up a good appetite.

Now the same kitchen stove was where they heated all the water used for cleaning up after coming down from the barn, washing the dishes etc., and for those Saturday night once a week baths, whether you needed it or not. In the winter it was used to heat that part of the house, with the stove loaded with wood and banked for the night. In the morning the fire was usually out and the kitchen was a little chilly, but a new fire would soon warm it up. Some had a large fireplace, with a pot hanging from a hook, for cooking soups etc. In the winter it was not unusual to see a pot of baked beans setting on the back of the stove to cook all week, with a big piece of salt pork resting on the top, served Saturday night with homemade brown bread smothered with real homemade butter. What a meal! Makes me hungry just thinking about it.

These stoves did not have a thermostat that you could set or a timer. I watched my grandmother many times, open the oven door of her old black cast iron kitchen stove, put her elbow close to the opening to test the temperature, then either upping the fire or putting the cake or pie in. How she knew it was hot enough or is beyond me. However, it worked! Did she learn this from her mother?

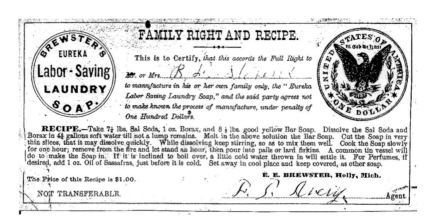

Great Grampa Benjamin Stevens, for a dollar, bought Great Gramma Ann a "Family Right and Recipe" for making soap. Did he think that she needed something else to do besides collecting the eggs, feeding the chickens, cleaning the hen house, cleaning the house, planting the garden and weeding it, canning the produce for winter eating, picking the berries and canning them, sewing and mending cloths for the family, taking care of the children, making butter and cheese, making and putting up sausage and mincemeat? All this plus the difficult and time consuming chore of preparing three hearty meals each day for the hungry clan. And that's probably not all she had to do.

Great Gramma Ann was probably looking for something new and different to feed her family, plus something to cure up her sick ones. Thus, her scrapbook

Great Gramma Ann came in to this world as Ann Hawkins Dailey in 1830, and passed away at the ripe old age of 39 in 1869, soon after the Civil War had ended. She was born in a backwoods area near Bridgewater, Vermont, known as Dailey Hollow, and the name still holds. Her body rests in the Bridgewater Hill Cemetery. She had two children, Walter Stevens (my grandfather) and a daughter, Alma A. Stevens.

Now, this book is different. The only excuse for putting "Great Gramma Ann's Scrapbook" before the public is to share these old recipes, cures and helpful hints of approximately 160 years, or more, ago, for your enjoyment. I hope you enjoy reading her "Scrap Book", and who knows, you might just find a cure for what's ailing you.....Lindy

Ann, Age 4 – 1834
(before photography was invented)

AIR FRESHENER

In the morning, before opening the house to air it, sprinkle a pinch of ground cloves on the stove. When the smoke has thoroughly permeated the house open the doors and windows, and after it has cleared away, close the house, which has a delightful, sweet, fresh spicy odor. This is an excellent way to fumigate a sick room.

AIR PURIFIER

A few drops of oil of lavender poured into a glass of very hot water will purify the air of a room almost instantly from cooking odors, and is especially refreshing in a sick room.

ALBANY CAKE

Two eggs, one and one-half cups white sugar, two-thirds cup of butter, one cup of sweet milk, two and one-half cups of flour, two teaspoonfuls of cream of tartar, one teaspoonful of soda. (Mrs. A. L. F.)

ALMOND CAKE

One pound of flour, one pound of sugar, the whites of one dozen eggs, the weight of six eggs in butter, cream the butter as light as possible, then add the sugar, next the flour stirred in gradually, adding the whites of the eggs beaten very light as needed, and season with one-half teaspoonful of ground mace and one teaspoonful of extract of almond.

ALMOND CAKE

Three cupfuls of flour, which should be sifted twice after measuring; one cupful of white sugar and one of butter, creamed together; the whites of eight eggs; one teaspoonful of cream of tartar and half that quantity of soda; one teaspoonful of almond extract. Beat thoroughly. Blanch a cupful of shelled almonds by throwing them into boiling water to remove the skin, dry, chop fine, and dredge with flour. Stir into your cake; pour the mixture into a buttered pan and bake nearly an hour.

ALMOND CREAM

Take one-half pint thick cream whipped stiff, one-third cup powdered sugar, one cup almonds chopped or pounded fine.

If this cream is whipped with the egg-beater it will remain stiff and will not fall nor turn to liquid. The sugar may be put into the cream before it is whipped or cut in lightly afterwards.

The almonds are blanched by being placed in boiling water till the skins slip off easily. Then throw into cold water and afterwards chop and pound till very fine. After the almonds are added this cream will remain stiff for a day if kept in a cool place.

Spread over a thin loaf of white cake and place another above, as for a Washington pie. Add plain frosting to the top, or whipped cream if preferred.

ALMOND CUSTARD

One pint of milk; half pint of cream; one ounce and a half of sweet almonds; five yolks, and two whites of eggs, and four ounces of white sugar. Boil the milk and cream with a small stick of cinnamon; pour into a basin, and when cool, take out cinnamon; set the milk on a slow fire, adding the sugar, the eggs, well beaten, and the almonds, blanched and chopped fine; stir on the fire till thick, but do not allow it to boil; pour into a jug or bowl, stirring it frequently till cold, and serve in custard glasses.

ALMOND PASTE

Almond paste is one of the best and simplest creams, and is made as follows: Two ounces oil of almonds, one ounce white wax, melt together and add ten drops attar of roses, beat until mixture cools.

AMMONIA

Ammonia is a useful thing in the home. It is an excellent cleansing agent. A little of it added to the water in which handkerchiefs or any clothes that may have become bloodstained are soaked, will take out the stains readily. It is also a good plan to add a half-cupful or so to the boiling suds, or to the water in which clothes are put to soak overnight. Again, it is a good remedy for headache; rub it on the forehead and temples, and inhale it. You will find it gives great relief. Use it for pains in the limbs, by adding hot water and wetting cloths in it for application to the affected parts, keeping them hot and moist. Ammonia is useful, too, for cleaning jewelry; dampen a flannel cloth with it, rub the jewelry, then polish with a dry flannel. Glassware or windows take on a beautiful polish when treated in like manner.

AMMONIA USES

Put a teaspoonful of ammonia in a quart of warm soap-suds, dip a cloth in it and go over your soiled paint and see how rapidly the dirt will disappear; no scrubbing will be necessary. To a pint of hot suds add a teaspoonful of the spirits, dip your forks or spoons (or whatever you have to clean), rub with a soft brush and finish with a chamois skin. For washing windows and mirrors it has no equal. It will remove grease spots from every fabric without injuring the garment. Put on the ammonia nearly clear; lay blotting paper over, and set a hot iron over it for a moment. Also a few drops in water will cleanse and whiten laces and muslins beautifully. A few drops in a bowl of water, if the skin be oily, will remove all uneasiness and disagreeable odors. Added to a hot bath, it entirely absorbs all noxious smells, and nothing is better to remove dandruff from the hair. For cleaning hair and nail brushes it is equally good. For heartburn and dyspepsia, the aromatic spirits of ammonia is especially prepared; ten drops taken in a wine-glass of water will give relief. For house plants, five or six drops to every pint of water once a week will make them flourish. It is also good to clean plant-jars. So be sure to keep a bottle of it in the house, and have a glass stopper as it eats away cork.

ANGEL CAKE

The whites of 8 eggs beaten to a stiff froth, 1 cup of white sugar, 1 teaspoonful of essence of lemon, 2 cups of flour, or flour till your spoon will stand in the middle of the dough without falling, as there is a difference in the many kinds of flour; frost with soft frosting, colored pink by adding a little beet juice.

ANGELS' FOOD CAKE

Find a tumbler which holds exactly two and one-fourth gills, or eighteen tablespoonfuls. Eight tablespoonfuls, liquid measure, is an accurate enough measure of a gill. One and one-half tumblers of white granulated sugar sifted several times before measuring, one tumbler of flour sifted four times before measuring, one teaspoon of cream of tartar sifted into the flour, no soda, whites of eleven eggs well beaten, and one and one-half teaspoonfuls of extract of vanilla. Beat the eggs very thoroughly and add easily the sugar, then, as lightly as possible, the flour, then the extract. The cake must be mixed in a platter (a large flat dish), and not in a bowl. Bake in a new pan, without a particle of grease, about forty minutes, and try with a straw. When done, invert the pan on two or three goblets. Let it cool, then with the assistance of a knife it is easily removed. Be sure to ice it.

ANISE TEA

Make a strong tea of sweet anise roots and drink it for cold, cough or croup. It is excellent.

ANNA CANDY

Two cups sugar, one cup of milk, two squares chocolate, small piece of butter; cook in a spider. When done, beat and flavor.

ANTS, BLACK AND RED

Ground cloves, sprinkled on pantry shelves or in other places infested with black ants, is an excellent remedy. I have tried this for the small red ants as well as black ones, and found it very helpful.

APPLE

Keep an apple in the cake box. It will impart moisture to the cake and keep it from drying.

APPLE AND BREAD PUDDING

Break and rub bread fine; peel and chop good, sweetish apples - sweet apples keep their flavor and take a little longer to cook; butter a pudding dish, then put in a layer of apples an inch deep, then a layer of bread crumbs not quite so thick, then another layer of apples until the dish is full; bread being last. A little butter may be added to each layer of bread, or a tablespoonful of cream sprinkled over each. Bake an hour or till the apples are thoroughly cooked. Serve with sweet sauce or cream.

APPLE BUTTER

Cook slowly until very soft sweet apples in boiled cider, and sift through a colander. Flavor with cinnamon or ginger root. Pack in stone or glass jars while warm.

APPLE BUTTER

Place a large copper or brass kettle, well cleaned, over the fire; fill the kettle with new cider in which fermentation has not begun. When it comes to a simmer, begin to skim off the scum. As it boils down, fill in more cider and skim as before until you have in the quantity you wish to boil. A barrel and a half can be nicely done in what is commonly called a barrel kettle. When the cider is boiled away one-half or more, dip out six or eight gallons into earthen or stone jars. then fill in for each barrel, or thirty-two gallons of unboiled cider, one and a half bushels of quartered apples, nicely washed and drained. If the apples are not all put into the kettle at the same time, replace the apples and the cider taken from the kettle as soon as there is space to receive it. Have a slow fire under the kettle while the apples are dissolving, to prevent running over. When once dissolved it must be constantly stirred until finished. This is done with an implement made as follows: Take a piece of soft wood, two feet long, one and one-fourth inches thick, two inches wide at top end, four at the bottom, which should be oval; now have a hole at the top one and one-fourth inches in diameter, and place a handle in it eight feet long. This will enable the operator to stand away from the fire and yet move it over every part of the bottom of the kettle and thus prevent its burning. No burning wood should touch the kettle, neither should the blaze rise above the boiling mass. One barrel of cider and one and one-half bushels of quartered apples boiled down to about ten gallons, can be kept for one or more years. For winter use, two bushels of quarters may be used, and less boiling is required. Before taking it from the fire, season with spice, cinnamon, and cloves to suit the taste. Remove the kettle from the fire, dip the apple butter, while hot, into well glazed crocks or stone jars, then set away to cool; when cold, cut paper covers for each crock or jar, lay it into the vessel on the apple butter, and the work is done. Cider made from sour apples, and sweet apples boiled in it, makes an excellent dish.

APPLE CHARLOTTE

Take two pounds of apples, pare and core them, slice them into a pan, add one pound of loaf sugar, the juice of three lemons, and the grated rind of one. Let these boil about two hours. Turn it into a mould and serve it with thick custard or cream.

APPLE CHARLOTTE

Pare and chop your apples fine, butter your earthenware baking dish first, and put a layer of bread crumbs in the bottom, then a layer of apples, then another layer of crumbs, sprinkle very thickly with brown sugar, nutmeg and pieces of butter; keep on so until your dish is filled, ending with crumbs and half a teacupful of water sprinkled over all. Bake and eat with rich cream - some add a little mace also.

APPLE-CORN PONE

One cup of finely chopped apples; one quart of Indian meal; scald with a pint of boiling water, add sweet milk to make a stiff batter, then stir in the apples; add a little salt. Bake in a close vessel three hours, or pour into a tin pail, cover tightly and boil in a kettle of water for the same time. Eaten with sweet milk or cream.

APPLE CUSTARD

Peel, quarter and bake rich, tart apples, or stew them slowly in a very little water; fill a pudding dish two-thirds full. When cold, pour over a custard made by stirring into a quart of boiling milk a tablespoonful of flour wet with a little milk, two spoonfuls of white sugar, and two eggs. Flavor with lemon. Bake in a quick oven. To be eaten cold.

APPLE CUSTARD PIE

The nicest pie ever eaten! Peel sour apples and stew until soft, and not much water left in them; then rub them through a cullender; beat three eggs for each pie to be baked, and put in at the rate of one cup of butter and one cup of sugar for three pies; season with nutmeg. One egg for each pie will do very well, but the amount of sugar must be governed somewhat by the acidity of the apples. Bake as pumpkin pies, which they resemble in appearance. Dried apples are very nice by making them a little more juicy. You can frost them, and return them to the oven for a few moments, which will improve their appearance.

APPLE CUSTARD PIE

Grate the apples, then make a custard of one pint of milk, three eggs, pinch of salt, small lump of butter, and a little grated nutmeg to flavor; for two pies.

APPLE DUMPLINGS

Apple dumplings, either baked or boiled, are nicest and healthiest if the crust is made of cream. Pare and core an apple, cover it with crust; put several such dumplings in a baking dish (earthen is much better than tin), add sugar between them and a little water. Eat with the same sauce given for bread pudding. If preferred, use sugar and butter beaten together.

APPLE FAVORITES

Pare and core medium sized apples; make a syrup of sugar and water deep enough to float them; cook until they can be easily pierced with a toothpick; remove, cook parings in syrup or add a little red coloring and when sufficiently boiled down, turn over the apples, put whipped cream and a small piece of jelly on each apple.

APPLES FOR DESSERT

Apples to be eaten with cream or custard; to be eaten cold: Two pounds fine firm apples, pare and core them; slice them in a pan; add one pound of loaf sugar, juice of three lemons, rind of one grated; boil two hours slowly, and turn into a wet mould.

APPLE FRITTERS

Two eggs, half a pint of milk, one teaspoonful of salt, two cups of flour, tart apples. Beat the eggs well, stir in the milk, salt and flour till you have a light batter, then pare nice tart apples, core and cut in pretty thick slices, dip them in the batter, being sure to have them well covered; fry in boiling lard. Serve with white sugar or any kind of sweet preserves.

APPLE FRITTERS

Make a batter, not very stiff, with one quart of milk, three eggs, and flour to bring it to a right consistency. Pare and core a dozen large apples, and chop them to about the size of small peas, and mix them well in the batter. Fry them in lard as you would doughnuts. For trimmings use powdered white sugar.

APPLE INDIAN LOAF

Scald three pints corn meal with one and a half pints of boiling water, and thin immediately with three pints of tepid water. Add four teacupfuls of graham flour (or other flour may do), three or four cupfuls of finely chopped sweet apples, a gill of molasses, and a little salt. Bake six to eight hours in a hot oven. The apples may be omitted. This gives a moist loaf, relished by many people.

APPLE JELLY

Slice thirteen apples very thin without paring them; then cover them with water, boil and strain; to the juice add a pound of sugar and as much lemon juice as your taste may direct. Clarify it with eggs, and boil it to a jelly. It is exceedingly delicate, palatable and beautiful dish, fit to grace any wedding table, the writer having partaken of it on such occasion, the housekeeper forming the centre of attraction at the time.

APPLE JELLY

Apples make an excellent jelly. The process is as follows: They are pared, quartered, and the core completely removed, and put into a pot without water, closely covered, and put into an oven or over the fire. When pretty well stewed, the juice is to be squeezed out through a cloth, to which a little white of an egg is added, and then the sugar. Skim it previous to boiling, then reduce it to a proper consistency, and an excellent jelly will be the product.

APPLE MARMALADE

Take any kind of sour apples, pare and core them, cut them in small pieces, and to every pound of apples put three-quarters of a pound of sugar. Put them in a preserving pan and boil them over a slow fire until they are reduced to a fine pulp. Then put them in jelly jars and keep them in a cool place.

APPLE MERINGUE ————————————————

Pare, core, and stew ten tart apples in a very little water, season as for pie, and put it in a fryit-pie dish into a cool oven. Beat up meanwhile the whites of four eggs, as for icing, piling it on the apples like rocks, or irregularly, avoiding the edge of the dish. Return it to a warm oven and brown macaroni color; slip all out carefully into a dish and serve with cream, or custard flavored.

APPLE MERINGUE ————————————————

Prepare six large tart apples for sauce and while hot put in a piece of butter the size of an egg; add a cup of fine cracker crumbs, the yolks of three eggs well beaten, a cup of sweet milk or cream, a little salt, nutmeg and sugar to taste. When cold bake in a large plate, with an under crust and rim of rich paste. When done take the whites of the eggs. half a teacupful of white sugar, and a few drops of essence of lemon, beat to a stiff froth, pour over and put back into the oven to brown lightly.

APPLE MERINGUE PIE ————————————

Stew and sweeten juicy apples when you have pared and sliced them; mash smooth and season with nutmeg, or stew some lemon peel with them and remove when cold; fill your pans and bake till done; spread over the apples a thick meringue, made by whipping to a stiff froth the whites of three eggs for each pie, sweeten with a tablespoonful of powdered sugar; flavor this with rose or vanilla; beat until it will stand alone and cover the pie three-quarters of an inch thick; set back in oven until the meringue is well set; should it color too darkly sift powdered sugar over it when cool; eat cold. Peaches are even more delicious when used in the same manner.

APPLE MERINGUE PIE

To a quart of nice apple-sauce (strained through a colander) put a cup of white sugar, a tablespoonful of butter, a teaspoonful of cinnamon, a pinch of salt and a little essence of lemon; beat the yolks of four eggs light and add to the apple-sauce. Fill the crusts and bake a light brown - no upper crust - then cover with meringue of the four whites beaten with four tablespoons of powdered sugar. Sift a little powdered sugar over the top and brown lightly.

APPLE MERINGUE PIE

Stew nice cooking apples, mash until smooth and season with nutmeg. Bake without a top crust, and when done, spread over the top a frosting made by beating the whites of three eggs with three tablespoonfuls of powdered sugar. Replace in the oven and slightly brown.

APPLE PIE

Take one egg and half a cracker, or if the plate is large, a little more, to a pie, and about two good sized, sour apples, which may be grated raw, or stewed and strained, with a little nutmeg and salt. Use but very little more sugar than for common custard pies, preparing with milk like them.

APPLE PUDDING

Make a paste with equal quantities of sifted flour and finely-chopped suet, a pinch of salt and a little water. Roll it out thin into a large piece; place this as a lining in a well buttered bowl, cut it off all round, leaving enough to fold over; roll out the trimmings to such size as to cover the top. Peel, core and slice a quantity of good sound apples, put them in the bowl with brown sugar to taste, some chopped lemon peel, two or three cloves and a little grated nutmeg; add a small piece of fresh butter, pack the apples tightly in, put on a cover of paste, turn up the edges and press them down, tie a floured pudding-cloth over, and put the bowl into a saucepan full of boiling water, which should come well over the pudding. Boil from two to three hours, according to size.

APPLE PUDDING

Place some nicely made applesauce, an inch or two thick, in the bottom of the dish in which you wish to serve your pudding. Make some corn starch blanc mange, or boiled pudding, according to the rules given on the package, with or without eggs as fancy dictates; pour this over the applesauce and eat with hot or cold sauce. If eggs are used, the whites of them may be used for frosting, or jelly may be spread over the top or dropped in small bits over it to make it look nicer. It is quickly made and quite nice.

APPLE PUDDING

About apple dumplings. I would like to say we make apple pudding that "grandmother appears to like rather well as the dumplings she used to make, "and 'pater familias', who is authority on this question, fears no consequent danger to the digestion, the only objection being that the crust will allow all of the good cream that you choose to put on it. I use a gallon milk pan similar to figure 3, page 184 of American Agriculturist for May. It should be heated gradually, and a little ashes put on the stove to prevent breaking. Work some good butter in sufficient light dough, yeast bread, no lard or soda, to make a cake nearly as large as the pan, and one inch thick. Set it to where it will rise. Fill the pan half full of apples, pared and cut in eighths. Add water to cook them, and set on the stove. Lay over them the cake, which should be quite light and gashed. Cover tightly. If the apples cook quickly, it will be done in half an hour. Turn quick on a large plate - sugar and cream.

APPLE RICE WATER

Half a pound of rice, boiled in apple water until in pulp, passed through a cullender, and drunk when cold. All kinds of fruit may be done in the same way. Figs and French plums are excellent; also raisins. A little ginger where desired may be added.

APPLE SAGO PUDDING

Take six heaping tablespoonfuls of sago, cover with water and let stand overnight; in the morning add nearly a quart of water, put over the teakettle and let it stand until it is clear; then add a little salt. Prepare six medium-sized apples (pleasant sour are nicest) by paring and digging out the cores; fill the apples with sugar and place in a nappy, pour the sago over them and bake slowly one and one-half hours. Serve with milk and sugar.

APPLE TAPIOCA - FOR INVALIDS

Pare, core and quarter eight apples; take half a spoonful of tapioca; put it to soak and swell all night in the water, put in half a teacupful of white sugar and a little lemon peel; put this into a stew pan and let the tapioca simmer ten minutes, then put in the apples and simmer ten minutes more. When the tapioca is clear, it will form a jelly around the apples.

APPLE TART

Peel and cut two dozen russet apples in slices, which put into your dish, interspersing them with lemon peel free from pith; cut into strips six cloves; add a little grated nutmeg; build the apples up in a dome to the center of your dish, and cover over with half a pound of powdered sugar; then have ready half a pound of puff paste, made in the usual way, with which make a band a quarter of an inch in thickness, laying it around the edge of the dish; roll out the remainder of the paste to the thickness of a quarter of an inch, and large enough to cover the fruit; wet the band of paste upon the dish with a little water, lay the cover gently over, pricking a hole with your knife at the top to let out the air, closing it gently at the edges, which trim neatly with a knife; egg the top over with a paste brush, and place in a moderate oven to bake, which will take about an hour; just before taking from the oven, sift a little sugar over, and let remain till melted, forming a nice glaze over the tart, which may be served either hot or cold.

APPLE TEA FOR THE SICK

Peel, core and quarter one pound of apples; boil for half an hour in a quart of water; strain and add juice of one lemon, and sweeten to taste. Rhubarb, strawberry, or other fruit, may be used in like manner; black currant tea is much recommended in England. Maid-of-all-Work.

APPLE VINEGAR

I use apple parings in making vinegar; put them in a jar and cover until sour, then drain and strain, and put the juice in a jar with a good "plant". In a few days you will have genuine "apple vinegar", ready for use.

ARRESTING FERMENTATION

Dissolve a small quantity of borax (half a teaspoonful) into a tablespoonful of boiling hot water, for every quart of cream or milk. To keep meat from spoiling, sprinkle on a little powdered borax like salt; then wash well in borax water before cooking.

AQUARIUM CEMENT

Use of litharge, fine white dry sand and plaster of Paris, each one gill, pulverized rosin one-third of a gill; make into a paste with boiled linseed oil containing drier. Beat it well and apply in about five hours. This cement has been successfully used in stopping leaks as well as in the construction of tanks.

ARROWROOT PORRIDGE

Mix one ounce of prepared arrowroot with a tablespoonful of cold water, then pour boiling water on it to make the required thickness, stirring it well at the same time. A slice or two of lemon with a little sugar will be found an improvement. To be eaten with crackers or bread.

ASH CAKE

Wet corn meal, salted to taste, with enough cold water to make a soft dough. Let it stand half an hour, or longer. Mould into a cake one or two inches thick, as you prefer. Place it on a clean spot on the hearth and cover with wood ashes. Bake from half to three-quarters of an hour. Wipe before eating. The alkaline properties left by the ashes in the crust render it especially good for dyspeptics with an acid stomach.

ASPARAGUS

Select green asparagus. If you have the privilege of cutting it from the bed, break or cut as close to the ground as it is tender. If you must buy from the markets, try several stalks and see that they are not woody and tough. The white ends are usually so, and are not eatable, being very bitter besides. After breaking off the hardest part, the asparagus may be improved by taking a thin sharp knife and stripping off the outside skin, beginning at the cut end and drawing the skin upward as far as it will go. The bitter lies next to the outside. Now cut the stalks into pieces an inch long, put into a saucepan, sprinkle over a little salt, and just cover with boiling water. Cook twenty minutes; add half a teacupful of sweet cream; rub together a teaspoonful of butter and a teaspoonful of flour and stir in; boil up a minute or two; toast a thin slice of bread a light brown; cut into several pieces; lay into the bottom of a dish, and pour the asparagus over. Or leave the asparagus without cutting up, lay it all one way in the saucepan, and otherwise prepare the same.

ASPARAGUS ON TOAST

Reject all the woody part and cut the stalks of equal length, scraping the white part and letting them lie in cold water an hour. Tie in a bunch and boil for half an hour in well salted water. Toast several slices of bread, dip them in the asparagus liquor and butter them. Drain the asparagus, untie and serve on the toast, peppering it lightly and putting on it a spoonful of butter and salt bits.

ASTHMA - A CURE FOR

Professor Germain See has recently read a paper before the Paris Academy of Medicine, in which he expresses himself very enthusiastically concerning the efficacy of iodide of potassium and iodide of ethyl in the treatment of asthma. He dissolves ten grams of iodide of potassium in two hundred of wine or water, and gives before each meal, twice a day, a dessert-spoonful (eight or nine grams}, so that the patient takes daily sixteen or eighteen grams of the solution, or 1.8 grams of the iodide. After some days, this quantity is gradually doubled. The same doses may be taken in syrup of orange peel. If the patient becomes disgusted with the taste, he may take the iodide in wafers. There is no definite time for the duration of the treatment, but generally at the end of two or three weeks, when the attacks are mitigated or abolished, the dose may be diminished to a gramme and a half per diem. From time to time the treatment may be interrupted for a day, but longer interruption may be followed by a relapse. In one case, a patient, who had been cured for a year, having given up the iodide for four days, was again attacked. Any accompanying cough may be relieved by the addition of a little extract of opium or syrup of poppies; while, when there is not much cough or catarrh, two or three grams of chloral given in the evening assist in diminishing the dyspnea. The general result is that a cure takes place in almost all cases, even when the patients are placed amid atmospheric conditions that are habitually injurious.

ASTOR-HOUSE ROLLS

Put two quarts of sifted flour in a deep bowl, make a hole in the center, put into it a level teaspoonful of salt, a teaspoonful of sugar, two gills of yeast, and one pint of warm milk. Put one tablespoonful of butter dissolved in it: mix a little of the flour with these ingredients to form a thin batter, and set the bowl in a warm place, covered with a thin cloth; as soon as the sponge is light mix in the rest of the flour, and knead the dough for fifteen minutes; let it stand again until it is plump and light, then roll out about an inch thick; cut with a large biscuit-cutter, put a small bit of butter on each round of dough, fold it half over on itself, lay the rolls on a floured baking pan, cover them with a cloth, let them stand until they rise plumply, and then bake them about twenty minutes in a quick oven.

ATTAR OF ROSES

Fill a large glazed earthen jar with rose petals. Pour upon them soft water just sufficient to cover them, and set the jar with its contents in the sun for two or three days, taking it under cover at night. At the end of the third or forth day small particles of yellow oil will be seen floating on the surface of the water, and within a week will have increased to a thin scum. The scum is the attar of roses; take it up with a little cotton tied to the end of a stick and squeeze it into a pail; lay the vessel in a south aspect exposed to the sun, and in fifteen days when opened a fragrant oil may be squeezed away from the whole mass, and but little inferior, if roses are used, to the expensive attar or odor of roses.

AUNT BETSY'S RECIPE FOR COOKING CODFISH

Pick the fish into little bits and soak half an hour in water, then put in a sauce pan and simmer until your meal is ready; if too salty pour off the water and pour in fresh, and when it boils add half a teacupful of cream and a piece of butter the size of an egg, thicken with flour and water, pour into a tureen and stir a beaten egg into it. This is a true Yankee mode, and is good.

BABIES

Babies that are destined to be born on the twenty ninth of February are entitled to a few kindly thoughts. Parents should be more careful about such things.

BABY CURES

How many mothers know that a pillow filled with hops, warmed and placed under baby's head when the little one is cross and restless, will soon bring slumber, sweet and soothing. Make onion poultices in case of colds, and see how quickly the trouble is relieved. If baby has a cankered mouth wash several times a day with a solution of boric acid or alum. These simple remedies are all tried and true.

BAKED APPLE PUDDING

Pare and quarter four large apples; boil them tender with the rind of a lemon, in so little water that when done no water may remain; beat them quite fine in a mortar; add the crumbs of a small roll, quarter pound butter, melted, the yolks of five and whites of three eggs, juice of half a lemon, sugar to your taste; beat well together, and bake in paste.

BAKED BATTER PUDDING WITH FRUIT

Take a half pound of flour; one pint of milk; the yolks of four, and the whites of two eggs, and half teaspoonful of baking powder. Rub the powder till smooth, mixing it well with the flour, and with as much milk as will make it a stiff batter; beat it till quite smooth, then add the remainder of the milk, and the eggs, well beaten. Put some apples, cut as for pie, into a buttered dish; pour the batter over, and bake in a moderately hot oven. Damsons, currents, gooseberries, or rhubarb may be made in the same way.

BAKED BEANS

One quart of small white beans, picked and washed clean. Pour over them two quarts of boiling water and let them stand overnight. In the morning, pour off the water and put the beans into a kettle with three quarts of cold water; and a teaspoonful of soda; boil fifteen minutes, then drain off the water; put them into a dish or kettle to bake; add a cup of maple sugar; a piece of pork as large as desired; cover with hot water and bake four hours. Just before the beans are dished, dip off all the fat that you possibly can with a spoon.

BAKED BEANS

Pick over one quart of beans; pour cold water over them and let them stand three hours; then set them on the stove, and let them boil until the skins begin to crack open; put them in the bean pot with a piece of pork, the rind cut in strips, and a piece of corned beef; add three tablespoonsfull of molasses, and a half teaspoonful of saleratus; cover with hot water and bake three hours in a moderate oven.

BAKED BEANS

Take one quart of beans - the smallest kind, I prefer; put them in warm water to soak during the night; pour off the water in the morning, and add about one pound of salt pork, and a little molasses, or sugar, if preferred. Cover the whole with warm water; set them in the oven and let them bake as long as you choose - three, four, five or six hours. Don't let them bake too dry.

BAKED BEETS

Wash a half dozen beets and bake until quite tender. This will require more time than to boil them. Pare, slice and cover with vinegar to which has been added little melted butter, salt and pepper. Beets cooked in this way have a decidedly different flavor. (Ima)

BAKED CABBAGE

Boil a firm head of cabbage, and when half done drain off the water and pour on more from the boiling tea kettle and slightly salt it. When tender, set aside until thoroughly cold; chop up fine, and add one-half teaspoonful of cream or rich milk, one teaspoonful of butter, pepper, two eggs, well beaten. Mix all well together, and bake until brown in a pudding dish. Serve hot.

BAKED CABBAGE

Baked cabbage is fine. Boil it ten minutes and finish cooking it in a covered baking dish in the oven. Season with salt, pepper and fresh meat fryings.

BAKED CHICKEN

Split the chicken open on the back and flatten them out with a cleaver; lay in a dripping pan with the inside of the chicken next to the pan; bake one hour and baste occasionally; when done make a gravy with the giblets and a little butter and browned flour.

BAKED CODFISH

Pick up the fish and freshen a little as for cooking, then into a dish put a layer of cracker crumbs, then one of fish, over each layer sprinkle pepper and butter, continue until you have two layers of fish and three of crackers; lastly, beat two eggs with milk enough to cover the whole, bake about three-quarters of an hour.

BAKED CORN

Take six ears of field corn, or twelve ears of sugar corn. Cut the grain partly off, and scrape the rest; add one tablespoonful of butter, a tablespoonful of sugar, and a tablespoonful of salt. Rub these well together, and add a pint of new milk. Bake in a dish that you can set on the table without disturbing it.

BAKED CREAM POTATOES

Peel and slice raw potatoes quite thin, and let remain in cold water an half hour or longer. Then put into a pudding dish, season with pepper, salt and butter, and add a pint of sweet milk to a quart of sliced potatoes. Put into the oven and bake an hour.

BAKED FISH

A fish weighing four to six pounds is a good size to bake. It should be cooked whole to look well. Make a dressing of bread crumbs, butter, salt and parsley; mix this with one egg. Fill the body and lay in a large pan; put across it some strips of salt pork to flavor it. Bake it half an hour. Baste frequently.

BAKED FISH

To make a delightful supper dish, take a salmon, trout or whitefish, steam till done, then remove all the bones and superfluous skin, and season with pepper and salt. Make a sauce of one quart of milk, one small cup of flour, a sprig of thyme minced fine, a slice of onion, if desired, and two eggs. Wet the flour and stir it in the boiling milk, add the seasoning, and let it again come to a boil; then remove from the fire and add the two eggs, thoroughly beaten. Have ready a well buttered dish, in which put a layer of the fish, then of the sauce, and so on until the dish is full, having a layer of sauce last. Cover with grated bread and a little grated cheese. Bake half an hour and serve hot. If trout to be used, some butter will be required.

BAKED GOOSE

A goose eight months old, and fat, is best for baking. Let it hang a day or two, then remove every fine feather, singe it well, and take away everything not edible, including all the loose fat. Stew the giblets all by themselves, and make a pie of them. Goose requires high flavored stuffing. Chop two large onions fine, add to them a tablespoonful of pulverized sage, a teaspoonful of black pepper and two of salt. Mix these ingredients with crumbled bread, put in the body of the bird, and sew up closely all the openings. This prevents the steam from getting out and the fat from getting in, and adds to the flavor and tenderness of the meat. Put no water in the pan. A slice of fat pork or some butter may be laid on the breast when it is put in the oven. Baste with its own fat every few minutes. Two hours will bake a goose if the oven is hot. When done it will be brown all over; then remove the bird to a platter, pour all the fat from the pan, add to the brown gravy in the pan the gravy from the giblets, but no flour, and bring to a boil, then serve from a gravy boat. Save the fat for medicinal and other purposes. It is not good for food. Goose should be served with applesauce, onions, and potatoes boiled and peeled, but not mashed.

BAKED INDIAN PUDDING

Boil one quart of milk and pour over a pint of sifted Indian meal; stir it well till the meal is thoroughly wet and scalded. Mix three tablespoonfuls of wheat flour with one pint of milk and beat to a smooth batter, until entirely free from lumps; then pour it in with the Indian batter, and beat well together. When the whole is lukewarm, beat three eggs and three tablespoonfuls of sugar and mix with the batter, together with two tablespoonfuls of molasses; add two teaspoonfuls of salt, two nutmegs, cinnamon or ginger if you prefer; two very large spoonfuls of suet chopped fine, or the same of melted butter; let it bake a few minutes and then add half a pound of raisins and half a pint of milk, which the raisins will soak up. Bake until the pudding is of a rich color, but do not let it whey.

BAKED OMELET

Boil half a pint of cream, or rich milk; beat six eggs thoroughly - they will be nicer if the whites and yolks are beaten separately; have a deep dish hot and buttered; stir the beaten eggs, with a little salt, into the cream; put all quickly into the dish, and bake from five to ten minutes, depending upon the condition of the oven. It should be lightly browned, and taken directly to the table in the dish.

BAKED POTATOES

Wash and pare rather small potatoes and boil ten minutes, then strain off the water. Then melt two tablespoonfuls of butter in a baking pan, put in the potatoes whole and baste and turn them frequently until nicely brown, which will take about twenty minutes in a hot oven. This is a new way, but a great improvement on the old fashion.

BAKED RHUBARB

The man that found out that rhubarb was good to eat was probably a grocer with an over stock of sugar. Still he merits a little gratitude, for rhubarb is good, especially when prepared as follows: Cut the pieces about an inch in length; weigh; allow as much moist sugar as rhubarb, and bake in an earthen dish; put into the dish in layers; add a little water; cover closely and bake.

BAKER'S GINGERBREAD

One cup of good molasses; half a cup of butter; one teaspoonful of ginger; one teaspoonful soda; half as much powdered alum; dissolve the soda and alum separately, in one-third of a cup of boiling water; have enough flour to roll out.

BAKING APPLES

To bake an apple perfectly, can only be done by giving it time, keeping it under heat - steady at that - from four to six hours, depending upon the size and quality of the fruit. It requires this length of time to reduce it to a fine pulp and destroy all rawness. The flavor is changed and improved, making one of the choicest and daintiest dishes. The point in baking is to give all the heat that can be borne without bursting the skin, thus retaining the moisture.

BAKING CAKE

More cake is spoiled in baking than is dreamed of in the philosophy of most women. After a recipe which is known to be good has been carefully followed, some mysterious power seems to interfere to prevent success, whereas it is very likely true that when the cake had risen to the top of the tin, and the crisis had come, the oven door was opened and a piece of cold newspaper was laid over the tin, the cake fell, and the inexperienced cook wondered why the cake was so poor. The oven door should never be opened unless there is really danger of the cake burning, and if a paper is laid over it, be sure to see that it is first heated. When baking a nice cake, a cook should try to arrange her work so to have nothing else of importance on her mind.

BAKING A TURKEY

After it is dressed, salt and pepper it inside; make a force-meat of bread or cracker crumbs, season with summer savory or sweet marjoram. To this force-meat chestnuts may be added. They are put over the fire in a saucepan to burst the skins, then boiled in salt water. Or whole oysters, well seasoned, may be added to the stuffing. Truffles are also used. A couple of eggs added to any stuffing improves it. Boiled mashed and seasoned Irish or sweet potatoes are also used for turkey stuffing. When stuffed, tie it in shape, lard the top, or lay slices of bacon over it, wet the skin, and sprinkle it well with salt, pepper and flour. Have the oven not very hot till the turkey gets heated through, then increase the heat. While the fowl is cooking boil the giblets, neck, liver, gizzard, sweetbread, chop them fine, and when the gravy is made add them to it. To make the gravy, after the turkey is removed from the baking pan, put the pan over the fire, dredge flour into it, and when browned pour in boiling water or stock; skim off every bit of fat, add the giblets, and season with salt and pepper. If chestnuts are used in the stuffing, add them also to the gravy. Oyster stuffing should be used just before the turkey is baked; with other stuffing it is well to let it remain a number of hours before cooking, that its flavor may permeate the bird. Turkey is served with cranberry jelly or with currant or plum jelly.

BAKING POWDER HOME-MADE

No. 1 - 16 ounces of corn starch, 8 ounces of bicarbonate of soda, 5 ounces tartaric acid; mix thoroughly.
No. 2 - 8 ounces of flour, 8 ounces of English bicarbonate of soda, 7 ounces of tartaric acid; mix thoroughly by passing several times through a sieve. These have been tested.

BANANA SKINS

Use banana skins for cleaning tan leather suitcases and other articles. Rub well with the inside of the skin, then wipe with a dry cloth and give some good polishing with the same.

BARLEY AND BREAD SOUP

Take three ounces of barley, one and one-half ounces of butter, one-half ounce of salt, and one-quarter ounce of parsley. Wash and steep the barley for twelve hours, in one-half pint of water, to which a piece of carbonate of soda, the size of a pea, has been added; then pour off the water not absorbed, and add the crumbs of stale bread, three quarts of boiling water, and the salt. Digest these in a salt-glazed covered jar, in the oven, or boil them slowly in a well tinned covered pan, for from four to six hours, adding the chopped parsley, with the butter, thirty minutes before the expiration of the time of boiling.

BARLEY SOUP

Two pounds of shin of beef, quarter of a pound of pearl barley, a large bunch of parsley, four onions, six potatoes, salt and pepper, four quarts of water. Put in all the ingredients, and simmer gently for three hours.

BARLEY TEA

Boil half a teaspoonful of the best pearl barley in a quart of water till smooth; then strain through muslin; add the juice of one lemon, and sweeten to taste.

BATTER TO FRY WITH SALT PORK

This is where anyone has few eggs. Beat together four eggs; three spoonfuls of flour; one-half pint new milk. Add a little salt. After taking your pork out of the spider, pour this mixture in, and fry a light brown.

BAY RUM

The ingredients can be had at any drug store. Take a pint bottle and drop seventy five drops of bay, five drops of oil of orange and five drops of oil of allspice into it, and pour on it nine fluid ounces of 95% alcohol, and shake the bottle well to cut the oils. Fill the bottle with water and put a pinch of cleavers into the bottle to color the liquid, cork it securely and stand for eight days, shaking it frequently. Filter or strain and you will have a most excellent article of bay rum.

BEAN SOUP

Put one quart of beans to soak overnight in lukewarm water. Put over the fire next morning with one gallon cold water and about 2 lbs. salt pork. Boil slowly about three hours, add a little pepper. It is better to shred into it a head of celery. Strain through and serve with slices of lemon to each guest.

BEAN SOUP

Look over a couple of quarts of last year's beans (those which are older must be cooked a long time, four or five hours at least, and then are likely to prove strong and unpalatable); sort out all the poor and dark ones; wash the remainder and put into a kettle; fill the kettle half way up with cold water; stir into a half teaspoon of saleratus; bring to a boil, and let it simmer or boil slowly about an hour; then turn off all this water, add fresh boiling water, and salt enough to season, and boil two hours longer, or until the beans are every one entirely soft. Water should be kept in so there will be about two quarts of the broth when done. Serve hot with a few of the beans, and to each plate of soup add a dusting of pepper and two or three tablespoonfuls of cream from the mornings milk. Crumb in your crackers or bread, and you have a dish that, if not equal to oyster soup, comes very nearly up to it.

BEATEN BISCUIT

Mix two pints of flour, one tablespoonful of lard and one teaspoonful of salt, into a very stiff dough with equal parts of sweet milk and water; beat thirty minutes with an axe kept for the purpose; or, if you use a kneader, run the dough back and forth through it until soft and perfectly smooth. Break off small pieces, and roll into shape and bake twenty minutes.

BEATING EGG WHITES

A pinch of salt added to the whites of eggs while beating makes them froth quicker.

BEDBUGS

For that dreaded pest, the bedbug, I have found nothing better than a solution of one teaspoonful of corrosive sublimate to a pint of wood alcohol. Use a small spray pump such as is used for spraying "dip" on horses and cattle. Get one with a glass reservoir, as the sublimate eats metal. I was careful not to spray directly on the springs, but it can be used on mattress, quilts and around door casings, and not injure paper or paint. After having been troubled four years, and using turpentine and gasoline by the gallon without relief, I gave everything the application suggested twice, thoroughly, and our troubles, so far as bedbugs are concerned, are at an end.

BEDBUGS

Fill up the cracks with plaster of Paris. This is how I got rid of the bedbug pests in a rented house. We found one sleeping room literally swarming with the vermin, in crevices and under loose edges of the wall paper. The wall paper was completely torn off and burned. Insect powder was blown into all cracks. After that every possible resting place for a bug was filled with plaster of Paris mixed with cayenne pepper and water. It was crowded into the cracks, under the base boards, in the floor etc. It will harden directly. We painted the woodwork and repaired the walls. It was a thorough job, for never again did we see a bug.

BEDBUGS

Bedbugs will quickly disappear if alum water is used in their haunts. Hot water is best. Even powdered alum, dusted in, is good.

BEDBUGS

A lady keeping a lodging house in a large city told us how to get rid of bedbugs. By her direction I bought at the druggist ten cents worth of blue ointment, thinned it with kerosene to the consistency of thin paint and applied it with a small brush to their favorite haunts. It proved to be most efficacious. A bug touched with it will die dead within a minute or two (not simply faint away and then recover, as when given a bath with kerosene). It kills all the eggs and tiny ones. And in my experience none of the tribe will ever return to a crack or crevice once treated in this manner even after a year has passed. The mixture, of course, is poisonous and must be kept out of the way of children.

BEE STING

When stung by a bee, always remove at once the sting which was left in the wound, and over the latter squeeze the juice of a red onion, if convenient, or apply a little hartshorn. Baking soda, moistened with a little water, is another excellent remedy.

BEEF AND VEGETABLE SOUP

Two pounds beef, a good size bone, salt and pepper, one turnip, one carrot, one onion, one leek, two sprigs parsley, one sprig celery, two tomatoes; put the beef (free from bones) in your soup pot with almost two quarts of water; put the bones and marrow in a separate vessel with two quarts of water, and when boiled strain and add to the beef; cut the vegetables in small squares, and about half an hour before you want to use the soup put them in with the beef; toast bread and cut it into small squares: put in the soup just before dishing.

BEEF AND VEGETABLE SOUP

Get six to eight pounds of beef - cut from the leg - with the marrow bone left in; wash it in cold water; put in a pot containing six or eight quarts of warm water; set it on the stove to boil; as soon as it comes to a boil place it on the back of the stove, where it will boil slowly; any scum rising to the surface must be taken off; add one tablespoonful of salt; after the beef has boiled two hours and a half add one small onion and turnip, also three carrots, cut fine or chopped, about one cupful barley or rice, well washed; boil half an hour; add two sliced potatoes and a little celery or parsley cut fine;

let it boil half an hour, and the soup is finished. If the water boils away too much add more or less water to your taste.

BEEF COLLOPS

Cut the inside of a sirloin into circular shapes the size and the thickness of a quarter of a dollar, flour and fry them; sprinkle with salt, chopped parsley; make a gravy and serve with tomato sauce.

BEEF PIE

Take cold roast beef or steak, cut it into thin slices, and put a layer into a pie-dish; shake in a little flour, salt, and pepper; cut up a tomato or onion, chopped very fine, then another layer of beef and seasoning, and so on until the dish is filled. If you have any beef gravy put it in; if not, a little beef drippings, and water enough to make sufficient gravy. Have ready one dozen potatoes, well boiled and mashed, half cup of milk or cream, and a little butter and salt; spread it over the pie as a crust, an inch thick; brush it over with egg, and bake about 25 minutes.

BEEF SOUP

Crack the bone of a shin of beef and put it on to boil in three quarts of water. To every pound of meat add one large teaspoonful of salt to every quart of water. Let it boil two hours and skim it well; then add four turnips pared and cut into quarters, four onions pared and sliced, one root celery cut into small pieces. When the vegetables are tender, add a little parsley chopped fine, with salt and pepper to the taste. Serve hot.

BEEF SOUP

3 lbs. beef, 3 onions, 3 quarts water, 1/2 pt. pearl barley. Boil beef slowly about an hour and a half, then add onions, sliced, and pearl barley (previously well washed and soaked ~ half an hour); then boil about an hour longer. More water may be added, sufficient to have two quarts of soup when done. Season to taste with pepper.

BEEF STEAK

To cook beef steak, slit the outside or fat part, say every four inches, cutting through to the lean, which prevents contraction and increases its tenderness. Have a bright fire and gridiron hot before putting it on; turn over to prevent burning. A steak an inch and a half thick will be cooked in from seven to ten minutes. To fry, prepare the same way; put a little butter on pan or griddle, and let it get brown before putting on the meat; cook quickly, and, whether broiled, fried, roasted or baked in the oven, if you want juicy, tender beef, never salt it before it is cooked; otherwise it loses its flavor. (Erin.)

BEEF STEAK

Heat a cast-iron frying-pan, lay on beef steak free from fat; before turning sprinkle on a little salt, and do not scorch it. When done it should be juicy. Put upon a warm plate, then put crumbs or potato in the frying-pan and add hot water, stirring them to absorb the juice of the meat. Do not use too many bread crumbs, and when brown put them in a dish beside the meat, adding pepper and salt if necessary.

BEEF STEAK STEW

Take some finely chopped beef fat or a piece of butter, heat it in the stew-pan, and sprinkle some flour in, brown and add some water. Place into this gravy the steak, which must be a thick cut, and in one piece if possible. Add salt, pepper (whole black), three cloves, a small piece of mace, and a bay leaf if it is handy. Close up tight and let gently simmer for three-quarters of an hour, shaking the stew now and then. After that time put in two tablespoonfuls of mushroom catsup or any dark sauce and allow the stew to simmer another quarter of an hour. It should then be done and served upon a hot dish, the gravy being poured over it. To this stew steamed rice makes an excellent adjunct. It is optional to brown the steak a little in the fat, but it must be done with a closed lid, else some of the best nutrition will be lost. Beefsteak stew is very nourishing with vegetables. Melt the fat and brown slightly in it small cut onions; add flour and warm water, the meat and salt and pepper. Instead of flavoring with spices, put in small cut carrots and turnips; let gently simmer and add two spoonfuls of dark sauce.

BERLIN PANCAKES

One pint flour, quarter cup sugar, one saltspoonful salt, one teaspoonful baking powder, one saltspoonful mace, one egg, about quarter cup milk, one teaspoonful butter. Mix in order given, roll thin, cut in rounds, put together with jam between and fry like doughnuts. Mix the dry ingredients and sift. Beat the egg and add it to the milk with a tablespoonful of butter, melted. Please note the distinction between a tablespoon of melted butter and one of butter melted. This mixture makes a stiff dough which you may roll out thin, using half the dough at a time. Cut, fry, etc., as directed above. Raspberry jam is good for this, though any may be used. Press the edges of the rounds together well after wetting with the fingers dipped in water. If you are making these all alone, better cut and prepare all before beginning to fry, as they need pretty constant attention. Have the lard hot enough to brown a piece of bread while you count sixty. Or hot enough to make the pancake rise immediately on being put in. The kettle can be drawn back a little till the cakes are brown. As soon as taken from the kettle, roll in powdered sugar and spread on brown paper. These are delicious.

BERRY SAUCE

One teaspoonful of corn starch, wet with cold water and pour over it one pint of boiling water, add one cup of sugar, and butter size of a nutmeg; boil ten minutes, then pour over one pint of chopped berries. This sauce is nice with several kinds of puddings.

BERWICK SPONGE CAKE

Three eggs beaten one minute, two cups of sugar beaten five minutes, one cup of flour with one teaspoonful of cream of tartar beaten five minutes; dissolve one-half teaspoonful of soda in one-half cup of cold water just stirred in, then stir in one more cup of flour and it is ready to bake.

BEST ICING

For one large cake use a pound of pulverized sugar, rolled or sifted, and the whites of two eggs. Stir the sugar gradually into the whites; when nearly stiff enough, squeeze in the juice of half a lemon. When all the sugar is in, stir it well; put the icing in the center of the cake, spread it with a broad bladed knife dipped in water. Put the cake on the stove hearth till the icing is firm.

BIRD'S NEST PUDDING

Pare and core apples sufficient to fill a pudding dish. Make a batter of one quart of milk, three eggs, two cups of flour. Pour over the apples, and bake in a quick oven. Eaten with a sauce.

BIRD'S NEST PUDDING

Peel and core with a scoop enough apples to cover the bottom of your dish, and fill up the holes with sugar, sprinkle one ounce of sugar over them, add a little lemon peel and nutmeg, cover the whole with water and bake an hour. If eaten hot let it stand five minutes.

BISCUITS WITHOUT CREAM

Some time ago a lady asked what she could use instead of sour cream in cookery. For biscuits I take two cupfuls of sour milk {buttermilk is best) and add salt and soda as when cream is used. I mix this together, and when of the consistency of good thick batter, add half a cupful of melted drippings. This must be turned on the dough, a few drops at a time, stirring vigorously all the time. More shortening can be added if one desires them richer. Properly mixed they cannot be told from cream biscuits. I used to find it a great deal of trouble to use beef drippings in baking, as the fat would harden so much sooner than lard or butter, but after a few failures I tried this way of adding it, and was much pleased with the result.

BISMARK PUDDING

One cup of molasses, one of boiling water, three of flour, one of fruit, one tablespoonful of suet, or same quantity of butter, two large teaspoons of baking powder; steam three hours. Sauce for the pudding: A large tablespoonful of sugar, butter the size of an egg; stir to a cream; when cold add a well beaten egg and a little boiling water; flavor with nutmeg and wine, if desired.

BLACK PEPPER

Remember that a tablespoonful of black pepper will prevent gray or buff linens from spotting if stirred into the first water in which they are washed. It will also prevent the colors running in washing black or colored cambric or muslins, and the water is not injured by it, but just as soft as before the pepper was put in.

BLACKBERRY CORDIAL

To one quart of blackberry juice add one pound of white sugar, half an ounce of grated nutmeg, and half an ounce of pulverized cinnamon. Tie the spice in a fine muslin bag, boil the whole and skim it. When no more scum rises set it away to get cold, and add one pint of best brandy. Cloves and allspice may be added in the proportion of a quarter of an ounce each.

BLACKBERRY WINE

Measure the berries and bruise them. To every gallon add one quart of water and let the mixture stand for twenty-four hours, stirring occasionally; then strain off the liquid into a cask, adding two pounds of sugar to every gallon of the mixture. Let it stand till the following October, when the wine will be ready for use without further straining or boiling. It may be improved and perhaps kept better by adding a small quantity of pure French brandy.

BLACKBERRY WINE

Mash the berries and pour one quart of boiling water to each gallon; let the mixture stand twenty four hours, stirring occasionally; then strain and measure into a keg, adding two pounds of sugar to each gallon; let it stand till done fermenting, then cork tight or draw it off and bottle.

BLACKBERRY WINE

I think you will like my way of making blackberry wine. Pick the berries over, and if you have no fruit press use a bag of new, unbleached, coarse cotton cloth. A bushel of juicy berries will yield about three gallons of juice. Pour one quart of boiling water over three pounds of granulated sugar and add it to the juice just as soon as it is pressed, for there must be no fermentation before the sugar is added. Put the prepared juice in a large stone jar, cover with cheese cloth, so the flies cannot get in, and set in a cool, dark cellar. Skim daily until all fermentation ceases, then empty into a demijohn well bunged if you have one. I use fruit jars. The wine will be ready for use about Christmas time. Age, however, will improve this as well as other wines. (L., Chinchester, N.H.)

BLACK COLOR RESTORATION

To restore the color of black goods use bruised galls one pound, logwood two pounds, green vitriol half pound, water five quarts. Boil for two hours and strain.

BLACK CURRENT VINEGAR

To four pounds of fruit, very ripe, put three pints of vinegar; let it stand three days; stir occasionally; squeeze and strain the fruit. After boiling ten minutes, to every pint of the juice add one pound of lump sugar. Boil twenty minutes.

BLACK MERINO

Black merino grows rusty when seldom worn, but by carefully observing the following formula it can be made to look like new.

Rip the dress apart; then soak the goods in warm soap-suds two hours; dissolve one ounce of extract of logwood in a bowl of warm water, add sufficient warm water to cover the goods, which are to be taken from the suds without wringing; let the dress stand in the logwood water all night; in the morning rinse in several waters without wringing in the last water; add one pint of sweet milk; iron while damp.

BLACK PUDDING

One cup of chopped suet, two cups of chopped raisins, one cup of molasses, one teaspoonful each of soda and salt, four cups of flour and one cup of sweet milk; mix well together and steam for five hours. Make a sauce.

BLANC MANGE

Mr. Crowell: I will send Mrs.H.J.H. a good recipe for Blanc Mange. Take a handful of Irish moss, (it can be obtained from her grocer) wash it, put in about three pints of milk, let it boil fifteen minutes, stirring all the while to prevent scorching, then pour it through a colander; when it is thoroughly cold it is ready for the table. Serve with cream or sugar. (Della M. C.)

BLANC MANGE

Four tablespoonfuls, or three ounces of corn starch to one quart of milk, two eggs. Dissolve the corn starch in some of the milk. Put into the remainder of the milk four ounces of sugar, a little salt, a piece of lemon rind or cinnamon stick, and beat to near boiling. Then add the mixed corn starch, and boil (stirring briskly) four minutes; take out the rind, and pour into a mould or cup, and keep until cold. When turned out, then pour round it any kind of stewed or preserved fruits, or sauce of milk and sugar.

BLANC MANGE

Try this in preference to all others. To one quart of milk take three eggs and six tablespoonfuls of prepared corn starch, beat the eggs well and stir in the milk, when near boiling add the corn starch, previously dissolved in part of the milk, stir constantly until it boils, then turn into a deep dish, to be eaten cold with sugar and cream, or sweeten while cooking and pour cream over when served. Flavor with lemon or vanilla.

BLEEDING

To stop bleeding from a wound, bind on equal parts of wheat flour and salt.

BLOOD

For the blood. - Drink red clover blossom tea. This was recommended by a noted traveling doctor. - Yours for health, E.P., Pennsylvania.

BLOOD MEDICINE

Two parts sulphur and one part pure cream of tartar, with sufficient syrup to blend them well, is excellent blood medicine for either children or grown people. It is the old-fashioned "spring remedy" of our grandmothers, with the addition of cream of tartar, in itself cooling and purifying to the blood. One taking this should be very careful not to expose one's self to wet and cold, however; be sure to keep the little ones in out of the rain.

BLOOD STAIN REMOVAL

Blood stains may be removed by rubbing with a piece of cotton batting soaked in chloroform.

BLUE STARCH

To blue starch properly the water should be colored before the starch is added to it.

BOILED BREAD PUDDING

To one quart of bread crumbs, soaked in water, add one cup of molasses, one tablespoonful of butter, one cup of fruit, one teaspoonful each of all kinds of spices, one tablespoonful of soda, about one cup of flour. Boil one hour.

BOILED CIDER

Boiled cider is prepared by boiling sweet cider down in the proportion of four gallons into one. Skim it well during boiling, and at the last take special care that it does not scorch. A brass kettle, well cleansed with salt and vinegar, and washed with clear water, is the best thing to boil it in. For tart pies for summer use it is excellent; and for mince pies it is superior to brandy, or any distilled liquor, and in fruitcake it is preferable to brandy. It is a very convenient article in a family.

BOILED CIDER SAUCE

I saw an inquiry some time ago about making boiled cider sauce; and as no one else has answered I will send my recipes. Four gallons of cider boiled to one is strong enough to keep well though some like it stronger, some not as strong. The scum should be removed from the top while boiling, and when done the cider should be strained. Take as many dried sour apples as you can heap on a quart measure. Soak overnight and if the apples are not very sour cook in the same water, but if quite tart use a different one. (The water you drain off will do to make jelly.) When partly cooked add two cups of boiled cider, one cup of molasses, one cup of sugar, and a piece of orange or lemon peel for flavoring. If not juicy enough add more water and cook slowly that the apples may retain their shape.

BOILED CIDER SAUCE

To one peck of sweet apples (measuring them before they are cut) use a little more than a quart of boiled cider. If you make it in large quantities remove the wood from under the kettle after the sauce gets well to boiling, and cook slowly over the coals. You can replenish as necessary from your stove and not burn your sauce.

BOILED COD

When cod has been thoroughly cleaned, washed and dried, then put into a fish boiler in cold water, adding a gill of vinegar, or, better still, the juice of a good lemon. It should first be wrapped in cloth and wind twine around to keep it in shape. Put two teaspoonfuls of salt to every quart of water, having it covered with not more than two inches of water. As soon as the water begins to boil set the kettle to one side and let it simmer till done. If boiled too fast the skin will break and the fish will come to the table in a ragged condition. When the fish can be separated easily from the bone it is done. If it falls from the bone it is over-done, and will be watery and insipid. When done lift the cloth covering the fish with care from the kettle, cut the twine, and turn it upon a napkin, which should be in the platter. Serve with drawn butter, egg or caper sauce, or shrimp-oyster pequante or anchovy sauce; slice some hard boiled eggs and lay over the fish.

BOILED CORN

Select from the lots or patches of early sugar corn destined for table use, ears with the sap or milk running full. Husk and silk the tender ears and boil in a kettle of water slightly salted. Many persons deem the sweetness greatly enhanced by this method of serving, which certainly preserves all the current juices intact.

BOILED EGGS

Boil three minutes by the watch, and you have the central or yellow part soft boiled, while the white is hard, unpalatable, and difficult of digestion. Place the eggs in water "milk warm" or a little warmer. In four or five minutes pour off the water, and immediately pour on boiling water to cover the eggs, and in five minutes they will be cooked. If boiling water is poured on cold eggs in a cold dish, it will be so suddenly cooled that the eggs will not be cooked, but treat them as above directed and you will find them thoroughly cooked, yet soft and palatable.

BOILED FROSTING

Boil about one-half cup sugar and about two tablespoonfuls of water. When quite a thick syrup, add the beaten white of an egg and beat until cool.

BOILED FRUIT PUDDING

One quart crushed wheat, one teaspoonful cinnamon, half teaspoonful cloves, two cups of sugar, two eggs, half pound suet chopped fine, one teaspoonful cream of tartar, half teaspoonful soda, half cup molasses, half pound raisins chopped fine, citron or lemon peel if desired. Boil two hours.

BOILED HADDOCK

Scrape clean and empty the fish, and fasten the tail firmly in the mouth. Tie in a well floured cloth, and lay it in the fish kettle or ordinary saucepan. Cover it with cold water, and let it heat slowly. When it simmers, push the kettle back to prevent boiling, and simmer gently for twenty minutes; or, if the fish is very large, half an hour. Serve with melted butter, parsley, and slices of hard boiled eggs.

BOILED HOMINY

Have a quart of boiling water in a saucepan; take a cupful of hominy and stir it up into the water gradually, put a little salt into it, and add hominy until it is as thick as desired. Let it boil one hour; stir often to prevent its burning.

BOILED ICING

Two and one-fourth cups of sugar, two-thirds of a cup of cold water; boil together until it candies when dropped into cold water; beat lightly the whites if three eggs, then stir into the sugar and beat twenty minutes, add the juice of one lemon.

BOILED INDIAN PUDDING

One quart of sweet milk; one cup of flour; Indian meal to make not a very stiff batter; two teaspoonfuls of cream of tartar, one teaspoonful of saleratus; boil three hours.

BOILED LEG OF LAMB

Time, one hour and a quarter after the water simmers. Select a fine fresh leg of lamb, weighing about five pounds; soak it in warm water for rather more than two hours, then wrap it in a cloth and boil it slowly for an hour and a quarter. When done, dish it up and garnish with a border of carrots, turnips, or cauliflower around it. Wind a cut paper around the shank bone, and serve it with plain parsley, and butter sauce poured over it.

BOILED STARCH

A lump of lard the size of a walnut put in boiled starch keeps it from sticking to the irons.

BOILS - ABSORBING

An early application of ointment of nitrate of mercury is recommended as an effective means of absorbing boils.

BOILS - REMEDY FOR

Peel a boiled egg and remove the tough skin, wet it and apply to the boil. It will draw out the puss and relieve the pain in a few hours.

BOLOGNA SAUSAGE

Ten pounds of beef, two and one-half pounds of pork, chopped fine; 1/4 ounce of cloves, 1/4 ounce of mace, 2½ ounces black pepper, powdered; salt to taste. Mix well together and let stand for twelve hours; stuff and lay in a ham pickle five days, after which thoroughly smoke.

BOOT AND SHOE CLEANER

Milk applied once a week with a soft brush cleanses and softens boots and shoes.

BORAX ON MEAT

If powdered borax is sifted thickly over on meat when it is taken from the salt and hung up, the "skippers" will not bother it.

BOTTLE CLEANING

Bottles may be cleaned by putting fine coals into them and well shaking either with water or not, hot or cold, according to the substance that fouls the bottle.

BOTTLE CLEANING

Take a raw potato, cut it in small pieces, put them into a bottle with a tablespoonful of salt and two tablespoonfuls of water, and shake vigorously, and every stain will be removed from the glass.

BOWEL LOOSENESS

Anxious Mother, do try giving your little daughter a tea made of red raspberry leaves for looseness of the bowels which seems likely to become chronic. It has a pleasant taste and is perfectly harmless. Children like the tea, if a little cream and sugar are added. It will not check the trouble all at once, but gradually, which is the proper way.

BRASS CLEANING

To clean brass, make a mixture of one part common nitric acid and one part sulfuric acid in a stone jar, having also ready a pail of fresh water and a box of sawdust. The articles to be treated are dipped into the acid, then removed into the water, and finally rubbed with sawdust. This immediately changes them to a brilliant color. If the brass has become greasy it is first dipped in a strong solution of potash and soda in warm water; this cuts the grease, so that the acid has the power to act.

BRASS AND COPPER CLEANER

Half a lemon dipped in salt will do the work of oxalic acid in cleaning brass and copper.

BRATTLEBORO PUDDING

1 cup of milk (or water), 1 cup of molasses, 1 teaspoonful of soda, 1 teaspoonful of salt, 1 pound of raisins, flour to make a stiff batter

41

and 1/4 cup of mixed spices. Boil 4 hours. Leave sufficient room in the bag or mold to allow for swelling, as it will double in size when boiled, if allowed room to expand. By adding more fruit (such as currents or citron), it makes a most excellent plum pudding.

BREAKFAST BACON

For 100 pounds of meat use seven pounds of fine salt, two quarts of molasses and four ounces of saltpetre. Pack closely with this mixture between the layers of meat; add sufficient water to cover the meat. Let it remain thus six weeks and then smoke. After smoking sew the pieces up in bags made of cotton cloth, first wrapping a piece of paper around each piece and hang it up in a dry cool place. This is for summer use. For immediate use six pounds of salt, and put the meat in pickle for four weeks, or rub the mixtures of salt, molasses and saltpetre on the fleshy side, and pile the meat up one piece above the other, dividing the mixture into three parts and rubbing it on with three days intervening, letting it remain in the pile until the salt is absorbed, then smoke.

BREAD

To a quart of warm milk or water stir in flour to make a thick batter, and add one teacupful of yeast. Put in a warm place to rise. When risen stir in flour sufficient to knead and make into loaves. Set them by the stove, and bake soon after they begin to rise.

BREAD AND BUTTER

The girl engaged in moulding bread
Shall make some heart flutter,
With hope to get that dairy maid
To make his bread and butter.
She may not play the game croquet,
Or French or German stutter,
If well she knows the curd from whey
And makes good bread and butter.

In meal and cream she's elbow deep,
And cannot stop to putter,
But says if he will sow and reap
She'll make his bread and butter.
The dairy maid, the farmer's wife,
Shall be the toast we utter;
Alone, man leads a crusty life,
Without good bread and butter.

BREAD AND BUTTER PUDDING

Cut slices of thin bread and butter, lay them in a dish with currents or marmalade between them, and covered with a thin custard rather sweet; bake about half an hour. This is excellent cold.

BREAD PUDDING

Take one pint of bread crumbs soaked in one quart of sweet milk; one-half cup of white sugar; two eggs, beaten thoroughly; one cup of raisins if desired; heaping teaspoonful of butter, and salt to suit the taste; stir well together and bake.

BREAD PUDDING

Take stale bakers' bread a good handful to a pint of milk, pour over it boiling water to just cover it; cover with a tin lid tight; when almost cold beat out all the lumps; add a small piece of butter, one pint of milk, one or two eggs, one-quarter pound of sugar, and some grated nutmeg or cinnamon; currants or raisins may be added; bake until lightly browned.

BREAD WITH POTATOES

Potatoes assist fermentation, and render the dough lighter and more tender when we wish to make bread in haste. Peel and boil, or steam, a quart of potatoes, mash them very fine, or, what is better, press them through a colander while they are hot, add half a pint of water and a saltspoonful of salt, stir them into a batter, and then put in a yeast cake previously softened, or a teacupful of lively yeast, and make into a dough with two quarts of sifted flour. Knead it half an hour, put plenty of flour on your board, and knead it until it cleaves from the board with a light tearing sound. Be careful not to let your dough grow very cold while you work it. Divide into loaves, and set to rise in a warm place. Watch the process, and when the loaves are quite light have your oven in good heat and bake three-quarters of an hour. This bread is very nice if well made, i.e., the potatoes made very fine and kept hot, and perhaps the flour warmed also; but it is not so good when stale as that made with a scalded sponge.

BREADED LOBSTER

Lobster meat, egg, bread crumbs, salt and pepper. Cut the meat in large pieces, and season well with salt and pepper; dip them in beaten egg and then in fine bread crumbs or pounded cracker, let them dry, then dip them again; fry them in a boiling fat till a nice brown - serve with tartar sauce, or with vinegar and pepper.

BREAKFAST CAKES

One cup and a half of flour, one cup and a half of Indian meal, one tablespoonful of molasses, one egg. Two teacupfuls of sour milk or buttermilk, in which dissolve one teaspoonful of saleratus. Bake in the oven.

BREAKFAST GRAVY

Dried beef makes a very nice gravy for breakfast cooked in this way: Shave off the beef thin, and put it in the frying pan, with nearly as much water as you wish for gravy; let it boil a few minutes, keeping it covered. Then thicken with a little flour moistened with cream; add butter, pepper and salt to taste.

BREAKFAST INDIAN CAKES

As we are now able to get Indian meal from the new crop, I will tell your readers how they can have excellent cakes for breakfast which

I call mush-cakes. It is this: Take as much meal as may be required, scald it partially; then take some drippings or lard, and with warm water - melt the fat with it, then take the meal and mix it with milk to the proper consistency; add a little salt and a beaten egg, or the egg may be omitted. Bake on the griddle and you will have an excellent cake. (Germantown Telegraph)

BREAKFAST MUFFINS

This recipe will be valued by housekeepers as a dainty substitute for bread at breakfast or tea. Two eggs, well beaten, with a cup of sugar and a lump of butter the size of an egg; to this add one pint of milk, with a teaspoonful of soda, one quart of meal, and two tablespoonfuls of cream of tartar; bake in muffin rings on top of the range, or in gems in a quick oven.

BREATH FRESHENER

Leaves of parsley eaten with vinegar will remove the odor of onions from the breath.

BREWERS YEAST POULTICE

Pour one quart of boiling water over two packages, or two handfuls of dried hops. Cover tightly and set to cool. When almost cool drain off the water and in it soak two cakes of yeast foam. When the yeast is soaked with it mix one teaspoonful of salt and rye flour enough to make a thick batter. Set in a warm place and let it rise two or three hours and use as a poultice. Any flour will do, but rye flour is better for this purpose. My mother had a severe gangrenous carbuncle in the palm of her hand. She had diabetes and a weak heart, so the physicians did not dare operate. They told me to use poultice of brewer's yeast for a few days. I secured yeast from the brewery, but did not dare use as it was full of dead flies and all sorts of dirt. Then my neighbor told me how to prepare this yeast, and I used it and am sure it saved my mother's life. The hand improved so that it was not necessary to amputate it. (S.G. F. ,Bradford, Pa.)

BRICK KINDLING

Have any of the readers who make their own fires tried kindling them with a brick soaked in coal oil? It saves using other kindling. This is the way it is done. Soak pieces of broken building brick for a few days in coal oil; lay a piece under the wood, in each stove, set it on fire with a match, and a good fire is the result; probably coal could be ignited in the same way. Several pieces of brick should be kept covered with oil, in an old vessel, so as to have them ready when needed. Before putting in wood for a new fire take out the brick last used and soak it again. Bricks soaked in oil for three days make good illuminators for lawn or garden parties; they are to be placed on an elevation with an unsoaked brick or some stones under them, so as to prevent danger from fire.

BRIDE'S CAKE

Mr. Editor: - As I have read your paper with much interest, and I am one of your Western subscribers, I would like to contribute my nice recipe for bride's cake, hoping it will be a benefit to some fair maid who is contemplating marriage. Ten eggs, four cups of sugar, two cups of butter, four cups of flour, two cups of corn starch, two cups of milk, two teaspoonfuls of cream of tartar, and one teaspoonful of soda. This makes a large cake. You can frost it yourself and purchase the ornaments at your city bakery, and then you will have as nice a cake as though made at the bakery, and it will cost only about one-half what they will charge. (J.A.W.)

BRIDE'S CAKE

Two cups of sugar, one-half cup of butter, the whites of five eggs beaten to a stiff froth, one cup of cold water; mix well together; then add three cups of flour into which one teaspoonful of soda and two of cream of tartar have been stirred; beat briskly for two minutes; flavor with almond and bake in a quick oven; frost the top.

BRIGHT SILVER

Use the water in which potatoes were boiled for brightening your silver.

BRIGHTENING STEEL KNIVES

To brighten a discolored steel knife, draw it back and forth between two sections of raw potato.

BRINE FOR PRESERVING BUTTER

The "Duchess Farmer" says: "To three gallons of brine strong enough to bear an egg, add a quarter of a pound of nice white sugar and one tablespoonful of saltpetre. Boil the brine, and when it is cold strain carefully. Make your butter into rolls, and wrap each roll separately in a clean white muslin cloth, tying up with a string. Pack a large jar full, weight the butter down, and pour over the brine until all is submerged. This will keep really good butter perfectly sweet and fresh for a whole year. Be careful not to put upon ice butter that you wish to keep for any length of time. In summer, when the heat will not admit of butter being made into rolls, pack closely in small jars and using the same brine allow it to cover the butter to the depth of at least four inches. This excludes the air and answers very nearly as well as the first method suggested."

BRITTLE FINGER-NAIL CURE

To cure brittle finger-nails anoint them at the roots every night with Vaseline, or dip them in warm sweet oil. This will cause them to grow better and prevent splitting.

BROILED BEEF STEAK

Have your round steak cut from one and a half to two inches thick, put it on your meat board, trim all the fat from it, and with a sharp pointed bread knife, or a beef steak hatchet, cut the steak every imaginable way on both sides, to make it tender, then put it on your gridiron and broil over a clear fire, turning it very often. Put a lump of butter, some salt and pepper, into a flat tin or plate, and set your china steak dish in some place to get it warm. When the steak is cooked, put it into the tin plate, double it over, and press on very hard with a knife, to get out all the juice you can, double, turn and press it every way, then with your cooking fork, lay it on your china dish. Put the tin plate with the juice, butter, pepper, and salt, on top of the stove and stir it all the time until it boils up and thickens, then pour it over the steak.

BROILED CHICKEN

Clean and split open the chicken and broil it on the gridiron over a clear fire. Sprinkle with salt and pepper, spread it with the best fresh butter and serve on a hot platter with a few sprigs of watercress around it. Serve lettuce salad with it. Dress the salad with oil, salt, pepper and vinegar.

BRONZE RENOVATED

Bronze may be renovated and recolored by mixing one part of muriatic acid and two parts of water; free the article from all grease and dirt and apply the diluted acid with a clean cloth; when dry polish with sweet oil.

BROOMS

Remember that if brooms are dipped for a minute or two in a kettle of boiling suds once a week they will last much longer. It makes them tough but pliable, and a carpet is not worn half so much by sweeping with a broom cared for in this manner. A good housekeeper will see that her brooms are all thus scalded.

BROOMS

Dip your brooms in hot water occasionally to straighten and stiffen it, and make it last longer.

BROWN BREAD

One quart of graham flour, one teaspoonful corn meal, one-half cup of molasses, one teaspoonful of saleratus; mix quite thin with warm water. Steam in a two quart basin three hours.

BROWN BREAD

Two cups of Indian meal, two cups rye meal, one cup of molasses, one cup of sour milk, one large teaspoonful of soda, a little salt, warm water sufficient to have the dough stir easily with a spoon. Steam three hours, and bake half an hour in a moderate oven.

BROWN BREAD

One cup of Indian meal, one cup of rye meal, one-half cup of molasses, one-half cup of whole raisins, one-half teaspoonful of soda, a little salt; mix very thin with milk or water and steam three hours.

BROWN BREAD

Two cups of Indian meal, one cup of rye meal, one cup of flour, one-half cup of molasses, a little salt, one teaspoonful of soda, mix with sour milk very soft. Bake two hours or steam one hour and bake one hour.

BROWN BREAD

Two quarts Indian meal, new; 1 quart rye meal; 1 cup molasses; 1 cup good yeast: pour enough boiling water upon the Indian meal and molasses to scald it; cool; then add the rye, yeast, and enough water to mix it. Let it stand and rise until it is light; work over and bake immediately.

BROWN BREAD

A pint basin twice heaping full of corn meal, which is ground very coarse, scald with boiling water, using as little water as you can, with much stirring, get the meal all wet; when cool add a pint dish not quite even full of rye meal; one teacup of hop, or hop and potato yeast: one cup and a half of molasses. Mix very soft, with tepid water. Rise about two hours or till it cracks, then bake four or five hours, very slowly at the last.

BROWN BREAD

Among the recipes for brown bread, I find none which suits me any better than mine. I do not think sweetening improves the bread enough to pay for the molasses used. I prefer mixing at night. For two loaves, I take five pints of Indian meal, nearly the same of rye, full two-thirds of a cup of yeast (I like Ruby's way of making yeast very much); mix with warm water. In summer I use cool water. In extreme hot weather I took cold water. When I do mix at night, I scald the Indian meal, and use warm water.

BROWN BREAD

One quart of rye, two of Indian meal, sifted together; one pint maple molasses; one quart good buttermilk, not old and bittery; two teaspoonfuls soda; water sufficient to make a batter that can be stirred easily with a spoon. If baked from two to three inches thick, in shallow pans, bake two hours.

BROWN BREAD

Take equal quantities of Indian meal and wheat flour (rye is better), mix it quite soft with sour milk, or buttermilk, add one cup of molasses for two small loaves, and saleratus. It is excellent eaten warm, for dinner; at least, so testifies my family.

BROWN BREAD BREAKFAST CAKES

Mix up brown bread over night as usual, then in the morning instead of putting all into one loaf, put it into the "cast iron roll pan," now sold everywhere. Bake half to three-quarters of an hour, and you have a nice thing for breakfast, sure to be light and wholesome.

BROWN GRAVY

When making brown gravy, after putting the flour in the grease, add all the cold water or milk you will need all at once, stir mixture until it thickens, and see how free from lumps and smooth it will be.

BROWN SPOTS ON FACE AND HANDS

Several have asked the remedy given by March Fourth in the May issue repeated, and here it is: Put one ounce of common Epsom salts into a wide-mouthed bottle and add ten tablespoonfuls of soft water. When dissolved the lotion is ready for use. Wash face and hands in warm soft water, rinse and wipe dry; pour a little of the lotion into the palms of your hands and wet the face with it, letting it dry, then rub gently until the skin has the appearance of being powdered, and dust off with a piece of fine flannel or chamois.

BROWNING FLOUR

Put into an ordinary baking pan a pound of rice flour, spread it out evenly, and set the pan in an oven hot enough to bake bread. When the top is of a brownish yellow mix it with a spoon to brown the whole quantity evenly. When done let it cool and put in wide mouthed bottles till wanted. A small quantity of it is excellent for coloring and thickening many dishes that are usually fortified with caramel and espanole.

BUCKWHEAT CAKES

Are improved for some people by mixing the buckwheat with graham flour. Put about one-third of graham with it. Start the cakes at night with yeast - a small teacup of yeast to one quart of flour - mix with cool, not cold water, and set in a warm corner. Griddle cakes can be made of oatmeal by putting one-third of wheat flour with it. They require more for cooking than buckwheat cakes do, and should be browned thoroughly.

BUCKWHEAT CAKES

Take two quarts of water, blood warm; one pint of brewer's yeast; make a thin batter, let them rise as far as they will; then add three-fourths of a tablespoonful of carbonate of soda, dissolved in a little water; then fry them as quick as you like.

BUFFALO MOTHS

Before laying a carpet, wash the floor thoroughly with water to which a tablespoonful of turpentine has been added; this serves to prevent the depredations of buffalo moths. If your carpet is laid, go around the edge of the room with turpentine, applying by means of a small paint brush. It will not harm the carpet and the odor soon disappears.

BUG POISON

A good bug poison is made of proof spirit, one pint; camphor, two ounces; oil of turpentine, four ounces; corrosive sublimate, one ounce. Mix and apply.

BUNION OINTMENT

An excellent ointment for bunions is made of iodine, twelve grains, lard or spermaceti ointment half an ounce. It should be rubbed on two or three times a day.

BUNION REMEDY

Paint the bunion with a mixture consisting of one part of tincture of aconite root and three parts of tincture of iodine.

BUNS

A pint of warm milk; two eggs; cup of yeast; cup of shortening; flour enough to make a batter. Let this stand until light, then add one pint of sugar; one cup of currents; tablespoonful cinnamon; mould with flour. Let this rise again; then take it in small pieces, roll lightly in the hand, put in shoal baking pans, (sheet iron preferred), and let rise the third time. Touch over the tops with the white of an egg; bake quickly.

BUNS

Break one egg into a cup and fill with sweet milk; mix with half cup of yeast, a half cup of butter, one cup of sugar, enough flour to make a soft dough; flavor with nutmeg. Let rise the second time in pan, bake and when nearly done, glaze with a little molasses and milk.

BUNS

At night take three cups of warm milk, one cup of sugar, one-half of a cup of good yeast. Make batter then let it stand overnight, in the morning it should be very light; then add one cup of sugar, and one cup of butter. Mould it well and let it rise again; when well risen cut in small pieces and roll them in the hand; put them on tins just to touch, let them rise again and rub over the top with the white of an egg and bake a light brown. This quantity will make sixty buns; currents or chopped raisins improve them.

BURN

Do the sisters know that common baking soda mixed with molasses and applied to a burn, will give quick relief?

BURN AND SCALDING CURE

For burns I find lime-water and linseed oil just the thing, also in case of scalding. I severely scalded my hand with boiling water, and after holding the hand over red-hot coals, using scraped raw potatoes, molasses and soda, and other remedies, I resorted to lime-water and oil, as suggested, and my hand was well, without a scar, in four or five days. Keep a bottle at hand, sisters.

BURNED FRUIT OR VEGETABLES

When cooking apples, peaches, or any kind of fruit or vegetables, should they happen to burn on, do not pour them out of the kettle but just set the latter right off into a vessel of cold water for a few minutes, and there will be no scorched taste to the contents, as there will surely be should you turn them out at once.

BURNED VEGETABLES

My folks have found out that if any kind of vegetable boils down on the stove, it helps to lift the kettle out and let it stand in a big basin of water a while. This almost takes out the burned taste and smell.

BURNS

Sisters, keep a bottle of lime-water and linseed-oil, mixed in equal parts, ready for application to a burn. I want to thank you for all your good remedies; my husband says our paper saves him many a doctor's bill.

BURNS

I want to give my remedy for burns. Take a knife having a thin blade and with it spread pure lard or other unsalted grease over the burned surface, cover thickly with flour, wrap with a soft cloth, and you will be surprised to see how quickly the pain will cease. Then remove the flour, put on a little lard or Vaseline, sprinkle with boric acid powder (which may be had at any druggist at ten cents an ounce) and again wrap with a cloth. The burn will give no more trouble and will be quite well almost before you know it.

BURNS

It may not be universally known that there is nothing more soothing for either a burn or a scald than the white of an egg. It is contact with the air which makes a burn so painful, and the egg acts as a varnish and excludes the air completely, and so prevents inflammation.

BURNS

Raw potato, scraped and bound upon a burn, will give quick relief. Apply at once and change often, replacing with freshly scraped potato, when the first becomes dry. The fire will be drawn out and the burn will heal quickly, leaving no scar.

BURNS AND CRUSHED ICE

The value of crushed ice as a dressing for burns and scalds, first pointed out by Sir James Earle, is confirmed by Dr. Richardson. The ice, after being reduced, by crushing or scraping, to as fine a state of division as possible, is mixed with fresh lard into a paste, which is placed in a thin cambric bag and laid upon the burn. This is said to banish all pain until the mixture has so far melted that a fresh dressing is necessary.

BURNS AND SCALDS

The following is one of the best applications in case of burns or scalds, more especially where a large surface is denuded of the cuticle. Take one drachm finely powdered alum, and mix thoroughly with the whites of two eggs, and one teacup of fresh lard; spread on a cloth, and apply to the parts burnt. It gives almost instant relief from pain, and, by excluding the air, prevents inflammatory action. The application should be changed at least once a day.

BURNS - SCARLESS

Weak lime water applied to burns will cure without leaving a scar.

BURNS - SODA FOR

All kinds of burns, including scalds and sunburns, are almost immediately relieved by the application of a solution of soda to the burnt surface. It must be remembered that dry soda will not do unless it is surrounded with a cloth moist enough to dissolve it. This method of sprinkling it on and covering it with a wet cloth is often the very best. But it is sufficient to wash the wound repeatedly with a strong solution. It would be well to keep a bottle of it always on hand, made so strong that more or less of it always settles on the bottom. This is what is called a saturated solution, and really such a solution as this is formed when the dry soda is sprinkled on and covered with a moist cloth.

BUTTER

Stir the cream every day - always churn within a week.   The first and most important thing is to have everything sweet about the milk-room, and the air pure. We wash our dairy utensils, by first using warm water to wash off the milk, and then in another water, as hot as the hand can be borne in, using soap and washing thoroughly. Never wash the churn or tray with soap. Scald all with boiling water and put out-doors in the sun to dry in warm weather.

Strain the milk into the pans half-full. A moveable cupboard, with a screen door and slats, instead of shelves, is an admirable contrivance for dairy use, as it can be put into the coolest place in summer and the warmest in winter, or its place changed according to the temperature, as milk ought to be kept warm enough for the cream to rise in thirty-six hours. It should always be skimmed as soon as it sours, as no cream rises after, and it very soon injures if not skimmed then. If you have neglected to skim any, and it is too old, do not skim it into your cream jar, as it will injure the flavor of the whole. Have a smaller cream jar for immediate use in skimming, and when full empty into a larger one, being careful not to let any splatter up on the sides of the larger jar, for if allowed to remain there it becomes mouldy, and imparts its odor to the whole of the cream. The smaller jar can then be washed after each skimming. Set the large jar into the cellar, summer or winter. Do not cover air-tight, as it causes the cream to be bitter, but lay over a cloth or board to exclude flies or dust.

STIR THE CREAM EVERY DAY

And, if you have neglected to do so, remove a thin skim before stirring, as there is a bitter taste to this skim. I think the neglect of these little things is the greatest cause of so much second class butter in the market. Always churn within a week. Put cold water into the churn in summer, and hot in winter; churn a few minutes and draw off the water just before putting in the cream. In cold weather set it in a warm place awhile before churning, in order to raise the temperature to about 60, which is about half-way between milk-warm and stone cold. When the butter has come draw off the buttermilk, put in cold water and churn a few times and draw off. Having had the tray previously soaked in cold water, now take it out into it and work over and salt. Use a heaping tablespoonful to a pound of butter. Place in the cellar covering with a cloth or board. On the next day work until you have only pure "beads" clear as rain water, but do not work so much as to break the grain, causing it to be greasy. To prevent butter from sticking to the hands wash first in strong suds, rub them in salt, then in cold suds, and last, in clear cold water. When butter is made into lumps it should be constantly be kept in good salt brine.

This is a way to prepare butter tubs for use: Scald with clear water; put three or four quarts of salt in the tub, then fill full with boiling water, putting the cover on tight, shaking once in a while to stir up the salt, and let it set a few days until wanted for use. Burn a little brimstone in the tub after the brine is out. Fill the tub within an inch of the top. Keep strong brine on the top of the butter at all times.

BUTTER AND CHEESE

It takes the same amount of milk to make one pound of butter that it does for three pounds of cheese. Just now butter brings 25 cents a pound to the farmer, while cheese is worth 12 cents.

BUTTER BISCUIT

Mix a cup of melted butter with a pint of milk, a half-cupful of yeast, a half-teaspoonful of salt, two eggs, flour enough to knead. Set in a warm place to rise; roll out and cut; let them rise, and bake in a buttered pan.

BUTTER DRESSING

Four tablespoonfuls of butter, one of flour, one of salt , one of sugar, one teaspoonful of mustard, a dash of cayenne, one cup of milk, half a cup of vinegar, three eggs. Let the butter get hot in a pan, stir in the flour until a smooth paste, without browning, add milk and let come to a boil; beat eggs, salt, mustard, sugar and pepper together and add the vinegar; stir this into the boiling mixture until it thickens as soft custard; take off immediately or it will curdle. Set away to cool; bottle it if you wish and it will keep for two weeks.

BUTTER STORAGE

Butter put in clean pots and well surrounded with charcoal will keep good for several months.

BUTTERMILK BISCUITS

Those who remember the "good old-fashioned" buttermilk biscuits, will find this a trusty recipe. Rub a tablespoonful of butter into a quart of flour, into which a teaspoonful of salt has been sifted. Dissolve an even teaspoonful of soda in a large cup of buttermilk, mix very soft, handle as little as possible, roll out at once, cut into small biscuits, and bake in a quick oven.

BUTTERMILK BLEACH

Buttermilk will bleach clothes. Soak the soiled or discolored pieces for several hours in buttermilk, then wash, blue, and dry in the usual way. After boiling the cloths will be the traditional whiteness.

BUTTERMILK BREAD

Put three or four pints of fresh buttermilk into a saucepan and boil it. Stir it pretty constantly while it is heating, to keep it from separating into whey and curd. Have a quart of flour sifted into a suitable vessel, pour the boiling buttermilk on the flour and scald it thoroughly. Stir until all the flour is mixed, and set to cool. When sufficiently cool, add a teacupful of good yeast, and let it rise over night; in the morning sift and mix into the sponge enough flour to make a stiff dough; knead well, and set to rise for two hours, then divide into loaves and knead lightly. At this time use as little flour as possible. Set to rise again, and bake as soon as light enough. Bake in a steady oven three-quarters of an hour. This is a good sponge for dark or runny flour. The bread will be white and moist. Graham flour, prepared with scalded buttermilk, mixed a little stiffer than where sweet milk or water is used, is very sweet and good. Do not put soda into the milk or sponge. It will be perfectly sweet when it is baked if the yeast is fresh, and if the whole process is carefully attended to in the right time.

CABBAGE

Cabbage is one of the few winter vegetables whose possibilities are only half understood by many housekeepers. There are delicious ways of preparing this sturdy standby. In salad it can be eaten with benefit every day. Try cooking an onion with boiled cabbage; this prevents the strong cabbage odor that some fastidious folks object to. When cabbage seems rather "wilty" in winter, soak it for half an hour in cold water before cooking.

CABBAGE SALAD

One small head of cabbage, one-half bunch of celery, one-quarter cup of vinegar, one tablespoonful of mustard, one egg well beaten, one tablespoonful of sugar, pepper and salt. Take a little of the vinegar to wet the mustard, put the rest over the fire; when boiling, stir in the ingredients and cook until it becomes thick; pour it over the cabbage while hot, and mix well. When cold it is ready for the table. The same sauce, when cold, will do for lettuce.

CABBAGE SALAD

Take one teacupful of sour cream that has no bitter taste, and beat into it two raw eggs; half a teaspoonful of raw mustard, rubbed smooth in cold vinegar; two-thirds of a teaspoonful of salt and a dash of pepper. Put upon the stove or range and let it boil up, stirring as it begins to boil, to prevent the egg from curdling. When thick as custard, take from the fire; add a teacupful of strong vinegar to it, let it cool, and turn it over a dish of finely chopped raw cabbage, and see if you have not a dainty dish to go with the Sunday's dinner of cold meat. Potato salad dressing can be made in the same way. Slice very thinly cold boiled potatoes, sufficient to fill a dish; chop a small raw onion, and scatter through the slices. Then turn the sour cream dressing over the whole.

CALF'S HEAD CHEESE

Boil a calf's head in cold water enough to cover it, after you have let it lie in clean, hot water to soak for an hour. Add salt; this will send the scum to the top of the water, which must be taken off as fast as it rises. Let it boil gently until done, or until the meat leaves the bone, when take it up, dividing the meat from the bone. Season with salt, pepper and sweet herbs, and a little grated nutmeg if liked. Place in a deep dish or basin, putting a plate and a gentle weight over the top of it. When cold it will be nice sliced for supper or sandwiches.

CAMPHOR ICE

To make this excellent ointment, melt one drachm of spermaceti with one ounce of almond oil, and add one drachm of powdered camphor; mix well together and let it harden in small cakes.

CAMPHOR-GUM

Camphor-gum will keep rats or mice out of closets and drawers; scatter the bits of camphor about.

CAMPHOR OINTMENT

One tablespoonful of brandy, two tablespoonfuls of beeswax, three tablespoonfuls of sweet oil, one teaspoonful of strong spirits of camphor.

CAMPHORATED OIL

Excellent in cases of pneumonia or rheumatic pains, colds, etc. One cup home made lard, one tablespoon kerosene oil. Two teaspoons sassafras oil, one cake (5c worth) camphor gum cut in small pieces. Dissolve the camphor gum in the lard by setting on the back of the stove till all is melted, then put in the other ingredients and stir well. If this is to be used by grown people I add one tablespoon turpentine and put away in tight jars. (Mrs.J.M.S.,Pa.)

CANCER

Mrs. David Warnock. Roast the common polk root, make a poultice of it, rub sweet oil on the skin around the cancer, apply the poultice, putting on a new one twice a day until the cancer drops out. Then heal by washing with alum water and anointing with sweet oil.

CANCER REMEDY

Now let me give you a remedy for cancer, which I saw tried some years ago with perfect success. Bind a fresh piece of lemon on the cancer, changing it morning, noon and night. In a very few days the cancer will drop out, "root and branch", never to return; at least it did so in the case referred to.

CANDIED FRUITS AND NUTS

For candied fruits and nuts boil one cup of granulated sugar and one cup of boiling water together for half an hour. Then dip the point of a skewer or the tip of a spoon into the syrup, and then into cold water. If the thread formed breaks off brittle the syrup is ready. The syrup must never be stirred, and must boil slowly, not furiously. When done set the saucepan in boiling water, or pour the syrup into a bowl placed in hot water to keep the syrup from candying. Take the prepared fruit or nuts on the point of a large needle or fine skewer, dip them into the syrup and then lay them on a dish which has been lightly buttered or oiled; or string them on a thread, and after dipping in the syrup suspend them by the thread till dry. When oranges are used, divide carefully into eighths and wipe away all moisture. English walnuts are especially nice prepared in this way.

CANDLE GREASE SPOTS

Candle grease yields to a warm iron. Place a piece of blotting or other absorbing paper under the fabric; put a piece of the paper also on the spot, apply a warm iron to the paper, and as soon as a spot of grease appears move the paper and press again until the spot disappears. Lard will remove wagon grease. Rub the spot with lard as if washing it, and when it is well out wash in the ordinary way with soap and water until thoroughly cleansed.

CANE-CHAIR BOTTOMS

The elasticity of cane-chair bottoms can be restored by washing the cane with soap and water until it is well soaked, and then drying thoroughly in the air, after which they will become as tight and firm as new, if none of the canes are broken.

CANE SEAT TIGHTENING

Cane-seated chair bottoms that have sagged may be made as tight as ever by washing them with hot soap suds and leaving them to dry in the open air.

CANKER - CURE FOR

Wash a small stove shovel and place upon it a piece of alum the size of an egg, and place it over red hot coals. Let it boil until all the water evaporates, leaving it a dry mass. Now take the alum from the shovel and pulverize it with a case-knife; then add as much sulphur as there is alum; add to this honey or white sugar dissolved in water to the consistency of honey (about half a teacupful), and stir thoroughly before taking. Take a half a teaspoonful three times a day, before eating, until a cure is affected.

CANKER SORE MOUTH

One tablespoonful of borax in half pint of water, use as a wash.

CANNED FRUIT

Put the prepared fruit in a jar, and cover with boiling syrup sweetened to taste; on three successive mornings drain off the syrup, boil again and pour over the fruit; the last morning let the fruit and syrup come just to the boiling point, but do not boil; then seal immediately. Fruit prepared in this way has been tested by the author and found perfect; strawberries preserve their shape and never ferment.

CANNED MILK

A method of saving milk against a time of scarcity would be useful at this time of the year. This is the way several families have tried and found successful. Save a few quarts at a time as it can be spared and prepare it as follows: Place the milk in a tin pail, and set the pail in a kettle of boiling water; let it remain there until the milk is nearly or fully boiled; have your cans hot; pour in the milk and seal tightly. The boiling kills all germs and sealing keeps fresh ones from entering, consequently the milk keeps for a long time.

CARAMEL CAKE

The following receipt makes an excellent cake: Two eggs, one cup of butter, one cup of sugar, one-half cup of milk, two cups of flour, one teaspoonful of cream tarter, and one-half teaspoonful of soda. The following is used in the filling of the above: Two cups of sugar, two-thirds cup of milk, butter the size of an egg. Boil ten minutes; stir until thick, then flavor. Spread between layers and also on outside, as in jelly cake. Mrs.C.F.J.

CAROLINA WAY OF COOKING RICE

Pick rice over carefully, wash in two or three waters, drain dry, and put it into a pot of boiling water with a very little salt; allow a quart of water to half pint of rice. Boil twenty minutes or more, drain off the water as dry as possible, set it on a hot place with cover off, let it dry thus for fifteen minutes; then turn it into a deep dish, and toss it up with forks in each hand until each kernel seems to stand alone.

CARPET CLEANING

We have before spoken of the value of ox-gall for cleaning carpets and reviving their colors. There is nothing better and it is also very cheap, as a gall bag can be purchased at a city market for fifteen or twenty cents, and for next to nothing of a country butcher. Add a tablespoonful of the gall to a quart of water, or use a little more gall if the carpet is very badly off. Rub the fabric a little piece at a time with a linen cloth wet in the gall water, wash off with another cloth wrung out in fresh water, and finally rub with a dry cloth. In case you can't procure fresh ox-gall, soft soap with fuller's earth in equal parts, beaten up with a little oil of turpentine, will answer. First moisten a small square of the carpet, rub with the cake, allow it to become nearly dry, when rub with a little warm water and a brush or piece of woolen cloth, afterwards rinse in clean water, finally rub dry, and smooth off with a dry brush.

CARROT PIE

Scrape, slice, boil tender, and rub through sieve or colander. Take one tablespoonful of carrot, one egg, and one cup of milk to each pie, and sugar, salt and spice to taste. I prefer ginger and nutmeg. Don't omit a pinch of salt to each pie.

CASSEROLE OF POTATOES

Peel and boil some good mealy potatoes, mash them with a little salt, butter, cream, and the yolk of one egg to every pint of potatoes. Beat them two or three minutes over the fire to dry thoroughly, then place them in a shallow dish, and work into the shape of a raised pie. Leave a hollow in the middle, ornament it with flutings, etc., brush it over with beaten egg, and brown it in a quick oven. Fill the inside with beef, minced and well seasoned, and serve hot.

CASTOR OIL FOR LEATHER

Castor oil is much better to soften and redeem old leather than any other oil known. When boots or shoes are greased with it the oil will not interfere at all with the polishing afterwards.

CATARACT

This remedy for cataract was tried by a dear friend of mine, and helped her very much, she said. Mix one teaspoonful each of salt and baking soda in one pint of rain-water, boil and bottle for use. Put one or two drops in the eye. It can do no harm, I should say, and my friend recommends it heartily.

CATARACT OF THE EYE

The following is the "goose-oil remedy for cataract of the eye," requested by one of the sisters: Procure pure goose-oil and drop it in the eye, one or two drops at a time, once or twice a day. It cannot be other than harmless.

CATARRH

Fill a pint cup half full of vinegar. Heat it until it steams, then inhale it through the nose.

CATARRH

For many household purposes the onion is extremely useful; its healing properties are notorious. There is nothing to surpass it in its good effects in cases of catarrh. Peel and slice it, boil till tender, strain off the liquor, sweeten it with sugar candy, and the result will prove the best cough mixture in the world. It should be taken in desertspoonfuls when the cough is troublesome.

CATARRH - SIMPLE CURE FOR

Many persons in this climate afflicted with catarrh and bronchitis have not the money to pay a physician. Let them try this simple, harmless, home treatment, and, if faithfully followed, it will afford relief or effectual cure: Take a common pitcher, holding two quarts or more, heat it thoroughly and fill three-quarters full with steaming, boiling water; add instantly a teaspoonful of oil of tar; then inhale the steam through the nostrils and exhale through the mouth; put the nose well into the mouth of the picture and take a deep, full inhalation, letting the air pass out through a very small opening of the lips. Continue this ten or twenty minutes at a time two or three times daily. Drink a cupful of hot water after each treatment; also a quarter or half hour before breakfast. Physicians often charge $3 or $5 a visit for treatment not as effectual as the above.

CATFISH SOUP

Take two large or four small white catfish, cut off the heads, and skin and clean them. Cut each in three parts, put them in a pot with a pound of lean bacon, a large onion cut up, a handful of parsley chopped small, some pepper and salt; pour in a sufficient quantity of water and stew them until the fish are quite tender, but not broken; beat the yolks of four fresh eggs, add to them a large spoonful of butter, two of flour and a half a pint of rich milk. Make all of these warm, thicken the soup, take out the bacon, put some of your fish in the tureen, pour in the soup and serve it up.

CATNIP TEA

Catnip tea will produce sleep in adult or infant, and is excellent to quiet the nerves. If it is not convenient to steep the catnip, eat a bit of the herb before retiring. It is much better than opiates and perfectly harmless.

CATSUP

Catsup made by the following recipe, provided the directions are followed exactly, will keep perfectly, and it certainly could not be nicer. Scald, peel and take the cores from one peck of perfectly ripe, sound tomatoes. Mash them up thoroughly as if for stewing. Season with salt to your taste, one tablespoonful of finely pounded black pepper, half a teaspoonful of Cayenne pepper, one tablespoonful each cracked (not pounded) mace, allspice and cloves, three large onions thinly sliced and minced fine. Put it in a porcelain lined kettle and set it on the stove to boil. When the tomatoes are thoroughly done, remove the kettle from the fire, and rub the catsup through a sieve to get out the seeds and pieces of spice. Return it to the kettle when strained and let it boil until it is as thick as cream. Let it get perfectly cold and put it in clean, sweet bottles. Pint bottles are best. Fill the bottles to within half an inch of the cork, pour into each one a teaspoonful of salad oil, cork tight with new, sound corks, pressing the cork in until it refuses to go in further. With a sharp knife cut it off level with the neck of the bottle and seal all over the cork and down for an inch on the neck of the bottle with canning wax put on boiling hot. Lay the bottles away on their sides in a cool, dry, dark place.

CEDAR BOX

A desirable article to add to the regular furnishing of a house is a cedar box, in which to lay all the woolen goods and garments during the summer. You can feel sure that your blankets, furs, etc., are not fretted by moths. Country housekeepers can have theirs made at quite a low cost. A wardrobe lined with cedar, and with a division containing deep drawers of that wood, is of equal efficacy and much greater convenience, but will be a rather costly affair.

CELEBRATED ONION STEW

There are people who despise one of the most valuable vegetables we have, that is, the onion, and let the tomato replace it; but pleasant and stimulating as is the flavor of the tomato, it cannot replace the onion for muscle workers. The unpleasant smell caused by onions is far less powerful when these have been stewed whole, or stewed after having been fried. Take finely chopped beef suet or other fat and warm through; slice in a good many onions right across in rings, let them just change color in the fat, sprinkle over some flour and add warm water. Place into this gravy small pieces of steak, cut thick; add pepper and salt and cover up close to stew for twenty minutes. Place then over the stew as many potatoes as will be required for dinner, pretty well of one size, and close up again allowing the whole to simmer gently till done. Do not stir at all, so that the potatoes remain whole. Add the last ten minutes two spoons of sauce or mushroom catsup, and let simmer for that time. Turn out carefully, placing the potatoes, which will be whole, round the dish. This stew has been very successful.

CELERY SOUP

Two heads of celery, one quart of milk, cup of rice, veal or chicken broth, pepper and salt. Grate or cut fine the celery, and boil it in the milk with the rice very slowly till soft enough to run through a coarse sieve, adding more milk if too thick; then add an equal quantity of veal or chicken broth; pepper and salt to taste. Serve very hot with toast cut dice shape.

CEMENT

If for glass or earthenware, the white of an egg makes a transparent and durable cement; if for iron, the white of an egg and lime mixed makes a valuable cement, as fire and water make no impression upon it. It must be used immediately after mixing as it hardens quickly. Southerner will find it nice to fasten her lamp burners on with.

CEMENT FOR STOVES

When a crack is discovered in a stove, through which the fire or smoke penetrates, the aperture may be effectually and readily closed with a composition consisting of wood ashes and common salt, made into a paste with water. Plaster this over the crack.

CHAMBER TOWEL RENEWAL

When chamber towels get thin in the middle cut them in two, sew the selvages together and hem the sides.

CHAPPED HANDS

For badly chapped hands, use a mixture of glycerin and lemon juice, applying at night after thoroughly washing and rinsing the hands, and while they are wet. The lotion will make the skin smart at first, but one application affords great relief if not a cure; then keep the bottle on your wash stand and use occasionally. I have also found that a great help in keeping the hands smooth in cold weather is to wash them in cornmeal and vinegar.

CHAPPED HANDS

Three ounces white wine vinegar; three ounces lemon juice; one-half pint white brandy. Rub this liquid on the hands frequently, especially after washing with soap.

CHAPPED HANDS

Quarter of an ounce of camphor, the same of sweet oil and wax; place together in a cup to melt until thoroughly mixed. Wash the hands clean and wipe dry; apply before retiring.

CHAPPED LIPS

For those sore lips, rub your finger behind your ear until it is greasy, then rub lightly across the lips. I think I hear some of you laughing at this "old woman's whim," but please try it. Rub the lips as directed several times a day, or whenever you think of it; it will entirely cure them and prevent them cracking in future - at least it proved a cure in my mother's case, as she was always troubled with chapped, bleeding lips before trying this simple remedy.

CHAPPED LIPS - A GOOD LIP SALVE

Useful for chaps etc., is made of equal parts of almond or olive oil, and the best white wax; melt the latter in a clean gallipot, set at the side of the fire, then add the oil.

CHARD

Chard is the bleached leaves, leafsticks, or midribs of certain plants, as the globe artichoke, and white beet; also a variety of white beet; Swiss chard beet; leaf beet. In cooking Swiss chard for greens the wide, white midribs are cut out, and the green leaves served alone, the ribs being cooked separately and served like asparagus, for which they are an appetizing substitute. Then, for a change, a dish of leaves and ribs together are served as greens, but this always seems a waste of good material when either is better alone. The hens greedily eat any that may be left when the table is cleared or the cows and pigs will dispose of it, so that not a leaf need be wasted. All things considered, Swiss chard is one of the most satisfactory plants a gardener can raise.

CHARLOTTE RUSSE

It will cost thirty cents for the charlotte russe. One quart of sweet cream whipped, half a package of gelatin, soak fifteen minutes in cold water; pour off the water; flour the gelatin and put it on the stove in a dish of hot water to dissolve. Beat three eggs until very light: add three-quarters of a pound of sugar, mix well, and put in the gelatin; keep it warm, then stir in the cream.

CHEAP DOUGHNUTS

One cup molasses; one cup sour milk; one teaspoonful saleratus; a little cinnamon or nutmeg; make a little stiffer than you would if you used eggs; fry quick, and they will not soak.

CHEAP FRUIT CAKE

To one quart of sifted flour, add a teacup of sugar; half a cup of butter; two teaspoonfuls of cream tarter; one of soda; rub them all thoroughly together into the flour; stir in cold water sufficient to make a stiff batter; pour it into a small tin pan; bake one hour, in a quick oven the first half hour, then quite slow; spice with any kind to suit the taste and add a teacup of raisins.

CHEAP SMALL BEER

To twelve quarts of cold water, add a pint and a half of strong hop tea, and a pint and a half of molasses. Mix it well together, and bottle it immediately. It will be fit for use the next day, if the weather is warm.

CHEESE SOUFFLE

Melt two tablespoons of butter, add three tablespoons of flour. Then pour on ½ cup of scalded milk. Add ½ teaspoon of salt, a few grains of cayenne, 1/4 cup of grated American cheese. Remove blazer from flame, add the yolks of three eggs well beaten. Cut and fold in the whites of three eggs until stiff. Place blazer over hot water pan and cook until mixture is firm.

CHERRIES PRESERVED

Take fine large cherries, not very ripe; take off the stems, and take out the stones; save whatever juice runs from them; take an equal weight of white sugar; make the syrup of a teacup of water for each pound, set it over the fire until it is dissolved and boiling hot, then put in the juice and cherries, boil them gently until clear throughout; take them from the syrup with a skimmer, and spread them on flat dishes to cool; let the syrup boil until it is rich and quite thick, set it to cool and settle; take the fruit into jars and pots and pour the syrup carefully over; let them remain open till the next day; then cover as directed. Sweet cherries are improved by the addition of a pint of red-currant juice, and half pound of sugar to it, for four or five pounds of cherries.

CHERRY JAM

To every pound of fruit weighed before stoning, allow half a pound of sugar; to every six pounds of fruit allow one pint of red currant juice, and to every pint one pound of sugar. Weigh the fruit before stoning, and allow half the weight of sugar; stone the cherries, and boil them in a preserving-pan until all the juice is dried up; then add the sugar, which should be crushed to powder, and the currant juice, allowing one pint to every six pounds of cherries (original weight), and one pound of sugar to every pint of juice. Boil all together until it jellies, which will be in from twenty minutes to half an hour; skim the jam well, keep it well stirred, and, a few minutes before it is done, crack some of the stones and add the kernels;

these impart a very delicious flavor to the jam.

CHERRY PUDDING

To make cherry pudding, take two eggs (one will answer) and beat till very light; add one teacupful of good buttermilk, not too sour, half a cupful of sweet cream of medium richness, a pinch of salt, a good level teaspoonful of soda, and flour to make a batter about as stiff as can be easily stirred with a spoon. Do not get it too stiff, or the pudding will be hard and dry. Add a couple of handfuls of dried cherries, and stir till the fruit is evenly distributed through the latter; then put into a greased pudding-dish or basin, set into the steamer, and steam about three-fourths of an hour. Have the water boiling before the pudding goes in, and do not let the boiling cease till done. Eat with cream and sugar, maple syrup, or any pudding sauce that is preferred. Twice the above quantity will be required if the family is a large one.

CHERRY PUDDING

One teacup cream, 1 teacup milk, 1 egg, 1 teaspoon soda, 1 teacup fruit and flour enough for thick batter - adding fruit last. Bake in buttered baking dish and serve with sweetened cream.

CHICKEN BROTH

Chicken broth, both delicate and nourishing, is made by cutting in parts the wings, legs and neck of a fowl, and simmering in a quart of water for three hours; then strain the broth and add to it a desertspoonful of farina, blended with a cup of cold cream; season with celery, salt, but no pepper.

CHICKEN CHEESE

Did you, reader, ever eat any? Boil two chickens till tender; take out all the bones and chop the meat fine; season to taste with salt, pepper, and butter; pour in enough of the liquor they are boiled in to make it moist. Mould it in any shape you choose. When cold, turn out and cut in slices. It is an excellent traveling lunch.

CHICKEN CHEESE

Two chickens, boiled tender, chopped not too fine, and seasoned with salt and pepper. Boil 3 or 4 eggs and slice, with which line moulds and pour in the chickens, and add liquor they were boiled in. Slice cold.

CHICKEN CROQUETTES

Boil one chicken with an onion thrown in the water; add some bones and pieces of beef also. Cut the chicken, when cooked, into small dice; mince half a large onion, or one small one and two sprigs of parsley together. Put into a saucepan a piece of butter the size of a small egg; when hot put in the minced onion and parsley, and half a cupful of flour. Stir well until it is well cooked and of a light brown color; then add a cupful and a half of stock, or the stock in the kettle, boiled down until it is quite strong, then freed from fat; the stronger the stock, the better; stir it into a smooth paste, and pepper, salt, not quite half a grated nutmeg, and the juice of a quarter of a lemon. When all is well stirred mix the pieces of chicken. Mold into croquette shape or into the forms of pears. When they are dipped in egg and fine cracker crumbs, fry them in boiling hot lard. If they are pear shaped put a stem of parsley into the small end of each pear.

CHICKEN GELATIN

Slice cold roast chicken and lay in a mould with alternate layers of cold boiled tongue and occasional slices of hard-boiled egg; season with celery salt. Dissolve a half ounce of Cooper's gelatin in a pint of clear brown gravy, and pour over the meat. It must stand twelve hours to harden before cutting.

CHICKEN POT PIE

Prepare and cook chicken until within twenty minutes of being done. Prepare a dough of one quart flour, butter to make as short as biscuits, salt, a teaspoon of baking powder, and cold water. Roll and cut in small squares, place in a steamer over boiling chicken and steam. When done remove, and prepare chicken as for fricassee and serve.

CHICKEN POT PIE WITHOUT CHICKEN

I take a piece of the neck of veal or beef, cut it up in small pieces; put that, potatoes and dumplings, with pepper and salt in alternate layers; put some water in the boiler first, and keep adding boiling water to prevent its sticking. I make the dumplings in this manner: Put a small piece of lard in some flour, add a little salt, mix with water and roll out thin. This makes a good dinner. Ger. Telegraph.

CHICKEN PUDDING

Cut up a tender fowl into small pieces and boil slowly one-half hour. Season with pepper and salt. Put the pieces into a dish to cool, and set the liquor aside for gravy. Make a batter of a quart of milk, three cups of sifted flour, two tablespoonfuls of melted butter, four well beaten eggs, two teaspoonfuls of baking powder and a little salt. Put a layer of chicken into the bottom of a baking-dish, pour a cupful of batter over it, then another layer of chicken and batter until full. Have batter for the upper crust. Bake in a moderate oven for about an hour. Skim the gravy saved, boil down, thicken, season, add a little chopped parsley and pass with the pudding.

CHICKEN SALAD

For one good sized chicken take one bunch of celery chopped fine, a little pepper and salt. For dressing for the above quantity take the yolks of two eggs boiled hard, make them fine, and add mustard, vinegar, oil, and a little Cayenne pepper and salt, to suit taste, and the liquor of the chicken boiled in is very nice to use, mixing it. Put in just enough to moisten it nicely. When it becomes cold it is just like a jelly, but it is a great improvement to the salad.

CHICKEN STEW

Chicken stews are generally prepared with white sauce. The gravy made, the chicken should be cut in pieces and a couple of slices of lemon (without the peel), some mace and pepper and salt. If lemon is not used, milk can be added instead of water. It will enhance the nutritiousness of the stew if a small piece or two of veal is added to the chicken.

CHICKEN STEW

Boil a chicken until tender; remove and chop fine; have ready a deep dish; put in the pieces of chicken with the liver in layers, with salt, pepper and butter; make a gravy with the liquor; pour over the chicken and cover with a suet crust.

CHILBLAINS

Two tablespoonfuls of lime water mixed with enough sweet oil to make as thick as lard. Rub the chilblains with the mixture and wrap up with linen.

CHILBLAINS

Chilblains are often cured by soaking the feet in water in which potatoes have been boiled, also by applying copperas water.

CHILBLAINS

Any person with chilblains will feel grateful indeed if they will use a lotion composed of equal parts of turpentine, ammonia and raw linseed-oil rubbed in, three or four times a day. There is nothing that equals this liniment for the purpose. It gives relief as soon as applied.

CHILBLAINS

The following recipes have been found effective in relieving the pain of these troublesome affections:

1. Take of sulphurous acid one ounce, glycerin one ounce, and

distilled water two ounces. Apply night and morning.

2. White wax, two drachms; spermaceti, two drachms; balsam Peru, one drachm; olive oil, three ounces; muriatic acid, two drachms; water, six drachms. Make plaster and apply.
3. Rubbing the feet with snow often effects a cure.
4. Bathing them in strong oak leaf tea is good, and almost equally as good as bathing them in liquor from tan vats heated hot.
5. Copperas water applied to them often relieves.

CHILBLAINS

Simply heat it as a blacksmith heats a burned finger to take the fire out. Let the sufferer take off his boot and hold his foot, with the sock on, as near the fire as he can stand it; if it gets too hot, withdraw it and put it near the fire again as soon as he can. Heat it this way for five or ten minutes, keeping it as hot as the pain will permit, without blistering. He can then go to work, and have no more trouble that day. A second application may be necessary the next day, but one or two applications will complete the cure.

CHILBLAINS - A SURE CURE FOR

Boil one pound of alum till dissolved, place the feet in the water as hot as it can be borne, and keep there till the alum has solidified. Two applications cured the worst case I ever knew. Mine were disposed of effectively at one trial.

CHILBLAINS - REMEDY FOR

If they are very bad, apply at night a plaster of brown sugar, mixed with scrapings of common soap; wash the feet daily with brown soap and water.

CHILBLAINS - TO CURE

The following mixture is useful for allaying intense itching caused by chilblains: Sulphurous acid three parts and glycerin one part, diluted with the same quantity of water. Apply with soft camel hair pencil.

CHILI SAUCE

Eighteen large ripe tomatoes, two onions as large round as a common teacup, four green sweet peppers; chop onions and peppers fine; four cups of vinegar, two tablespoonfuls of salt, four of sugar, two of ginger, two of cinnamon, one of clove, one of allspice, and one of nutmeg; boil one hour. This makes three quarts.

CHILI SAUCE

This is a little different from catsup, but is equally nice. Skin twenty four ripe tomatoes, and chop them finely, with six green onions and six green pickles. Put upon the fire and boil and skim for half an hour. Then add five or six cupfuls of strong vinegar, four tablespoonfuls each of ground mustard, cinnamon, ginger and turmeric, one tablespoonful of ground cloves, and three tablespoonfuls of white mustard seed, and the same of celery seed. Boil an hour slowly, and bottle tightly. It is delicious with bread and butter for lunch.

CHILI SAUCE

Forty-eight ripe tomatoes, ten peppers, two large onions, two quarts vinegar, four tablespoons salt, two teaspoons each of cloves, cinnamon, nutmeg and allspice; one cup sugar. Slice the tomatoes, chop peppers and onions together; add vinegar and spices, and boil until thick enough. Mustard and curry powder improve this.

CHIMNEY FIRE

A fire in the chimney may be extinguished by throwing powdered brimstone on the fire in the grate or stove. Close the grate or stove to prevent the fumes from coming out into the room.

CHINESE PUDDING

Melt half an ounce of fresh butter in a saucepan; stir in a tablespoonful of flour; when the two are well amalgamated, put in a small quantity of milk and about three ounces of grated Parmesan cheese. Stir the mixture on a slow fire till it assumes the appearance of thick cream, but be careful not to let it boil; then add some white pepper; mix thoroughly, and, if required, add a little salt; keep on stirring the mixture at a very moderate heat for about ten minutes; take the saucepan off the fire and stir the contents occasionally until quite cold, then stir into them the yolks of three eggs beaten up with a little milk and strained; and finally, the whites of five eggs whisked into a white froth. Put the mixture into a pudding dish and put it into the oven at once. Serve quickly, as soon as the pudding has risen and the top is well browned.

CHOCOLATE BLANCMANGE

Grate a quarter of a pound of sweet chocolate into one quart of milk; add a quarter of a pound of gelatin, and a quarter of a pound of powdered sugar. Mix all in a farina kettle or a pitcher, and stand in a kettle of cold water over the fire. Stir occasionally until the water boils, and then stir continuously, while boiling, for fifteen minutes. Dip a mould into iced water, pour in the blancmange, and stand aside to cool. When cold, turn out of the mould, and serve with sugar and cream.

CHOCOLATE CAKE

Two cups of sugar, one of butter, yolks of five eggs and whites of two, one cup of sweet milk, three and a half cups of flour, two teaspoons of baking powder. For the frosting: One and one-half cups of sugar, two squares of chocolate, one cup of sweet milk; cook a little and spread between the layers.

CHOCOLATE CARAMELS

One cup chocolate, one cup sugar, one cup milk, one cup molasses, butter the size of an egg, one tablespoonful flour. Boil twenty minutes.

CHOCOLATE CARAMELS

For chocolate caramels take one cup molasses, half cup of sugar, one quarter of a pound of chocolate cut fine, half a cup of milk, and one heaping tablespoonful of butter. Boil all together, stirring all the time. When a bit of the syrup will harden in cold water pour into shallow buttered pans and as it cools cut into small squares. Cut evenly so that the squares will break evenly.

CHOCOLATE CARAMELS

One cup of milk, two cups of sugar, two cups of molasses; one cake of chocolate grated fine. Boil till it candies. Pour out on a flat dish and cut in squares.

CHOCOLATE CREAM DROPS

One cake vanilla chocolate, three cups powdered sugar, one cup soft water, two tablespoonfuls corn starch or arrowroot, one tablespoonful butter, two teaspoonfuls vanilla.

Wash every grain of salt out of the butter. Stir the sugar and water together; mix in the corn starch, and bring to a boil, stirring constantly to induce granulation. Boil about ten minutes, when add the butter. Take from the fire and beat as you would eggs until it begins to look like granulated cream. Put in the vanilla; butter your hands well; make the cream into balls about the size of a large marble, and lay on a greased dish. Meanwhile the chocolate should have been melted by putting it, grated fine, into a tin pail or saucepan and setting this into another of boiling water. When it is a black syrup add about two tablespoonfuls of powdered sugar to it, beat smooth, turn out upon a hot dish and roll the cream balls in it until sufficiently coated. Lay upon a cold dish to dry, taking care that they do not touch each other.

CHOCOLATE CREAM DROPS

Two cups granulated sugar, one-half cup of water, cream tarter size of a large pea; boil exactly five minutes after beginning to boil freely in a covered basin without stirring. Pour out into a dish to cool, and when quite cool work it on the side of the dish with a spoon to a creamy texture; flavor with vanilla and roll into balls and lay aside to harden. Take not quite half a cake of Baker's chocolate; grate it into a vessel that will fit into the teakettle. When it is dissolved by the steam dip the balls into it and lay on brown paper to cool. Fifty balls can be made from this rule.

CHOCOLATE CREAMS

Two cups powdered sugar, one-half cup of milk. Boil five minutes then add one teaspoonful vanilla, set into a dish of cold water and beat to a cream. Roll in balls and drop in chocolate; melt a little over half a cake of Baker's chocolate while cooking cream, drop them on paper and put away to harden.

CHOCOLATE CREAMS

For the cream: Boil two cups of sugar and one-half cup of milk or water for five minutes, add one teaspoonful of vanilla, then beat for half an hour or till stiff enough to hold, then make into drops. For the chocolate: Take three-fourths of one-half pound of unsweetened chocolate, grate and steam over the teakettle. Drop the creams when hard (one at a time) into the hot chocolate, using two forks to take them out (quickly), set the drop on one fork" on the bottom, using the other fork to scrape the chocolate off the cream, gently slip the drop on to a buttered dish. If when cool the chocolate drops stick to it, hold the dish for a second over the steam of the teakettle, then slide them off.

CHOCOLATE CUSTARD FROZEN

Break up and cook to a smooth paste in a pint of water a half-pound of chocolate. Put a half-gallon of new milk into a double boiler. When it has just come to a boil stir in the chocolate. Then add the well beaten yolks of four eggs, a little bit at a time, carefully stirring all the while. Flavor slightly with vanilla. Have in the freezer a quart of cream beaten to a stiff froth, then add the chocolate custard sweetened with a pound and a half of sugar. Add the four whites of egg just as the freezing well begins.

CHOCOLATE DROPS

In the February issue of The Household, Abby wishes for a recipe for chocolate drops such as confectioners have. Here is one which is sure to please if directions are strictly followed. Two cups of granulated sugar, one-half cup of water, and one-half cake of Baker's chocolate. Boil sugar and water together exactly five minutes after commencing to boil; should be boiled in a porcelain lined dish. Stir constantly while boiling, also while cooling. While cooling add extract of vanilla to taste. Roll up into fifty balls size of a marble as soon as cool enough to handle. Scrape the chocolate into a small tin dish and place over the teakettle until the steam has dissolved it, then roll the balls separately in the chocolate (using a fork for the purpose), then lay them on buttered paper to cool.

CHOCOLATE FROSTING

Three cups of crushed sugar, with a little water to dissolve it, boiled to a syrup till it will hair on the spoon, whites of two eggs beaten stiff. When sugar is boiled, pour into it the eggs, beating all the time; then put in chocolate enough to taste, and color nicely; add a small pinch of tartaric acid.

CHOCOLATE ICE CREAM

Add to the pint of sweetened cream four ounces of the best chocolate dissolved in a little water, mix it well in, strain through a sieve, and freeze.

CHOCOLATE MARBLE CAKE

Two cups of sugar, one cup of sweet milk, half cup of butter, two and one-half cups of flour, two eggs, and three teaspoonfuls of baking powder. Dissolve one-third cake of chocolate, mix with one-half cup of the cake, then marble through the whole.

CHOCOLATE PASTE

One cup of boiled milk, and when boiled stir in two tablespoons corn starch dissolved in one half cup cold water; then add two ounces Baker's flavored chocolate grated, the yolk of one egg beaten, twelve teaspoons vanilla; stir this over the fire, and when a little cool add one cup of powdered sugar. This will make a thick paste to spread between layers of cake

CHOLERA INFANTUM

Take the inside lining of a chicken's gizzard, make a tea of it, and give one teaspoonful at a time. It is a sure cure for cholera infantum.

CHOPPED PICKLES

One-half bushel of green tomatoes, one dozen green peppers, two cabbages and one ripe cucumber; chop all together and sprinkle over it one pint of salt; let it stand overnight, then drain and pack in a jar; take two pounds of brown sugar, two tablespoonfuls of cinnamon, one tablespoonful of allspice and pepper, one-half cup of mustard, one pint of grated horseradish, and vinegar enough to mix; pour the vinegar, when boiling hot, over the contents of the jar and cover closely.

CHRISTMAS PUDDING

Five eggs; spoonful of sugar to each egg; a heaping coffee cup of boiled rice ; a teacup of thin cream; a teaspoonful of salt; spices to suit the taste; and raisins. Then fill a six quart pan within two inches of the top with new milk, and bake until done. Take from the oven and spread the top over with currant jelly. Then beat the whites of four eggs until it will stand alone, and add two tablespoonfuls of white sugar; beat awhile, and spread over the top of the jelly, and put it into the oven and let it just brown over, which it will do in a very short time, and you have a most excellent pudding. This is sufficient for a family of twelve.

CIDER JELLY

The juice of the apples was very abundant last season, and the housewife can, with little labor, prepare many luxuries that are both healthy and palatable. Jellies made from cider are very nice, and it is little trouble to make them. Take a gallon of cider, before fermentation has commenced, and boil it down in a porcelain kettle to two quarts, skim it frequently, and then strain it through a jelly bag. Add one quart of granulated sugar, and boil slowly for fifteen minutes, and dip into jelly glasses. It is pure fruit jelly that is remarkably nice for either invalids or table use. Those who do not like very sour jelly can add more sugar.

CIDER JELLY

Soak one box of Cox's gelatin in half pint of cold water until soft, then add one quart of granulated sugar, mixing thoroughly with the gelatin, then pour over the mixture one pint of boiling water, stir thoroughly, add one quart of cider, stirring well; strain into your moulds and put in a cold place.

CIDER JELLY

Soak an ounce of gelatin in a quart of sweet cider for quarter of an hour; put it over the fire in a clean saucepan with six tablespoonfuls of sugar and a glass of apple jelly, and stir the whole until quite liquid; then cool in tin or earthen moulds, rubbed with a little salad oil, so that the jelly will turn out easily. Unless the moulds are oiled they must be dipped for an instant into hot water before the jelly is taken out of them.

CIDER VINEGAR

Cider vinegar is almost a necessity in housekeeping, and is easily prepared. After cider is fermented, draw it off into a keg, and take strips of straw paper, dipped either into West India molasses or maple syrup and put them into a keg of cider, and set in a warm place, near a stove or chimney, where it will not freeze, and in a few weeks you will have a sharp, pure vinegar. If one needs to use it in a short time they can fill a jug with cider, and turn into each gallon of cider a pint of molasses and a cupful of lively yeast. Have a jug full of liquid, let it stand uncorked back of the stove, where it will keep warm. It will commence fermenting in twenty-four hours, and will not take over a week to make splendid sharp vinegar. It must be drawn off into another jug, leaving the dregs, and kept in a tight corked jug or bottles, where it will not freeze. If one has good cider, there need be no trouble about vinegar, as it can be made into sharp vinegar in a short time by using a little labor, and taking care of it. Straw paper saturated with molasses acts upon cider like mother, and in a few weeks has every appearance of that article, only a little firmer in consistency, and rather thicker in texture.

CINCINNATI STEW

Cut into pieces three pounds lean, fresh beef, veal or pork; peel and slice a quarter of a peck of tomatoes, and season the whole with pepper and salt; put the whole into a stewpan and cover it close, but put in no water, as the juice is enough; stir in a piece of butter, dredge it with flour and cook till meat is tender; toast some bread, cut in three-cornered pieces, soak in water and butter; then set up around the inside of a deep dish and pour the stew in and serve hot.

CINNAMON BUNS

One pound flour, one gill yeast, half pint milk, two ounces butter, two ounces sugar, three eggs beaten to a cream, one teaspoonful salt, one grated rind of lemon, one tablespoonful cinnamon, one handful Zante currants, picked, washed and dried. Set a sponge with yeast, the milk lukewarm, and enough of the flour to make a smooth batter, and set it in a warm place to rise. Cream the butter and sugar, add the eggs, the salt, and the lemon, and work well into the sponge as soon as it is light. Mix in the rest of the flour with milk, to a dough a little softer than bread dough, and set aside for a few minutes. Dust a pie-board with flour, put the dough in the middle, dust it on the top, roll it out into a sheet twelve by six inches and a quarter of an inch thick; brush it with melted butter, leaving a margin of one inch all around unbuttered. Wash the margin with white of an egg. Strew with currants and dust with powdered sugar mixed with cinnamon. Roll over like roly-poly, cut into cakes across the roll, an inch thick, set them flat on a square pan and bake like bread. Turn out the pan while hot.

CITRON PRESERVES

Take citron and sugar equal weight, put the citron in a kettle or stewpan, boil until tender, then put in a colander to drain. I often leave mine until morning to well drain, then take this water, put it in your kettle with sugar, and boil until well done, flavor with lemon if you like. This has been my plan for over thirteen years, and to my remembrance, I have never had any sour. I also preserve watermelon rinds the same way.

CITRON PRESERVES

Cut the citron in thin slices, boil in water with a small piece of alum until clear and tender, then rinse in cold water. Make a syrup allowing three-fourths of a pound of sugar to a pound of citron; boil a piece of root ginger in the syrup; then pour the citron in and let it boil for a few minutes. Put in one lemon to five citrons.

CLAM CHOWDER

Chop fifty clams, peel and slice eight raw potatoes, mince six onions, slice a quarter of a pound of fat salt pork, slice half a dozen tomatoes (two cupfuls canned tomatoes), a pound of crackers (butter are best) rolled fine, butter and season to taste. Put pork in the bottom of the kettle and try out, removing the bits. Partially cook the minced onion in this fat, then turn on to a plate. Put the ingredients into the kettle in layers, season with pepper, salt, bits of butter, cover with water and simmer two hours. An iron kettle is not a good thing to make the chowder in, as it is apt to give it an unpleasant flavor.

CLAM CHOWDER

Put in a pot a layer of sliced pork, chopped potatoes, chopped clams, salt, pepper and lumps of butter, and broken crackers soaked in milk, cover with the clam juice and water, stew slowly for three hours, thicken with a little flour, it may be seasoned with spices if preferred.

CLAM SOUP

Boil fifty clams in two quarts of water; mix together, and add to it a little butter and flour. Just before it is taken of the fire, stir in the yolks of two eggs, and some cream, with a few sprigs of parsley and pepper; after these are added, let it simmer a few minutes, and then serve it. If preferred the parsley may be omitted.

CLARIFYING SUGAR FOR PRESERVING

For each pound of sugar allow one-half pint water; for every three pounds of sugar the white of one egg. Mix when cold, boil a few minutes, and skim it. Let it stand ten minutes, skim it again, and strain it.

CLEANING CARPETS, CLOTHING, ETC.

For cleaning carpets, clothing, and wool fabrics generally.- Take four ounces of white Castile soap; four ounces of aqua ammonia; two ounces sulphuric ether; two ounces alcohol; two ounces glycerin; cut the soap fine and dissolve in one quart of water over the fire; add four quarts of water, and when nearly cold, add the other ingredients and immediately bottle or can and keep tight, as it will loose its properties if allowed to evaporate. Apply with a brush or a soft cloth to soiled parts, and rinse if necessary. This makes a very useful article to keep on hand in every household.

CLEANING FLUID

A cleaning fluid or "Javelle water" which is a great help to the busy housekeeper, is made as follows: Dissolve two pounds of sal soda in a gallon of water (rainwater is best), boiling thirty minutes, then add a ten cent can of bichloride of lime. For washing clothes add one-third cup of the fluid to a boiler of water. For cleaning white-lined granite ware fill with water, add a tablespoonful or two of the mixture, according to the size of the utensil, and boil for three or four minutes. Keep the fluid in bottles labeled "POISON" since it is very caustic.

CLEANING GILT FRAME

To clean gilt frames rub them with a little sal volatile mixed with cold water; or, after dusting the frames well, paint the gilding with a camel's hair brush dipped in the following mixture: One gill of water in which one ounce of common salt, one ounce of alum and two ounces of purified nitre have been dissolved.

CLEANING KID GLOVES

A piece of white soap, a little sweet milk in a saucer and a clean cloth folded two or three times. On the cloth spread out the glove smoothly. Take a piece of flannel, dip it in the milk, then rub off a good quantity of soap on the wetted flannel, commence to rub toward the fingers holding it firmly with the left hand. Continue the process until the glove, if white, looks of a dingy yellow, if colored, till it looks spoiled; lay it to dry and you will soon see that the glove looks nearly new. It will be soft and elastic.

CLEANING OIL PAINTINGS

To clean oil paintings wash them with a sponge and dry them by rubbing with a silk handkerchief. When the picture is very dirty remove it from its frame, lay a wet towel on the face of the picture, sprinkling it from time to time with clear, soft water. Let it remain wet for two or three days. Then remove the towel and wash the picture well with a soft sponge. When quite dry rub it with some clear nut or linseed oil.

CLEANING OLD LAMP BURNERS

To clean old lamp burners, wash and boil them in ashes and water, then rub them with oxalic acid, then dry and polish with fine coal ashes, and they will be clean and bright. Wash the wicks and dry. Many times the burners are condemned when only the wicks are at fault.

CLEANING PLUSH

To clean plush, use lightly a soft sponge dipped in a weak solution of borax and water.

CLEANING SILVER

To clean silver or plated ware, wash in clean hot water or lay in hot soda water a few minutes; then wipe dry with a canton flannel cloth, and polish with chamois skin. Never use soap in washing silver.

CLEANING SOILED LACE

Steam in a steamer over a kettle of strong soap suds. This is a good way to treat soiled lace.

CLEANING TINWARE

The best thing for cleaning tinware is common soda; dampen a cloth and dip in soda, rub the tin briskly, after which wipe dry, and black and dirty tinware can be made to look like new.

CLEANSING COLLARS AND WRISTBANDS

Grease the soiled parts before wetting, with any kind of fat or drippings; let them remain a few hours, or overnight; wash with soap in hot water. They will become wonderfully clean.

COAL-OIL

When wash-day comes, try putting a little coal-oil in the ' boiling water. It is a great loosener of dirt, and the clothes will require far less rubbing.

COAL-OIL FOR CLEANING

Coal-oil is good for cleaning zinc or galvanized iron tubs, and the outside of water buckets made of the same material.

COCOANUT BREAD PUDDING

Soak half a cup of desiccated cocoanut in boiling hot milk for half an hour or more, then add to it the usual bread pudding preparation (the quantity of bread being about three times as much as the cocoanut. Enrich and flavor to suit. This you will find to be a very pleasant and economical dessert.

COCOANUT BUTTER DROPS

1 cup sugar, ½ cup butter, well blended; 2 eggs, ½ cup milk, 2 level teaspoons of baking powder, sifted with 2 cups flour; 1 teaspoon vanilla, 1 cup cocoanut; drop on buttered tin and bake in quick oven.

COCOANUT CAKES

For cocoanut cakes take the grated meat of two cocoanuts, their weight in sugar, loaf if you have it, one cup flour and whites of two eggs. Shape into balls and bake for twenty minutes.

COCOANUT CANDY

Four pounds standard A sugar, two good cocoanuts, one teaspoon best cream tarter, one quart water; boil the sugar, water and cream tarter to a ball; that is, until it feels soft on being taken out of water; then remove from the fire and stir until it grains. Add the grated cocoanut and stir well before pouring out. Let it stand till cold and cut into squares.

COCOANUT CANDY

Rasp very fine a sound, fresh cocoanut, spread it on a dish, and let it dry naturally for three days. Four ounces will be sufficient for a pound of sugar for most tastes, but more can be used at pleasure. Boil the sugar, and when it begins to be very thick and white strew in the nut; stir and mix it well, and do not quit it for an instant until it is finished. Keep the pan a little above the fire to prevent the nut from burning.

COCOANUT COOKIES

One egg, one cup of sugar, one-half cup of butter, one cup of cocoanut, four large spoonfuls of milk, one teaspoonful of cream of tartar, one-half teaspoonful of soda, and flour to roll out thin.

COCOANUT CUSTARD

To 1 lb grated cocoanut allow one pint of new milk and six oz. of sugar. Beat well the yolks of six eggs, and stir them alternately in the milk with the cocoanut and sugar. Put the mixture into a pail or pitcher, set it into boiling water, and stir all the time, till very smooth and thick; as soon as it comes to a hard boil, take it off, and serve in cups or glass tumblers.

COCOA-NUT PIE

Cut off the brown part of the cocoa-nut, grate the white part, and mix it with milk, and set it on the fire and let it boil slowly eight or ten minutes. To a pound of the cocoa-nut allow a quart of milk, eight eggs, four tablespoonfuls of sifted white sugar, a glass of wine, a small cracker pounded fine, two spoonfuls of melted butter, and half a nutmeg. The eggs and sugar should be beaten together to a froth, then the wine stirred in. Put them into the milk and cocoa-nut, which should be first allowed to get quite cool; add the cracker and nutmeg, turn the whole into deep pie-plates, with a lining and rim of puff paste. Bake them as soon as turned into the plates.

COD AU COURT BOUILLON

A favorite way among professional cooks to cook cod is to boil it in water saturated with vegetables, called court bouillon, and so it would be called cod au court bouillon, which is in good English simply cod cooked in broth.

CODFISH BALLS

Peel the potatoes the night before you wish to make the   balls, and put them in clean water. Put the codfish also in water to soak. In the morning boil both, and after picking up the codfish very fine and mashing the potatoes. Mix about two-thirds of potato with one-third fish, and fry the balls with thin slices of nice pork just taken from the brine. The making of the balls from fresh cooked potatoes and fish adds very much to their excellence. When warmed up they are called codfish balls.

CODFISH ON TOAST

Take a pint of shredded codfish that has been soaked in cold water long enough to freshen; drain, put into a skillet with a little cold milk, season with butter and pepper, mix a spoonful of flour smooth in a little milk, add, boil up and turn on to buttered toast on a platter.

COFFEE

I have tried with success and pleasure this recipe. I make coffee after mother's way, that is, by stirring an egg into as much ground coffee as is required for strong coffee, and letting it boil a few minutes, set it off to settle.

COFFEE

When eggs are high priced, and you do not feel rich enough to use a whole one every time you make coffee, try beating an egg thoroughly with a large cup of sugar, and use a small spoonful of the mixture; it will clear the coffee as though the whole egg were used. Keep in a cool place and it will not spoil until entirely used.

COFFEE

Heat the grounds hot in a mess-pan, one tablespoonful for each person and add one for the pot or kettle; then pour on boiling water, one cupful for each spoonful of coffee. Cover tight and stand where it will keep hot, but not boil, for fifteen or twenty minutes. Then strain into the cups. The coffee should never be boiled. "Coffee boiled is coffee spoiled."

COFFEE CAKE

One cup of strong coffee, one cup of molasses, one cup of butter, two cups of brown sugar, three eggs, four cups of flour, one nutmeg, one teaspoonful of cinnamon, one cup of raisins, one cup of currants, and one-half teaspoonful of saleratus. This makes two loaves.

COFFEE CAKE

One cup of clear, strong coffee, one cup of sugar, one cup of molasses, one-half cup of butter, two eggs, three cups of flour, one nutmeg, one teaspoonful of cinnamon, one teaspoonful of clove, one teaspoonful of allspice, one-half pound of chopped raisins, one teaspoonful of saleratus, one teaspoonful of cream of tartar, and a little citron. This makes two loaves. Bake in a moderate oven.

COFFEE CAKE

One cup sugar, one cup molasses, one cup butter, one cup strong coffee, two eggs, cream tarter and saleratus, one teaspoonful each. Cloves, cinnamon and nutmeg, raisins or currants, and citron (if you can afford it); six cups flour. Will make two good-sized loaves.

COFFEE ICE CREAM

To a pint of sweetened cream add a cup of strong infusion of Mocha coffee, and freeze.

COFFEE IN A FEW MINUTES

Put an ounce of good ground coffee near the fire, or in the oven, to get hot, but not on any account to burn. Scald your coffee-pot to make hot, as you do your tea-pot; tie up your ounce of hot coffee in a bit of clean coarse muslin, it must be loosely tied, not in a hard ball; put it into the pot and pour a quart of boiling water over it, put on the lid directly, and let the pot stand by the hot fire for ten minutes or more. Have ready some good boiled milk, add half coffee; sugar to taste. This will be really good coffee.

COFFEE MAKING

In making coffee observe that the broader the bottom and the narrower the top of the vessel, the better it will be.

COFFEE MAKING

A professional caterer makes the assertion that the cook who uses eggs in making coffee does not understand his business; and recommends that the coffee be put into a thick flannel bag and suspended in the coffee-pot, so as to prevent its scorching.

COFFEE STAINS

For coffee stains try putting thick glycerin on the wrong side and washing it out with lukewarm water.

COFFEE SYRUP

An exchange gives the following rule for preparing a syrup of coffee, which would be very convenient for long journeys, or for summer jaunts by carriage, or for camping out: Take half a pound of the best coffee; put it into a saucepan containing three pints of water, and boil it down to one pint. Cool the liquor, put it into another saucepan, well scoured, and boil it again. As it boils, add white sugar, enough to give it the consistency of syrup. Take it from the fire, and when it is cold put into a bottle and seal. When traveling, if you wish for a cup of good coffee you have only to put two teaspoonfuls of the syrup into an ordinary coffee-pot, and fill with boiling water. Add milk to taste if you can get it.

COLD

Camphorated oil is one of the best of remedies for a cold - try it sisters: Put ten cents' worth of pure olive oil in a bottle and drop into it five cents' worth of camphor gum. It will not take long to dissolve. Bathe the little one's sides, chest and joints, also soles of feet and palms of hands at bedtime, and see what a help it will be.

COLD

As a mustard plaster is one of the common household remedies extensively used for the cure of a cold after it has settled on the lungs it will be of considerable benefit to know that if it is made from pure lard and mustard only it will not blister the skin even if kept on from six to twelve hours at a time, but will impart a pleasant, glowing warmth to the body where it is placed.

COLD BEEF WITH MASHED POTATOES

Mash potatoes, either in a plain way or with hot milk and the yolk of an egg, and add some butter and salt. Slice the cold beef, and lay it at the bottom of a pie dish, adding to it some pepper, salt and a little beef gravy. Cover the whole with a thick paste of potatoes. Score the potato crust with the point of a knife in squares of equal size. Put the dish in an oven, and brown it on all sides. When nicely browned serve immediately. This, with an apple tart or dumpling to follow, is a capital dinner for a small family.

COLD FEET

J.M.K. says: "If you have cold feet wear sulphur in your shoes. You will think you are walking on velvet."

COLD FEET - SIMPLE CURE FOR

The following remedy for cold feet is recommended for sedentary sufferers, as well as policemen, cab drivers and others who are exposed to the cold: All that is necessary is to stand erect and to very gradually to lift one's self up upon the tips of the toes, so as to put all the tendons of the foot at full strain. This is not to hop or jump up and down, but simply to rise - the slower the better - upon tiptoe, and to remain standing on the point of the toes as long as possible, then gradually coming to the natural position. Repeat this several times, and, by the amount of work the tips of the toes are now made to do in sustaining the body's weight, a sufficient and lively circulation is set up. A heavy pair of woolen stockings drawn over thin cotton ones is also a recommendation for keeping the feet warm.

COLD ON THE LUNGS

I have found no better remedy for cold on the lungs than camphorated lard. Put a heaping tablespoonful of lard into a can with a cover - I use a baking powder can - add five cents worth of camphor gum, and place the can, tightly covered, on the back of the range, where the lard will keep hot without boiling. Shake the can once in a while until the gum, which should be shaved in small pieces, is dissolved, and remove from the stove, but do not take off the cover until cold. A little turpentine may be added but it is good if made as directed. Apply to throat or chest and cover with a flannel cloth. It is really a "one night cure".

COLD REMEDY

For colds in head and chest. Dissolve a small amount of gum camphor in a small bottle of olive oil and rub well into throat, lungs and temples.

COLOGNE

I. One quart of alcohol, one-quarter ounce oil of lavender, one-quarter ounce oil of rosemary.
II. One quart alcohol, one ounce of lemon, one-half ounce oil of bergamot; Shake well.

COLORING BROWN

Take a peck of hemlock bark steeped in brass, add a little alum to set the color; after the goods are taken out dip in lime water; this makes a dark tan color, if something darker is wished dip the goods in a weak black dye, then put them in the brown dye. To color drab, take willow bark -- and a little copperas; for gray, put in some blue vitriol with the drab dye.

COLORING BROWN

C.P.S. wishes a recipe for coloring brown; here is one from "The Druggists" Circular, which I think is good. For ten pounds of yarn or cloth, boil two pounds of prepared catechu and three ounces of blue vitriol together. Put the yarn or cloth into the hot liquid and let it remain over night. In the morning prepare a hot solution of seven ounces of bichromate of potash - just by dissolving the bichromate in water - into which put the goods after wringing it from the first preparation; let it remain in this solution till the right shade is acquired; then rinse and dry. This is for dying cotton or linen.

COLORING COCHINEAL

One pound of yarn to one of cochineal, two ounces cream of tarter, two ounces muriate of tin; wet the yarn in clear water, pulverize the cochineal and sift, put in soft water, also the cream of tartar; when it begins to boil put in the muriate of tin, then the yarn, simmer one hour; air frequently, and rinse in clear water.

COLORING CUCUMBER PICKLES

The bright green color is given to cucumber pickles by scalding them in a copper kettle, which imparts its verdigris to the pickle in sufficient quantity to color them. The color is attractive to the eye and probably harmless, though the fear of poisoning has no doubt had something to do with the unpopularity of green pickles. Of late years they are little called for. Beans, peppers, onions, martinias, etc., are pickled the same way as cucumbers. See cucumber pickles.

COLORING PICKLES AND SWEETS GREEN

The following green coloring extract is said to be destitute of any poisoning properties: Dissolve five grains of saffron in one-fourth ounce of distilled water, and in another dish dissolve four grains indigo carmine in one-half ounce of distilled water. After mixing thoroughly let stand twenty four hours, then put together, and the results will be a green solution capable of coloring four or five pounds of sugar.

COLTSFOOT LOZENGES

To one pint of spring water add one handful of coltsfoot leaves: boil this down to a gill, and let stand till cold. Then strain it through a fine woolen cloth (without pressing), and add half a pound of sugar. Boil to a syrup. Strain it again through a woolen cloth, and put to it as much common black liquorice as may be found necessary to give it consistency. Then form it into any shape or form that you may fancy.

COMPLEXION

Ninety-nine out of every hundred complexion powders prevent healthy action of the skin, and therefore bring on wrinkles or blotches. Pure blood gives the only perfect complexion, and "Dana's Sarsaparilla" makes pure blood.

COMPLEXION

Make a linen bag large enough to hold a quart of bran, put it in a vessel and pour two quarts of boiling water on it; let it stand all day, and at night, on going to bed, take the bag out and wash the face with the bran water; in the morning wash it off with rain water. In a short time it will make a coarse skin feel like velvet.

COMPLEXION

Here is what is necessary to practice the very simple art of grooming: One jar of guaranteed cold cream, one cake of pure olive oil soap, three Turkish toweling wash cloths, one box of pure talcum powder, and a half-pint bottle of alcohol. Ten minutes at night will cleanse the face and massage it sufficiently with the cream, and in the morning still less time is required, for cream is not used save for an exceptionally dry skin.

COMPOSITION RECIPE

Four ounces of bayberry bark, two ounces of ginger and one drachm of cayenne.

CONSTIPATION

By the way, try a cup of hot water with a pinch of salt in it, taken as warm as you can sip it comfortably, for constipation; it is excellent, and tones up the system as well.

CONSTIPATION

Pure olive oil is an excellent remedy for constipation, and is perfectly harmless. It must be taken regularly, say a teaspoonful at night and in the morning for a time, and then only at night. A child would not, of course, require so large a dose as an adult; you can easily gauge the amount after trying it for several days.

CONSUMPTIVES - RELIEF FOR

The common mullein, steeped strong and sweetened with coffee sugar, and drank freely. The herb should be gathered before the end of July. Young or old plants are good, dried in the shade and kept in clean paper bags. The medicine must be continued from three to six months, according to the nature of the disease. It is good for the blood vessels also; it strengthens the system, and builds up instead of taking away strength. It makes good blood and takes inflammation from the lungs.

COOKIES

One cup of butter; one of cream; two of sugar; one egg; a teaspoonful of soda; flour enough to roll. These are very nice, and will keep a long time.

COOKIES

Take one and one-half cups of white sugar; one-half cup of lard; one-half cup of butter; sufficient caraway seeds or nutmeg to season, to suit the taste; one cup of sour milk, with teaspoonful of soda and flour sufficient to make dough; mix thoroughly, roll very thin, and bake quickly.

COOKIES

Two cups of sugar; two eggs; one cup of butter; one cup of milk;

one-half teaspoonful saleratus and flour sufficient to roll; roll in sugar.

COOKIES

One teacup of butter, 2 of sugar, 2 eggs, 4 tablespoonfuls of sour milk, 1 teaspoonful of saleratus, put in the milk, with spices.

COOKING CALF'S HEAD

Remove the brains, soak in salted water half an hour, then place in a little boiling water and simmer till thoroughly done; now remove the bones and chop the meat fine, season with salt, pepper, parsley, or whatever herb preferred. Add to this a little of the meat liquor, then put in a porcelain or earthen basin, mix a two egg omelet, pour over it, and bake only so long as to heat the meat through and nicely brown the omelet. Send to the table in the dish you bake it, and serve with a sauce made of the brains. Tie them in a cloth and boil fifteen or twenty minutes, then beat smoothly with butter, salt and pepper. Should any of the family be fastidious about brains when they are to be eaten, I would say do not announce "calf's head" until all have partaken, and you will have them converted to an economical and elegant dish.

COOKING EGGS

When properly cooked, eggs are done evenly through like any other food. This result may be attained by putting the eggs into a dish with a cover, as a tin pail, and then pouring upon them boiling water, two quarts or more to a dozen eggs, and cover and set them away from the stove for fifteen minutes. The heat of the water cooks the eggs slowly and evenly and sufficiently and to a jelly-like consistency, leaving the center or yolk harder than the white, and the egg tastes as much richer and nicer as a fresh egg is nicer than a stale egg, and no person will want to eat them boiled after having tried this method.

COOKING FISH

Fish should not be put in to fry until the fat is boiling hot. It should be dipped in Indian meal before it is put in, the skinny side uppermost when first put in, to prevent its breaking. It relishes better to be fried after salt pork than in lard alone. Never put fresh fish to soak in water. If you want to keep it sweet, clean and wash it; wipe dry with a clean towel, sprinkle salt inside and out, put in a covered dish and keep on the cellar bottom until you want to cook it. If you live remote from the seaport, and cannot get fish hard and fresh, wet it with an egg (beaten) before you meal it, to prevent its breaking.

COOKING PEASE

Boil until tender in very little water. Drain off the water and for every quart add two tablespoonfuls of butter, half a tablespoonful of flour rubbed into the butter, half a teaspoonful of sugar and one of salt. Mix thoroughly, simmer a few minutes, add a cup of cream or rich milk to each quart, heat and serve. This will be found very fine if the pease are not too old.

COOKING SMALL NEW POTATOES

1. Select the very smallest, scrape and drop into cold water; have ready a saucepan of hot lard or drippings; drain the potatoes, dry them on a towel and drop into the hot fat; cook until easily pierced with a fork. The fat should not be too hot or the potatoes will be too deeply browned before cooked through; drain, sprinkle with pepper and salt and serve at once.

2. Another good way of using the smallest potatoes is to scrape and boil them until almost tender, and then put them into a frying pan having a few spoonfuls of hot drippings or butter; sprinkle with salt and pepper and cook until nicely browned; only enough fat is required to keep them from burning. 3. Or boil until tender, drain, and cover with a white sauce made of a pint of new milk, a large spoonful of butter, pepper and salt, and thickened with a spoonful of flour, rubbed smooth in a little milk. This quantity of sauce answers for a quart of potatoes. The sauce should be made first, the potatoes added, and then leave on the back of the range ten minutes before serving. Small potatoes will be found very palatable,

and altogether too good to throw away, as is often the case from a lack of patience in preparing.

COOKING STEAK

Take beef, pork, lamb, or any kind of steak, lay it in a sauce pan and lay upon it a few slices of salt pork. Set it in a stove oven until done.

CORK STOPPERS

Corks warmed in oil make good substitutes for glass stoppers.

CORN AND CHICKEN

Several delicious dishes can be made by combining corn with other ingredients in the form of stews and ragouts. An exceedingly nice dish of corn and chicken may be made as follows: Prepare a chicken as for fricassee by carefully removing the feathers and entrails and cutting it in joints; fry it light brown in a little butter, add a quart of milk and the grains cut from a dozen ears of corn; season the stew with salt and pepper, and cook it slowly for half an hour; serve hot with small pieces of toast, or bread fried in hot fat.

CORN AND RYE BISCUITS

Pour boiling water on coarse yellow corn meal, and stir to the consistency of a thick batter. Immediately add coarse rye meal to make it into a very soft dough; form into small, flat biscuits (fifteen to a baking pan) with the hands frequently wet in cold water, and bake immediately in a hot oven. They are very nice for variety, and are best made of equal parts of corn and rye. Bake thirty minutes or more.

CORN BATTER CAKES

One pint of gold corn; a small teaspoonful of soda and salt; pour on enough boiling water to make it like mush; let it stand a few minutes to cool; then take four eggs; put the yolks in with the meal; a handful of flour, with two teaspoonfuls of cream tarter; stir in enough milk or water (either will answer) to make the batter suitable to bake; beat the whites of the eggs last, and put in just before baking.

CORN CAKES

Three cups of corn meal, one cup of graham flour, two teaspoonfuls of cream yeast powder sifted together, one cup of cream, and half a cup of milk, one egg, well beaten; stir together well and quickly; heat your gem irons hot; butter and fill; bake with a brisk heat. Gem tins or forms do not need to be heated before filling, they may be oiled and filled on the table, and put into a quick oven.

CORN BREAD

Three and one-half cupfuls of milk, 2 cupfuls of Indian meal; 2 cupfuls of wheat flour, into which sift 2 teaspoonfuls of cream tartar and 1 of soda; 2 eggs; a lump of shortening the size of an egg; 1 tablespoonful of molasses; a little salt. Pour into a well-buttered tin about two inches deep, and bake half an hour.

CORN BREAD

Two cups of Indian meal, one teaspoonful of salt, two teaspoonfuls of baking powder, one cup of molasses, one quart of sweet milk, two eggs; stir with wheat flour about as stiff as for cake and bake in a deep dish.

CORN BREAD

Take four quarts Indian meal; pour on boiling water and let stand twenty minutes; then add four quarts of fine rye flour; one cup yeast; one-half cup molasses; mix with warm water; put it in large six quart pans, and let rise two hours, then bake two and one-half hours.

CORN BREAD

Here is one of the best rules for the corn bread: 1 cup Indian meal, 1 cup flour, 1 spoonful melted butter, 1 tablespoonful sugar, 1/2 teaspoonful soda, 2/3 teaspoonful cream of tartar, 1 2/3 cups sweet milk. Bake in a quick oven, in either sheet or roll form.

CORN BREAD

Three cups of corn meal, two cups of wheat flour, three eggs, one pint of sour milk, lump of butter the size of a walnut, one teaspoonful of soda.

CORN CHOWDER

Cut half a pound of salt pork in little pieces not more than a inch square; slice four onions very thin, as if you were to fry them; boil the pork and onions for twenty minutes in two quarts of water; cut six medium sized potatoes in rather thick slices so they will keep their shape; add them to the soup and boil ten minutes (meanwhile scald one quart of milk); after the potatoes have boiled, add one quart can of corn, and lastly the milk, and let all come to a boil; cover the bottom of the soup dish with buttered crackers, and pour the soup over them.

CORN CUSTARD

One pint (heaping) corn meal, two tablespoonfuls white flour, one quart sour milk, or buttermilk, three egg yolks and whites separate, two teaspoonfuls soda, dissolved in boiling water. Time - twenty minutes. See that the oven is just right; then stir together the meal, flour, milk and beaten yolks. When these are well mixed, add the dissolved soda, and the whites cut to a stiff froth, and beat hard. Pour into two pans, well oiled, and bake immediately. The custard should not be more than an inch in thickness when done; it should bake in about twenty minutes.

CORN DODGERS

Two pints of corn meal, one tablespoonful lard, two eggs, and one teaspoonful of salt. Scald the meal with the lard in it; cool with a very little milk; add the eggs, and beat hard for ten minutes. If too thick, add a little more milk. They must be just thick enough to retain their shape when baked.

CORN FRITTERS ━━━━━━━━━━━━━━━━━━━━━━━

Take one dozen ears of young, tender corn, cut the grains down the middle, and cut carefully off the cob. Add the yolks of two eggs and one-half cup of sweet milk, a lump of butter the size of a walnut, a pinch of salt, pepper, and a small cup of flour; beat to a stiff froth the whites of two eggs, add to the compound and fry in a skillet with fresh lard and serve hot. I need scarcely add that a proportion of baking powder and sugar will form a most palatable cake to be eaten hot with coffee.

CORN FRITTERS ━━━━━━━━━━━━━━━━━━━━━━━

Two teacups of corn meal and one of flour, two eggs, a teaspoonful of soda, and buttermilk sufficient to make the consistency of easily baked batter; beat the compound thoroughly.

CORN FRITTERS ━━━━━━━━━━━━━━━━━━━━━━━

Grate six ears of corn; add one tablespoonful of flour, and two eggs; Pepper and salt to your taste; to be fried like oysters.

CORN MEAL CAKES ━━━━━━━━━━━━━━━━━━━━━

Take one cup of sweet milk, and boil with half a cup of sugar and half a cup of butter. Add enough Indian or southern corn meal to make a stiff batter. Beat three eggs to a foam; add a little pinch of salt, and bake in shallow pans for half an hour.

CORN MEAL MUSH ━━━━━━━━━━━━━━━━━━━━━━

Mix a batter with corn meal and water; stir into a saucepan of boiling water, slightly salted, until it is perfectly smooth. Serve with milk as oat meal, or dress on the plate with butter and syrup.

CORN MEAL PUDDING ━━━━━━━━━━━━━━━━━━━

Beat the yolks of two eggs, and stir them into a quart of milk, with a pinch of salt; set the milk over the fire, and when it comes to a boil stir in dry meal, sifting it through your fingers until you have it as thick as mush, stirring all the time, and keeping it boiling all the time. When thick enough, it is done. To be eaten with butter and syrup, and can be made during dinner.

CORN OYSTERS

One pint of grated green corn, one cup flour, one spoonful salt, one teaspoonful pepper, one egg. Drop by the spoonful in hot lard, and fry.

CORN OYSTERS

Six ears of grated corn, one-half cup of sweet milk, three tablespoonfuls of flour, salt and pepper. Fry in lard.

CORN OYSTERS

To one quart of grated green corn, having carefully scraped the milk from the tender cobs, add three eggs and three or four grated crackers, beat well, with salt and pepper and drop with a spoon in a hot pan containing hot lard or butter. An instant serves to crisp and cook them, and they become feathery and savory as an oyster.

CORN PANCAKES

One cup of corn meal, one cup of flour, one cup of sour milk, one cup of water, one-half teaspoonful of soda, and a little salt. A well beaten egg makes them richer, but they are good without it.

CORN PORRIDGE

Take young corn, and cut the grains from the cob. Measure it, and to each heaping pint of corn allow not quite a quart of milk. Put the corn and the milk into a pot; stir them well together, and boil them till the corn is perfectly soft. Then add some bits of fresh butter dredged with flour, and let it boil five minutes longer. Stir in at the last some beaten yolk of egg, and in three minutes remove it from the fire. Take up the porridge, and send it to the table hot, and stir some fresh butter into it. You may add sugar and nutmeg.

CORN PUDDING

Twelve ears of corn, four thoroughly beaten eggs, one quart of milk, three tablespoonfuls of sugar and salt to taste. Grate the corn, add the other ingredients and pour into a pudding dish; bake slowly.

CORN PUFFS

Scald five tablespoonfuls of corn meal; while hot, add a piece of butter the size of an egg; when cool, two eggs beaten separately, eight table-spoonfuls of wheat flour, two cups of milk, and a little salt; bake half an hour in a hot oven, in round tins the size of muffins.

CORN STARCH CAKE

One cup of sugar, one and one-fourth of cup of butter; beat to a cream; add two eggs, one-half cupful of corn starch, two tablespoonfuls of baking powder, a half cupful of milk, one cupful of flour.

CORN STARCH CAKE

Eight ounces of corn starch and eight ounces of sugar, four ounces of butter, three eggs, and a teaspoonful of baking powder. Bake in patty tins.

CORN STARCH MERINGUE PUDDING

One and one-half pints of milk, two eggs, three tablespoonfuls of sugar, two tablespoonfuls of corn starch, and a pinch of salt. Boil the milk, stir in the corn starch wet with water, then add the yolks of eggs and sugar and salt. Boil a few minutes, put in the pudding dish, cover with the whites of eggs, beaten, and sugar. Brown in the oven. Serve with jelly dotted over the top.

CORN STARCH PUDDING

Scald one quart of milk. Have three tablespoonfuls of corn starch dissolved in a little cold milk, and the yolks of six eggs well beaten with four tablespoonfuls of sugar. Stir the dissolved starch, the beaten eggs, a little butter and a little salt together, and just as the milk boils, pour it in, stirring briskly. Boil two minutes, stirring all the time to prevent scorching. Remove from the fire, and flavor. Pour into a dish, the same in which it is to be served; beat the whites of the eggs with a little sugar to a stiff froth, spread upon the pudding, set in the oven and brown delicately. The above tastes as well as it looks.

CORN SOUP

Green corn, two quarts water, two spoonfuls butter, large spoonful flour, one pint hot milk, cupful cream, salt and pepper. Cut off the top of the corn from the cob, and scrape off the rest; to a quart of this add the two quarts of boiling water, and let it boil one hour; then strain through a colander; put the butter in a stew pan; when it melts add the flour; stir in the corn, milk and cream when it boils; add salt and pepper; serve very hot.

CORNS

Dissolve in spirits of camphor all the baking soda it will take up, and apply night and morning.

CORNS - CURE FOR

Soak the feet well in hot water before going to bed, then pare down the soft corn, and, after having just moistened it, rub a little lunar caustic on the corn and just around the edge till it turns a light grey.

CORNS - CURE FOR

If your corn is hard soak it, pare it slightly, take hog's lard and chalk, equal parts, spread on a rag, tie on and let it remain three days, when it will be dead.

CORNS - CURE FOR

Wet common cooking soda with water, so that it will spread easily on a bit of cloth, and bind it on the corn. Keep it on till the corn is loosened and comes out. It is simple and sure.

CORNS - CURE FOR

Soak the feet in warm water, pare off as much of the corn as can be done without pain and bind up the part with a piece of linen or muslin thoroughly saturated with sperm oil, or, what is better, the oil from herring or mackerel. After three or four days' dressing may be found a soft and healthy texture and less liable to the formation of a new corn than before. We have obtained this recipe from a reliable source which we cannot well doubt, and we publish it for the benefit of many readers.

CORNS - PROMPT RELIEF AND REMOVAL OF

The useful onion - there is nothing better for the prompt relief and removal of corns. The onion, after soaking in vinegar for three or four hours, can be tied on the painful part over night, and will so loosen the hard substance that it can easily be removed with the hand. It has the same effect on old standing warts; and it is also excellent as stickphast-nay, more so, since it has been known to secure broken metal of all kinds. The article which needs mending should first be thoroughly washed with soda and water, then the onion juice may be painted on, with excellent and unfailing results.

CORNS REMOVED

Corns may be removed by applying the milky juice of common dandelion.

CORNS - TO TAKE SORENESS OUT OF

August Flower writes: To take the soreness out of corns in one night bind on a poultice of strong vinegar and bread. By using this occasionally you can keep your corn any length of time with little inconvenience, but poultice it every night for a week and you will probably loose it.

COTTAGE BREAD

One quart of flour, one egg, one tablespoonful butter, one of sugar, half cup of yeast; use milk or water, one pint.

COTTAGE PUDDING

One cup of sugar, one egg, two tablespoonfuls melted butter, one cup sweet milk, two cups flour, one teaspoonful cream tarter, half teaspoonful soda. Bake one-half hour. Eat with hot sauce.

COTTAGE PUDDING

Take one quart of flour, rub in four teaspoonfuls of cream tarter; stir in two cups of sweet milk, one cup of sugar, two eggs, two small teaspoonfuls of soda; bake in two loaves, half an hour. To be eaten with sauce.

COUGH CURE

A sure cough cure. Every night upon retiring take from three to five drops of camphor on a lump or teaspoonful of sugar, and let it melt gradually in the mouth.

COUGH DROPS

Here is a homemade remedy for relieving coughs: Take three ounces of pulverized licorice-root, one ounce of cubebs, pulverized, two ounces of gum arabic and one ounce of chlorate of potash, mix well with one cup of pulverized sugar, and just enough water to form a paste of a consistency so that you can roll it out thin, or to be the thickness of any troches, and cut with a thimble or into squares.

COUGH REMEDY

An excellent remedy for cough is as follows: Take a cupful of ginger and put it into a little cloth bag, tie around the throat and chest and wet with alcohol on going to bed.

COUGH REMEDY

When the baby has a severe cough there is a simple remedy to be found that does not require the attendance of a physician. Grease the baby between the shoulder blades in the back and across the lungs in the front with pure lard. It will cure the most clinging cough. (Mrs.G.)

COUGH SYRUP

A strong tea of mullein and hoarhound, sweetened to make a syrup and taken in generous doses, is an excellent remedy for the cough that usually follows the influenza.

COUGH SYRUP

One ounce each of thoroughwort, slippery elm, stick licorice and flax seed. Simmer in one quart of water till the strength is extracted. Strain carefully. Add one pint best West India molasses and one-half pound loaf sugar. Simmer well together. When cold, bottle tight. Must be kept cold or it will sour in warm weather. Use freely as required.

COUGH SYRUP

An ounce of flax-seed boiled in a pint of water, with a little honey, rock candy and lemon-juice added is excellent for a cough.

COUGH SYRUP

Here is a recipe for cough syrup that is the best of any I have used: 3 ounces of pure glycerin, 3 of extract of wild cherry, and 5 drachms of paregoric. Take a teaspoonful of the mixture before meals and upon retiring. Paste this in your scrapbook.

COUGH SYRUP

Boil a quarter of a pound of raisins, broken and a handful of licorice root in two quarts of water until the strength is extracted, then add a cup of flaxseed and the water in which it has been soaked overnight and boil half an hour, stirring to prevent burning; strain, add the juice of a lemon and sweeten to taste.

COUGHING

Try this syrup for a troublesome cough. Simmer two ounces of balm of Gilead buds in a quart of water until reduced to a pint, then strain and add one pound of honey in the comb with the juice of three lemons and boil until the comb is dissolved.

COUGHING

It is said that a small piece of resin dipped in the water which is placed in a vessel on the stove, will add a peculiar property to the atmosphere of the room, which will give great relief to persons troubled with a cough. The heat of the water is sufficient to throw off the aroma of the resin, and gives the same relief as is afforded by combustion of the resin. It is preferable to the combustion, because the evaporation is more durable. The same resin may be used for weeks.

CRAB APPLES

With the limited supply of the late varieties of apples, it will be the part of prudence to well stock the store closet with crabs. They furnish a bright palatable jelly, excellent sweet pickle, marmalade, etc., and are tempting canned. The Russian is the best variety for canning. There is no objection to removing the core, but it is unnecessary to take the trouble to excavate the apple to that extent. Select fair apples, take out the eyes and wash, they are ready for the preserving kettle. A quarter of a pound of sugar to a pound of fruit satisfies the lover of acids, and the allowance of half a pound makes a syrup rich enough for those fond of sweets. Cook slowly and the pulp will not burst its boundaries and cloud the syrup.

CRAB APPLE MARMALADE

Remove the eyes from Russian crabs, wash the apples and cook until soft; strain through a sieve and weigh. To every pound of fruit allow half a pound of sugar, half a pint of plum syrup and a gill of water and cook until thick, stirring often to prevent scorching. Put up in cups or glasses and protect from dust by pasting paper over the tops.

CRAB APPLE PICKLE

Bring to a boil a quart of vinegar, skim, and add four pounds of sugar and a small bag of spices, cinnamon and a few cloves giving a desirable flavor. Cook about eight pounds of apples in this, leaving the stems on, and seal.

CRAB APPLE PIE

Make some puff paste and line deep tins; fill with the pulp after it has been sifted, season with nutmeg and sprinkle thickly with sugar. Bake with an upper crust; or, when done, add a meringue of the whites of two eggs and one cupful of sugar and brown slightly in a hot oven. (See "CRAB APPLES" for the pulp.)

CRAB APPLE PRESERVE

Select only the best fruit, leaving the stems on, the Russian crab being the most desirable variety. Put the apples into the preserving kettle, with sufficient water to cover them, and heat it slowly, letting it just simmer until the skins begin to crack. Then drain and peel them, the skin will be just ready to slip off; leave the stem and very carefully extract the core through the blossom end, using a very sharp knife for the purpose. As soon as you have them all peeled and cored, weigh them, and to every pound of the fruit allow 1 1/4 pounds of sugar and a teacupful of water. Boil the water and sugar together skimming carefully until the scum ceases to rise and the syrup is perfectly clear. Now put in the fruit, cover the kettle, and boil until the apples are a clear red, and so tender that they may be pierced with a broom straw and not broken. Take them out of the syrup with a skimmer, and spread them on flat dishes to cool and harden. Add to the syrup the juice of one lemon to three pounds of fruit, and boil until it is clear and quite thick. Fill glass jars three-quarters full of the fruit, pour the syrup in, and when cool put on the tops and screw them down, and set away in a cool, dark, dry place.

CRAB APPLE PUDDING

Take one quart of crab apples, well cored, place over the fire with one pint of sugar and three cupfuls of cold water; cook until clear and thick. Place in a deep pudding dish, and pour over a batter made as follows: One-fourth of a cupful of butter, one cupful of sweet milk, two eggs, a spoonful of baking powder, and flour to make a thin batter. Bake one hour. Serve with sweetened whipped cream. This is a delicious pudding with other kinds of fruit.

CRAB APPLES WITH RAISINS

With a sharp knife remove the cores from large, crimson crab apples, fill the holes with raisins, sprinkle thickly with sugar, add a little water, and cook quickly. When cool and thick place in a glass dish and cover with the whites of two eggs, beaten stiff with a cupful of pulverized sugar.

CRACK FILLER

Cracks in floors, around the mould-board or other parts of the room, may be neatly or permanently filled by thoroughly soaking newspapers in paste made of one pound of flour, three quarts of water and a tablespoonful of alum, thoroughly boiled and mixed. This mixture will be about as thick as putty, and mix may be forced into the cracks with a case-knife. It will harden like paper mache. After getting it into good shape let it dry thoroughly, and then color it to conform to the woodwork around it.

CRACKED WHEAT

Put five large spoonfuls of wheat in a two-quart earthen jar which has a tight fitting cover; add a large spoonful of brown sugar, a small teaspoonful of salt and fill the jar with cold water. Place a few nails in a large iron kettle and set the jar in the kettle with cold water around it half way up the outside of the jar. Cover the jar and also the kettle and let it cook all day. If properly cooked the wheat will be like thick jelly. Eat with cream and sugar.

CRACKER MINCE PIE

Three large crackers; one cup of vinegar; one cup of molasses; two cups of sugar; a piece of butter the size of an egg; raisins and spice to your taste. This will make three pies.

CRACKER PIE

One soda cracker and a half, one teacup of white sugar, one lemon, one teacup of boiling water. Break the crackers into small bits, pour over them boiling water, cover and leave them to swell. Grate the yellow part of the lemon, add to it the juice and the sugar, mix with the cracker when it is sufficiently swelled; make a nice crust, and prepare as apple pies. Sift sugar over the pies when baked.

CRACKER PIES

Roll six crackers fine, and put them in a four quart pail or kettle; pour over them three-fourths of a pint of vinegar, two cups of molasses and a quart of boiling water. Boil on the stove half an hour, adding more water if necessary, to make quite thin. Add salt, raisins, and all kinds of spices, and make short crusts for four pies. Bake about twenty minutes, or until the top crust is put on.

CRACKER PLUM PUDDING

Split twenty-four crackers, place them in layers alternately with raisins, salt and cinnamon; that is, a layer of crackers, then one composed of raisins, salt and spice, then another of crackers, and so on until the crackers are all in. Fix three pints of new milk as you would for a rich custard, say four or five eggs to the quart, and sweeten to your taste; pour it over the crackers and let stand until morning. If the milk is then all absorbed add a little more, sweetened of course. Bake two hours and a half in a pretty hot oven. Let it stand in a cool place twenty four hours, then slip a knife round between the pudding and the pan and turn out upon a platter. Cut as you would cake, and eat with hot sauce made with sugar, a little flour and a bit of butter, with some grated nutmeg therein. This is a nice way to make plum pudding that will cut in slices, so much sought after at the present day. I should have said bake in a deep pudding pan. It looks very nice on the table if you put in plenty of plums, and tastes as nice as it looks.

CRANBERRIES

Put three pints of washed cranberries in a granite stewpan. On top of them put three cups of granulated sugar and three gills of water. After they begin to boil cook them ten minutes, closely covered, and do not stir them. Remove the scum. They will jelly when cool, and the skins will be soft and tender.

CRANBERRY TEA

For each quart of cranberries take one pound of sugar, boil to a pulp, and strain through a colander. For every two tablespoonfuls of the residue left in the colander, and being put into a mug, pour in one quart of boiling water; let stand for one hour and then strain. The jelly which passes through the colander can be used for cooking purposes, or tea can be made of it (like all other fruit jellies) by pouring boiling hot water upon it. Maid-of-all-Work.

CREAM

Beat well one egg, add to it one-half cup of sugar, one-third cup of flour, and a little milk to cause it to pour easily. Put into a kettle one and one-half cups of milk, when boiling add the above mixture, and let it boil enough to thicken, then take off, and when cool, add one-half teaspoon of lemon. This makes one large pie.

CREAM CAKE

Three eggs, one and one-half cups flour, one cup sugar, two teaspoonfuls baking powder, two tablespoonfuls water. Bake in jelly pans, making four cakes. Between the layers put a cream made of one pint milk, one egg, one tablespoonful corn starch and two tablespoonfuls sugar.

CREAM CAKE

One pint sweet cream; one cup white sugar; one cup currants;

wheat meal added to water, thin batter; bake in roll pans ½ inch deep, in quick oven.

CREAM CAKE

Four cups of sugar, three cups of flour, one cup of butter, one cup of sour cream, five eggs, one teaspoonful of soda dissolved in the cream; fruit if desired, though it is good without, and will keep a long time.

CREAM CAKE

One and one-half cups cream; one and one-half cups sugar; two eggs; spice as you please; make not quite as stiff as bread.

CREAM CANDY

Easily made and more wholesome than that which we buy. Four cupfuls of white sugar; half a cupful of milk; boil without stirring from ten to twenty minutes, or until it cracks in cold water. When done it will string off the spoon. Have ready half a pint of hickory nut meats, and, when taken from the stove, cool a little and beat until it sugars. Then put in shallow tins and grease.

CREAM CANDY

Put a pound of sugar in a saucepan with a teacupful of water, a tablespoonful of gum-arabic water and stir over the fire until the sugar dissolves; then boil without stirring until the syrup will harden when dropped in cold water. Take up, pour in grease plates and pour over it a teaspoonful of vanilla. Let cool and pull until white. Cut in sticks, put in a deep dish and cover; let stand two or three days before using.

CREAM CANDY

Take one-half cup of water and let it boil; then put in two cups of powdered or granulated sugar, one-half teaspoonful of cream of tartar, and butter large as a good size walnut; do not stir after it comes to a boil; try it and when it hardens in water, turn out and flavor with vanilla. Take chopping knife and cut in short pieces while pulling it; you can mix in chocolate if you wish.

CREAM CANDY

Boil one pint of granulated sugar and a pint of water, without stirring, until stiff enough to harden when dropped into cold water. Have prepared four teacupfuls of corn starch rubbed smooth in a very little cold water, and add just at this time. Stir constantly while boiling for a few minutes longer. Pour into a buttered dish, and when cool enough to handle work rapidly. Flavor as you pull it.

CREAM COOKIES

Two cups of thin cream, two cups of sugar, three eggs, a little salt, one small teaspoonful of soda, flavor to taste, add flour for a batter that can be dropped from a spoon on buttered tins. Bake fifteen minutes in a quick oven.

CREAM DRESSING

Two eggs, three tablespoonfuls of vinegar, one of cream, one teaspoonful of sugar, a little salt and one-fourth of a teaspoonful of mustard. Beat the eggs well, add sugar, salt and mustard, then vinegar, lastly cream. Place the bowl in a basin of boiling water and stir until it thickens, not longer. Cool and use when needed.

CREAM FOR CREAM CAKE

Let one coffee cupful of milk come to a boil, then thicken quite thick with one egg, two tablespoonfuls of sugar, one tablespoonful of corn starch. Salt the milk. Flavor and let cool.

CREAM PASTE

Mix half a teaspoonful of salt and half a saltspoonful of soda with one cup of cream, and stir in flour enough to mix to a stiff paste; roll half an inch thick; cut half a cup of butter into small pieces and put it on the paste; sprinkle with flour, fold and roll out thin, roll up, cut a piece from the end of the roll to fit the plate.

CREAM PITCHER DRIP

By rubbing a bit of butter immediately under the spout of the cream pitcher the disagreeable dripping of the cream can be prevented.

CREAM OF TARTER BISCUITS

One quart of sifted flour, mix with it thoroughly two teaspoonfuls of cream of tarter, one-half pint of new milk with two large tablespoonfuls of melted butter, one teaspoonful of soda; put the milk, butter and soda together, then mix with the flour, stirring and kneading as lightly as possible, so you can roll it out, bake in a quick oven. Great care should be used not to have the dough too hard; mix it just as soft as you can roll.

CREAM PIE

One cup of powdered sugar, three tablespoons of melted butter, two eggs, one-third cup of milk, one-half teaspoon of soda, one teaspoon cream tartar.

CREAM PIE

Boil one pint of milk, then beat together one egg, one cup of sugar, two tablespoons of flour, a little salt; add this mixture to the milk, and thicken over the fire. When cold flavor with lemon. Bake two crusts and put the cream between them, and I know you will have a good pie.

CREAM PIE

Two eggs, four tablespoonfuls of sugar, two of corn starch; mix yolks, flour and sugar together. Boil one pint of milk and stir in the above ingredients. Flavor with lemon and when baked frost with the two whites of the eggs whipped with a little sugar.

CREAM PIE

One cup of milk, one egg, one tablespoonful of sifted flour, and one tablespoonful of sugar. Put the milk on the stove and heat. Break the egg, separating the yolk from the white. Stir the flour into a little cold milk, add the yolk of the egg and beat well, stir into the boiling milk, and stir until it thickens. Flavor with one teaspoon of lemon. Pour into a crust previously baked. Beat the white to a stiff froth, adding two tablespoonfuls of white sugar. Spread over the pie. Put in the oven and slightly brown. Try these and you will find them good.

CREAM PIE

One cup of white sugar, two eggs, well beaten together, then cream a piece of butter the size of a hen's egg, add to the mixture, then sift 2 teaspoonfuls of cream tarter in two cups of flour and ½ cup of sweet milk and one teaspoonful of soda. Bake on round tins, in very thin layers; as soon as cold, beat one pint sweet cream until quite thick, add one cup of white sugar, then spread between cakes; any flavoring you prefer.

CREAM PIE

One cup of sugar; three eggs; one cup of flour; small piece of butter; one teaspoon of cream tarter; one-half teaspoon of soda. For the filling, one-half cup of white sugar; one small half cup flour; two eggs; a small piece of butter; one pint of milk; let the milk come to a boil, then add the rest; flavor to taste.

CREAM PIE

Take flour enough for the crust; salt it and mix with cream; roll the crust; sprinkle some flour between so that they need not stick together; bake in a quick oven. When done, separate the crusts, and take two tablespoonfuls of flour; the same of white sugar; one egg; beat all together. Boil one-half pint of milk; put in the batter of sugar and egg and stir till it thickens; then add some extract of lemon, and put it between the crusts, and you have a nice pie.

CREAM PIES

Four eggs beaten in one-half pint of cold milk, with six teaspoonfuls of flour, one teacup of sugar, little salt; heat one quart of milk to near boiling; then stir the eggs, etc., into the milk and stir rapidly until it thickens; add one teaspoonful of lemon extract; make the pastry, or crust, as for custard pies; when done, pour the cream on the pies and set away until cool.

CREAM SALMON

Take out the contents of a pint can and remove all bits of skin and bone, drain off the fluid and mince the fish fine. For a white sauce boil a pint of milk, thicken with two tablespoonfuls of corn starch, and add two tablespoonfuls of butter, with salt and pepper to one's liking; prepare one pint finely-powdered bread crumbs; put a thin layer of crumbs in bottom of pudding dish, then a layer of the minced fish, then a layer of the white sauce; repeat these layers for the whole, ending with crumbs; then bake in the oven until the top crumbs are a handsome brown. This is a delicious and nourishing dish for breakfast or tea, and is served as a fish course for dinner.

CREAM SAUCE

Boil a pint of rich cream with a few tablespoonfuls of powdered sugar, some grated nutmeg, and a dozen bitter almonds or peach kernels, or a dozen fresh peach leaves. As soon as it boils up take it off the fire and strain it. If it is to be used with boiled pudding, send it to the table hot, but if it accompanies pies or tarts, let it get quite cold.

CREAM SPONGE CAKE

Two eggs; one cup white sugar; one-half cup cream; mix thin with graham or white flour; bake in shallow roll pans.

CREAM TOAST

Boil a pint and a half of cream or new milk and thicken with a tablespoonful of flour or corn starch, add a little salt. Toast slices of stale bread quickly, of an even brown on both sides, lay them in the toast dish and dip over them a plentiful supply of the hot thickened cream; add another layer of toast and then more cream.

CREAM TROUT

Cut off the head and the tail, and put in boiling water slightly salted; let simmer five minutes, when, taking it out, let it drain, and put in a stewpan with some powdered mace, nutmeg and cayenne pepper; cover with cream and the fresh grated rind of a lemon; keep the pan covered and stew ten minutes; after dishing it stir in the cream a teaspoonful of arrowroot and pour over the trout.

CREAMED CABBAGE

Creamed cabbage has a delicate, delightful flavor and is more easily digested than boiled cabbage. Cut the cabbage fine and drop it in a stewpan of boiling water; add a pinch of ground cloves and a small onion. Cook it ten minutes; drain and add a tablespoonful of butter, the same of sugar, enough salt and pepper to suit your taste, and three tablespoonfuls of thick cream. Heat well and serve.

CREAMED SALT FISH

Soak one pint salt fish over night. In the morning pick it in small pieces and put it in a frying pan with sufficient water to cover it. Boil five minutes then pour off the water and add one pint of milk with cream if you have it. Let it boil five minutes, then thicken with flour and season with pepper and a little salt if required. Serve with plain boiled potatoes.

CREAMY TINGED STARCH

A faint, creamy tinge may be given to starch simply by omitting the bluing, and that a deeper yellow may be secured by mixing the starch with clear coffee.

CROCKERYWARE CEMENT

An easy way to mend broken crockeryware is by means of a cement made of lime and white of egg. Mix to form a paste and but a small amount at a time, as it hardens so quickly. Take sufficient quantity of the egg, mend one article, shave off a little lime, mix thoroughly, apply quickly to the edges, and place firmly together.

CROUP

Take a knife or grater and shave off in small particles about a teaspoonful of alum, mix it with twice the quantity of sugar to make it palatable and administer it as quick as possible. Almost instant relief will follow.

CROUP - CLARA'S REMEDY

In croup or lung trouble where there is difficulty in breathing, boil slack lime and let the patient inhale the steam. This has cured membranous croup and given great relief in lung trouble.

CROUP - INFLAMMATORY OR MEMBRANOUS

In inflammatory or membranous croup it is best to send for a physician at once. If it is a mild attack, mix equal parts of paregoric, sweet oil and syrup of ipecac, and give a teaspoonful every fifteen minutes until the child vomits, then once in three hours. Apply hot cloths to the chest.

CROUP REMEDY

Before putting the little ones to bed bathe feet and legs in as warm water as they can bear, rub neck, chest and back with kerosene, and give about a half a teaspoonful internally. This is the best remedy that I have found, and I have six little croupy fellows to doctor.

CROW- FEET

One need have no more "crow-feet" at 40 than at 14 if people would laugh with their mouths and not with the sides of their faces.

But the crow-feet are increased tenfold by burying the face in pillows at night. A looking-glass will prove this at any time. Wrinkles on the forehead are similarly invited, and with the crow-feet, can be sent away at any time.

CRULLERS

One cup of sugar, one cup of buttermilk or sour milk, three tablespoonfuls of melted butter, one egg, one teaspoonful of saleratus; flavor with nutmeg; a little salt. Mix as soft as possible, and cut any desired shape. Have your fat hot. If a piece of raw potato be peeled and thrown in the fat, it will keep the crullers from burning.

CRULLERS

Take three eggs; one teacup of sugar; a little salt; a piece of butter the size of an egg; knead in flour enough to make a stiff dough.

CRULLERS

A piece of butter the size of an egg, one cup of sugar, one nutmeg, three eggs; make stiff with flour and cut into fanciful shapes; fry in boiling lard.

CRUMPETS

Mix a quart of good milk with water to make a batter; add a little salt, and a tablespoonful of good yeast; beat well, cover it up, and let it stand in a warm place to rise. Clean the muffin plate, or, not having this, a frying pan, while warm, over the fire, and rub it with a greased cloth or a little butter tied up in a piece of muslin; pour a cupful of batter into the pan or on the plate; and as it begins to bake, raise the edge all round with a sharp knife. When one side is done, turn and bake the other side. Crumpets are generally now poured into proper-sized rings of tin, which makes them all of a size and thickness.

CRUST COFFEE

Take two cups of graham meal, three of corn meal and mix in one of molasses, burning carefully, like common coffee. Of this about one teaspoonful to a pint of water is sufficient to make a delicious and wholesome drink, not "bilious" in its tendency. To try it is to use it.

CRUSTS FOR TARTS

A.A.F. and Minnie H. want to know how to make crusts for tarts. Here is my way which we think excellent, for pies, tarts, etc. ; take one pint of flour to the pie, rub into it shortening of butter if you can afford it, if not, use good sweet lard, never drippings, enough to make it as short as you like, and a little salt. Mix up with pure cold water just enough so you can make it stick together by pressing between your hands, and roll out to the desired thickness, and bake in a quick oven. Never knead your pie crust, and be sure to bake pies, not dry them.

CUCUMBER CATSUP

One dozen of large cucumbers grated, one pint of grated onions and one pint of grated horseradish; put in a jar and - season with clove and pepper; scald vinegar and pour on hot.

CUCUMBER PICKLES

The brine for salting them should be strong enough to float a potato, and they must be kept under it. The brine will also need to be poured over every few days for two weeks, in order to prevent the fresh juice of the cucumbers rising to the top and becoming sour. The pickles ferment in the brine, and a dirty scum rises to the top of the barrel which should be removed. To keep the pickles under the brine, the barrels are provided with a loosely-fitted cover, which must be loaded with stone and watched as the pickles settle, and care taken to keep them from the air. Any pickle coming to the air will quickly soften and spoil, and should be promptly thrown away to prevent them from spoiling the brine. When the pickles are wanted for use they are taken out of the brine and placed in fresh water, which is to be frequently changed. In a day or two they will become fresh, and should then be placed in strong vinegar, spiced to suit the taste. This method will produce what are known in the market as English pickles. They are a dull yellowish-brown color, and very good.

CUCUMBER PICKLES

Let the cucumbers soak in a weak brine for twenty-four hours, then pack in cans or jars. Boil the vinegar, spicing to taste, and pour over the pickles while scalding hot, and seal. If the pickles are in stone jars they may be sealed by tying a cloth over the top and pouring melted wax over it. If for present use keep a plate with a weight on it over the pickles to keep them under the vinegar, and tie a cloth and paper over the top. Be sure to keep the jar closely covered. If a scum rises on the vinegar scald and skim it. Spices help to preserve the vinegar.

CUCUMBER PICKLES

Pick small cucumbers carefully, wash in water and fill your jars. Mix thoroughly one-half cupful each of salt and ground mustard, with one gallon of vinegar, cold; fill your jars to the brim, seal, and you have pickles that will keep the year around.

CUFF HOLDER

A small loop of elastic, sewed to the inner side of the sleeve so that it may be attached to the cuff button, will be found to be better than a pin to hold the cuff securely in place.

CUP CAKE

Four cups of flour, two cups of sugar, one cup of butter, one cup of sour cream, four eggs, one scant teaspoonful of soda, nutmeg; fruit if desired.

CURING BACON AND HAMS

Rub them thoroughly with perfectly clean, pure common salt. Let them lie for one day, and in that time prepare the following mixture: For every forty pounds of meat take a pound of common salt, three-quarters of a pound of bay salt, one ounce and a half of black pepper, half an ounce of allspice, and two ounces of saltpetre, all well ground together. After it has soaked one day, rub the meat well with this mixture, and let it lie in it four days; then repeat the rubbing and let it lie two days; on the third day pour over it three pounds of treacle or molasses for every pound of meat. Leave the meat in this, rubbing it well all over in the pickle three times a week for one month, turning it over each time. At the end of the month hang up each piece to drain. When thoroughly drained smoke them, or, if not convenient, rub them over with the essence of tar, which will give them the smoky flavor, if desired.

CURING BEEF

For a small family, where only a small quantity of beef is cured, this is the most excellent way: Take for twenty pounds of beef, one pint of salt, one teaspoonful of saltpetre, quarter of a pound of brown sugar, dividing the ingredients into three equal parts, rub them well into the beef on three successive days; the meat is ready to hang up in one week; in this way we dispense with pickle altogether.

CURRANT AND GOOSEBERRY COMPOTE

Put one quart of red currant juice to five pounds of loaf sugar; set it on the fire, and when the sugar is dissolved put in eight pounds of red, rough, ripe gooseberries, let them boil half an hour, then put them in an earthen pan and leave them stand for two days; then boil them again until they look clear; put them into pots and let them stand a week to dry a little at the top, then cover them with brandy papers. (Germantown Telegraph)

CURRANT CREAM

Take some currants, thoroughly ripe, bruise them in boiled cream, add beaten cinnamon, and sweeten to your taste; then strain it through a fine sieve, and serve.

CURRANT JAM OF ALL COLORS

Strip your currants and put them into your pan, with three-quarters of a pound of sugar to a pound of fruit; add your sugar after your fruit has boiled a few minutes; boil all together, mashing your fruit with a wooden spoon; boil all gently for half an hour, then fill your jars.

CURRANT JELLY

Let your currants remain on the bushes until perfectly ripe; pick carefully from them all leaves, but it is not necessary to pick them from the clusters: put them in a stone pot, and place them in a kettle of boiling water for a few minutes, then the juice may be pressed from them more easily; mash and strain. To each pound of juice add one pound of sugar; boil the juice separately five minutes; heat the sugar as hot as possible without burning or melting; pour into the boiling juice, and boil together two minutes; strain and cool in any form desirable.

CURRANT JELLY

Put your currants in a bell-metal kettle and scald them well; when cool press them through a sieve, getting out all the juice, (be careful not to allow any skin or seeds to pass through the sieve), measure the juice and put it back again into the kettle and let it boil hard for five or six minutes, skimming it well; then add while on the fire boiling one pound of sifted loaf sugar to every pint of juice; stir it till dissolved, which will be in a few minutes; it ought not to boil after the sugar is in, all that is necessary is to have it well dissolved, and then it is ready to put in the tumblers. It tastes much more of the fruit and is a beautiful light color. Will keep for years if necessary.

CURRANT JELLY

Pick fine, red, but long-ripe currants from the stems; bruise them and strain the juice from a quart at a time through a thin muslin; wring it gently to get all the liquid; put a pound of white sugar to each pound of juice; stir it until it is all dissolved; set it over a gentle fire; let it become hot, and boil for fifteen minutes; then try it by taking a spoonful into a saucer; when cold, if it is not quite firm enough, boil it for a few minutes longer.

CURRANT JELLY

Stem the currants; scald them in a porcelain kettle or in a crock set in a kettle of hot water. Do not let them boil. You can tell by the changed color when they are scalded. They must be stirred occasionally, as those at the bottom heat more rapidly than those at the top. When they are scalded mash them, and as soon as cool enough strain first through a course linen bag, and then through a flannel one. Allow one pound of granulated sugar to a pint of juice, but it will jelly with less. Five pounds of sugar to six pounds of juice will answer, but will require boiling a few moments longer. Measure your sugar, put it in the oven and heat it as hot as possible without yellowing it any; let your juice boil ten minutes; then throw in the hot sugar and it will probably jelly as soon as it dissolves. Try it by cooling a little in a tablespoon on a piece of ice, or by putting a little in a sauce dish and setting in cold water. If it stiffens even on the edge of the spoon or dish it is done; if not, boil it five minutes and try it again. Old and fully ripe currants should not be used for jelly. The color will not be fine and it will be more difficult to stiffen it. Have your jelly glasses warm and pour the hot jelly immediately in, and set them until the following morning where the flies will not have access to them. Then cut some white writing paper just the size of the top of your glasses, and lay a piece over each glass so that it will rest on the jelly; then pour on each a teaspoon of brandy, and paste a brown paper tightly over the glass. The brandy will prevent any mould gathering, and, if you keep the jelly until next summer, you will find it all right. The glasses should be filled as full as possible with the hot juice, as it shrinks in cooling. Jellies made of berries are improved by putting currant juice with them, without losing the flavor of the berries.

CURRANT, RASPBERRY OR BLACKBERRY JAM

Pick over and mash the fruit; allow one pound of sugar to a pound of fruit; put the fruit and one-quarter of the sugar into a granite or porcelain kettle; when boiling add another quarter of the sugar; boil again, add more sugar, and when it is all used let it boil till it hardens on the spoon in the air. Apples, pears, peaches and quinces should be pared, cut small and treated in the same way. Cooking in only a little sugar at a time prevents the fruit from becoming hard.

CURRANT WINE

Two quarts of currant juice, two quarts of water, and three pounds of sugar. Leave it in open jugs until well fermented, taking care to keep them always full. Then pour it off carefully, and bottle tight.

CURRANT WINE

Dissolve eight pounds of honey in fifteen gallons of boiling water, to which, when clarified, add the juice of eight pounds of red or white currants: then ferment for twenty-four hours; to every two gallons add two pounds of sugar, and clarify with whites of eggs.

CURRANT WINE

We believe that we have as good currant wine as is made by the generality of people - some think it is unexcelled. We confess we never drank better. The process of making is simple, but none of its requirements should be departed from. It is as follows:

First, crush the currants effectually, then place them in a strong bag, and press the juice out, by whatever means will effect it best; then, to each quart of juice, add three pounds of double-refined sugar, and as much water as will make one gallon. Good brown sugar will answer, but not so well in retaining the fine flavor of the wine, though it will give it more body.

To make a ten gallon keg of wine, it will require ten quarts of currant juice, and thirty pounds of sugar, filled up with water. Be sure that the sugar is well dissolved, by rolling over and shaking the cask; but we prefer mixing all together before putting into the cask, in an open vessel, in which it should remain forty-eight hours, and frequently skimmed. Fermentation will begin in one or two days, the bung being removed, and will continue some two or three weeks. After it has entirely ceased fermenting, rack off carefully, then scald out the barrel, return the wine to the cask, tightly bung up, and leave undisturbed for six months before using, when, if preferred, it can be bottled. It requires no clearing substance or spirituous liquor of any kind, as it is much better without either.

The keg, cask, or whatever vessel it may be made in, should be full, and as fermentation is going on, the extraneous substances thrown out of the bung, the vessel should be kept full by adding sufficient pure juice kept in reserve. (Germantown Telegraph)

CURRANTS PRESERVED

Take ripe currants free from stems; weigh them, and take the same amount of sugar; put a teacup of sugar to each pound of it; boil the syrup until it is hot and clear; then turn it over the fruit; let it remain one night; then set it over the fire, and boil gently until they are cooked and clear; take them into the jars or pots with a skimmer; boil the syrup till rich and thick, then pour it over the fruit.

CURRANTS PRESERVED

Currants may be preserved with ten pounds of fruit to seven of sugar. Take the stems from seven pounds of the currants, and crush and press the juice from the remaining three pounds; put them into the hot syrup, and boil until thick and rich; put in pots or jars, and next day secure as directed.

CURRIED CHICKEN

Cut a chicken into pieces, season and fry in butter. Slice an onion and fry in butter, add a teacupful of stock, one tablespoonful of curry powder mixed with a little flour, and rubbed smooth with a little stock; salt; boil five minutes.

CUSK A LA CREME

Clean a fish and put it into boiling water with one tablespoonful each of salt and vinegar; boil until the fish separates from the bone; remove the skin and bones and flake; season highly with salt and pepper; spread it on a platter and pour over it a hot cream sauce made with one quart of milk, three tablespoonfuls of flour and one-fourth cup of butter; season the sauce with salt, pepper, onion juice and one tablespoonful of finely chopped parsley; spread it over one cup of bread crumbs moistened in one-fourth of a cup of melted butter, and brown in the oven.

CUSK A LA CREME

If any housekeeper desires to make the best dish from fresh fish she ever saw or tasted, let her try the following:

Take a fish weighing from two to three pounds, rub it well with salt and put it into a kettle with enough water to cover it. When it comes to a boil set it off where it will cool. When cool enough take out the bones. Take a pint of milk or cream, and boil a large onion and a piece of mace in it. Rub a quarter of a pound of butter into some flour, strain off the onion from the milk, and mix smoothly, adding a little pepper. Put it on the fire and stir until like a thick sauce. Lay the fish in a deep dish and pour the sauce over it. Have some crumbs ready to sift thickly over the top. Then bake from half to three-quarters of an hour.

CUSTARD

Plain boiled custard: To one quart of milk add four well beaten eggs; sugar to taste; flavor with lemon or vanilla. Put it in a small pan and set this in a larger one with hot water in. Cook until it thickens. Take a little out on a saucer, let it cool, and you can judge from that how long to keep it in the hot water. If left in the pan until it cools, it will thicken some even after it is taken out of the water.

CUSTARD CAKE

One cup of sugar, one egg, and one-third of a cup of butter, put together and beat to a cream; then add one cup of sweet milk, two cups of flour, one teaspoonful of soda and two teaspoonfuls of cream of tarter. Bake in jelly tins. Custard for inside - one and one-half cups of milk, two eggs, (reserving one white if frosting is desired), one tablespoonful of corn starch and one cup of sugar. Flavor to suit the taste.

CUSTARD CORN CAKE

One-half cup of sour milk, one and one-half cups sweet milk, one-half teaspoonful of soda, one tablespoonful of melted butter, one tablespoonful of sugar, and about four small handfuls of Indian meal. This will seem thin, but when baked twenty minutes in a hot oven it is very much like a thick custard. It is very nice.

CUSTARD MAKING

If one has not the convenient double boilers, use a common iron kettle, put a stick across it and hang a tin pail on it. If you wish to prevent the eggs from curdling when making boiled custard, pour the boiling milk on the beaten eggs. A little gelatin, dissolved, added to a baked or boiled custard, improves it very much. Steamed cup custards are very nice. Make as you would for baking, fill tea or coffee cups (without handles) two-thirds full, set into a steamer over a kettle of hot water, watch carefully and take out the instant the custard has "set". You can reserve some of the whites if you wish; beat them to a stiff froth, sweeten with a little powdered sugar, and then when the custards are cold, put a spoonful on top of each cup. A bit of currant jelly in the center looks pretty.

CUSTARD PIE

Put one quart of milk over the fire in a farina boiler, or in some vessel in which there is no danger of scorching. As soon as it boils stir in a large tablespoonful of dissolved corn starch. Sweeten and flavor to suit yourself. Take the milk from the fire, and stir in three thoroughly beaten eggs. This must be done very gradually, beating the mixture constantly, to prevent the curdling of the eggs. Bake with only a bottom crust.

CUSTARD PIE (ANOTHER ONE)

Take one and a half tablespoonfuls butter, two cups sugar, four eggs, two teacups water, two level tablespoonfuls flour. Rub the butter and sugar together, and add to it the juice of four lemons, and the chopped rind of two, the yolks of the eggs, then the flour, and lastly the water. Bake in an under crust only, until it is of a light brown color. While it is baking, beat the whites of the eggs to a stiff froth with a teacup of fine sugar. Spread this over the top of the pie when done, and return it to the oven for five minutes, to brown.

CUSTARD PIES WITHOUT MILK

Beat together four eggs, 4 large spoonfuls of sugar; 1 small one of flour; 1 of butter; a pinch of salt, and spice to taste; add boiling water enough to fill a large sized pie pan and bake immediately. (Ellen)

CUT GLASS CLEANING

Cut glass should be washed with a small soft brush, and dried with soft tissue paper.

CUT JEWEL CLEANING

Cut jewels should never be wiped after washing. Wash carefully with a brush and Castile soapsuds; rinse and lay face down, deep into fine sawdust until dry; boxwood dust is best.

CUTLETS OF COLD MUTTON

The remains of cold loin or neck of mutton, one egg, bread crumbs, brown gravy or tomato sauce. Cut the remains of cold loin or neck of mutton into cutlets, trim them, and take away a portion of the fat should there be too much, dip them in a beaten egg, sprinkle with bread crumbs, and fry them a nice brown in hot drippings. Arrange them on a dish, and pour around them either a good gravy or hot tomato sauce.

DANDRUFF

A remedy for keeping the hair from falling out and to cure dandruff is one tablespoonful of salt and eight of alcohol to one pint of soft water. Dampen the roots every other day.

DARNING GLOVES

Try darning gloves in buttonhole-stitch, repeating until the hole is filled up.

DEAFNESS AND HEAD-NOISES

Put four tablespoonfuls of fresh goose-oil in a bottle with a piece of camphor gum as large as a marble; keep the bottle in a warm place until the camphor dissolves, then add five cents worth of oil of peppermint, shake thoroughly, and put three drops in each ear night and morning. Place a bit of cotton in the ear to keep the oil in and the air out.

DELICATE CAKE

Take the whites of four eggs well beaten, 1 cup of white sugar, half a cup of butter, half a cup of sweet milk, 2 cups of flour, 1 teaspoonful of cream tarter and half a teaspoonful of soda.

DELICATE CAKE

One-half cup of sweet milk; one cup of white sugar; one-fourth of a teaspoonful of soda; one-half of a teaspoonful of cream tarter; one and one-half tablespoonfuls of melted butter; whites of two eggs, and one cup of flour.

DELICATE RICE PUDDING

One cup of rice, cleaned, washed, put into one quart of milk, set in a kettle of boiling water. Keep the water boiling until the rice is soft, then add the yolks of three eggs, putting a very little cold milk to them, that they may not change at once, and a little salt. Bake about an hour in a pretty hot oven. Just before taking it up, allowing just time to fit it for the table, beat the whites of the eggs to a foam, and add 1 cup sugar; flavor it if you wish; when all beaten together, pour over the pudding, which should be baked in a shoal dish, as this is the sauce to be eaten with it. Put it in a brisk oven about five minutes, or until the foam begins to brown. There is so much difference in the length of time required in different ovens, it is impossible to give the exact time for finishing. (American Agriculturist)

DELICIOUS CAKE

One cup of sugar, half a cup of butter, two eggs, the yolks and whites beaten separately, half a cup of milk, 1 ½ cups of flour, and 1 ½ teaspoonfuls of baking powder. This is nice with caramel frosting, which is made with 1 cup of sugar, half a cup of milk, a piece of butter the size of an egg; boil hard for ten minutes; stir till nearly cold. If chocolate is preferred add one square of melted; stir well.

DELICIOUS CORN CHOWDER

One quart of raw sweet corn, or one can of corn, one-fourth pound of fat salt pork, one heaping tablespoonful of butter, three heaping tablespoonfuls of flour, one pint of raw sliced potatoes, one large onion, one pint of tomatoes, one pint of new milk, salt and pepper. Cut corn from cob, cover cobs with water, and boil twenty minutes. Take out cobs, peel and slice onion, fry half of it with pork, mix pepper, flour and salt together. Put corn, potatoes, tomatoes, and remaining onion in layers, sprinkle each layer with the flour mixture, strain the fat from the onion and pork into the kettle, add cob water. Cook until vegetables are done, then add butter and milk, serve hot with crackers. If canned vegetables are used add one quart of water. (Anna L. Judkins)

DELICIOUS GINGERBREAD

One cup of molasses, two of butter, two cups of sugar, one cup of sour milk, four eggs, three cups of flour, one tablespoonful of ginger.

DELMONICO PUDDING

Boil one quart of milk over a slow fire, stirring often; stir in the yolks of four eggs, well beaten, four tablespoonfuls of corn starch wet with milk, five tablespoonfuls of sugar, a pinch of salt; when the mixture thickens, pour it into a tin kettle, set in cold water on ice, to prevent curdling; beat the whites of the eggs to a froth; add four tablespoonfuls of sugar and one ounce of vanilla; put the pudding in a baking dish, frost with the egg, and then brown in the oven.

DELMONICO PUDDING

Three tablespoonfuls corn starch; one quart of boiling milk; three eggs, whites and yolks separated. Mix yolks with cornstarch and add milk gradually. Let it boil. Beat whites to a stiff froth, sweeten. Put in pudding dish, cover with frosting and set in oven to brown. To be eaten cold.

DEODORIZING WOOLENS

Woolen garments of any kind that are worn frequently require more than ordinary brushing or shaking out, for often unpleasant odors cling to them. After using the brush or whisk broom conscientiously in every wrinkle or fold, the garment should be turned inside out and hung for several hours in the wind and sun. No simple or more efficacious means of deodorizing could be found.

DESTROYING BED BUGS

There are innumerable receipts for the destruction of this household pest. One of the best is the following: Scald the bedsteads, and wipe them dry; mix ordinary lamp-oil with a little quicksilver, and apply this to the cracks with a feather.

DESTROYING MOTHS

Get two or three pounds of powdered borax; if necessary untack the carpets around the edges; sprinkle plenty of borax all around the outer edges of the carpet, and with a feather or brush try to shove as much as possible under the surbase; let the borax remain there, it will not injure the carpet. I also made a line of borax all around the surbase and on the carpet.

DEVONSHIRE JUNKET

Regular Devonshire junket is made by adding to two quarts of milk warmed, one glass of pale brandy, sugar sufficient to sweeten, and two tablespoonfuls of rennet. After it sets in a curd lay over the top thick rich cream, and grate over it a little nutmeg. Serve.

DIARRHEA

A tea made of mullein-leaves, taken strong, will cure severe diarrhea; and the tea is also most excellent for lung-trouble, having been known to cure incipient consumption.

DIARRHEA - CURE FOR

The small plant, commonly known by the name of Rupturewort, made into a tea and drank frequently, is a sure cure for the disease. Rupturewort grows in nearly every open lot, and along the roads. It is a small plant, throwing out a number of shoots in a horizontal direction, and lying close to the ground, something similar to the manner of the Pusleyweed, and bears a small dark green leaf, with an oblong purple spot in the center. When the stem is broken, a white milky substance will ooze from the wound. It is very palatable, and infants take it as readily as any drink. This is an old Indian cure, and may be relied on. The botanical name of the plant is Euphorbia Maculata.

DIPHTHERIA

A noted medical authority recommends the following in a case of diphtheria: Pour from twenty to forty drops of a mixture of equal parts of turpentine and carbolic acid into a kettle of water, keep simmering over a slow fire, so that the air of the sick room will be constantly impregnated with the odor of these two substances.

DIPHTHERIA - A SIMPLE REMEDY

Dr. Revillout states that lemon juice used as a gargle is as efficacious specified against diphtheria and similar throat troubles. He has successfully thus employed it for eighteen years.

DIPHTHERIA-CURE FOR

We publish the following because the experiment may be safely tried, and is worth trying. Diphtheria is becoming a dreadful scourge, and what the writer of what is here said saw the working of this cure in the hands of an English physician, at a time when the disease was prevalent in an English town. Speaking of the physician's application, the writer says: "All he took with him was powder of sulphur and a quill, and with these he cured every case without exception. He put a spoonful of the flour of brimstone into a wine glass of water, and stirred it with his fingers instead of the spoon, as the sulphur does not readily amalgamate with water. When the sulphur was well mixed, he gave it as a gargle, and in ten minutes the patient was out of danger. Brimstone kills every species of fungus in man, beast or plant, in minutes. Instead of spitting out the gargle, he recommends the swallowing of it. In extreme cases in which he has been called just in the nick of time, when the fungus was too nearly closed to allow the gargle, he blew the sulphur through a quill into the throat, and after the fungus had shrunk to allow of it, then the gargling. He never lost a patient from diphtheria. If a patient cannot gargle, take a live coal, put it on a shovel and sprinkle a spoonful or two of flour of brimstone at a time upon it, let the sufferer inhale it, holding the head over it, and the fungus will die. If plentifully used, the whole room may be filled almost to suffocation, the patient can walk about in it, inhaling the fumes with doors and windows shut. The plan of fumigating a room with sulphur has often cured most violent attacks of cold in the head and chest."

DIPHTHERIA - CURE FOR

Make a strong decoction of the bark of the root of wild indigo, and stir in pulverized slippery elm to make a poultice. Put it on the throat from ear to ear. Swab the mouth, or rinse it freely, with the decoction. It is good for croup. For common sore throat wet the bark with a little warm water, put it in flannel, and bind on the throat at night; there will be no soreness in the throat in the morning. It is good to use as a gargle for sore mouth, also as a wash for sore or weak eyes.

DIPHTHERIA - LEMON JUICE

Dr. J. R. Page of Baltimore invites the attention of the profession to the topical use of fresh lemon juice as the most efficient means for the removal of membrane from the throat, tonsils, etc., in diphtheria. In his hands (and he has heard several of his professional brethren say the same) it has proved by far the best agent he has yet tried for the purpose. He applies the juice of the lemon by means of a camel-hair probing to the affected parts every two or three hours, and in eighteen cases on which he has used it the effect has been all he could wish.

DIPHTHERIA - TARTARIC ACID

The topical use of tartaric acid in diphtheria has been successfully resorted to by M. Vidal who, in one of the foreign medical journals, remarks upon the necessity of thus making use of topical agents against the false membrane, as it has a great tendency to spread by a sort of autoinoculation, similar to what occurs in some coetaneous affections. His formula is ten parts, by weight, of tartaric acid, fifteen of glycerin, and twenty-five of mint water. The acid acts upon the false membrane, converting it into a gelatinous mass, and favors its expulsion.

DIRECTIONS FOR FREEZING CREAM

The essential points are to have the ice finely crushed, to use the right proportion of coarse salt, and to beat the mixture thoroughly during the freezing. The finer the ice is crushed, the quicker it melts; and melted ice and salt is many degrees colder than ice alone. The more the mixture is stirred, the sooner all parts become chilled. The melted ice and salt should surround the can, and not drawn off until it floats the ice. Use one part of salt to three or four parts of ice, packing each layer in closely with a wooden paddle. Be sure that the freezer works perfectly before adding the cream. When the cream is thoroughly cold, pour it into the can. Turn slowly at first, and after ten minutes more rapidly, till you can turn no longer. It usually takes about half an hour. Remove the beater, scrape off the cream, and beat and pack the cream closely in the can. Put a cork into the opening in the cover, and lay the cross piece over to keep the can down in the ice. If the ice and salt have been well packed, and the cream is to be served within an hour, no more ice will be needed; but if to be kept longer, draw off the water and pack again.

DISAGREEABLE SMELL REMOVER

Charcoal left in jars or bottles will remove disagreeable smells.

DISCOLORED ENAMELED KETTLES

If you have an enameled kettle which has become discolored, try boiling it in water to which a little chloride of lime has been added.

DISEASE PREVENTION

A little sulphur burned in each room during or after a rainy spell will often prevent disease.

DISINFECTANT - USING COFFEE

Coffee is an effective disinfecting agent, as the following experiment will show: A quantity of meat was hung in a room which was kept closed until the decomposition of the meat was well advanced. A chafing dish was then put in, and some half-roasted coffee thrown on the fire. In a few minutes the room was disinfected. The best way to effect this fumigation is to strew ground coffee on a hot iron plate.

DISINFECTING MIXTURE

This disinfecting mixture is very agreeable to use in the sick room. It is to be put in a porcelain vessel and allowed to evaporate gradually. From a dessertspoonful to two tablespoonfuls may be used according to the size of the room. Make a solution of one and one-half parts of nitric acid in thirty parts of water; mix with it ten parts of rosemary, two and a half parts of oil of thyme and two and a half parts of oil of lavender. Bottle the mixture, and, before using, shake thoroughly.

DIZZINESS AND NAUSEA

You may find a good remedy in aromatic spirits of ammonia. Take from one-half to a teaspoonful in a glass of Vichy water as required.

DOLLIE VARDEN WHITE CAKE

Cream together one cup of white sugar and one-third cup of butter. Stir in the whites of three eggs beaten stiff, and beat the whole together until smoothly foamy, then add a small cupful of sweet milk into which has been stirred one teaspoonful of soda and two teaspoonfuls of cream of tartar. If the butter be very fresh add a pinch of salt. Much of the insipidity of cake is the result of a lack of salt. Thicken with flour to the consistency of ordinary cup cake, and bake in a biscuit tin or sponge cake sheet. To the yolks of three eggs add a teaspoonful of pulverized Poland starch and sugar enough to beat very stiff. When the cake is still warm from the oven spread upon it the frosting thus made, and put in a cool place to stiffen. This cake is very ornamental, being of snowy whiteness, with bright yellow frosting.

DOTTY DIMPLE'S VINEGAR CANDY ━━━━━━━━━

For Dotty Dimple's vinegar candy, three cups of white sugar, one and one-half cups of clear vinegar. Stir the sugar into the vinegar until thoroughly dissolved. Heat to a gentle boil, stew, uncovered, until it ropes from the tip of the spoon. Turn out upon broad dishes, well buttered and cool. So soon as you are able to handle it without burning your hands, begin to pull it, using only the tips of your fingers. It can be pulled beautifully white and porous. Children who have Sophie May's "Little Birdy" and "Dotty Dimple" stories will remember the famous vinegar candy and be glad to test it for themselves.

DOUGHNUTS ━━━━━━━━━━━━━━━

By Jane E. Duffie. Take one pint of strained buttermilk, one teacup of sugar, one egg; one teaspoonful of soda, and a little salt. Add flour enough to make a stiff dough.

DOUGHNUTS ━━━━━━━━━━━━━━━

I would like the lady readers of the household to try my doughnut recipe and see if they do not pronounce it excellent, because the doughnuts absorb so little fat. One teacupful of sugar, one teaspoonful of sweet milk, one egg, one teaspoonful of soda, one teaspoonful of cream of tartar, one tablespoonful of sweet cream or lump of butter the size of a hickory nut and spice to taste, roll thin and cut with a round tin, making the hole in the middle with a thimble; fry in lard.

DOUGHNUTS ━━━━━━━━━━━━━━━

One cup of milk; one cup of sugar; one egg; one teaspoonful of saleratus; one of cream tarter; flour enough to make them stiff enough to roll.

DRESSING FOR FISH

Soak half a pound of bread crumbs in water; when the bread is soft, press out all the water; fry two tablespoonfuls of minced onions in butter; add the bread crumbs, some chopped parsley, a tablespoonful of chopped suet, pepper and salt; let cook for a moment, take it off the fire and add an egg.

DRESSING FOR FOWL

A sausage cut up with bread crumbs, wet with an egg and a little boiling water, will be found to be convenient and good.

DRIED AND CANDIED FRUITS

We will give the rule for candying and drying cherries. The same process would be followed with other fruits. Candied fruit is prepared until it has cooled in the syrup. It must then be taken out, washed in lukewarm water and dried in the mouth of the oven, not too hard; the syrup is then returned to the fire and boiled until it reaches what confectioners call the "blow", that is when, by dipping a skimmer in the boiling syrup, and blowing through the holes, little sparkling bubbles are formed over them; the fruit is then put into it and boiled until it again reaches the "blow"; the skimmer is rubbed against the side of it until the sugar begins to "grain" - that is, to grow white; the fruit is then dipped in that part of the sugar, taken out with a fork, and drained on a wire grating over the pan; the fruit dries quickly, and is then ready for use or preservation by packing in boxes between layers of paper.

DRIED-APPLE CAKE

Soak two cups of dried apples overnight. Chop fine and boil in two cups of molasses until soft. Drain off the molasses, add to it one cup of butter, two eggs, one cup of sour milk, two teaspoonfuls of saleratus, four cups of flour, spice of all kinds . Add the apples last.

DRIED APPLE FRUIT CAKE

One and one-half cups of molasses; one-half cup brown sugar; 3 cups of flour; 1 cup sour milk; 1 teaspoonful saleratus; 1 egg; one-half cup of butter; one and one-half cups of sweet apples, soaked and chopped, put into the molasses and boiled; spice to taste.

DRIED BEEF

Cut in tolerably small pieces, roll in salt, shake lightly, put the beef down in what salt remains on it, tight. Use no water; let remain three days in salt, then hang up to dry; smoke with wood smoke until a hard crust forms on the outside. Try it, and you will have an article fit for the gods. There is no use in keeping beef in brine until it is as salt as Lot's wife.

DRIED CORN

Sugar corn gathered early and scalded to preserve the milky substance intact, should be carefully cut from the cob and placed on trays in the sun till thoroughly dried for winter use. If soaked overnight and seasoned as per recipe, it is excellent, and very like fresh corn. As previously stated, corn differs much in size and quality of the grain. Only the perfect ears are selected and placed into a separate bin for grinding purposes.

DRIED SWEET CORN

Boil the corn as directed in the receipt for hot corn; as soon as it can be handled, take off the husks and cut the grains from the cobs with a sharp knife. Spread them on a sheet of cotton batting, and dry them in the mouth of a cool oven or in the hot sun. When the corn is thoroughly dry put in paper bags and keep it in a dry place. When wanted for use, soak overnight in water, and then boil it for five minutes in water or milk; season it with salt and pepper, add a little butter and serve it hot.

DRINKING CUP

People who are traveling and do not wish to use the public and dangerous drinking cup may improvise one by bending up a piece of foolscap.

DRIVING FLIES FROM A ROOM

Mix with half a teacupful of milk a tablespoonful of finely-ground black pepper, and the same quantity of sugar. Put this about where the flies are the most numerous.

DROPPED EGGS

Have ready a saucepan of boiling water. Drop fresh eggs carefully into the water so as not to break the yolks. Let them stand where they will keep hot, but not boil, until the white sets. Toast slices of bread and lay in a dish, and pour over it a gill of hot cream with a little salt, then take out the eggs with an ess-slice or tablespoon, and put on the bread with parsley, if you like.

DROPSY

About two years ago I was quite ill with dropsy and two doctors said that I would have to be tapped, but a lady told me a simple remedy that I believed cured me. Take black current leaves and make an infusion, and drink it freely.

DROPSY

I must give a tested remedy for dropsy: Take uncolored broom-corn, such as brooms are made of when ripe, cut fine, make a strong tea, and drink in place of water, a cupful at a time. I have known five persons cured by this simple remedy, one of them being my sister.

DRY YEAST

To make dry yeast, steep for half an hour a handful of fresh hops in a quart of boiling water. Sift two quarts of flour in an earthen or stone pan, and strain into the flour the boiling hop tea. Stir well and let it cool, when lukewarm add a cents worth of baker's yeast or a cupful of good home-made yeast, and put in a tablespoonful of brown sugar, a tablespoonful of ginger, a teaspoonful of salt, mix thoroughly and let it rise. It is best to prepare this sponge over night, and early in the morning it will be rounded up and light, and give you all day, which should be sunny and breezy, to make and dry the yeast cakes. Now mix into the sponge as much corn meal as will make stiff, firm dough, knead it well and make into a long, round roll three or four inches in diameter. Cut it into slices half an inch thick, spread a clean cloth or clean paper on a board and lay the cakes on and put into a light, airy place to dry. Turn them several times during the day, and speed the drying as fast as possible, as the fermentation goes on while they remain moist. When dry put into a bag made of firm linen or cotton, tie close, and hang high and dry.

DRYING CHERRIES

Take out the pits, and spread the fruit evenly on platters or plates. If very juicy turn over them only part of the juice. Sprinkle liberally with white sugar and set in the oven or about the stove, where they will dry quickly, but be very careful not to scorch, as this injures the flavor, in fact, utterly ruins the fruit. When partially dry loosen from the plates and stir occasionally. When fully dried pack in bowls or small jars and tie paper over the top to keep out insects and dust. A little sugar may be sprinkled between the layers, although, if the fruit is well dried, this is not important.

DRYING SALT HINT

When you dry salt for the table do not put it into the salt cellars until it is cold, otherwise it will harden into a lump.

DUBOIS FISH RECEIPT

Mince a carrot, an onion, and a nice stalk of celery; fry them in a little butter in a stew pan, adding some parsley, a few peppercorns and three or four cloves. Pour to these two quarts of hot water, one pint of vinegar (or we prefer the juice of three or four lemons). Let it boil fifteen minutes; skim till clear, salt to taste, and use for boiling the fish. It is improved, so Dubois says, by using white or red wine instead of vinegar. This stock may be easily preserved and used several times. Now, to boil the fish. Rub the fish with lemon juice and salt, put in a fish kettle after wrapping in a fish cloth, and cover with court bouillon. Let it only simmer, never boil hard, until thoroughly done. Serve in a fish napkin surrounded with parsley. Slice hard-boiled eggs, or cut in quarters and arrange neatly over the fish, and some caper, egg, oyster or other sauce in a sauce-boat.

DUMPLINGS FOR SOUP

One cup of cold water, two teaspoonfuls of cream of tartar, one teaspoonful of soda, and mix with flour to the consistency of dough as for biscuit; let this be done as quickly as possible, cut them out and lay them on top of the boiling soup, and on no account allow the cover to be lifted till they have cooked for twenty minutes.

DUST AND MARKS

Dust and marks of children's fingers can be removed from windows by rubbing them with a sponge which has been dipped in ammonia and water. To remove finger marks from and restore luster to the keys of a piano, wash off marks with a chamois skin wet with cold water; then rub the surface with sweet oil, mixed with half its quantity of turpentine.

DUSTERS

Pieces of cheese-cloth make the very best kind of dusters.
Hem the edges and have a large enough supply, so that one set can be washed each week.

DUTCH PUDDING

One pint of flour, teaspoonful of cream tarter, half teaspoonful of soda, half teaspoonful of salt, one egg, two-thirds of a cup of milk, two tablespoonfuls of butter, four large apples; mix salt, soda and cream tarter in the flour, and sift it, add eggs to the milk and rub the butter in the sifted flour, pour the milk and egg on it and mix thoroughly; spread this dough on a buttered baking pan about an inch thick; pare and core the apples, cut them in eight pieces and set them in rows on the dough; sprinkle them with sugar and bake in a quick oven. Serve with sauce.

DYEING RED

To dye a cotton fabric a durable red give it a bath of boiled oil; from this put it through another bath of beef galls, and lastly one of alum; then have a decoction of madder, which is commonly mixed with blood, and boil your goods for one hour in it, and, lastly, plunge it into lye made of soda; this, if properly done, will give a most beautiful, rich and permanent tint.

DYSPEPSIA

For dyspepsia burn alum until the moisture in it is evaporated; then take as much as you can put on a dime about half an hour before eating. Three or four days will probably answer, but take it until cured. (San Francisco Chronicle)

EARACHE

For earache, mix two teaspoonfuls of olive oil and one teaspoonful of laudanum, warm slightly, and put one drop in the ear every half hour until relieved.

EARACHE

Take a small piece of cotton-wool, make a depression in center, fill it with pepper; gather it into a ball and tie it up; dip it in sweet oil and insert it into the ear.

EARACHE - REMEDY FOR

Put some live coals in an iron pan, sprinkle with brown sugar, invert a funnel over it and put the tube in the ear. The smoke gives almost instant relief.

EARACHE - TREATMENT OF

It is said that by the following method almost instant relief of earache is afforded: Put five drops of chloroform on a little cotton or wool in the bowl of a clay pipe, then blow the vapor through the stem into the aching ear.

EASTER BUNS

Two cups warm milk, one cup of yeast, flour enough to make a thin batter. Let stand overnight. In the morning add one cup of sugar, a half cup of melted butter, two eggs, salt, nutmeg and flour enough to knead. Let rise five hours. Add a few currants and seeded raisins; mould into small balls, and set them closely together in a baking pan. Let them stand till very light, then bake. Wash them over while hot with the white of an egg beaten light with white sugar.

ECONOMICAL DOUGHNUTS

Two cups sweet milk; two eggs; one cup sugar; one teaspoonful soda: nutmeg; salt; flour enough to roll.

ECONOMICAL IRISH STEW

For an economical Irish stew take the scrag of mutton, together with any trimmings, bones, etc., from the best end. To one pound of meat put two pounds of old potatoes, peeled and cut in pieces, with two onions sliced, pepper and salt, cover with cold water or weak stock, and simmer gently for a couple of hours; when half done add a few whole potatoes, and when the ingredients are well amalgamated skim off superfluous fat, and serve very hot.

ECONOMICAL SOUP

Put into a saucepan one pound of pieces of stale bread, three large onions sliced, a small cabbage cut fine, a carrot and turnip and a small head of celery, or any remains of cold vegetables, a teaspoonful of salt, a teaspoonful of pepper, a bunch of parsley, a sprig of marjoram and thyme; put these into two quarts of any weak stock and let boil two hours, rub through a fine hair sieve, add a pint of new milk, boil up and serve at once.

ECONOMICAL STEW

Slice some cold beef or mutton, season the meat with pepper and salt, and dredge over it a little flour; put it in a stewpan with some of the cold gravy, or, if there be none left, add a little water; slice an onion fine, and add to it also a few potatoes; stew gently until the meat is quite tender; if there was no cold gravy, a little butter rolled in flour must be added a few minutes before the stew is served.

ECONOMY IN FOOD

One pound of whole rice boiled in five quarts of water, thickened with a pound of oatmeal, will make five pounds and a half of good food. Put the rice down first with one quart of water, and add the remaining four quarts as the rice swells, then put in the oatmeal, stirring all. Add salt or sugar, to suit the taste. If the rice is steeped for five or six hours, it will be better.

ECONOMY PUDDING

Half pound of rice, half pound of sugar, one pint of milk, some preserve; boil half pound of rice in water until nearly soft, then add the milk and boil again, stirring it all the time: add the sugar. Dip moulds in water, fill with rice, when hard turn on to a flat dish. Eat with preserve of any kind, sugar and cream, or custard. This is simple and very attractive to children.

ECZEMA

Someone asked a remedy for eczema. Steep green walnut hulls and wash the affected parts frequently with the strong tea. This is a most effective treatment.

ECZEMA

Try mixing powdered sulphur with unsalted butter until it becomes a golden colored salve, and apply at night. This has cured eczema in cases where expensive ointments failed.

ECZEMA CURE,

The following prescription, given me by a physician, cured my boy of eczema after two years; this was eight years ago, and there has been no return of the trouble. Any druggist will put up the prescription which is: Ten grains lead acetate, four drams of laudanum, and water to make one ounce. Shake well before using, and apply locally. Bathe the affected parts in weak carbolic water before using the medicine.

ECZEMA, DRY

Get an ointment consisting of one dram of oxide of zinc, one-half ounce of tar ointment and one ounce of cold cream and apply it twice a day.

ECZEMA OF THE SCALP

Steep celandine and use as a wash or make an ointment. For the latter take the tea, when the strength is thoroughly extracted, strain and boil it down, then add unsalted butter, Vaseline, mutton tallow or even pure lard, if nothing better is at hand, and beat until cool The settlings are strongest. Old sores which refuse to heal are cured by this simple remedy, also salt rheum, scald-hear, etc. Do not use a tin vessel in which to steep the herb, as it will spoil the tin as well as the celandine. It is harmless, the tea being taken internally many times in case of liver or kidney disorders.

EGG GRUEL

Beat the yolk of one egg, with a tablespoonful of sugar till very light; on this pour two-thirds of a cupful of boiling water; on the top put the white of the egg beaten to a stiff froth, with a teaspoonful of powdered sugar.

EGG SANDWICHES

Boil fresh eggs, and when quite cool, peel them, and after taking a little of the white off each end of the egg, cut the remainder in four slices. Lay them between bread and butter.

EGGS ATB.

Boil six eggs until very hard, remove the shells, and cut them across, preserving the whites in the form of cups, and cutting off a piece at the round end to make them stand; cut the yolks into small cubes, add some minced cold ham, parsley and salt. Mix these ingredients with cream until they form a thick paste; then fill the cups formed of the whites with this compound heaped up in the middle; place them in a dish, and pour white sauce over them.

EGGS a la LAVALETTE

Eggs ala Lavalette is the name of the following dish, although "why Lavalette," as Flora Finching would say, no one knows. Pour into a flat tin dish cream to the depth of a quarter of an inch; bring to a quick boil and then drop in the eggs and cook until the whites are hard; season to taste and serve in the same flat tin dish.

EGGS au MIROIR

Butter a small pie-dish, and break into it as many eggs as will lie, without breaking the yolks; cover them with chopped parsley, Cayenne and salt them; put a good layer of bread crumbs over; place them in the oven, taking care not to do them too much. Turn out on a flat dish, and garnish with parsley.

EGGLESS CAKE

Butter one-half size of an egg, one cup of sugar, cream well together, add one cup of sweet milk or water, two cups of flour sifted with two teaspoonfuls of baking powder, flavor with nutmeg and lemon, or to taste. This makes a really nice layer cake for tea, to be eaten fresh. It is also an excellent recipe for cottage pudding.

ELDERBERRY JELLY

Elderberry jelly is very nice, and is often much liked by one who is sick; cook the berries until they are soft; then strain them through a jelly-bag; to every pint of juice add a pint of white sugar; if you prefer to do so you may take two-thirds of the elderberries and one-third of green or ripe grapes.

ELDERBERRY WINE

To every quart of berries add one quart of water; boil half an hour; run off the liquor and break the berries through a hair sieve; then to every quart of juice add three-quarters of a pound of sugar; boil again one-quarter of an hour with Jamaica peppers, ginger and a few cloves. When sufficiently cool pour it into a barrel, with a cup of yeast and a piece of toast to assist the fermentation (to be kept in a warm place). When it ceases to hiss, add one quart of brandy to eight gallons of the liquor; then close the barrel perfectly air-tight, and keep in a cool place for six months, when it will be fit to bottle.

ELDERBERRY WINE

To one gallon of the ripe berries add one of water; let it stand twenty four hours, stirring it often: boil it half an hour in a copper or brass kettle, and strain through a sieve. Put it again in the kettle, and to each gallon of liquid add three and a half pounds of sugar; boil it twenty five minutes. Tie in a cloth half an ounce of ginger, the same of allspice; put it into the kettle and boil five minutes; then take out the spice. When cool add one teacupful of good yeast; keep it in a warm room to ferment a few days; then put it into a cask with the bung out for three or four months, when it will be ready to bottle. Wine made by this recipe is equal in flavor to port wine, and is far more wholesome for medical purposes than any commercial wine.

ELDERBERRY WINE

To ten quarts of berries put five quarts of water, and let it stand twenty four hours; then boil and skim it, strain it, and to every gallon of the liquor put three pounds of sugar, half an ounce of cloves, one ounce of cinnamon and two ounces of ginger; boil it again and ferment it by putting in it a slice of toast covered with fresh yeast; by leaving out the spices this wine is said to resemble port.

ELDERBERRY WINE

To make elderberry wine for medical purposes, mash the berries and to one peck add three gallons of boiling water, let stand twenty-four hours and then drain. To each gallon of juice allow three pounds of sugar, one-half ounce of ginger and six cloves. Boil all ingredients with the juice for one hour. When lukewarm add two cakes of dissolved yeast to every twenty gallons of wine. Let stand until it ferments and then skim and bottle.

EMBROIDERY IRONING

Embroidery should always be ironed on the wrong side, on a soft surface, such as heavy flannel or felting, with a clean white cloth over it, and should be ironed until thoroughly dry. In this way the design will be beautifully brought out.

EMMA'S CAKE

One cup of brown sugar and one egg beaten together; add to this one heaping cup of sweet apples, pared, cored, cut in thin slices like citron and cooked in molasses or a syrup of brown sugar till clear and tender; one cup of sour milk, half a cup of sour cream, one teaspoonful of soda, one teaspoonful of salt and one teaspoonful each of nutmeg, cinnamon, ginger, and allspice; stir in sifted flour carefully until the spoon will stand up in the middle.

ENGLISH LUNCH CAKE

Mix three heaping teaspoonfuls of baking powder into one pound of fine flour, rub in one-quarter pound of granulated sugar, one-quarter pound of butter, a little caraway seed, cinnamon and grated orange peel (dry). When ready to bake, stir in as quickly as possible two eggs mixed with half a pint of milk, put in to a well buttered tin and bake. Currants may be added at discretion.

ENGLISH OMELET

Two eggs, a teaspoonful of finely chopped parsley and thyme, a teaspoonful of chopped onions, if liked, salt, pepper, and a large lump of butter. Beat whites and yolks separately, the whites to a stiff froth. Mix the herbs, pepper, and salt with the yolks. Put the onions and butter, about one and a half or two ounces, into your omelet pan, and when the butter is quite melted, and very hot, mix whites and yolks together lightly; pour into the pan, and keep stirring the mixture with a spoon or knife till it begins to set; then merely shake it till it is done. Omelets made by this receipt are equal to those made by French cooks. Do not turn the omelet in the pan, not even over half, but turn it out upside down; they are lighter so. A wood fire is best for cooking them, over light chips thrown on the fire, so as to make a good wood blaze. You can make "scrambled" or "buttered" eggs in the same way by substituting a sauce pan for the omelet pan.

ENGLISH PEA PUDDING

Put a teaspoonful of carbonate of soda in two quarts of water, into which put three teacups of dry peas. Let them soak all night. In the morning put a thick pudding cloth into a tin pan, turn in the peas, and press them as tightly as possible together. Tie the bag tightly, put it in sufficient lukewarm water to cover well, and let them boil up for five or six hours. In England they always boil the pea pudding in the same pot with ham or pieces of salt pork, which greatly improves the flavor. When done, dish it on a neat dish. This is to be used as a vegetable.

ERUPTIONS

Mrs. Christine Edwards Hall, to cure your little girl of the eruptions bathe in warm water to which has been added one tablespoonful of soda, and a little alum, wipe dry and bathe in sweet oil freely, repeat once each day. It is perfectly harmless.

ESCALLOPED TURKEY

Moisten bread crumbs with a little milk; butter a pan and put in a layer of crumbs, then a layer of chopped fine (not very fine) cold turkey, seasoned with salt and pepper, then a layer of crumbs, and so on until the pan is full. If any gravy or dressing has been left, add it. Make a thickening of one or two eggs, half a cup of milk, and a quarter of a cup of butter and bread crumbs; season, and spread it over the top; cover with a pan, bake half an hour, and then let it brown.

ESSENTIAL SALT OF LEMONS

Take one ounce of oxalic acid, in fine powder, mix with four ounces of cream of tarter, and keep in a box. To remove ink, iron mould and stains from linen and cotton, wet the finger in water, dip it in the powder and rub it on the spot gently, keeping it rather moist. After the spots disappear wash the linen in clear water. It will not injure the fabric, but is poisonous if swallowed.

ETHER

Ether will take out water marks from silk.

EUFS BROUILLES

Mix a piece of butter the size of a walnut with a teaspoonful of milk; break in two eggs with some salt and pepper; keep stirring till they begin to set, then turn out instantly upon a slice of buttered toast. A little cold kidney or ham, minced, put in with the eggs, and seasoned accordingly, makes a savory dish.

EXCELLENT CUSTARD PIE

One pint of sweet milk, two even tablespoonfuls of sugar, the yolks of three eggs beaten light, half a teaspoonful of salt; line a large pie plate with a crust made of flour, lard, a pinch of salt, and just cold water enough to roll (roll thin), pour in the custard, and bake slowly until done. Beat the whites of the eggs to a froth, add one tablespoonful of white sugar, spread over the pie, grate on a little nutmeg, and let it stand in a cool oven until a light brown.

EXCELLENT MINCE MEAT

Seven lbs. of mince meat which is the round of beef usually, or the neck. Cook tender and chop fine. Add two lbs. of suet cut fine, one peck of apples pared, cored and chopped fine, two lbs. of seeded raisins and two lbs. of currants, one lb. of citron, one lb. of almonds blanched and chopped, four lbs. of sugar, one ounce of ground cinnamon, two grated nutmegs, one-half gallon or more of cider. The grated peel of two oranges and the juice and pulp of six. Mix all except the almonds and oranges and cook slowly till about right for pies. Then cool and add the almonds and oranges.

EXCELLENT TEA CAKE

Two cups of sugar, one cup of butter, one cup of cold of water, half a teaspoon of soda, mix stiff, roll thin, and bake crisp. (A Northerner)

EXCELLENT TOMATO CATSUP

Take a peck of perfect, ripe tomatoes; wash clean - they must be absolutely free from fermentation - cut in halves, put into a porcelain-lined kettle and boil until the pulp is dissolved. Strain and press through a colander and then through a fine sieve. Return to the kettle and add one ounce each of salt and mace, one tablespoonful each of black pepper and ground cloves, two of ground mustard and celery seed - the last tied in a fine muslin bag. Boil slowly for four hours, stirring almost constantly the latter part of the time. More salt may be added, if liked, and also a little cayenne. Turn into an earthen dish to cool, and when cold add a pint of strong vinegar. Bottle and seal the corks and keep the bottles inverted in a cool, dark place.

EXCELLENT TOOTH LOTION

It is generally admitted that the best way to prevent decay of the teeth is to use a good antiseptic lotion. The following is a good formula: Take of carbolic acid fifteen grains; thymol, eight grains; boric acid, seven drachms; essence of peppermint, twenty drops; tincture anise, two and a half drachms, and water two pints. Mix thoroughly, and use every night and morning with a brush, as you would any other dentifrice.

EXTERMINATING BEDBUGS

To exterminate bedbugs use kerosene or turpentine freely, if not quite successful with these remedies, try gasoline, applying to beds and slats. These insects will not stay where kerosene has been used, as a rule. A good insect powder is a help also.

EXTERMINATING BEDBUGS

For positively exterminating that pest of all house-keepers, bedbugs, mix one pint of kerosene, one-half pint of turpentine and ten cents worth of tincture of iodine; apply with a brush. One must be persistent in the use of the mixture, making a third or fourth application, if necessary; but it is sure to succeed.

EYES - INFLAMED EYELIDS

Cut a slice of stale bread very thin, toast both sides well, but do not burn; when cold, lay in cold water; put between a piece of old linen and apply, changing when it gets warm.

EYES - REMEDY FOR WEAK OR SORE ONES

Get a five cent cake of elder flowers at the druggist's and steep in one gill of soft water. It must be steeped in bright tin or earthenware. Strain nicely and add three drops of laudanum; bottle it tight and keep it in a cool place. Use it as a wash, letting some of it get into the eyes. Follow this and relief is certain. If the eyes are painful or much sore, make small, soft compresses, wet them in the mixture and bind over the eyes at night. I warrant the above as harmless and sure, having tried it in a number of cases where other skills and remedies had utterly failed. If the eyes are badly inflamed use it freely. A tea made of elder flowers and drank will help cleanse the blood. Pure rock salt and water will strengthen your weak eyes if you bath them daily in it .

EYES - STY ON THE EYELID

Put a teaspoonful of black tea in a small bag, pour on it enough boiling water to moisten it; then put it on the eye warm; keep it on all night.

EYES, WEAK OR INFLAMED

A raw potato, scraped and bound on as a poultice, is good for weak or inflamed eyes.

FACE WASH

To make a good face wash take two parts of pure glycerin and one part of peroxide, and shake well; apply to face and hands at night.

FACEACHE CURE

Apply hot bran poultices to the cheek or rub the face with camphorated oil and cover the part with a piece of flannel. A little warm laudanum dropped into the ear on the affected side often gives relief. If the pain proceeds from the jaw, put a few drops of tincture of cayenne on cotton wool and place it between the cheek and teeth.

FADED RIBBONS

By adding a little pearlash to soap lather, faded ribbons placed therein will be restored to their natural color, faded breadths of silk can be restored if treated to a bath of this kind.

FANCY CAKE

One and one-half cups of sugar, the same quantity of flour, one half-cup each of butter, corn starch and milk, the whites of four eggs, one-half teaspoonful of cream of tartar, and one-fourth teaspoonful of soda. Color one-third of the above with extract of cochineal, a harmless liquid to be obtained at any drug store. Arrange in a pan in three layers with red in the center.

FARMERS FRUIT CAKE

Soak three cups of dried apples overnight in warm water. Chop slightly in the morning and simmer two hours in two cups of molasses. Add two well-beaten eggs, one cup of sugar, one cup of butter, one desert spoonful of soda, flour enough to make a rather stiff batter. Flavor with nutmeg and cinnamon to the taste. Bake in a quick oven.

FARMERS FRUIT CAKE

Two cups of dried apples; soaked overnight, then chop or cut them, and simmer in two cups of molasses three hours; then cool and add one cup of brown sugar, one cup of butter, two eggs, one cup of sour milk, one large spoonful of cloves, four cups of flour, and one teaspoonful of soda.

FEATHER-BEDS

Feather-beds should be opened every third year, the ticking well dusted, scraped and waxed and the feathers dressed.

FEATHER CAKE

One cup of sugar; one-half cup of sweet milk; two eggs; not quite half cup of butter; one teaspoon of cream tarter; one-half teaspoon of soda; two cups of flour; nutmeg; bake in shallow tins.

FEATHER CAKE

1 cup sugar, 1 cup flour, 1 egg, ½ cup sweet milk, 1 tablespoon melted butter, 1 teaspoon baking powder, a very little salt and 1 teaspoonful lemon.

FELON

It is said that the painful sore finger known as the felon may be effectually cured in three hours, with a poultice of the size of a small bean, made of quicklime slaked with soap, bound on the spot, and renewed every half hour.

FELONS - CURING

Prof. Huter of Berlin cures bone felon or whitlow by first probing the swelling of the finger, making a small incision where the pain appears greatest. The pain of the operation may be lessened by the local application of ether or inhalation of chloroform. The after-treatment is equally simple. The small wound is to be covered with a lint and carbolic acid, and bathed morning and evening in tepid water. In a few days it is perfectly healed.

FELON - SURE CURE

Apply a poultice of onions; renew every morning, noon, and night, for three or four days. No matter how bad the case, lancing the finger will be unnecessary if this poultice is used. The remedy is sure, safe, and speedy.

FELON - TO CURE A

Take a teaspoonful of fine salt, a tablespoonful of black pepper, a tablespoonful of vinegar and the yolk of an egg, simmer together and bind on. Renew twice a day.

FELON - TO CURE A

As soon as there are indications of a felon apply a poultice of equal parts of saltpeter and brimstone, mixed with sufficient lard to make a paste; renew as soon as it gets dry.

FELON - TO KILL A

To kill a felon, or bring it to a head if too far advanced to kill, take a poke root and boil it till soft enough to make a poultice, apply, and if the felon is too far advanced it will scatter it; if it is, it will hasten suppuration. It will deaden the pain in a short time and save much suffering. I have used this myself and know it to be good.

FELT HATS

Use old felt hats for inner soles for shoes, and tack a piece of felt on door jam and that screen door won't annoy you so.

FERTILIZER FOR HOUSE-PLANTS

Here is a fertilizer for house-plants which those who have "window gardens" will appreciate. Dissolve four ounces of sulfate of ammonia and two ounces nitrate of potash in a pint of boiling water and bottle for use. When watering the house-plants add three-fourths of a teaspoonful of this solution to two quarts of water, and give only a few tablespoonfuls to each plant; be careful not to give too much. When the leaves have become dark-green, stop using it for a time. The preparation is not expensive, and is easily made at home; it has odor and should be applied to the soil, only, not being allowed to touch the plant.

FEVER - DRINKS FOR PATIENTS

Drinks made from fresh or preserved fruits are sometimes useful in fevers. Rhubarb tea is a very refreshing spring beverage. Slice about two pounds of rhubarb and boil for a quarter of an hour in a quart of water; strain the liquor into a jug, adding a small quantity of lemon-peel and some sugar to taste; when cold it is fit for use. Apple water may be made in the same manner. The apples should be peeled and cored. Sugar should not be added to either of the above until after the liquor is removed from the fire. In the absence of fresh fruit a pleasant beverage may be prepared by stirring sufficient raspberry jam or currant jelly into the required quantity of water, straining the liquor before giving it to the patient.

FIG CAKE

Two cups of sugar, three-fourths of a cup of butter, whites of six eggs, one cup of milk, one pound of chopped figs, one cup of corn starch, two cups of flour, two teaspoonfuls of baking powder.

FIG CAKE

Jennie asks for a receipt for fig cake. I have one I will send. Two cups of shortened dough as for bread, one and one-half cups of sugar, two-thirds of a cup of butter, one-half of a cup of suet, one-fourth of a pound of figs, one cup of raisins or without, three eggs, one small teaspoonful of soda, nutmeg and clove.

FIG CAKE

For the cake take one cup of butter, two cups of sugar, three and one-half cups of flour, one-half cup of sweet milk, whites of seven eggs, two teaspoonfuls of baking powder. Bake in jelly tins. For the filling take one pound of figs and chop them fine, and put in a stew pan on the stove; pour over it a teacup of water and add one-half cup of sugar. Cook all together until soft and smooth. Spread between the layers.

FIG CAKE

Five eggs, two cups of sugar, one cup of melted butter, one-half cup sour milk, three cups of flour, one-half teaspoonful of soda, one-half of a teaspoonful of cream of tartar, one-fourth of a pound of figs sliced thin, three-fourths of a pound of chopped raisins. Spice to taste and frost with the whites of two eggs.

FIG PUDDING

Take half a pound of the best figs, wash, then chop them fine, two teacupfuls of grated bread, half a cup of sweet cream, one cup of sweet milk, half a cup of sugar; mix the bread crumbs with the cream, then stir in the figs, then the sugar, the milk the last thing; pour into a pudding-dish and steam three hours.

FILLING CRACKS IN PLASTER

Use vinegar instead of water to mix plaster of Paris. The mass will be like putty and will not set for twenty or thirty minutes; push into the cracks and smooth off nicely with a table knife.

FIRE AND HORSES

In case of fire, if horses refuse to walk out of the stable with a blanket over their heads, try harnessing them. This has been known to induce many horses to let themselves to be saved.

FISH CHOWDER

Four pounds of codfish or haddock, quarter of a pound of salt pork, five potatoes, one onion, salt, pepper, one pint of milk, six crackers. Skin the fish, cut in pieces and wash in cold water, cut the pork in small pieces and fry brown in the kettle in which the chowder is to be made, pare and slice the potatoes and onion, put a layer in the kettle, then a layer of fish, a little salt, pepper and flour; repeat this until all the fish is used, cover with hot water and boil gently for half an hour, then add milk and split crackers, boil ten minutes longer.

FISH FRITTERS

Take the remains of any fish which has been served the previous day, remove all the bones, and pound in a mortar; add bread crumbs and mashed potatoes in equal quantities; mix together half a teacupful of cream with two well beaten eggs, some cayenne pepper and anchovy sauce; beat it all up to a proper consistency; cut into small cakes, and fry them in boiling lard.

FISH SAUCE

Yolks of two raw eggs. Add salad oil, drop by drop, until it is the consistency of thick cream; add the juice of half a lemon.

FLAKE PIE CRUST

Take one-half cup of lard to a pint of flour; rub well together; take water sufficient to make a dough (not too stiff); roll out and spread with butter; fold over evenly and make a second fold in the opposite direction; roll out again, being careful not to squeeze the butter out.

FLAKY PIE CRUST

Wet half pound of fine flour, dried before the fire and sifted, with as much water as will make it into a hard, stiff paste. Roll it one way. Divide six ounces of butter into little bits, and put it on the paste with a knife at three different times, sifting just a little flour over it, and be careful always to roll one way - the same way. Four ounces of lard may be used with two ounces of butter. If your butter is not salt, add a little pinch to the dry flour.

FLANNEL CAKES

Boil one pint of milk with two heaping tablespoonfuls of butter; add one pint of cold milk, and flour enough to make as stiff a batter as you can stir; turn in two tablespoonfuls of brewer's yeast, or a small cupful of homemade yeast. Set to rise in a cool place, if the weather is warm, over night. Pour the batter into small baking tins or "gem pans" and bake half an hour.

FLANNEL CLOTH TREATMENT

Flannel cloths, wrung from hot vinegar to which a pinch of cayenne pepper has been added will relieve pain in any part of the body, if applied often.

FLANNEL PETTICOATS

One flannel petticoat will wear nearly as long as two if turned hind part before when the front begins to wear thin.

FLANNEL WASHING

Flannels should always be washed by themselves in suds made especially for them, and well rinsed. Use warm water but not boiling water.

FLAT-IRONS

Flat-irons should be kept as far as possible removed from the steam of cooking, as this causes them to rust.

FLAT TABLE CONVENIENCE

One of the greatest conveniences a kitchen can have is a flat table, which, when not in use, can be folded up and fastened against the wall.

FLIES ON PICTURE FRAMES

To keep flies away from picture frames, boil three onions (or four) in a pint of water for half an hour. When cold, brush the frames with the water, and the flies will not settle on them nor will the former be injured by the application.

FLOATING ISLAND

The floating island, which will cost twenty cents is made as follows: Beat the yolks of six eggs with the juice of four lemons, sweeten to your taste, and stir it into a quart of boiling milk till it thickens, then pour it into a dish. Whip the whites of the eggs to a stiff froth and pour it on the top of the cream.

FLOATING ISLAND

This is a simple and pretty dessert dish. Cover the bottom of a large open glass dish with small square sponge cake - Savoy biscuit they are sometimes called - into which you have stuck a few spikes of candied citron. Make a soft custard of a quart of milk, the yolks of five eggs, sweetened with powdered sugar, and flavor with nutmeg or stick cinnamon. Simmer gently till it begins to thicken, and then pour over the sponge cake, and set away to cool. In the meantime whisk the whites of five eggs to a froth, sweeten in the proportion of a dessert-spoonful of powdered sugar to one egg. Flavor it with essence of lemon, and heap it in snowy piles upon the custard. It may be ornamented with strawberries in their season, or pieces of red currant jelly.

FLOUR BREAD

Take two quarts of flour; a little salt; one cupful yeast; mix with lukewarm water; knead well; set it in a warm place to rise; when ready for use, knead once more, and make into loaves or biscuit. If in loaves, let it stand one-half hour in the tins before baking; if in biscuit, ten minutes is sufficient; and you have nice light and healthy bread. You can also make cake and brown bread with this yeast.

FLOUR GRUEL

Let one quart of fresh meal come to a boil, and then stir in one table-spoonful of flour which has been mixed with milk enough to make a smooth paste; boil this mixture thirty minutes, being careful not to let burn. Season with salt and strain.

FLOOR CRACK FILLING

A very complete filling for open cracks in floors may be made by thoroughly soaking newspapers in a paste made of one pound of flour, three quarts of water and a tablespoonful of alum, thoroughly boiled and mixed; make the final mixture about as thick as putty, a kind of paper putty, and it will harden like papier-mâché.

FLOUR SACKS

Rip them, wash and boil them to get the printing out, and iron smoothly. The largest ones make into every-day pillow slips, hemstitching the hems of some of them, and ruffling others. For the ruffles use the thinner sacks, and when the slips are nicely laundered they look "nice enough for anybody." Make quilt linings of some of the sacks, and of others, or finer quality, cut and hemstitch squares for napkins.

FLUMMERY

Lay sponge cake cut in thin slices in the bottom of a deep dish. Turn over enough thin, sweet cream to moisten. Make a custard of the yolks of three eggs, one pint of milk and two tablespoonfuls of sugar. Beat the sugar and eggs together; boil the milk and turn the sugar and eggs in, and stir till thick; let cool and then turn it over the cake and cream. Beat the whites to a stiff froth and spread over the whole.

FLY PAPER

If anyone is so unfortunate as to get into the sticky fly paper, a liberal rubbing with butter will dissolve the sticky stuff, so that it can be washed off.

FLY REMOVAL

Flies do not like the odor of clover, and a bunch of these blossoms left drying in a room will effectually expel them.

FOOTSORE

Try sprinkling oxide of zinc in your shoes, after bathing the feet in clean water and putting on clean hose; I am sure the result will please you.

FOUL WELL OR CISTERN

A peck of unslacked lime thrown into a foul well or cistern is an effectual cleanser.

FRECKLE REMEDY

Lemon juice and home-made elder-flower water are harmless remedies for freckles.

FRECKLES

To get rid of aged, faded, freckled or discolored complexion, buy an ounce of common mercolized wax at any drug store and apply nightly as you would cold cream, erasing this in the morning with soap and water. This will slowly absorb the undesirable surface skin, revealing the younger, brighter, healthier skin underneath. I know of nothing to equal this treatment as a facial rejuvenator.

FRECKLES - TO REMOVE

Cosmetics sold for this purpose are often dangerous. The best plan is to make a lotion of a teacupful of sour milk and a small quantity of scraped horseradish; let this stand from six to twelve hours, then use it to wash the parts affected twice or thrice a day.

FRECKLES - TO REMOVE

To remove freckles apply a lotion composed of equal parts of lemon-juice and glycerin.

FRENCH CAKE

Five cups of flour; 3 cups of sugar; 1 ½ cups of sweet milk; one-half cup of butter; 4 eggs; 2 teaspoonfuls cream tarter; 1 of soda.

FRENCH CHOCOLATE CAKE

One tablespoon butter, one and one-quarter cups sugar, two eggs, one cup milk, two and three-quarters cups flour, small teaspoon soda, two teaspoons cream of tarter. Slightly melt the butter and mix it with the sugar and the two eggs beaten, add the two and three-quarters cups of flour and cream of tartar therein, then the milk with soda therein, and one teaspoon vanilla. Bake in four jelly pans well buttered, and in a quick oven.

FRENCH CREAM

One and one-half pints of milk boiled; add the sweetened yolks of three eggs beaten in a little cold milk. Let all boil at once; place it in a dish and throw gradually in the stiffly beaten whites.

FRENCH CUSTARD

Have ready ten custard glasses, or small coffee cups, measure one of them ten times full of milk, which place in a stewpan, and set upon the fire till boiling, when add a quarter of a pound of powdered sugar, and the rind of two lemons, free from pith; place the lid upon the stewpan, take from fire, and let infuse ten minutes, then in a basin have ready the yolks of eight eggs, with which stir in the milk by degrees; pass through a strainer, and fill the cups. Have ready upon the fire a large flat stewpan, containing water sufficient to cover the bottom two inches in depth, and just simmering; stand in the cups and let remain still simmering until the custards are quite firm, then take them outside, dress them upon a napkin, and serve; any kind of flavor may be introduced into the above, but for coffee custard, proceed as follows: Make half pint of strong coffee, according to the usual method; add half a pint of thin cream, or milk, previously boiled; sweeten to palate, mix with the yolks of eggs, pass through a strainer, and proceed precisely as directed for French custard.

FRENCH DRESSING

Three tablespoonfuls of oil, one of vinegar, one saltspoonful of salt and a speck of cayenne. Put salt and pepper in a cup with one tablespoonful of oil. When thoroughly mixed add remainder of oil and the vinegar. Add a little onion juice if desired.

FRENCH HONEY

Break one pound of lump sugar into pieces, put it into a pan, and the yolks of six eggs, and the whites of four, the juice of four lemons, and the grated rind of two, and three ounces of butter. Stir this mixture over a slow fire, until it becomes thick like honey. It will keep a year, put into a dry, cool place. This is nice for a variety of tarts and shells.

FRENCH LOAF

Three teacups of light bread, two cups of white sugar, one cup of butter, one cup of raisins, three eggs, one nutmeg and one teaspoonful of saleratus. Rub the butter and sugar together, then add the eggs, lastly the bread and fruit. Bake in two loaves one hour and a half.

FRENCH MUSTARD

Take four spoonfuls of ground mustard, one spoonful of fine salt, one of granulated sugar, and six spoonfuls of sharp vinegar. Mix thoroughly and beat smooth, and you will have a toothsome preparation to give a relish to your cold or hot meats, hash, or anything you choose to spread it on.

FRENCH ROLLS

One quart of flour, rub it thoroughly through a piece of butter the size of an egg, one teaspoonful of salt, now pour in half a teacup of yeast and sufficient tepid water for a soft dough; knead it at least half an hour, and set it in a warm place to rise. When light, roll out without kneading again, cut with a biscuit cutter, put together, and only grease the top of one, using butter for the purpose; now set them again in a warm place to lighten, and when sufficiently risen bake in a quick oven.

FRENCH ROLLS

One quart of flour, one-half pint of milk, one-half cup of yeast, two tablespoonfuls of butter, two tablespoonfuls of sugar, raise over night, and bake in a quick oven.

FRENCH TOAST

Beat your eggs very light, and stir with them one pint of milk; slice some nice white bread, dip the pieces into the egg and milk, then lay them into a pan of hot butter and fry brown. Sprinkle a little powdered sugar and cinnamon or nutmeg on each piece and serve hot.

FRICASSEE CHICKEN

Cut up a pair of chickens, take off the skin, wash them and let them remain in water half an hour to make them white, drain them, sprinkle them with salt and put them in the skillet with two ounces of butter, a teaspoonful of lard to keep the butter from burning, and a cup of water, cover tightly to keep in the steam, turn them often and watch that they do not burn, and add more water when necessary. When they have cooked until tender, which should be an hour and a half for young chickens and double the time for old ones, add salt and pepper to taste, a pint of milk or cream, half a tablespoonful of flour, rubbed very smooth with a little milk, stirring all the time until the gravy thickens and browns. You may add more butter if you wish it richer. (Emily)

FRICASSEE CHICKEN

Soak the cut up chicken in salt water twenty minutes. Then put in a kettle in cold water enough to cover and cook until tender. Then season with pepper and salt and butter, and thicken with flour and water.

FRICASSEE OF CHICKEN

This fricassee of chicken will cost 75 cents. Cut two chickens into pieces. Reserve all the white meat and the best pieces for the fricassee. The trimmings and the inferior pieces use to make the gravy. Put these pieces into a porcelain kettle with a quart of cold water, one clove, pepper, salt, a small onion, a little bunch of parsley and a small piece of pork; let it simmer for an hour and a half, and then put in the pieces for the fricassee; let them boil slowly until they are done; take them out then and keep them in a hot place. Strain the gravy, take off all the fat and add to it a mixture of half a cupful of flour and a small piece of butter. Let this boil; take it off the stove and stir in three yolks of eggs mixed with two or three tablespoonfuls of cream; also the juice of half a lemon. Do not let it boil after the eggs are in, or they will curdle. Stir it well, keeping it hot a moment; then pour it over the chicken and serve.

FRICASSEE OF OYSTER

Put a quart of oysters on the fire in their own liquor. The moment it boils up turn into a colander. Put into a saucepan a piece of butter the size of an egg, and when it bubbles up sprinkle in a tablespoonful of sifted flour. Let cook for an instant without browning, then add a cupful of oyster liquor. Mix together, take from the fire, add salt, a dash of cayenne pepper, the beaten yolks of two eggs and a tablespoonful of lemon juice. Beat together, return to the fire to set the eggs (without boiling), put in the oysters, and as soon as heated through pour over buttered toast.

FRIED CHICKEN

After neatly dressing and carving in pieces of proper size, parboil a half-hour or longer, until tender; take out with a fork, and place in a frying-pan of melted butter; fry brown by frequent turning to keep from burning. A nice gravy is made by pouring the broth in which it was boiled into the frying-pan, with a thickening of flour and any seasoning preferred. Curled parsley, arranged as a garnish, adds to the general effect.

FRIED CORN

Prepared like stewed corn with the milk omitted. Turn it into a skillet into which butter has been melted, with a slice of bacon or salt pork which has previously been browned to a crisp.

FRIED CUTLET AND STEAKS

Cutlets and steaks may be fried as well as broiled, but they must be put in hot butter or lard. The grease is hot enough when it throws off a bluish smoke.

FRIED DUMPLINGS

One pint of milk; two eggs; a little saleratus; flour sufficient for drop cakes; fry in lard; when done pour over them sweet sauce; serve hot.

FRIED EGG SANDWICHES

Beat some eggs well; fry them in butter as a pancake. When cold, cut in small square pieces, and lay them between brown bread and butter.

FRIED MEAT BALLS

Mince some cold meat finely, and if very dry add a little fat bacon with some parsley and a little onion. Soak a large slice of bread in water, squeeze the water from it, and put the bread to the meat; add two raw eggs, pepper, salt, and a little grated nutmeg; mix all well together, make into small balls like foremeat; fry in drippings, and serve hot with brown gravy.

FRIED MUSH

Cut in slices a mould of cold mush, and fry in butter to a rich brown color. This makes an excellent breakfast dish.

FRIED PIGS FEET

Make a batter, dip the feet into it; fry in hot fat until brown; make a little drawn butter, then add a spoonful of vinegar to serve with them.

FRIED POTATOES

Pare and cut the potatoes in thin slices, over night, let them stand in cold water. In the morning shake them in a dry towel, till perfectly drained. Then drop them into very hot fat, enough to float them. (The fat from beef suet is best.) Shake and turn them till brown, keeping them very hot. Dip out with a skimmer and salt them a little. If properly done they will be crisp and delicious.

FRIED TRIPE

Get the thickest honey-comb tripe to be found, two pounds will do. For the batter beat up one egg with a tablespoonful of flour and a little salt. Try out a piece of clear pork, dip the pieces of tripe in the batter and fry, taking care to have the fat very hot.

FRITTERS

One pint of sweet milk, the yolks of three eggs stirred into a thick batter with flour, a pinch of salt and three teaspoons of baking powder; lastly, add the whites of the eggs well beaten. Drop in hot lard and cook until done; about a tablespoonful of dough for a cake.

FROST

To keep frost from forming on your windows, rub the inside and out with glycerin.

FROZEN PUDDING SAUCE

This is made of one-half pint cream, whipped, sweetened and flavored with brandy or Jamaica rum.

FROSTBITE

Mrs. C.L., an infallible remedy for frostbites and chilblains is as follows: Bathe the feet in pure linseed-oil; at night wet cloths with the oil, wrap them around the feet, and put on a pair of stockings. This will stop the itching and draw the frost out. Two or three applications should effect a complete cure.

FROSTING FOR CAKE

For the white of one egg take nine heaping teaspoonfuls of white sugar and one teaspoonful Portland starch. Beat the eggs to a stiff froth, so the plate can be turned upside down without the egg falling off; stir in the sugar slowly with a wooden spoon, ten or fifteen minutes, constantly. To frost a common sized cake one and one-half eggs will suffice.

FROSTING WITHOUT EGGS

I have a frosting without eggs that is so much better than the frosting with eggs that I am sure it will please all who try it. I use it altogether. One cup of granulated sugar, or any white sugar, five tablespoonfuls of milk, boil four or five minutes, then stir until cold, and put on a cold cake.

FROZEN APRICOTS

One can of apricots, one quart of water and one pint of sugar, mixed well and frozen like ice cream. Serve with whipped cream, one pint being sufficient for this quantity.

FRUIT CAKE

Two cups sugar; one cup molasses; one of butter; one of cream; five eggs; one pound of raisins; one of currants; spice to taste. Those who like can frost it, which is still better.

FRUIT CAKE

Mr. Editor: M.M.M. asks for a recipe to make fruit cake. Please permit me to send her mine, which I call good. Four eggs, two cups of sugar, one cup of molasses, one-half pint of sweet milk, one and one-half cups of butter, one large tea-spoonful of soda, one tablespoonful of cinnamon, two nutmegs, one-half pound of stoned raisins, and four cups of flour. This makes enough for two loaves.

FRUIT COOKIES

Two cups of sugar, one cup of butter, two cups of chopped raisins, two eggs, two tablespoonfuls of sour milk, two tablespoonfuls of nutmeg, cloves and soda, flour to roll out. Bake the same as other cookies.

FRUIT CUP CAKE

Five eggs, one and one-half cups of sugar, one cup of currants, one of milk, six of flour, juice and rind of one lemon, one-half glass of wine.

FRUIT STAINS

Fruit stains are usually best removed from white goods by pouring boiling water through them, provided the spots have not first been wet in cold water. If they have or are long standing dip them in water to which has been added chloride of lime in the proportion of one tablespoonful of the chloride to each quart of water. If the stains are very deep let the article remain in the water for ten or fifteen or twenty minutes, then hang in the sun without wringing. Or pour boiling water on chloride of lime, in the proportion of one gallon to a quarter of a pound, bottle it, and in using be careful not to stir it. Lay the stain in this for a moment, then apply white vinegar and boil the linen. For raspberry stains, weak ammonia and water is the best. If fruit stains get upon colored goods, remove at once with boiling water. Other remedies usually take out the colors.

FRY BREAD

Beat an egg with milk and sugar, cut in slices a stale French twist, soak them in the milk, when soft have hot lard in a pan and fry till brown.

FRYING FISH

Wash and wipe perfectly dry; rub them over lightly with flour, cover them with yolk of egg and bread crumbs; place them in a pan of boiling lard or drippings, having sufficient to completely cover the fish; cook a nice fine brown. When done, place them on a hot dish in a warm place until taken to the table. Be sure to have plenty of fat and that it is hot, or your fish will not be nice.

FUR PRESERVATION

To preserve furs from moth, wash them in warm water, one pint, corrosive sublimate, twelve grains. Dry thoroughly after washing. Handle mixture carefully as it is poison.

FURNITURE POLISH

Melted beeswax, turpentine, and sweet oil, well mixed together, are excellent for polishing furniture, stained floors, and picture-frames. It should be rubbed on with a piece of soft cloth.

FURNITURE POLISH

Have a cloth moistened with linseed-oil and use it to wipe over your furniture occasionally. It will keep it looking like new.

FURNITURE REFINISHER

To make old furniture look nearly like new, take equal parts of linseed-oil and turpentine, stir in burnt umber until the mixture is about as thick as molasses, and apply to furniture that has been thoroughly cleaned. It gives a beautiful walnut color.

GALL STONES

I had gall stones for nine years, and after trying many remedies and doctors without avail, I was told the following: Take beets and boil them as for table use, peel and slice them, place in a jar and add as much good brandy as you would use of vinegar if you were pickling them. Let stand two or three days, ten take a tablespoonful of the liquid three times a day.

GALL-STONES

An Interested Reader, have you tried pure olive-oil for gall-stones? I have a friend who was so severely afflicted with this distressing ailment that everyone thought every attack would be the last. She began using the oil, taking a teacupful every day, and now she is seventy years young, and she is entirely cured.

GAME OR POULTRY SOUP

An excellent, clear soup can be made with scraps and bones of game or poultry, boiled down with a little bacon, vegetables, such as carrots, onions, leeks, turnips, tomatoes, celery, parsley, etc., cunningly proportioned, and spices and sweet herbs. When the whole is well boiled clear and strain it. Then serve either plain or with macaroni or crackers.

GARGLE

A gargle of hot claret often affords much relief in cases of acute sore throat.

GAS GLOBE SAFETY

Do not screw gas globes tightly to the fixtures, as the heat expansion will crack them. The same is true of lamp chimneys which are kept in place by screws, as many are.

GELATIN

Gelatin should be soaked in cold water for two or more hours, and then have boiling water or milk poured on it, in which case it will dissolve immediately, and be almost free from the taste and odor which will be present if the process is less careful, and the gelatin is dissolved in 15 or 20 minutes by pouring hot water over it, covering it, and setting it on the back of the range.

GEMS

Make a batter about as thick as for griddle cakes, with graham flour and cold milk or water and salt. Beat well and bake in a very hot oven, in cast iron gem irons which have been heated. No gem with eggs, baking powder and butter can excel these simple and healthful ones.

GEMS

Take one quart graham flour, one egg, a little salt, two teaspoonfuls baking soda, rub into the flour a small piece of butter and add sufficient water to make a stiff batter.

GERANIUM LEAVES

One or two geranium leaves, bruised, and applied to a bruise or cut will cause it to heal in a short time.

GILDING RESTORATION

To restore gilding to picture frames, remove all dust with a soft brush, and wash the gilding in warm water in which an onion has been boiled; dry quickly with soft rags.

GILT FRAME PROTECTION

A safe protection to gilt frames and other articles from flies and dust is oiled tarlatan. If it cannot be purchased already prepared, it may be prepared by brushing boiled oil over cheap tarlatan.

GILT FRAMES

Gilt frames may be cleaned by rubbing with a little sal volatile mixed with cold water.

GINGER BEER

Brown sugar, two pounds; boiling water, two gallons; cream of tarter, one ounce; bruised ginger, two ounces. Infuse the ginger in the boiling water, add the sugar and cream of tartar; when lukewarm strain; then add one-half pint of good yeast. Let it stand all night; then bottle. If desired, a lemon may be added, and it may be clarified by the white of one egg.

GINGER BEER

The proportions of this may be varied to suit the taste. Granulated sugar is best. If you wish it very sweet put a pound and a half to the gallon, otherwise a pound will be sufficient. Half an ounce to an ounce of bruised ginger to the gallon may be used, and a lemon to the same quantity is the usual allowance; some would add from a quarter to half an ounce of cream of tartar. The white of an egg to each gallon is useful for clarifying, but not absolutely necessary. Some persons use brandy to preserve the beer; hops will answer the same purpose; half an ounce to every four gallons. The following proportions will be found very good: To four gallons of water put five pounds of sugar and the well-beaten whites of two eggs. Boil and skim carefully. Add four ounces of bruised ginger, the thin, yellow rind of four lemons and half an ounce of hops; let boil half an hour; remove the tough white skins and seeds from the lemons and put the balance in the beer; put an ounce of cream of tarter in a stone jar and pour the boiling liquid over it; when cool stir in two tablespoonfuls of yeast for every gallon; put it into a keg without straining and bung close; in two weeks draw off and bottle, cork and wire down, and in two weeks longer it will be fit for use. If a quicker beer is desired it may be made without boiling and bottled immediately.

GINGER BEER QUICKLY MADE

A gallon of boiling water is poured over three-quarters of a pound of loaf sugar, one ounce of ginger, and the peel of one lemon; when milk-warm, the juice of the lemon and a spoonful of yeast are added. It should be made in the evening, and bottled next morning in stone bottles, and the cork tied down with twine. Good brown sugar will answer, and the lemon may be omitted if cheapness is required.

GINGERBREAD

One and one-half cup of molasses, one cup butter, one tablespoonful ginger, one tablespoonful soda, and one teaspoonful alum powdered. Dissolve the soda and alum in each one-third cupful of water. Add soda water first, and stir well; then alum water, the last thing before the flour. Mix so as to roll out, but not very hard. Cut into cakes the size of baking tins, having the dough from one-half to three-quarters of an inch thick. Cross the top in lines, and bake fifteen minutes.

GINGERBREAD

Melt a teacup of butter and mix it with a pint of molasses, a tablespoonful of ginger, a pint of flour, and two beaten eggs; dissolve two teaspoonfuls of saleratus in half a pint of milk, and stir it into the cake; add flour to make it the proper thickness. Bake in deep tins.

GINGERBREAD

Take two coffee cups, put in each one tablespoonful of soda, four tablespoonfuls of boiling water, three tablespoonfuls of melted butter or lard, then fill with molasses. Stir until it foams, then add ginger to taste. Flour either hard or soft.

GINGER COOKIES

One cup of molasses, one cup sugar, one egg, two-thirds cup lard, two teaspoonfuls soda, one tablespoonful vinegar, and one tablespoonful ginger. Roll thin and bake in a quick oven.

GINGER CRISPS

Two cups of molasses, one cup of sugar, one cup of butter, one egg, two tablespoonfuls of soda, and use just a little water, boiling, as will dissolve the soda. Do not mix hard. Roll thin and bake in a quick oven.

GINGER LAYER CAKE

Half a cupful of brown sugar, the same of cooking molasses, one egg, two tablespoonfuls of butter, one and one-half cupfuls of sifted flour, half a cupful of sour milk, one teaspoonful of soda and the juice of a small lemon. Cream the butter and sugar, stir in the molasses and lemon juice, then the egg and flour, lastly the soda, dissolved in the sour milk. Bake in three layers.

Now for the filling; dissolve half a cupful of brown sugar and butter the size of a walnut in one cupful of boiling water, add also one teaspoonful of ginger and a little nutmeg. Mix one tablespoonful of flour in cold water and add to the mixture. Let it boil five minutes, then stir in one well beaten egg just before removing from the stove.

GINGER POP

Allow a pound of light brown sugar, two ounces of cream of tarter and an ounce of bruised ginger to every gallon of water. Stir all well together in a stone jar and cover up to cool, so that the flavor of the ginger will not evaporate. Do this the last thing at night and it will be ready to set to working early in the morning. Take out a teacupful for each gallon of the mixture, and to each teacupful add two tablespoonfuls of yeast; let it stand fifteen minutes in a warmish place, and mix it with the balance of the liquid in the jar. Stir it well and cover up for exactly eight hours; skim, strain, bottle in stone bottles, cork and wire down without delay. The corks should not touch the beer. Care should be taken to observe the exact time. The bottles will be apt to fly if the beer is put into them too soon; if the liquid stands too long it will become vapid. It will be fit for use the next day and does not keep as well as ginger beer made the other way. The bottles, as soon as empty, should be soaked in cold water, well rinsed and scalded, together with the corks. In this manner they may be made to serve many times in succession.

GINGER SNAPS

Take one cup of white sugar; take of butter and lard of each one-half coffee cup; one cup of molasses; one-half cup of water; one table-spoonful of ginger; one teaspoonful of soda; mix thoroughly and bake quickly.

GLAZE

Sisters, just try putting a little cream, sweet or sour, on top of the upper crust of pie or on baking-powder biscuits, and see what a nice, rich glaze it gives.

GLUE

Furniture so frequently needs a drop from the glue-pot, this article should be found on the repair shelf. The double one - one pot within the other - is decidedly the best. Put the broken white glue in the inner tin, cover with water and partly fill the outer pot; place on the stove, and when the glue is of the consistency of thin cream apply it hot to the wood; press the parts firmly together and let the article remain several hours before using. A glue which, it is said, will resist the action of water is made by boiling a half-pound of glue in skimmed milk. For a strong glue for veneering use the best glue, dissolve it in water and to every pint add one-half gill of the best vinegar and one-half ounce of isinglass. A good glue, insoluble in water, and suitable for sealing bottles containing volatile liquids such as ether, alcohol, etc., is prepared by soaking glue in water, adding tannin (about two ounces for every pound of glue) and heating the mixture in a dish of water until quite thick.

GLYCERIN USES

Glycerin is excellent for rubbing into shoes as the preventive of wet feet, as well as to soften the leather and keep it in good condition.

If you want to show your husband a little attention, place a bottle at his hand of equal parts of glycerin and bay rum, for use after his morning shave, and he will rise up and bless you.

Another use may be added, which is not generally known. When you are about to seal fruit-jars, drop in half a dozen drops of glycerin, and it will help to keep the contents and prevent mold from gathering on the top.

GOITRE

Despondent asks a home cure for goitre. I have been troubled with this for some time, and a friend advised me to try coal-oil, which I did and was greatly benefitted. Simply saturate your neck in coal-oil (or kerosene oil) every night and morning, rubbing in well with your fingertips. It has helped me and others.

GOITRE

A home cure for goitre is the following. I had this disease, and the bunch had grown large and troublesome, but I cured it by eating burnt sponge! Do not laugh, but try it. Take a large brown sponge, singe it on a hot stove and scrape it off on a plate as fast as it singes, until it is all in powder. Eat a teaspoonful of this night and morning.

I have cured others in this way, also. Will someone send in good recipes for making lemon pies? Mrs. O.H.M.

GOITRE

And do you know that frequent application of spirits of camphor will cure swelled neck, goitre?

GOLD CAKE

Two cups of white sugar, the yolks of eight eggs, three-fourths cup each of butter and sour milk, two cups of flour, one-half teaspoonful of soda, and one teaspoonful of cream of tartar.

GOLD CAKE

The yolks of four eggs and one extra egg, one cup of sugar, one and three-fourths cups of flour, one-fourth cup of melted butter, one-half teaspoonful of cream of tartar, one-fourth teaspoonful of soda, and three-eighths cup of milk.

GOLD CAKE

Yolks of eight eggs , half cup of sugar, one teaspoonful of cream of tarter, half cup of milk, half spoonful of soda, half cup of butter, two cups of flour.

GOLDEN BROWN BREAD

Take hot water, not scalding, and stir in corn meal until half thick enough for batter; cool it with cold water; put in graham flour to make a thick batter; then stir it all; put in pans two or three inches deep; let it stand for an hour or two, and bake in a hot oven two and a half hours. Cool under thick cloths an hour or two when taken out, and it is good - hot or cold - light, moist and sweet.

GOOD, AND CHEAP MUTTON STEW

A good and cheap mutton stew is made with a piece of breast or neck of mutton by placing it in a saucepan with the usual gravy or warm water, and slicing over it turnips and carrots, also a parsnip and onion if desired. Cover this with a suet crust made of flour, finely chopped beef suet and warm water. Put the crust right over the stew, and now let it simmer till done. It will make an excellent meal for a large family of small means.

GOOD AND CHEAP SOUP

Cut in slices four pounds lean beef or mutton, fry them brown, and lay them with their gravy in the stew-pan; cut six carrots, and as many turnips in slices (the latter may be quartered), three tolerably sized onions, two tablespoonfuls of black pepper, whole, and two heads of celery, with the green tops on; let it boil, and then simmer till the meat is reduced to pulp; strain it, and serve with or without vegetables.

GOOD CEMENT

A Southerner wishes a good cement to fasten a burner on a kerosene lamp. I have used alum and think it good. Clean the lamp and burner good, get all the old cement off and then melt the alum, put it in the burner, and put it on as quick as possible, for as soon as it is cold it is ready for use. It is also very good to fasten knife and fork handles with.

GOOD CEMENT FOR CHINA

A good cement for mending china is made in the following way: Make a thick solution of gum arabic and warm water, and stir in a sufficient quantity of plaster of Paris to make a thick paste; then, with a small brush apply the paste very carefully to the fractured edges of the china, pressing them tightly together, and leave the mended dish untouched for two or three days.

GOOD CHRISTMAS PUDDING

One pound of flour, two pounds of suet, one pound of currants, one pound of plums, eight eggs, two ounces of candied peel, almonds and mixed spices according to taste. Boil gently for seven hours.

GOOD CAKE

Take the yolks of eight eggs, 1 ½ cups of sugar, half a cup of milk, half a cup of boiling water, 1 teaspoonful cream tarter, half a teaspoon of soda, 2 cups of flour; flavor with vanilla. For frosting, allow 3 tablespoonfuls of sugar to the white of one egg, beat the egg to a stiff froth, then stir in the sugar, spread it on the cake, then set in the oven to brown.

GOOD-ENOUGH CAKE

Cream 1 ½ cups flour and one teaspoon of baking powder with cup shortening. Beat together 2 eggs and 1 cup sugar, add to flour and shortening and beat; add ½ cup milk, 1 teaspoon each of salt and vanilla. Beat well, bake in moderate oven.

GOOD FROSTING FOR LAYER CAKE

First beat the whites of two eggs to a stiff froth, next take 1 1/3 cups of granulated sugar, put in a basin and pour nearly half a cup of water in, and boil it until it becomes a little waxy. Then put in about a spoonful of the egg and beat a little; put in a little more egg and beat; and lastly put in all the egg and beat fast until cold. This will be enough to put between two layers and the top of one cake. I hope some of the sisters will try this receipt, as it is splendid and it can be made quickly and with so little trouble. -Jack.

GOOD GIRLS CAKE

The whites of six eggs, one and one-half cups of sugar, half a cup of butter, half a cup of sweet milk, two and one-half cups of flour, one teaspoonful of cream of tartar, one-half teaspoonful of soda, flavor with rose or vanilla. Rub the sugar and butter to a cream, then add the milk and flour containing the cream of tartar and soda, and at last the whites well beaten. Bake until the cake shrinks from the pan.

GOOD PEA SOUP

In an article on "Summer Soups" Mrs. Beecher gives the following as a recipe for "a most delicious pea-soup": Put half a pound of butter into a soup-kettle, over the fire, and add to it a quart of green pease. Shake them round constantly for fifteen minutes to prevent their browning. Then take out half the pease and set aside; then pour in two quarts of vegetable stock, or some prefer boiling water. Cut fine about a pint of spinach, half a dozen green onions, a little mint, if agreeable, and a head of celery. Set the kettle where this will stew slowly two hours, till all the materials are reduced to a jelly, then add the pint of pease reserved, three teaspoonfuls of sweet butter rolled in flour, two tablespoonfuls of salt and one of black pepper. Let it just boil up, and then pour into a hot soup tureen and serve immediately.

GOOD PIE CRUST

A quart of flour will make two large pies. Sift the flour. Take a large, strong spoon, and stir into the flour one quarter pound of butter and a teaspoonful of yeast powder; then moisten with cold water - ice water if you have it - using just as little as will make the flour stick together. Sprinkle some of the shortened flour on the pie board, and roll the crust large enough for the pie-pan; do not try to make smooth edges until you have put in the filling and the upper crust; then press the edges firmly together and cut off the rough edges with a knife. The secret of good, tender, plain pastry is speedy work - no working with warm hands.

GOOD SMELLING SALTS

One gill of liquid ammonia, one quarter of a drachm each of English lavender and of rosemary, and eight drops each of oil of bergamot and cloves. Mix all these ingredients together in a bottle and shake them thoroughly. Fill the vinaigrette, or any small bottle which has a good glass stopper, with small pieces of sponge, and pour in as much of this liquid preparation as the sponge will absorb, and cork the bottle tightly.

GOOD WHITE BREAD

Take one cup of yeast, add warm water enough to make it lukewarm, two tablespoonfuls of sugar and enough flour to make a thick batter. Set it in a warm place and cover closely. This should be raised in about four hours. About four pounds of flour will be needed for this amount of batter. Use cold water in warm weather and warm water in cold weather. Knead the dough well, set in warm place to raise, knead again, put into pans and let it rise two hours before baking.

GOOD WHITE HARD SOAP

Use five pounds of clear grease melted but not hot, a ten cent can of caustic potash (lye) and a tablespoonful of borax. Dissolve the potash over night in a quart of cold water, then add the melted grease and stir the mixture constantly for about ten minutes, or until it looks likes honey. Pour into a vessel with greased paper in the bottom. When partly hardened, mark it off into squares and turn it out. Pile it log-cabin fashion to dry.

GOOSEBERRY CREAM

Take a quart of gooseberries and boil them very quick in enough water to cover them; stir in a half ounce of good butter; when they become soft, pulp them through a sieve; sweeten the pulp while it is hot, and then beat it up with the yolks of four eggs. Serve in a dish or glass cup.

GOOSEBERRY JAM

Stalk and crop as many as you require of ripe, red, rough gooseberries; put them into the preserving-pan, and as they warm, stir and bruise them to bring out the juice. Let them boil for ten minutes, then add sugar in the proportion of three-quarters of a pound to every pound of fruit, and place it on the fire again; let it boil slowly, and continue boiling for two hours longer, stirring it all the time to prevent its burning. When it thickens, and is jelly-like on a plate when cold, it is done enough. Put it into pots, and allow it to remain a day before it is covered.

GOOSEBERRY JAM

Three-fourths of a pound of sugar to a pound of gooseberries; boil the berries alone one hour, then add the sugar and boil another hour. The berries should be fully ripe.

GOSSAMER GINGERBREAD

One cup butter, two cups sugar, well worked together; one cup milk, three and two-thirds cups flour, a tablespoonful of ginger, two eggs; use tin sheets, cool, and rubbed with butter; place one tablespoonful of mixture on tin and spread as thin as possible with a thin bladed knife; bake in a well but not overheated oven; cut on the tins into any shape desired; remove at once from tins, and it will soon become crisp. Keep in a dry place and it will remain so, but not long as it is so good.

GRAFTING WAX

For grafting, take four parts of mutton tallow, eight parts of rosin and two parts beeswax. Melt them all together over a slow fire. When thoroughly melted and mingled, pour the mixture off in small quantities into a tub of cold water. As soon as the masses thus poured into the cold water cool down sufficiently to be handled, work precisely in the same manner as you would candy, by drawing it out and doubling over, until the whole presents a uniform color, and becomes hard enough to mould into balls or sticks. This wax, when it is cold, should be quite hard, but it should be tough at any ordinary summer temperature. If, however, it is found for the climate where it is to be used it is too soft, more rosin should be used. Tallow will soften it, rosin will harden it, render it more infusible, and the beeswax will toughen it. By slightly varying proportions of these ingredients any desired consistency may be obtained.

GRAHAM BREAD

Two cups of graham flour, one cup of white flour, one-half cup of yeast, salt, one cup of water (warm) in which one-half teaspoonful of soda has been dissolved, and one tablespoonful of molasses, stir with a spoon and let rise in the pan it is baked in. Mrs.E.M.W.

GRAHAM BREAD

One pint of milk, one cup of sugar, one teaspoonful of soda, two teaspoonfuls of cream tarter, enough flour to make it stiff as a cake; have tin hot and bake immediately.

GRAHAM BREAD

Make a thin batter of flour, warm water and yeast, let the batter rise, then add sugar or molasses to taste, and make rather stiff with graham flour, then put in baking pans and set to rise. When light bake in a moderate oven. I sift my graham flour and mix thoroughly. When thickening the batter I add a little at a time and beat it well.

GRAHAM CUP CAKE

Unbolted wheat meal, two cupfuls; buttermilk, one cup; molasses, half cup; butter, quarter of a cup; eggs, two; soda, half a teaspoonful. Bake half an hour.

GRAHAM MUFFINS

Dissolve a half cake of yeast in a little warm water, scald a quart of milk and pour it into two quarts of graham flour, stir well, and let cool sufficiently, and then put in the yeast and a spoonful of brown sugar, make a very thick batter, which will heap on the spoon; set to rise overnight. In the morning have a good oven, butter your rings and pan well with cold butter, fill the rings two-thirds full, let them stand a few minutes in a warm place, then put into a brisk oven and bake half an hour.

GRAHAM ROLLS

To one quart of thick sour milk add one teaspoonful of soda, the same of salt, and as much graham flour as will form a batter sufficiently thick to drop from the spoon into the roll pan; have the pan sizzling hot and slightly buttered; bake immediately.

GRAHAM ROLLS

Take one pint of sweet milk, one teaspoonful of salt, and stir in graham flour to form a thick batter. Mix this at night, and in the morning have your roll-iron smoking hot; pour in the batter, and bake in a quick oven. They are delicious.

GRANDMOTHER'S GINGERBREAD

One and one-half cupfuls of sugar, one cupful New Orleans molasses, one cupful of lard, three eggs (save whites to frost the tops), one-half cupful strong coffee, two tablespoonfuls of vinegar, one tablespoonful each of ginger, cinnamon, allspice and soda.

GRAPE CATSUP

Five pounds of grapes, boiled and sifted, three pounds of sugar, one pint of vinegar, two teaspoonfuls of all kinds of spice, one teaspoonful of black pepper, and one teaspoonful of cayenne. Boil one hour. This is very nice to eat with meats.

GRAPE JAM

Boil grapes very soft, and strain them through a sieve. Weigh the pulp thus obtained, and put a pound of crushed sugar to a pound of pulp. Boil it twenty minutes, stirring it often. The common wild grape does extremely well for this use.

GRAPE JELLY

Boil green grapes in cold water till tender; take them out and strain them; rub through a sieve; add their weight in sugar, and boil fifteen minutes. Set in proper dishes to cool.

GRAPE JELLY

Select the grapes when not fully ripe. Wash and drain, then put them in a preserving kettle, mash well and heat till all the skins are broken and the juice flows freely. Strain and use the juice only with an equal part of sugar.

GRASS STAINS

Grass stains may be removed by washing with alcohol. Or apply soda and soap, wetting the spot, rub over with common soap wet in warm water and as much common baking soda as will adhere; let it remain on the stain half an hour or more, then wash out in warm water. Whiting and soap will also remove grass stains.

GRAVY

Add a pinch of salt to the flour used for thickening gravy before mixing with water and it will not "lump"; a fork is better to beat it smooth with than a spoon, and the egg-beater quicker than either.

GRAY MARBLE HEARTHS

Hearths of gray marble may be cleaned by rubbing them with linseed oil.

GREASE REMOVAL FROM KITCHEN FLOOR

To remove grease from kitchen floors pour on cold water, let it stand until it dries, repeat until the grease disappears.

GREASE SPOT AND STAIN REMOVAL

A mixture, which is excellent for removing grease spots and stains from carpets and clothing, is made of two ounces of ammonia, two ounces of white Castile soap, one ounce of glycerin, one ounce of ether. Cut the soap in small pieces and dissolve it in one pint of water. This should then be mixed with more water, in the proportion of a teacupful to one ordinary-sized pail of water. The soiled articles are then washed thoroughly in this. If grease or oil is spilled on a carpet, sprinkle flour or fine meal over the spot, as soon as possible; let it remain for several hours, and it will absorb the grease.

GREASE-SPOT REMOVAL

A better plan for removing grease-spots than by applying a hot iron is to rub in some spirits of wine with the hand until the grease is brought to powder, and there will be no trace of it.

GREASE SPOT REMOVER

A mixture of spirits of turpentine, three ounces, with one ounce essence of lemon will remove grease spots.

GREEN CORN AND HOW TO COOK IT

What Juliet Corson, Supt. of New York Cooking School, says in the Christian Union.

The colored cooks of the south believe that green corn is much more wholesome and nutritious when cooked with the husks on; it is certainly much sweeter than when entirely stripped of its covering. Select full ears, but see that the grains are tender and full of milk; strip off the outer husks and remove all the silk; put the corn into a pot of boiling water and boil it fast until tender, about twenty minutes; then drain the ears and serve them in a covered dish or folded in a napkin. Before eating each ear should be buttered and seasoned with pepper and salt. When hot corn is not served on the cob the grains should be seasoned with salt and pepper, mixed with butter and heated before they are placed on the table.

GREEN CORN DUMPLINGS

A quart of young corn grated from the cob, half a pint of wheat flour sifted, half a pint of milk, six tablespoonfuls of butter, two eggs, a saltspoonful of salt, a saltspoonful of pepper, and butter for frying. Having grated as fine as possible sufficient young, fresh corn to make a quart, mix it with the wheat flour, and add the salt and pepper. Warm the milk in a small sauce-pan, and soften the butter in it. Then add them gradually to the pan of corn, stirring very hard, and set away to cool. Beat the eggs light, and stir them into the mixture when it has cooled. Flour your hands, and make it into little dumplings. Put into a frying-pan a sufficiency of fresh butter (or lard and butter in equal proportions), and when it is boiling hot, and has been skimmed, put in the dumplings, and fry them ten minutes or more, in proportion to their thickness. Then drain them, and send them hot to the dinner-table.

GREEN CORN MARYLAND STYLE

Take six ears of boiled green corn when cool enough to handle, and cut off the kernels. Cut one-quarter of a pound of fat bacon in little strips, then in very small dice and fry them crisp. Take them out of the fat and add the corn to the hot fat, toss it about for a few minutes, add salt and cayenne, and turn out on a hot dish, strew the bits of bacon over the top and serve.

GREEN CORN PATTIES

Grate as much corn as will make one pint, add one teacupful of flour and one teacupful of butter, one egg, pepper and salt to taste. If too thick add a little milk. Fry in butter.

GREEN CORN PUDDING

This is made of green corn cut down fine, two eggs, one pint of milk, butter the size of an egg, three tablespoonfuls of flour; salt and pepper to taste, if served as a vegetable; if not, omit the condiments, substitute sugar in the seasoning, beat well, bake one hour and serve with sauce.

GREEN CORN RAGOUT

Cut a pound of fresh pork in pieces an inch square, fry it brown in the bottom of a saucepan, add to it six large ripe tomatoes, peeled and sliced, and the grains cut from six ears of corn, cover these ingredients with boiling water, season the ragout highly with salt, pepper, and sweet red pepper, and cook it slowly for half an hour; serve it hot, with toast or fried bread.

Ham or bacon, cut in half inch dice and fried, may be substituted for the pork in the above dish. In fact, corn cooked in combination with any meat and highly seasoned makes a palatable dish.

There is hardly an American farm or homestead where this delicious vegetable is not abundant, and it can be made as enjoyable a dish as it is wholesome, abundant and cheap. We advise our farmers' wives not to confine themselves to boiled corn, but to try these combinations for the purpose of varying their list of summer dishes.

GREEN CORN, TO COOK

A delicious way of preparing corn is the following: Cut off the kernels from six large ears of corn. Boil until tender in salted water about twenty minutes. Drain and then put in a saucepan with a cup of milk, into which one tablespoonful of cornstarch has been smoothly mixed. Add two beaten eggs. Cook until cornstarch is done and serve.

GREEN PEA SOUP

Boil one quart of shelled pease and an onion until the pease are very tender. Mash, and add a pint of stock, two tablespoonfuls of butter and one of flour rubbed together; boil up and add two cupfuls of rich milk; season, strain and serve. Small pieces of fried bread are nice served with the soup.

GREEN-PEA SOUP

Take two quarts of green-pease, one small onion, and a sprig of parsley cut fine; add two quarts of hot water, and boil slowly for half an hour, then add a pint of small new potatoes which have been peeled and laid in cold water for an hour; Put in a tablespoonful of sugar and a little salt, boil till the potatoes are done, now add a teacupful of cream or a pint of milk, boil a minute or two, and serve with small slices of toasted bread or gems cut in half.

GREEN PEAS

These should be boiled in very little water with a teaspoonful of salt to a pint of water, and if the peas are not very sweet add a little sugar. When they are young fifteen minutes is sufficient to boil them.

Drain them and add butter, pepper and salt to taste.

GREEN PEAS

The most important part is to get the peas fresh from the vines. They loose their delicious flavor in a very short time after picking. Wash before shelling, not after. Shell the peas, then select the tenderest pods, and put in just water enough to cover them, and after boiling them ten or fifteen minutes, skim out the pods and put in the peas. Boil them slowly twenty minutes, trim with a little rich cream and salt. They should be boiled in so little water that there will not be more than a half teacupful around them when they are cooked, and this should be seasoned and dished with the peas. Those who must depend upon the market for peas often find them very insipid and tasteless, notwithstanding their care in selecting and cooking. Sometimes a spoonful of sugar will add to the flavor. Boiling the pods adds much to the richness and sweetness of the peas.

GREEN PEASE

A peck is sufficient for the ordinary family of four or five. Shell the pease, but do not wash them, as it robs them of much of the flavor. If carefully shelled there will be no necessity for it. Put them in boiling salted water, add a teaspoonful of white sugar and cook for half an hour; then drain off the water, stir in a tablespoonful of butter with a dust of pepper and a saltspoonful of salt and serve hot.

GREEN PEPPER CATSUP

Very charming to those who like hot things. Fill a porcelain lined kettle of ten pounds capacity with green peppers - the hot kind. Crack up a tablespoonful each of the following spices - mace, allspice and cloves - and strew among the peppers, also slice up four large onions and mix with them. Now fill the kettle with good vinegar and set it on the stove to boil until the peppers will mash up readily.

Lift the kettle off, cover it up and set it away for the contents to get cool. When cool, dip up the peppers and vinegar with a teacup, pour into sieve, (I use an ordinary sifter for the purpose) and rub them through with a spoon until nothing is left in the sieve but skins and seeds. Throw those aside and repeat until all the peppers have been rubbed through. The catsup is now complete. Bottle and cork tight. There is no necessity for sealing it.

GRIDDLE-CAKES

Mrs. G. inquires how she can make buckwheat griddle-cakes "Which can be eaten", it being winter and she having no sour milk, and raised cakes proving disagreeable to the stomachs of her men folks. Let her try the following recipe: Three cupfuls of finely-sifted buckwheat flour, one teaspoonful of Cleveland's superior baking powder added before wetting, one egg, one scant teaspoonful of salt, and sufficient water or sweet milk to form a batter. Five things are to be well guarded against, viz.: I. Never mix wheat or corn (meal) flour with the buckwheat; 2. If mixing rye flour with it, only use a very little; 3. Do not make the mistake of adding buckwheat flour to "thicken up," but learn to get the right consistency at first; 4. Never put the baking powder into the batter, but always into the dry flour; 5. Fry as soon as you can after making the batter, and never "keep over" for economy's sake.

GROUND RICE PUDDING

Boil one pint of milk with a little piece of lemon-peel; mix one-quarter pound of ground rice with a half pint of milk, two ounces of sugar, and one of butter; add this to the boiling milk, keep stirring, take it off the fire, break in two eggs, one after the other; keep stirring, butter a pie dish, pour in the mixture, and bake until set. This is one of the quickest puddings that can be made.

GROWING PAINS

A cloth wrung out of cold water and wrapped around the knees will relieve the growing pains children are so often troubled with, and one laid on the throat will often prevent that dose of "nasty medicine" from coming up again.

GRUEL

An egg added to gruel just before taken from the fire adds to its nutritive qualities.

GUMBO

Slice a large onion and brown it in a skillet with a slice of fat bacon or ham; peel and slice two quarts of tomatoes, cut thin one quart of okra, put all together with a little parsley into a stew kettle, add three quarts of water, season to taste, and stew slowly for two or three hours.

HAIR AND SCALP CLEANER

For cleaning the scalp, keeping the hair to its natural color and promoting growth, use a mixture of white cornmeal and fine table salt, two parts of meal to one part of salt. Rub it through the hair, then shake and comb it out well.

HAIR CLEANSING

Barbers and ladies' hair-dressers sometimes use carbonate of potash in solution in cleansing the hair; but on account of its alkaline nature it is especially objectionable. It will be found that a teaspoonful of powdered borax in a quart of warm water is far better.

HAIR DRESSING

Equal parts of glycerin and bay rum, mixed well together, make a dressing that will keep the hair fine and soft.

HAIR FALLING OUT

To stop hair falling out and cure baldness - rub Vaseline thoroughly into the scalp two or three times a week for a month. This will not cure baldness where the roots of the hair have become dead. If the spot on the head where there is no hair looks as if it has been polished, this is a sure sign that the hair roots are dead. A most necessary thing to keep the hair in a healthful condition, is to see that the scalp is loose upon the skull. A tight cap prevents circulation. Nothing can grow without circulation. This is why rubbing the head and working the scalp loose with the fingers is always practiced by those whose business it is to take care of the hair. Keep your scalp loose.

HAIR GROWTH

A tea made by steeping equal parts of sage and box-wood leaves is fine to promote the growth of hair.

HAMBROS PICKLE FOR BEEF

Put five pounds of salt, four ounces of saltpetre, and a pound of brown sugar to four gallons of water; boil all together for two hours, carefully removing the scum as it rises. When cold pack the meat in this pickle, sinking it down under the pickle with some heavy weight. Let it remain six weeks, and then pour off the pickle and boil it again, removing every particle of scum, and again pour on the meat. After this drain it off and reboil every month. In this way it will keep good four or five months. Beef used out of this pickle is said to be much more delicious than when dried or hung.

HARD GINGERBREAD

Rub 2 ½ tablespoonfuls of lard into a pint of flour; take 2 cups of molasses; half a teaspoonful of saleratus; 2 ½ tablespoonfuls of hot water. Stir well together, add a little ginger, then stir into the flour, and mould as soft as it will roll into cards. Bake quick.

HARD GINGERBREAD

One and one-half cups of white sugar, one-half cup of butter, one-half cup of sweet milk, one-half teaspoon soda, one of cream tarter, one egg, ginger to suit the taste, or nutmeg and cinnamon. Knead in flour enough to make a very hard dough, and roll it out to the thickness of pie-crust.

HARD OR CHEMICAL SOAP

Six pounds of clean fat or tallow; six pounds of sal soda; three pounds of lime and four gallons of water. Melt the fat, dissolve the lime and soda in boiling water, and let it remain overnight to settle; then strain the water into the grease, not disturbing the sediments, and let boil until done or until thick; take it out to cool. When cold, cut in bars.

HARD SOAP

Six pounds sal soda, six pounds of grease, three and one-half pounds of new stone lime, four gallons of soft water, and two pounds of borax. Put soda, lime and water into an iron boiler, or large kettle, and boil until all is dissolved. When well settled, pour off the clear lye, wash out the boiler or kettle, put back in the lye, put in the grease and borax, boil till it comes to soap, pour into a tub make it ferment, place in a gallon jug, set it in a warm place to ferment; cork to cool, and when hard, cut into bars, and put on boards to dry. I have put in as much as four pounds of borax. I use the ground borax, not the powdered, and find it all the better.

HARD SOAP FROM REFUSE GREASE

This recipe, which has been used in my mother's family for several years, will be found excellent for all household purposes, except for the toilet, and it may be for very nice paint, and the beauty of it is that refuse grease which is needed for nothing else can be used. Materials are three pounds of solid grease, three pounds of common washing soda, one and three-fourths pounds of lime, one-half pound of lump borax, two gallons of soft water; boil water, lime and soda all together, until the soda and lime are melted, then pour into a pail, leaving it to stand until next morning that it shall be settled; then pour off the water into the vessel you intend boiling it in, place on the fire, adding grease and borax, let it boil slowly for two hours without a cover, then pour into pans, or a shallow box, let stand until firm, cut into pieces about four inches square, and put away to harden. If soft soap is needed let the above boil only about an hour, then turn into a tub slowly, stirring in about six quarts of water or enough to make a hard, white jelly. The grease should be well melted and allowed to stand after straining, then only the hard cake on the top used, scraping away any dirt or extraneous matter. We use the skimmings of everything, not fit for other purposes, even candle ends and grease, and if mutton fat predominates the soap is harder. Of course, like other soap, the older it is, the better.

HARD TIMES FRUIT CAKE

I will send a recipe for hard time's fruit cake. Two cups dried apples, soaked overnight, chopped rather course, three cups of molasses, one egg, two-thirds of a cup of butter, one teaspoonful of soda, all kinds of spices, and flour as you would for cup cake. This will make two loaves.

HARNESS DRESSING

One gallon of neat's-foot oil, two pounds of beeswax, four pounds of beef tallow; put the above in a pan over a moderate fire. When thoroughly dissolved add two quarts of castor oil; then, while on the fire, stir in one ounce of lampblack. Mix well, strain through a fine cloth to remove the sediment, and let it cool.

HASH

Put a teacupful and a half of boiling water into a sauce-pan, and make a thin paste with a teaspoonful of flour, and one tablespoonful of water. Stir it, and boil it three minutes. Add half a teaspoonful of black pepper, rather more salt, and one tablespoonful of butter. Then chop the cold beef into a fine hash, removing all tough, gristly pieces; put the meat in a tin pan, pour over it the gravy above mentioned, and let it heat ten minutes or so, but not cook. The reason so many people have poor hash is that they cook it too much, making it hard and unpalatable, or they use tough pieces of cold meat, or they put in too much water, and make it vapid. If preferred, add equal quantities of chopped boiled potatoes: and if you have gravy of the meat of yesterday's dinner, you may use that instead of the made gravy, and you will need less salt, pepper and butter.

HASH FROM COLD POULTRY

Cut the meat in pieces, put the trimmings and bone in a saucepan, with some pepper, salt, and a slice of lean ham, and a little onion; simmer this for half an hour, thicken it with a little butter rolled in flour, then put in the meat; before serving squeeze in a little lemon-juice.

HAY CAPS

Thick, brown sheeting, one and one-half yards in width, make handy hay caps. This should be cut into squares and a cord hemmed in at the edges. A loop in the cord at each corner is desirable, as wire or wood pins can be thrust through the loops into the haycocks and hold the caps in place. A coating of linseed oil should be given them to render them waterproof and durable. If preferred apply the following mixture: Four ounces of pulverized rosin, one of powdered sugar of lead and one quart of linseed oil. Heat sufficiently to dissolve the materials.

HEADACHE CURE

A towel dipped in hot water, wrung out and applied to the back of the neck, will cure the severest headache.

HEADACHE

To cure a simple headache, put the feet in very hot water, and keep them there for fifteen minutes. This will often afford immediate relief.

HEADACHE

You may not think it, but when you have a bad headache try a hot-water bottle on the calves of your legs. Magic!

HEADACHE - FOR NERVOUS

A simple but often effective way of relieving a nervous headache is to bathe the head freely in water as hot as can be borne. This should be applied not alone to the temples, but to the back of the ears and the back of the neck, where the nerves are very numerous. The effect is, in most cases, soothing and beneficial.

HEAVY CAKE AND BREAD

Much of the heavy cake and bread is the result of the oven door being banged in closing. It should be closed as gently as possible.

HELPFUL HINTS

Scald the teapot and use fresh water just brought to a boil for tea.

A little molasses upon the mustard draft will prevent blistering.

A bit of soda dropped into the cavity of an aching tooth will afford relief.

Tissue or printing paper is the best thing for polishing glass or tin ware.

Water in which meat has been boiled should be saved for broth after removing the fat.

Egg shells crushed and shaken in glass bottles half filled with water will clean them quickly.

When eggs are used for raising mixtures the whites and yolks should be beaten separately.

Unvarnished furniture is easily cleaned by rubbing it with a piece of flannel moistened with kerosene.

Spots may be removed from wash goods by applying the yolk of an egg before putting the article in the tub.

The aroma of coffee overpowers, in a measure, the odor of onions while cooking and an after dinner cup of the beverage renders the breath less disagreeable after indulging in this assertive vegetable.

HEMORRHAGES - LUNG OR STOMACH

Hemorrhages of the lung or stomach are promptly checked by small doses of salt. The patient should be kept as quite as possible.

HICCOUGHS

Dr. Henry Tucker recommends, in the Southern Medical Record, the following very simple treatment of hiccoughs: Moisten granulated sugar with good vinegar. Of this give to an infant from a few grains to a teaspoonful. The effect, he says, is almost instantaneous, and the dose seldom needs to be repeated. He has used it for all ages, from infants of a few months old to those of the down-hill side of life, and has never known of it to fail. The remedy is a very simple one, and merits trial.

HICKORY NUT CAKE

Take four eggs well beaten; reserve whites of two eggs for frosting; one cup of sugar; one-half cup of butter; one cup of sweet milk; two cups of flour in which two tea-spoonfuls of baking powder has been mixed; one and one-half cups hickory nut meats, selecting and reserving some of the whole ones for decorating the top, and stirring the balance of them into one-half cup of flour. Stir the butter and sugar together, then stir in the milk, next the flour, then the eggs, and lastly the mixture of the hickory nuts and flour with salt and flavoring. After baking, dress the top with frosting heretofore described, decorating it with the reserved hickory nut meats.

HINTS FOR THE LAUNDRY

A practical laundress says that all towels should be thoroughly dried before they are put in the hamper.
That clothes-pin are made much more durable by boiling for ten minutes before they are used.
That linen may be made beautifully white by the use of a little refined borax in the water instead of using a washing fluid.
That blankets should be washed in moderately warm water, in

which a teaspoonful of ammonia has been put to each gallon of water.

That washing fabrics that are inclined to fade should be soaked and rinsed in very salt water, to set the color, before washing in the suds.

That calicoes, ginghams and chintzes should be ironed on the wrong side.

HOARSENESS

Take a pinch of powdered borax, let it slowly dissolve and run down the throat. Repeat it often. It is also good to keep the throat moist at night and prevent coughing.

HOARSENESS

For hoarseness take sugar and squeeze enough lemon juice to make a syrup and then add a few drops of glycerin.

HOARSENESS - BAKED LEMON

Bake a lemon or sour orange twenty minutes in a moderate oven; when done open at one end and take out the insides; sweeten with sugar or molasses. This is excellent for hoarseness and pressure on the lungs.

HOARSENESS - MIXTURE FOR

When hoarse, avoid using the voice as much as possible, meanwhile taking the following mixture: Beat well the whites of two eggs, then add two tablespoonfuls of white sugar, stir this into a pint of lukewarm water, grate in half a nutmeg and mix thoroughly. Drink often. This usually acts like a charm in banishing the troublesome affliction.

HOGSHEAD CHEESE NO. 1

Take a hog's head, ears and feet, and clean thoroughly; boil them till you can pick all the bones out; chop the meat, add a cup of vinegar, a little salt and pepper, and pack in a pan or cheese-hoop;

when cool it is ready for use. It is very nice served in slices cold for the tea-table, or fried for breakfast.

HOGSHEAD CHEESE NO. 2

Have the head cut open and put into cold water and soak overnight; then take out the eyes and the ears with a sharp-pointed knife; remove the brains and clean thoroughly the head; boil in salted water until very tender; then pick from the bones and chop; season with pepper, sage (some prefer savory) and a little clove; press into a colander, set on a plate and place in the oven with the doors open, for an hour, to let the fat run out.

HOMEMADE POLISH

Mix together in a bottle equal parts of vinegar and paraffin, cork and put away for use. It is splendid for pictures, mirrors, pianos, floors, etc. If used regularly on a soft duster for gilt picture frames, silver photo frames and the like, they will never tarnish.

HOMINY - IMPROVED WAY OF COOKING

Wash thoroughly, then put into a large pan or pot filled with water; then set in the oven and bake for four hours about as you would beans; it needs no stirring, will not burn down, and is a great improvement over the old way of boiling.

HONEY

When honey is taken from the hive, keep it in the driest and warmest room in the house. It absorbs moisture in a damp place or cellar and loses its flavor.

HONEY AS A MEDICINE

Dr. Bonney, an Iowa physician, has discovered that honey taken in two tablespoonful doses, five times a day for ten days to twenty days, will cure rheumatism. There is but one thing to observe: The honey must be taken between meals, the last dose at bedtime, and no fluids must be ingested for at least one hour after taking a dose. Either strained or comb-honey will do to take. Honey is often recommended by physicians for colds, coughs, etc. It is also beneficial to patients afflicted with kidney trouble. Dr. Gandy of Nebraska, says that honey is a sure preventive of that dreaded Bright"s disease of the kidneys. Honey has a good effect on dyspepsia, if eaten on graham gems. In cases of erysipelas, immediate relief of pain is secured by spreading honey on a cloth and applying it to the affected part.

HONEY SOAP

Cut two pounds of bar soap into thin shavings, and put in a pail with barely hot water enough to cover it; place the pail in a kettle of boiling water, and when its contents are melted stir them thoroughly and add one-fourth of a pound of strained honey, one-fourth of a pound of almond oil, and one-fourth of a pound of powdered borax; mix all well together by stirring ten minutes; then add oil of cinnamon, or oil of bergamot, a few drops, or any scent which is preferred; mix it well and turn the soap into a deep dish to cool, then cut it into squares. It can be made into sand soap balls by adding equal quantities of pure white sand and Indian meal, until it is so stiff you can roll it in your hands. There is no soap that will whiten the hands like this.

HOP BEER

Sugar, four pounds; hops, six ounces; ginger, bruised, four ounces. Boil the hops for three hours with five quarts of water, then strain; add five more quarts of water and the ginger; boil a little longer, again strain; add the sugar, and when lukewarm add one pint of yeast. After twenty-four hours it will be ready for bottling.

HOP YEAST

Put two ounces of hops in four quarts of cold water and boil it three hours. Then take three large tablespoonfuls of flour, mix with cold water, and strain the water from the hops on it, stirring at the same time.

Add a tablespoonful of salt; this will make one gallon of yeast. When lukewarm add one pint of yeast to tightly, put in a cool place to keep.

HOPS

How many mothers know that a pillow filled with hops, warmed and placed under baby's head when the little one is cross and restless, will soon bring slumber, sweet and soothing.

HORNLESS CATTLE

If you want hornless cattle, buy a stick of white potash and rub the incipient horn of a young calf, after dampening it. This is an effective method of preventing horn growth and is painless to the calf.

HORRIBLE DEATH

An urgent invitation to a horrible death is the washing of goods in a pan of gasoline in a room in which there is a fire. Goods washed in gasoline should not be taken to dry into a room in which there is a blaze of any kind. In Columbus a barber carried a fresh washed wig into a room heated by a stove and put it in a bureau drawer. In a while he saw a flash from the stove to the bureau fourteen feet away and found the wig afire. In Ohio one year five women were burned to death for adding gasoline to the clothes in a washer-boiler while it was on the stove - an act almost invariably disastrous.

HOT CROSS BUNS

Three cups of sweet milk, one cup of yeast; flour enough to make a stiff batter; set this as a sponge overnight. In the morning add one cup of sugar, one-half cup of melted butter, one-half nutmeg; saltspoonful of salt; flour enough to roll out like biscuits; knead well and set to rise for five hours. Roll half an inch thick; cut into round cakes and put in the pan. When they have stood half an hour make a cross on each one and put into the oven instantly.

HOT PUDDING SAUCE

To four large spoonfuls of rolled, clean brown sugar, put two of butter, and stir it together in an earthen dish until white; then put it into a saucepan with a teacup of hot water, and set it upon the coals. Stir it steadily till it boils, and then add a spoonful or two of wine, lemon juice, or rose water, and let it boil up again. Pour it into a sauce tureen and grate nutmeg over the top. The advantage of stirring the butter and sugar together before melting it, is, that it produces a thick white foam upon the top. The reason for stirring it steadily while on the coals, is, that it would otherwise become oily.

HOW TO COOK RICE

Rice is becoming a much more popular article of food than heretofore. It is frequently substituted for potatoes at the chief meal of the day, being more nutritious and much more readily digested. At its present cost it is relatively cheaper than potatoes, oatmeal or grain grits of any kind. In preparing it, only just enough cold water should be poured on to prevent the rice from burning at the bottom of the pot, which should have a close fitting cover, and with a moderate fire the rice is steamed rather than boiled until it is nearly done; then the cover is taken off, the surplus steam and moisture allowed to escape, and the rice turned out a mass of snow-white kernels, each separate from the other and as much superior to the usual soggy mass as a fine mealy potato is to the water-soaked article. The above facts are of general interest to the "poor and prudent", and therefore worthy of note.

HULLED CORN

K., Saratoga Springs, N.Y.: Let me tell you how Aunt Joshua hulls corn. Select the nicest ears, rejecting the small grains at the ends; shell two quarts, blow out the hulls and beards; that will be as much as an eight quart pot will accommodate. Tie three pints of fresh wood ashes in a bag and place with the corn in as much water as the pot will hold without boiling over; put over the fire, cover up and boil until the hulls separate from the grains. This can be ascertained from inspection. Then remove the corn and wash in cold water until no hulls remain. Replace on the fire in clean water, salt to taste, and boil until soft.

HULLED CORN

For one quart of nice kernels take three quarts of weak lye; boil until the stage when, if you put in cold water, you can wash off the little black hulls at the points. Wash in ten clean waters, then put the corn into three quarts of hot water in a tin or earthen dish and boil until soft; then salt to taste. Boil ten minutes, stir to keep from scorching; if the water gets low at any time add more. Serve with sugar and milk, or either alone; or eaten without either it is very good. Wheat may be hulled in the same way and then used in place of rice. (Sarah A. Fowl, Elmira, Ohio)

HUMBUG PIE

One cup of molasses, one cup of sugar, one cup of chopped raisins, two-thirds of a cup of rolled crackers, one cup of cold water, one-half cup of vinegar; spice like mince pies and a piece of butter the size of a walnut. Annie R. H.

HUNTERS PUDDING

1 cup of finely chopped suet, 1 cup molasses, 1 cup milk, 3 cups flour, 1 tsp soda, 1½ tsp salt, ½ tsp each clove, cinnamon, allspice, 1 cup raisins. Add milk and molasses to suet; mix and sift dry ingredients and add raisins; combine mixtures. Cover and steam for 3 hours.

HUSBAND (AT BREAKFAST TABLE)

"Oh for some of the biscuits that my mother used to make!"
Wife (sweetly): "I'm sorry you haven't them, dear. They would be just about stale enough to go well with that remark."

HYGIENIC BREAKFAST CAKES

One pint of fresh oatmeal, one quart of water, let it stand overnight. In the morning add one teaspoonful of fine salt, one teaspoonful of sugar, and the same of baking powder, and one pint of graham flour. If the above proportions make a batter too stiff for griddle cakes, add more water. If gems are preferred instead of cakes, the addition of a little more flour is all that is required to produce an extra article.

ICE CREAM

One pint milk, one cup sugar, two tablespoonfuls flour, one salt spoonful salt, two eggs, one pint to one quart of cream, one-half to one cup sugar, one tablespoonful flavoring extract. Boil the milk. Mix the sugar, flour and salt; add the whole eggs and beat all together. Add the boiling milk and when well mixed turn out into the double boiler and cook twenty minutes, stirring constantly till smooth; after that, occasionally. When cool add the cream, flavoring and sugar to make it quite sweet. This makes a smooth and delicious cream, and if the milk be boiling and the custard cook fully twenty minutes, there will be no taste of the flour.

ICE CREAM

Fill the pail two-thirds full of the custard to be frozen; set it, tightly covered, in a wooden bucket, pack the space between the two with a mixture of one part salt to two parts ice broken in small bits. When the space is full to within an inch of the top remove the cover and stir with a wooden spoon or paddle, keeping the freezing cream detached from the sides till the whole is stiff; replace the cover, pour off the water, repack, cover the whole with a blanket and set in a cool place.

ICE CREAM CAKE

Three eggs well beaten, a cupful of sugar, a half teaspoonful of soda dissolved in a half-cupful of rich milk, a half teaspoonful extract of lemon or vanilla, two cupfuls of flour; beat all thoroughly together; bake in a sheet in a slow oven. Serve cold with ice cream.

ICE CREAM CANDY

Take two cupfuls of granulated sugar, half a cupful of water, and one-quarter of a teaspoonful of cream tarter dissolved in a teaspoonful of boiling water. Put in a porcelain kettle and boil ten minutes without stirring it. Drop a few drops into a saucer of cold water or in snow. If it is brittle it is done; if not, boil till it is. Add a piece of butter half as large as an egg while it is on the fire and stir it in. Pour into a buttered tin, and set on ice or snow to cool enough to pull it white. Flavor with vanilla just before cool enough to pull. Work into strands and cut into sticks.

ICE HOME-MANUFACTURED

Place the water to be frozen in a tin bucket, put this bucket into a larger vessel containing a weak dilution of sulphuric acid and water, into this throw a handful of common Glauber's salt, and the resulting cold will be so great that water immersed in the mixture will be frozen solid in a short time, so that ice-cream or ices of different varieties may be quickly prepared. In making the sulphuric-acid solution always put the acid into the water - never pour the water into the acid. The acid should be added gradually to the water. Be sure to keep everything of this sort out of the reach of children - this cannot be too strongly emphasized. Sulphuric acid is one of the strongest caustics. Sister Talkative.

The following was the editors' reply to the above: The experiment suggested, of making artificial ice, is a most interesting one. Have you ever tried it, so that you may vouch for its verity? Glauber's salt is, we think, the ordinary sulphate of soda, and we are not sufficiently well versed in chemistry to be quite sure of the result of mingling this with the sulphuric-acid solution. We mean to know, however - by actual test! If it is possible to "freeze a pail of water solid in a few minutes" by this method, we can laugh in our sleeve at the dilatory ice-man, who neglects to bring ice for Sunday's ice cream!

ICED APPLES

Pare and core one dozen large apples; fill with sugar, very little butter, and cinnamon; bake till nearly done; let them cool, and if you can without breaking, put on another dish; if not, pour off the juice; having some icing prepared, lay on top and side, and set in oven a minute or two to brown slightly. Serve with cream.

ICED COFFEE

To make coffee, always have the water freshly boiled. Allow one tablespoonful of coffee and one inch of isinglass to one-half pint of water. Put in the coffee and isinglass after scalding the coffee first, add the boiling water and boil five minutes. Pour out a little to clear the spout, and pour back again; add one-half cup of cold water. When it has settled pour carefully off into a pitcher to cool. Serve in goblets in which are chopped ice, and add sugar and cream to each glass to suit your taste.

ICING RUN-OFF

To prevent icing running off a cake, rub a little dry flour over the latter and pin a band of oiled paper around it.

IMITATION CORN STARCH PUDDING

One quart of milk, and a little salt. Thicken one-third of the milk to quite a thick, smooth paste, with flour; add two eggs well beaten, and stir in the remainder of the milk, when it boils. To be eaten cold with cream and sugar.

INDIAN BATTER CAKES

To about a pint of Indian meal pour a little boiling water on to scald it, then add a handful of wheat flour and a little salt; thin it with cold milk; add two or three well-beaten eggs. They are very nice and tender.

INDIAN APPLE PUDDING

Turn three pints of scalding milk into a pint of sifted Indian meal; stir in two large spoonfuls of sugar, two teaspoonfuls of cinnamon or ginger, a teaspoonful of salt, one teaspoonful of soda and one dozen sweet apples, pared, cored and sliced thin. Bake three hours. To be eaten with nice syrup of any kind, or is good without addition.

INDIAN CAKES

Mix up Indian meal with water or milk, with or without an egg, into a batter, rather thicker than for griddle cakes, add a trifle of flour, salt well, and pour it into the cast iron roll pan, previously greased.

INDIAN GRIDDLE CAKES

Two cups of sweet milk, the same of sour, one teaspoonful of soda, salt; one-third flour, two thirds Indian meal; mixing a little thicker than when all flour is used. The flour sifted from the meal will make them better, if anyone has a fine sieve.

INDIAN MEAL GRUEL

One quart of boiling water; stir into this one tablespoonful of flour and two of Indian meal, mixed with a little cold water. Boil thirty minutes. Season with salt and strain. Use sugar and cream, if you choose. If flour is not liked, use an other spoonful of meal instead.

INDIAN MUFFINS

One quart of Indian meal; one quart of flour; eight eggs; two gills of yeast; a little salt; as much warm milk as will make the whole into a thick batter; mix the Indian and wheat flour together; stir in the milk, then the yeast, and lastly the eggs. After they have been well beaten. When the batter is light, grease the griddle and muffin rings, pour in the batter and bake brown on both sides, and serve hot. If for breakfast, set to rise the night previous; if for tea, about one o'clock.

INDIAN PUDDING

Take an earthen bean pot with a wide top, butter it well and leave in it a piece of butter, size of a large egg, then put in a full cup of molasses, a scant cup of meal, one teaspoonful ground cinnamon; mix well and pour onto it one quart scalding milk; stir well and put in moderate oven for half an hour, then pour in one pint cold milk without stirring, and bake slowly three and one-half hours. I prefer the coarse to the fine meal.

INDIAN PUDDING

For a two quart pudding, put to boil three pints of milk; when at boiling point stir in one teacupful of Indian meal thoroughly; then remove from the fire and add one teacupful of New Orleans molasses, one large teaspoonful of salt, one-half cup of butter, or one full cup chopped suet. Pour it into a deep brown earthen pudding-pot and let it stand half an hour to cool. Then add one pint of cold milk, without stirring; bake in a range oven three hours with a steady fire, and not too hot.

INDIAN PUDDING

Into a quart of boiling milk stir a coffee cup of Indian meal, sifted; a coffee cup of molasses, a teaspoonful of salt, a piece of butter the size of an egg. Butter the dish well and pour the above into it; stir it well from the bottom to prevent its settling.

After it is in the oven pour over the whole, without stirring, carefully a pint of cold milk; bake three and a half hours in a moderate oven.

INDIAN PUDDING

Two quarts of milk; when it boils, stir in a medium-sized cupful of Indian meal; stir until it thickens a little, take off the range, add little more than a cup of molasses and some salt; pour this into a deep earthen pudding dish and bake three hours - four is better if it is desired dark and wheyed. After it has been baking an hour and a half, pour into the pudding, without stirring at all, one pint of cold milk. This is the good old-fashioned pudding, such as our grandmothers used to make, and if made and baked according to this rule, the pudding will be very palatable.

INDIAN PUDDING

One quart of milk, small one-half cup Indian meal stirred into the milk while boiling, boil from five to ten minutes, then set off from the fire and add one cup molasses (dark molasses is best), three-fourths cup nice beef suet chopped fine or one-half cup of butter, salt, cinnamon or ginger to taste. Stir all together and pour into a buttered baking dish, then add a large pint cold milk and do not stir. Bake very slowly six to eight hours.

INDIAN PUDDING

Take two cups of Indian meal; two teaspoonfuls of salt; put it in your pudding pan, and then put molasses enough to moisten the meal; heat two quarts of milk to boiling, and pour it on the meal; stir it quickly till thoroughly mixed, and bake three hours.

INDIAN PUDDING

Two quarts milk, scalding hot; stir in one cup Indian meal, and let it stand to cool 30 minutes; beat two eggs together with one cup of molasses, ginger, nutmeg and salt; bake one and one-half hours. Cool one hour before eating.

INDIAN PUDDING

Boil a quart of milk, stir in a quart of corn-meal, a teaspoonful of salt and a half-pound of beef suet chopped to a powder. When cold add the yolks of three eggs, beaten light, with three heaping tablespoonfuls of sugar, and lastly add the beaten whites. Dip the bag into hot water, flour it inside, fill but half full of the mixture, as it will swell. Boil it five hours and eat it with butter and sugar. Instead of boiling it may be baked for an hour and a half.

INFLAMMATION

Here is a tested remedy for inflammation and nearly every pain and ache: Mix the white of one egg, a half teaspoonful of turpentine, a scant half-cupful of vinegar and sufficient flour to make a paste that will not run, spread this on a cloth as large as required to cover the part affected, and over it put another cloth to prevent soiling the clothing. Remember mothers and all, this is just fine for earache, toothache and lung trouble.

INFLAMMATION REMOVAL

A thin piece of salt pork bound onto a wound caused by stepping on a nail or carpet tack will remove the inflammation almost immediately, and prevent serious consequences.

INK-SPOTS

Every schoolboy is not aware that ink-spots can be removed from the leaves of books by using a solution of oxalic acid in water; nor does every housemaid know that "spots" are easily cleaned from varnished furniture by rubbing with spirits of camphor.

INK STAINS

Ink stains may be removed from colored table-covers by dissolving a teaspoonful of oxalic acid in a teaspoonful of hot water, and rubbing the stained part well with the solution. Ink stains may be taken out of anything white by simply putting a little powdered salts of lemon and cold water on the stain, allowing it to remain about five minutes, and then washing it out with soap and water, when the stains will disappear. Ink stains on silver or plated articles may be effectually removed without injury to the articles by making a little chloride of lime into paste with water, and rubbing the stains until they disappear, and afterwards washing the article with soap and water. To remove ink stains from a mahogany table, put a few drops of spirits of nitre into a teaspoonful of water, and touch the part stained with a feather dipped into the mixture. Immediately the ink stain disappears the place must be rubbed with a cloth dipped in cold water, or there will be a white mark.

INK STAINS AND SCORCHES

Scorches may be removed from linen by spreading over them the juice of two onions and half an ounce of white soap. Lemon juice and salt will remove stains of rust and ink. The articles should be exposed to the sunlight after being well saturated in the mixture.

INK STAINS ON MAHOGANY

Ink stains may be taken out of mahogany by applying spirits of salt.

INSECT REPELLENT

To keep insects away from bird cages suspend a little bag of sulphur in the cage.

INSECT STINGS

To insect stings apply soda moistened, or tobacco.

IODINE FOR CORNS AND CHILLBLAINS

One of the best remedies for allaying the inflammation of corns and chillblains is iodine and aconite in equal parts. The mixture is poisonous and should always be so marked, but for external use it is of great value in allaying the burning and itching of chilblains and soreness of corns.

Many people object to using iodine on account of the brown stain which it leaves. Colourless iodine may be had of your druggist, but as he will ask you more for it than the coloured, you can quite as well make it colourless yourself. This is done by dropping ammonia into the iodine, one drop at a time, until the liquid becomes white. This bit of information was learned from a druggist.

IODINE STAINS

This information is of value as a bit of household wisdom. If iodine is by accident spilled upon clothing, table linen or any article which will bear wetting, the stain may be entirely removed by soaking the article in ammonia water. An entire bottle of iodine was spilled upon the front of a linen dress skirt, and of course the owner thought it was ruined beyond the possibility of restoration. But it wasn't. A friend, who happened to know how iodine was made colourless, suggested that the skirt be soaked overnight in ammonia water. It was tried, and in the morning the skirt was taken out with no trace of the recent accident upon it. The secret is worth remembering.

IRISH CABBAGE

Chop fine a medium-sized head of cabbage, and season with butter, pepper and salt; add water enough to cook until very tender; then, when almost dry, add a cup of thick, sweet cream, and simmer a few minutes longer. A good way is to use half cream and half vinegar, or for those who have no cream use milk thickened with a little flour.

IRISH STEW

Cut up into cutlets about three pounds of the best end of a neck of mutton, saw off the chine bone and trim off the fat; season the cutlets well with pepper and salt and put them, with the bones, into the stewpan, just covering them with cold water; stew gently for half an hour, remove from the fire, skim the fat from the gravy, and then return it with the chops into the stewpan; add about eight potatoes cut in halves, four onions sliced, a couple of turnips, and one and a half pints of either stock or water; cover the stewpan and simmer gently for one and a half or two hours. Serve with the potatoes in the centre of the dish, the cutlets arranged all round, and with the onions and gravy poured over.

IRISH TOAST

One cup buttermilk; one egg; one-half teaspoonful soda; mix hard with flour; cut in six pieces; roll thin as pie crust, and fry in lard, like doughnuts. Make a sauce of flour, water, butter, sugar and a little nutmeg, boiled together. Pour some of the sauce over each cake; as soon as fried put it into a large nappy; cut like a pie and serve hot.

This is an excellent substitute for pudding and is well liked.

IRON HANDLED KNIVES

Knives with iron handles, which have become loosened, or have fallen out entirely, can be cemented at home and with small expense by using this cement: Take four parts of rosin, one part of beeswax, one part of plaster of Paris, fill the hole in the handle with the cement, then heat the steel of the handle and press it firmly into the cement.

IRON RUST REMOVAL

A widowed mother asks how to remove iron-rust. Lemon juice, applied either with or without salt will prove effective; but the washing of the spots in warm juice of freshly stewed rhubarb (pie-plant) is better, both in case of old and new stains.

IRON RUST REMOVAL

To remove iron-rust, place the fabric where it will be exposed to the sun, cover the rust spot with a small quantity of oxalic acid, pour on boiling water and allow a short time for action. If the stain does not disappear with one application, repeat, allowing a short time to dissolve.

IRON RUST REMOVAL

Sister May, to remove iron rust, cover with salt and squeeze on enough lemon-juice to wet it thoroughly, then place in the hot sun; it may require a third application to take the spots out of badly rusted goods - we are told "the third time is the charm".

ITALIAN CREAM OF RICE

The cream of rice is made by boiling the breast of a fowl and a cup of rice in chicken broth until soft enough to rub through a fine sieve; the paste thus formed is used to thicken boiling milk, season with salt, pepper and nutmeg, to the consistency of thick cream; it is one of the most delicious and nutritious of all soups.

ITCH

One way to deal with winter itch is to grin and bear it in public and scratch in private.

ITCHING

Here is a tried and true remedy for all itching diseases of the skin: Mix white Vaseline and boric acid, equal parts, or use any kind of petroleum jelly and finely powdered boric acid, in equal parts, mixing thoroughly. This is absolutely safe and sure as a healing antiseptic salve.

IVORY-HANDLE KNIVES

Ivory-handle knives should never be put in hot or greasy water. If servants will do such careless things, the only remedy, then, is to scrape the handles with glass or sandpaper.

IVORY POLISHING

To polish ivory first smooth the surface with the finest sand-paper, then apply whiting on a bit of flannel, rubbing it well. The whiting may be wet with oil or water. Finish by rubbing the ivory with a slightly oiled bit of linen cloth. All scratches must be fairly rubbed out in the process.

Ivory, when not stained, may be restored to its former whiteness by cleaning with powdered burnt pumice-stone and water, and then placing it under glasses in the sun's rays.

JAMAICA GINGER BEER

Put two ounces of the extract of Jamaican ginger, a pound of sugar, an ounce of cream of tartar, and the grated yellow peel of a lemon into six quarts of water. Stir until the sugar is melted, and heat until the mixture is lukewarm, then add a quarter of a cup of yeast. Let it stand two or three hours, stir, bottle and wire the corks. It will be fit for use in four days. One of the best and most harmless drinks for the harvest field.

JAVELLE WATER

Javelle water, often met with in works and articles on cleaning and dyeing, is made of one gallon of water and four pounds of ordinary washing soda; boil five or ten minutes, then add one pound of chloride of lime. Let cool, and keep corked in a stoneware jar or airtight vessel.

JAVELLE WATER

Javelle water will remove almost any stains, but one cannot always obtain it ready made at the apothecary's. It can be prepared very easily, however, in the following manner: Put a pound of sal soda into a kettle over the fire, add one quart of boiling water, let it remain ten minutes, then add a quarter of a pound of chloride of lime; stir it until there are no lumps. A larger quantity can be made by using four pounds of soda, one pound of lime and one gallon of water. Use when cool. This water will remove almost any stain. Of course the cloth needs to be rinsed clean afterwards.

    This will remove tea stains, fruit stains, some kinds of ink and almost everything of the sort. It is also excellent for bathing purposes, a few drops added to the water removing at once all ink spots, stains from colored stockings, etc., from the flesh.

JELLY CAKE

Three eggs well beaten, one cup of powdered sugar, one cup of flour, one teaspoonful of cream of tartar, one-half teaspoonful of soda dissolved in three teaspoonfuls of water; spread thin on shallow tins and bake in a moderate oven. When done turn upon a towel, spread the cake with jelly, roll up, and wrap in the towel.

JELLY CAKE

Three eggs, one cup of sugar, two-thirds cup of milk, two cups flour, a piece of butter the size of a butternut, two even teaspoonfuls of cream of tarter, and one even teaspoonful of soda. This makes an excellent jelly cake, and does not break when taken from the pan.

JELLY CAKE

1 cup sugar, 1 cup sweet milk, 1 cup flour, 1 egg, 1 teaspoon butter, 3 teaspoons baking powder. Bake in jelly tins and spread jelly when warm.

JELLY MAKING

When making jelly, if a few marbles are thrown in it they save the necessity of frequent stirring, as they roll around when it boils, and thus prevents the jelly from burning.

JENNY LINDS' PUDDING

Grate the crumb of half a loaf, butter the dish well and lay in a thick layer of the crumbs; pare ten or twelve apples, cut them down, and put in a layer of them and sugar; then crumbs alternately, until the dish is full; put a bit of butter on the top, and bake it in an oven, or American reflector. An excellent and economical pudding.

JERSEY PUDDING

One pint of sweet milk, five Boston crackers rolled fine and soaked in it over night; half a cup of butter, three-quarters of a cup of sugar, four eggs, one cup of raisins, half a teaspoonful of cloves, half a teaspoonful of cinnamon, half a nutmeg. Bake and serve with "yellow sauce" made as follows: One-third of a cup of butter, beaten light, two-thirds of a cup of sugar and the yolk of one egg. Mix well, and pour on it one cup of boiling water. When it cooks a little add the beaten white of the egg, stirring in a spoonful at a time. (Susan Anna Brown's Book of Forty Puddings)

JERUSHA CAKE

Three eggs; two cups of sugar; beat well together; half cup of butter; cup and a half sweet milk; two teaspoonfuls of cream tarter; one of soda; one quart of flour; and spice to your taste.

JEWELRY CLEANER

Tooth-powder is an excellent thing, applied with a brush, to clean filagree jewelry.

JOB'S TEARS

In reply to the sister who asked about raising Job's tears from seed? We planted some last spring, have made some pretty necklaces, and have quite a quantity of "tears" left. Plant them about six inches apart, so they will have room to grow. The plants resemble corn when they come up. The seeds ripen in early fall, and are pearly-gray color, very hard and lustrous.

JOHNNYCAKE

One pint of corn meal scalded with one cup of boiling water, one-half cup of flour, one cup of sour milk, one tablespoonful of shortening, one-half tablespoonful of molasses, one-half teaspoonful of soda, one teaspoonful of salt and one egg well beaten.

JOSEPHINE CAKE

Four eggs, two tablespoonfuls of sugar, three of butter, two of cream, two cups of milk, a little grated lemon peel and nutmeg, two teaspoonfuls of cream of tartar, one of soda. Bake half an hour. Eat while warm.

JUMBLES

Three eggs, one and one-fourth cups sugar, one cup butter, three tablespoonfuls sour milk, a little saleratus, flour to mix hard. Roll on sugar after it is kneaded and rolled.

JUNKET

Junket is a most delicious dessert dish and easily made. It must be prepared several hours before it is needed.

A plain junket is made by warming two quarts of fresh milk till it is a very little warmer than when just from the cow. Pour the milk into a large ornamental bowl or dish in which it can be brought to the table, and while the milk is warm stir into it two tablespoonfuls of prepared rennet; stir gently for two minutes, then set away in a cold place. It will soon become a solid sweet curd. Serve by dipping the curd out in large slices with a small flat ladle or broad spoon. It may be eaten with rich cream alone, or with cream and powdered sugar.

KEEPING BUTTER SWEET

If your butter seems likely to spoil, immerse the vessel which contains it in cold lime-water and keep it there until the sweetness of the butter is restored.

KEEPING CIDER

Let the cider reach the point of fermentation. Then to one bbl. add 1 pint of alcohol, 3/4 ounce of wintergreen, 1/4 ounce sarsaparilla. Keep tight for ten days when it will be fit for use.

KEEPING DUST DOWN

Moistened corn meal, sprinkled on the carpet you wish to sweep, will keep the dust down and will not make the rug or carpet look streaked. Sawdust answers the same purpose; be careful not to get it very wet.

KEEPING EGGS

A western egg merchant gives the following rule for keeping eggs: "To one pint of salt and one pint of lime add four gallons of boiling water. Slack the lime first in a small quantity of hot water. When cold put it in stone jars, or anything that will not absorb the liquid (a vessel of wood or brown earthenware will not do). Then, with a dish, let down your fresh eggs into it, tipping the dish after it fills with water, so that they will roll out without cracking the shell, for if the shell is cracked the egg will spoil. Put the eggs in whenever you have them fresh (they should not be over two or three days old). Keep them covered in a cool place, and they will keep fresh for a year."

KEEPING MILK SWEET

To keep milk sweet, stir into it a tiny pinch of borax.

KENTUCKY FRIED CHICKEN

After thoroughly washing the chicken drain all the water off; never let chicken soak in water. When you are ready to fry it take a clean towel, lay it on the table, lay the pieces of chicken on it, and turn the towel over them, so as to soak up all the moisture; then pepper and salt it and dip lightly in flour; fry in lard and use plenty of it; lard is better than butter to fry chicken in; have your frying-pan hot when you put the chicken in, and give it plenty of time to cook; when it is done, if it is not browned evenly, set it in the oven a few minutes; take it up as soon as done; never let it stand in the grease. To make the gravy put a sufficient quantity of flour in the grease to make a thin paste, and stir it until it is perfectly smooth; then put in sweet milk until it is the right consistency; do not get it too thick, and let it boil about five minutes, and season to taste; then pour it over the chicken.

KENTUCKY POTATOES

Raw potatoes, milk, pepper, salt, teaspoonful of flour, butter. Slice the potatoes very thin, put them in your baking-dish and just cover them with milk, add a little salt and pepper and a few bits of butter, mix the flour in the milk, bake a nice brown. Do not put the potatoes in water after they have been sliced.

KEROSENE ODOR

Hot vinegar removes the odor of kerosene from earthen, glass or tin.

KIDNEYS

For the kidneys - Eat plenty of beans. Where the kidneys are already affected eat the beans without parboiling. This is a very good remedy where the disease has not reached its last stages.

KISSES

Five ounces of sugar, three eggs, six ounces of flour, pinch of salt; to be dropped and sugar sprinkled on before baking.

KISSES OR CREAM MERINGUES

To make kisses or cream meringues beat the whites of three eggs stiff and flaky, add three-quarters of a cup of powdered sugar, sifting and cutting it in lightly. Drop by spoonfuls on paper placed on boards. Put in the hot closet or oven with the door open for half an hour. Then brown slightly. Put two together, or put them on the paper in oblong shape, dry one hour, then remove the soft part and fill with whipped cream. To make these successfully, a very steady moderate heat is required, and it is a waste of time to attempt them unless this can be secured.

LAMP CHIMNEYS

Polish lamp chimneys after washing with a bit of old newspaper. Boil them when new in sweet milk or salt-water (put in of course while the milk or water is cold), and they will not break so easily.

LAMP WICKS

Lamp wicks should have the charred part rubbed off with a rag kept for that purpose. They should very seldom be cut.

LAMP WICKS

Old cotton stockings may be made into lamp wicks which answer very well.

LEATHER CHAIR-SEATS AND BOOK BINDINGS

Leather chair-seats may be brightened and revived by rubbing them with the white of an egg; leather book bindings will also be improved by the same treatment.

LEMON BEER

Sugar, one pound; boiling water, one gallon; one sliced lemon; bruised ginger, one ounce; yeast, one teacupful. Let stand twelve to twenty hours, after which it may be bottled.

LEMON CREAM

Steep the rinds of four large lemons in a pint of water for twelve hours; strain and dissolve in it three-quarters of a pound of loaf sugar; add the strained juice of the lemons and the beaten whites of seven eggs and the yolk of one. Boil it over a slow fire, stirring constantly, till it is like thick cream. Serve in a glass dish.

LEMON CREAM CANDY

To make lemon-cream candy take six pounds best white sugar; strained juice of two lemons, grated peel of one lemon, one teaspoonful of soda, three cups clear water.

Steep the grated peel of the lemon in the juice for an hour; strain, squeezing the cloth hard to get out all the strength of the flavor. Pour the water over the sugar, and when nearly dissolved, set it over the fire, and bring it to a boil. Stew steadily until it will harden in cold water; stir in the lemon, boil one minute; add the dry soda, stirring well to avoid lumps; and, instantly, turn out upon broad shallow dishes. Pull as soon as you can handle it into long white ropes, and cut into lengths when brittle.

Vanilla cream candy is made in the same way, with the substitution of vanilla flavoring for the lemon juice and peel.

LEMON CREAM PIE

One cup sugar, one raw potato grated, one cup water, one lemon grated and juice added, bake in pastry top and bottom. This quantity will make one pie.

LEMON CUSTARD

Eight eggs; six ounces of sugar; two lemons; a tea-cupful of cream;

one pint of boiling water; and two table-spoonfuls of orange-flower water. Beat the yolks of the eggs till quite frothy; pour on them the boiling water, stirring quickly all the time; add the sugar, and the rinds of the lemons, grated; stir it over a slow fire till thick, adding the cream and orange-flower water; when hot, stir in the lemon juice; pour it into a basin; stir till nearly cold, and serve in custard glasses.

LEMON FOAM

Beat well together the yolks of six eggs, half a pound of powdered sugar, two grated lemons, half ounce of gelatin dissolved in cold water. Simmer over the fire until thick. Beat the whites of the eggs to a stiff froth, add them to the mixture, beat together and pour into moulds.

LEMON HONEY

Have you ever tried lemon honey? Nothing can be nicer. Three lemons, three eggs, three cups of sugar, two cups of water, small piece of butter; boil gently twenty minutes.

LEMON JUICE

How many know that if a lemon is well heated before being squeezed, nearly twice the quantity of juice will be obtained that would be if the lemon were not heated?

LEMON LEAVES

Lemon seeds, if planted and treated as house plants, will make pretty little shrubs. The leaves can then be used for flavoring. Tie a few in a cloth and drop in apple sauce when boiling and nearly done. It is a cheap essence.

LEMON MINCE PIE

Chop three large apples with four ounces of beef suet, squeeze the juice from a lemon and boil the lemon till soft; then make it fine and add the apples; put in half a pound of currants, four ounces of white sugar and one ounce of candied orange and citron; line plates with nice puff paste, fill with meat, cover with paste and bake.

LEMON PIE

M.E.M. wishes to know how to make lemon pie. Take two yolks and one white of eggs to a pint of sweet milk, add the juice of half a lemon and sweeten to taste, take the other white, beat to a froth, adding some white sugar, and pour on top, and bake as common custard. I.A.C.

LEMON PIE

Pare one apple and two lemons, taking care to remove all the white of the rind from the latter. Cut them all in small dice, and put them over the fire with one cup of molasses, half-cup of sugar, butter the size of an egg and one cup of hot water. Let the mixture come to a boil and stir in one tablespoonful of corn starch that has been dissolved in cold water. Take from the fire and add a beaten egg. Bake between two crusts.

LEMON PIE

Two fresh lemons, either grated or chopped very fine, two eggs, one Boston cracker rolled fine, one cup of milk or cream, and one cup of white sugar. Bake this in the form of a custard pie, and when cold finish with the white of one egg, beaten to a froth, and five spoonfuls of frosting sugar added.

LEMON PIE

Take the juice and grated rind of one lemon, stir together with three-fourths of a cup of white sugar and one cup of water; lastly, stir in four well-beaten eggs (reserving the whites of two for frosting). Fill into crust and bake. For frosting, beat the whites of two eggs, reserved, to a stiff froth, with a tablespoonful of powdered sugar; spread over the top evenly and return to the oven till slightly browned.

LEMON PIE

For each peeled and grated lemon add one teacup of sugar, and one tablespoonful of cornstarch dissolved in cold water. Crust - One part white flour, one part graham flour, one part corn meal. Shorten it with butter or condensed milk, reduced one-third. Use two crusts.

LEMON PIE

The juice and grated rind of one lemon, one cup of water, one tablespoonful corn starch, one cup sugar, one egg, and piece of butter size of small egg. Boil the water, wet the corn starch with a little cold water, and stir it in; when it boils up pour it on the sugar and butter; after it cools, add the egg and lemon. Bake with an under and upper crust.

LEMON PIE

Cut one lemon fine; scald in one cup of water; add when boiled, one cup of sugar; the yolks of three eggs and the white of one; stir in a trifle of flour; put in the crust and when baked cover with a froth, consisting of the whites of two eggs and four tablespoonfuls of white sugar. Melvina.

LEMON PIE

Juice and grated rind of one lemon, 1 tablespoon cornstarch, 1 cup sugar, 1 egg, piece of butter the size of an egg. Boil the water, wet the cornstarch with a little water and stir in when it has boiled up. Set off and add butter and sugar. When cool, add beaten egg and lemon. Bake with upper and under crust.

LEMON PIE

Yolks of three eggs, juice and grated rind of 1 lemon, 1 and 1/4 teacup sugar, 1 teacup water, 3 tablespoonfuls flour. When done, add the well beaten whites of the eggs, 6 tablespoonfuls sugar. Cover the pie and brown nicely.

LEMON PIE

One lemon, one cup of sugar, two eggs, a little salt, one cup of cold water, one cracker, rolled; first beat sugar and eggs very light, then add the juice of the lemon and chop the rind and the pulp very fine. This will make two pies with cover. H.E.H.

LEMON PIE

Juice of one lemon, and a little of the peel grated; 1 cup of sugar; 1 of water; 1 cracker; 1 egg; put the yellow part of the egg into the pie, and save the white, and put some more sugar into it. When the pie is done, spread the frosting on to it, and set it into the oven until brown.

LEMON PUDDING SAUCE

One large cup of sugar, nearly half a cup of butter, one egg, one lemon - all the juice and half the grated peel, one teaspoonful nutmeg, three tablespoonfuls boiling water. Serve as lemon sauce.

LEMON SAUCE

Half cup of butter, one cup of sugar, one egg, one grated lemon, three tablespoonfuls of boiling water; put in a tin pail and set in a pan of boiling water to thicken.

LEMON SAUCE

Two cups hot water, one cup sugar, three heaping teaspoonfuls corn starch, grated rind and juice of one lemon, one tablespoonful of butter. Boil the water and sugar five minutes, and add the corn starch wet in a little cold water. Cook eight or ten minutes, add lemon rind and juice and the butter. Stir till the butter is melted, and serve at once.

LEMON STAINS

Lemon stains on cloth may be removed by washing the goods in warm soap suds, or in ammonia.

LEMONS

Lemons will keep good for months by simply putting them into a jug of buttermilk, changing the buttermilk about every three weeks. When the lemons are required for use they should be well dried with a cloth.

LEMONS

Here are a number of uses for lemons:

Lemon juice will bring out the flavor of fresh fruit cakes, especially those with molasses.

Chew a tiny bit of lemon rind and sweeten the breath.

Remove tarter from the teeth and warts from the hands.

Sometimes rubbing a slice of lemon on forehead will cure an ordinary headache.

Juice of one-half lemon in a cup of tea or coffee will often relieve a sick headache.

Chilblains will respond quickly if a slice of lemon is bound on when retiring.

Lemon juice, sugar and white of eggs will relieve a racking cough.

Lemon juice will remove fruit, mildew and ink stains from white fabrics, and iron or rust from marble or any household article.

LIGHT BISCUIT

To one pound of flour allow two ounces of butter, half a teaspoonful of salt, two eggs, and one gill of baker's yeast; mix it to a soft dough with new milk. Let it stand two hours in a warm place to rise, make it into biscuit, glaze the top with white of egg, and bake twenty minutes in a quick oven.

LIGHT DUMPLINGS

Some months since Ruth inquired how to make light dumplings. Please tell her to take to each cup of cold water one teaspoonful of cream of tartar, one-half teaspoonful of soda, and flour sufficient to mix a little harder than common biscuit. Cut out and boil twenty minutes. These never fail to be light. An Old Cook.

LIGHT TEA CAKE

One cup sugar, two eggs, one-half cup melted butter, one and one-fourth cup milk, two teaspoons cream tarter, one teaspoon soda, flour to make a stiff batter. It will bake in twenty minutes if the oven is hot.

LINIMENT

For a good all-round household liniment which will keep and not require bottling, the following is very useful: Bring one quart of clean soft water to the boiling point, add one pound of Ivory soap (shaved very thin); stir until smooth. Dissolve two ounces of camphor-gum, crumbled, in one pint of turpentine. While the soap mixture is hot add the turpentine in which the camphor-gum has been dissolved; stir until cool. This may then be poured into glass jars. For about fifty cents a large quantity of good "solid" liniment may be made. When using, rub well into the affected part.

LIPS - HARD AND DRY

Q. What is good to moisten the lips of a fever patient so that they will not become hard and dry? A. Glycerin and lemon juice, half and half, on a small piece of absorbent cotton, is very good to moisten the lips and tongue of a fever-parched patient.

LIP SALVE

A good lip salve may be made by melting beeswax in sweet oil.

LIQUOR

Take the liquor that you have boiled poultry or meat in; in five minutes you may make it into a very palatable soup.

LIQUOR-HABIT

A friend tells me of a young man who was weaned from the liquor-habit by eating oranges and drinking the juice of that fruit. When he felt the craving for strong drink he took instead an orange - sometimes two or more - with the result that he was able to break away from the chains which had held him in such unhappy bondage.

LIQUOR-HABIT REMEDY

Discouraged, I am sure that this is the remedy for the liquor-habit to which you refer. It is recommended by a man who was cured of a consuming appetite for intoxicants by its use. He, of course, desired to be cured, because I do not think this remedy could be secretly administered: Steep one ounce of quassia in a quart of vinegar, and when the craving for liquor comes on take a teaspoonful of the decoction in a little water. In a comparatively short time the craving will have entirely disappeared, growing less and less continually until this happy consummation. There can be no harm in this, surely, even though it may not in all cases have the longed-for result. I think it is safe to say that if one who really desires to be cured will persist in this simple treatment he will eventually succeed.

LOBSCOUSE

Mince, not too finely, some cold roast beef or mutton. Chop the bones, and put them in a saucepan with six potatoes peeled and sliced, one onion, also sliced, some pepper and salt; of these make a gravy. When the potatoes are completely incorporated with the gravy, take out the bones, and put in the meat; stew the whole together for an hour before it is to be served.

LOBSTER SOUP

To make the soup chop the lobster fine and make like an oyster stew.

LOCKJAW - POSSIBLE WAY TO WARD OFF

It has been found that a number of viruses are taken up by charcoal so rapidly that they lose their toxic properties for the tissues. Berlin scientists are now experimenting to see whether lockjaw cannot be warded off by the simple expedient of applying charcoal to the infected wound.

LOTION FOR FRECKLES

A lotion consisting of equal parts of lactic acid and glycerin will remove freckles.

LOTION - HARMLESS FOR THE FACE

The following lotion, used as a face-wash, is harmless, and is highly recommended by those who have used it: Boil 600 grains of barley down to one-half, with twelve quarts of soft water; strain the decoction through a cloth, and add twenty-five grains of Peruvian balsam. Use morning and night with a flannel cloth.

LOUISIANA CREAM CHEESE

Have a clear white cotton bag in which pour a large bowl of clabber; hang it up and let it drip for two hours; then empty into perforated cheese moulds of different shapes - stars, flowers or fruit; let it remain in them until wanted for tea. Carefully turn it upon a plate, and have a pitcher of rich sweet cream with sugar and nutmeg in it. Serve the cheese in saucers, and cover with cream and sugar.

LOUSE, NITS AND LICE

Put a teaspoonful of sulphur in a nest as soon as hens or turkeys are set. The heat of the fowls causes the fumes of the sulphur to penetrate every part of their bodies; every louse is killed, and as all nits are hatched within ten days, when mother leaves the nest with her brood, she is perfectly free from nits and lice.

LOWELL PUDDING

One coffee cup of milk, one cup raisins, half cup molasses, half teacup brown sugar, one teacup suet, one teaspoonful saleratus, half teaspoonful salt; flour to make a stiff batter. Boil three hours. Serve with sauce.

LYE USE

Keep a can of lye handy and when you have the misfortune to burn something in your granite kettles, just add a bit of the lye to the water in which you soak the kettle and see how quickly the crust will come off, leaving the vessel "nice as new".

LYFORD SPONGE CAKE

One and one-half cups of sugar, two eggs, a piece of butter the size of an egg, one cup of new milk, nutmeg, a small teaspoonful of soda; just before putting into the oven put in a teaspoonful of cream of tartar and two and one-half cups of flour.

LYONNAISE POTATOES

Cut an onion into rings and fry in butter until nicely browned. Cut cold boiled potatoes into thin slices and fry in the butter until brown on both sides. Then put back the onions and stir all together, adding a little chopped parsley, a sprinkling of marjoram, salt and pepper.

MADELINE CAKES FOR DESSERT

One half pound of egg (four), one-half pound of butter, one-half pound of sugar, one-half pound of flour. Mix the butter, sugar and the yolks of the eggs thoroughly; then add the flour and mix again; then the whites of the eggs beaten to a thick froth. Grate in a little lemon rind. Put into little dishes, each about one-third full, and bake till done.

MAHOGANY FURNITURE

Mahogany furniture should be washed with warm water and soap; an application of beeswax and sweet oil upon a soft cloth, and polished with chamois, gives a rich finish.

MAINE PLUM CAKE

A pound of butter, sugar and flour, ten eggs, one pound of raisins, two of currants, half a pound of citron, a teaspoonful of powdered clove, half a teaspoonful of mace, a nutmeg, the juice of a lemon and grated peel, and half a teacup of good molasses. Stir the butter and sugar to a cream, beat the whites and yolks separately and add them to the butter and sugar, then by degrees put in two-thirds of the flour and one teaspoonful of cream of tartar sifted in; the last thing, before adding the fruit powdered with the remaining third of the flour, dissolve a half-teaspoonful of saleratus in a spoonful of boiling water, and stir into the dough. Bake in two loaves an hour and a half. Mrs. Cornelius.

MAKING JELLY WITHOUT BOILING

To one package of Cox's sparkling gelatin put a pint of cold water, the juice and rinds (pared fine) of three lemons; let it stand one hour, then add three pints of boiling water and one pound of crushed sugar. When the sugar is dissolved strain the mixture and set away to cool.

MANICURE AID

For a manicure aid I have discovered that lemon-juice is all that is necessary for loosening the cuticle and for brightening and cleansing the nails. M.A.P.

MARBLE CAKE

One cup of white sugar, one-half cup of butter, one-half cup of sour milk, whites of three eggs beaten to a froth, one teaspoonful of cream of tartar, one-half teaspoonful of soda, one and one-half cups of flour.

Brown Part: One cup of brown sugar, one-half cup of molasses, one-half cup of butter, one-half cup of sour milk, yolks of three eggs, two and one-half cups of flour, one teaspoonful of cinnamon, one-half spoonful of cloves and allspice, one-third of black pepper, one-half of a nutmeg, one-third teaspoonful of soda. Put in the baking-pan first a layer of dark and then a layer of white, and so on, finishing with a layer of dark.

MARBLE CAKE

One-half cup of butter, two cups of white sugar, two eggs, one cup of milk, one-half tea-spoonful of soda, one tea-spoonful of cream of tartar; this makes the light; the following is the dark; one-third of a cup of butter, one cup of brown sugar, two eggs, one-half of a cup of milk, one-half of a tea-spoonful of soda, two cups of flour, one-half a pound of chopped raisins, one dessert-spoonful each of clove and cinnamon, one-half a nutmeg. Drop into your pan a tea-spoonful of one and then the other.

MARBLE CLEANING

To clean old marble or alabaster immerse the objects for two or three days in water to soften the dirt, lime, etc. Then take them out and clean with a brush. When cleaned in this way as well as possible put them in a mixture of one part of concentrated muriatic acid and three parts of water, until they appear perfectly clean. Sometimes it may be necessary to increase the "biting" property with nitric acid. Finally, soak the articles in water till they are perfectly free from acid. The appearance may be improved by rubbing them with almond oil.

Or marble may be cleaned in the following way: Take two parts of common washing soda, one part finely-powdered chalk, one part of pumice-stone; mix all together and sift through muslin; afterwards mix the powder with some water, and rub the marble with this; to add a gloss wash the marble with fullers' earth and hot water.

MARYLAND BISCUITS

Rub one tablespoonful of butter and one lard into a quart of sifted flour; add one level teaspoonful of salt, and milk enough, gradually poured in, to make a stiff dough; when the milk, flour and shortening have been thoroughly mixed, flour the bread board, lay the dough on it, and beat it with a rolling pin until it blisters and cracks loudly. This beating will generally occupy at least half an hour. When the blisters are abundant, tear off pieces of the dough as large as an egg, mould them with the hands in the form of biscuits, prick the tops with a fork and bake them in a moderate oven. These biscuits are so popular that they form a part of the regular market supply in Washington and several other southern cities.

MASHED POTATOES

Where the economy is a great object, and for those who can not digest rich dishes, the following is an admirable mode of mashing potatoes: Boil them thoroughly done, having added a handful of salt to the water, then dry them well, and with two forks placed back to back, beat the whole up till no lumps are left. If done rapidly, potatoes thus cooked are extremely light and digestible.

MAYONNAISE

A tablespoonful of mustard, one of sugar, a speck of cayenne, one teaspoonful of salt, yolks of three uncooked eggs, juice of half a lemon, a quarter of a cup of vinegar, a pint of oil and a cupful of whipped cream. These quantities may be increased or diminished according to judgment and needs of family. Beat the yolks of eggs and dry ingredients until very light and thick with wooden spoon, or, better, a Doyer egg beater. It greatly facilitates matters to set the bowl in which the dressing is made in a pan of ice-water during the beating. Add a few drops of oil at a time until the dressing becomes very thick and rather hard. After this add the oil more rapidly until it gets so thick the beater turns hard, then add a little vinegar. When all the oil and vinegar is used it should be thick and stiff. Now add the lemon juice and whipped cream and set on ice until ready to use. The cream may be omitted without injury.

MAYONNAISE DRESSING

Mix together one teaspoonful of mustard, one teaspoonful of powdered sugar, one-half a teaspoonful of salt and a speck of cayenne. Add the whole yolks of two raw eggs and stir well; add slowly one pint of oil, the juice of one lemon and two tablespoonfuls vinegar; add the oil slowly, stirring all the while, until it is very thick, then add the lemon and oil alternately, stirring vigorously all the time; then add the vinegar, taking care not to make it too thin. Just before serving add one cup of whipped cream. Give sufficient time to make this dressing, as it requires time, patience and an untiring right arm.

MEAD

To each gallon of water put four pounds of honey; boil it one hour; when the scum has done rising, pour the liquor into a tub, and when cool put a toast with yeast spread over it into the tub; allow it to stand until the next day, then pour into a cask and put the bung lightly over it; let stand one year in the barrel.

MEASURE CAKE

One teacupful of butter stirred to a cream, two teacupfuls of sugar, then stir in four eggs that have been beaten to a froth, one pint of flour, any kind of flavoring; beat it until it is ready to go into the oven.

MEASURES

1 finger and thumb is a pinch. 2 fingers and thumb is a dib. 3 fingers and thumb is a dab. 4 fingers and thumb is a smidgen .

MEAT PIE

Mince some cold meat very fine; cut an onion in very fine slices; put the onion in a sauce-pan with a piece of butter, fry it brown, then put in the meat, and some curry powder. Mix this well in the sauce-pan, with some milk, so that it is not dry; let it simmer a few minutes over the fire; then take two eggs, beat them up, put the meat in a pie dish, and then pour the eggs over it. Bake in a slow oven.

MEAT PIES OR PATTIES

Mince the meat fine, with a little fat, and season with pepper, salt, and chopped herbs; have ready some nice puff paste, put the meat into small rolls, or one large one, and bake for half an hour; or patties may be made by baking the same in small patty-pans. A leg of mutton will cut nicely into two or even three joints, and the same can be done with sirloin or ribs of beef; the latter are very nice boned and rolled, either stewed or roasted. Too much twice-cooked meat is very unwholesome for anyone, especially children.

MEAT STEWS

To make a good stew the meat must be tender and not too fat, and the vessel in which it is cooked bright inside. To begin by putting in the meat with cold water and thickening it afterwards will never make a good stew. A stew should be commenced in gravy. Most people use stock for stews; I prefer butter or suet, but never lard. Take a small piece of butter and melt it; when it is quite melted stir in a little flour gradually and combine thoroughly till it has well amalgamated. Now add warm water gently, while stirring all the while over the fire, till a smooth, even consistency is arrived at. Put in the meat to be stewed and allow it to get thoroughly warm till you add the vegetables, condiments and flavoring required. Keep the vessel well shut, and only open the lid when absolutely necessary, shaking the stew now and then in preference to stirring it with a spoon. This is the simplest and original form of stew, from which many deviations may be made.

MEAT STEW

Another form of meat stew is made by putting butter or fat in a saucepan, melting it thoroughly, and placing pieces of meat in to brown the outside; if this is done, a little flour should be sprinkled over the meat, and warm water be gradually added, while stirring all the time to make the gravy at once.

MEAT STEW WHITE OR BROWN

For white stews butter only must be used, and only just melted to retain a light color before adding flour and watered milk; for brown stews, butter or suet or drippings can be used, and be allowed to get a deeper color before being mixed with the water.

The cooking vessel is of great importance for stews; it must be clean and bright within, and the most nutritious stew will be that which is cooked in an inside vessel, and surrounded by steam engendered in an outside vessel.

MEDICAL VALUE OF SPICES

While not food, they are essential elements in diet.

The spices are a very interesting group of substances; they are the foundation of a considerable industry, they have their medical uses and finally are of special importance in dietetics.

Their value resides in their richness in aromatic substances and essential oils; strictly speaking, they are not foods, but often enough they are essential elements in the diet.

Spices have been the subject of classic research, as for example, in the clever and important investigation which Pawlow undertook as to the psychic influences of food and as to the value of zest in nutrition.

Spices were shown to arouse appetite and to promote the secretion of the gastric juice, and the role they play therefore in dietetics is a very important one. The medicinal action of some of them is further of value.

Allspice, for example, is used as an aromatic and has been successfully administered for flatulency or for overcoming griping due to purgatives, and occasionally it is reported that the oil gives relief in rheumatism and neuralgia.

The medicinal uses of cinnamon are well known.

Cardamoms are used in the form of tincture as aromatic and stomachic and they are also employed as a flavoring agent in curry powder, cakes and liquor.

The applications of capsicum and the peppers generally are well known.

Cloves are aromatic, carminative and stimulant and have been

244

used in dyspepsia, gastric irritation and in cases of vomiting.

Oil of cloves is also a popular remedy for toothache. It has also its uses in microscopy, as a preservative and for clearing sections.

The uses of nutmeg are wide, vanilla has an enormous application as a flavoring agent, while turmeric enjoys a similar patronage on account of its bright yellow color and pleasant musky flavor. The Lancet.

MELTON VEAL

Take any cold veal, either roast or boiled; chop it fine and season to the taste with salt, pepper and lemon juice; add two or three tablespoonfuls of cracker crumbs and moisten with soup stock or hot water. Take one-third the amount of finely chopped ham, seasoned with mustard and cayenne, add a tablespoonful or two of the cracker crumbs and moisten as you did the veal. Butter a mould and line it with slices of hard-boiled eggs. Put in the two mixtures irregularly, so that when it is cut it will have a mottled appearance; press in close and steam three-quarters of an hour. Set away to cool, remove from the mould and slice before serving. This is a very nice dish for summer and for a tea also, and is a capital way of using up bits of veal that cannot otherwise be utilized.

MENDING BROKEN GLASS, CHINA, ETC.

A good process for mending broken glass, china or earthenware is to dissolve shellac in alcohol until it is about the consistency of molasses. Take a piece of wood or brush and touch the edges of the broken ware. It will stand every contingency, except a heat equal to boiling water. Another method is to mix some egg and lime. Apply this quickly to the edges and place firmly together. It will soon become set and strong. You must be careful to mix only a small quantity at once, as it hardens very soon, so that it cannot be used.

MENDING CHINA

Take a piece of flint glass , beat it to a fine powder, and grind it extremely fine on a painter's stone with the white of an egg, and it joins china without riveting, so that no art can break it in the same place. This may be done in a mortar if a suitable stone is not to be had.

MENDING CHINA AND EARTHENWARE

To mend china or broken earthenware, take a very thick solution of gum arabic in water, and stir into it plaster of Paris until the mixture becomes of the consistency of cream, apply with a brush to the broken edges of the ware, and join together. In three days the article cannot be broken in the same place. The whiteness of the cement makes it doubly valuable.

MERINGUE

Many cooks do not know that half a teaspoonful of cream of tarter added to the whites of three eggs for meringue on pies is an improvement.

MILDEW

Mildew may be removed by dipping the stained part in buttermilk, and then put the article in the sun.

MILDEW AND FRUIT STAINS

To remove mildew and fruit stains from white goods slice green tomatoes and rub on the stains until the cloth looks green; allow the article to remain rolled up for about an hour, then wash as usual and the stains will disappear.

MILDEW REMOVAL

Take equal parts of lemon juice, salt, starch, and soft soap; rub on thickly, lay on the grass in the hot sun. Renew the application two or three times a day.

II.-Take five cents worth of lime, dissolve in a pail of water, put in the clothes; let them remain three or four hours, then wash and the

246

mildew will all disappear and does not injure the cloth.

MILDEW REMOVAL

Mix soft soap with powdered starch two parts, salt one part, and the juice of a lemon, to a paste. Lay it on both sides of the material and let it lie on the grass until the stain comes out.

MILK COOKIES

Two cups of sugar, one cup of butter, one cup of sour milk, three eggs, one teaspoonful of soda. Mix the butter and sugar together; add the milk and soda and the eggs well beaten; mix soft, roll thin. When the cookies are cut out, sift granulated sugar over them and roll by pressing the rolling-pin gently over the cakes, taking care not to flatten them too much.

MILK-CRUST

I agree with Mrs. M.A.S. that soap and water will not prevent real "milk-crust" on baby's head, although it will assuredly prevent the accumulation of dirt so often seen there. As she did not give an ointment I will tell you one that I have used with success on three little heads. Mix in the proportion of four teaspoonfuls of pure lard, two of sulphur and one of baking-soda. Apply morning and evening to baby's head, using as little water as possible; and do not stop its use too soon, as the head looks clean and well, but continue for four or five days. Then the trouble will not return. This simple ointment will cure any save the worst case in less than two weeks, if used as directed.

MINCE MEAT

Six pounds of currants, three pounds of raisins stoned, three pounds of apples chopped fine, four pounds of suet, two pounds of sugar, two pounds of beef, the peel and juice of two lemons, a pint of sweet wine, a quarter of a pint of brandy, half an ounce of mixed spice. Press the whole into a deep pan when well mixed.

MINCE -MEAT

One pound of raisins chopped fine, one pound of currants, half a pound of suet, three-fourths of a pound of sugar, one pound of apples, chopped, half a pound of mixed peel, quarter pound of sweet almonds, a gill of pale brandy, the juice of one or two lemons, according to taste.

MINCE PIES

Have a piece of puff paste, which roll out to the thickness of a penny-piece; have also a dozen tartlet-pans, which lightly butter; cut out twelve pieces with a round cutter from the paste, each the size of your tartlet-pans, lay them upon the slab, roll the trimmings of the paste to the former thickness; cut twelve other pieces, with which line the tartlet-pans; put a few pieces of mince meat in each; wet them round, place on the lids, pricking a hole with a pin in the center, and close them well at the edges; egg over lightly, and bake about twenty minutes in a moderate oven.

MINCE PIES

Take a pound of beef, free from skin and string, and chop it very fine; then two pounds of suet, which likewise pick and chop; then add three pounds of currants nicely cleansed and perfectly dry, one pound and a half of apples, the peel and juice of a lemon, half a pint of sweet wine, half a nutmeg, and a few cloves and mace, with pimento in fine powder; have citron, orange, and lemon peel ready, and put some in each of the pies when made.

MINCE PIES

Boil until tender three pounds of beef or heart, then chop as fine as possible, add half a pound of beef suet cleansed from its skin and filaments, one pound of brown sugar, two pounds of raisins, one tablespoon each of cinnamon, clove, ginger and mace, one pint of molasses, and salt; stir well together. This mixture should be very moist, but not thin. If you wish to use this mince immediately, add two pounds of finely minced apples and one pound of citron cut in slices. If you wish to keep this mince for future use it is best not to add the apples and citron until you are ready to bake. This mince confined and kept in tight jars will be good for two or three months. It rather improves by keeping. Cover the mince with syrup.

MINCE PIES WITHOUT APPLE OR MEAT

Two crackers rolled; two eggs; one large cup of sugar; one cup of molasses; one cup of boiling water; one-half cup of butter; one-half cup vinegar; one teaspoon of all kinds of spices. This is enough for three common sized pies.

MINUTE SOUP

Excellent for supper, where something warm is desired, or for the little folks when they return from school "almost starved to death." Light bread or crackers crumbled in a bowl or deep dish, add a lump of butter, half a cup of sweet cream, plenty of pepper and salt; if fond of onions, cut a few slices and lay over the top and pour over plenty of boiling water, and you will be surprised to see how good it is. If not fond of onions add a egg well beaten, after the water is poured over, and stir well.

MIRROR REPAIR

For repairing mirrors accidentally scratched, clean the bare portion of the glass by rubbing it gently with fine cotton, taking care to remove any traces of dust and grease. If the cleaning is not done very carefully defect will appear around the place repaired.

With the point of a knife cut upon the back of another looking-glass a portion of the silvering of the required form, but a little larger. Upon it place a small drop of mercury; a drop the size of a pin's head will be sufficient for a surface equal to the size of a nail. The mercury spreads immediately, penetrates the amalgam to where it was cut off with the knife, and the required piece may now be lifted and removed to the place to be repaired. This is the most difficult part of the operation. Then press lightly the renewed portions with cotton, and the glass presents the same appearance as when new.

MISSOURI CORN BREAD

Sift one quart of corn meal; beat three eggs very light, and stir well into it, with one pint of buttermilk, or sour milk, half a teaspoonful of salt, and a small teaspoonful of soda. Set an iron or tin baking pan on the stove, into which put a tablespoonful of lard or butter; when melted, and the pan is hot, toss it around the pan until it has touched all parts, then stir it quickly through the mixture, pour it into the pan while it is hot, and bake an half hour in a quick oven.

MIXED YELLOW PICKLE

Two cabbages, green tomatoes and cucumbers, either pickled or from the brine, in equal quantities, horse radish to taste, several pods of green peppers and two or three ears of corn; these ingredients must be minced fine and mixed together; pour boiling vinegar over the pickles and let it stand fifteen minutes, then strain off the vinegar; let the pickle get cold and then pour the following mixture over it: One box of mustard, one pint of olive oil, one-half pound each of white and black mustard seed, one and one-half pounds of turmeric, two teacups of sugar, one tablespoonful of celery seed, salt and black pepper to taste; mix mustard and oil together; add sugar and turmeric; mix all well and add cold vinegar to cover them; set away for a week.

MOCK APPLE PIE

For a large pie-plate, two crackers (milk or soda), one egg, one cup of sugar, one of water, and the juice of one lemon; add a pinch of salt, and spice with nutmeg and the rind of the lemon. This is quite a tolerable counterfeit.

MOCK MINCE PIE

One cup of bread crumbs, one cup of boiling water, two-thirds of a cup of boiled cider filled up with hot water, one cup of molasses, one cup of sugar, one cup of raisins, one-half cup of butter, of cinnamon, allspice, nutmeg each a teaspoonful, one-half teaspoonful of cloves. This quantity makes three pies.

MOCK OYSTERS

Grate enough young green corn to fill a pint measure, add to it two tablespoonfuls of butter, the yolks of four eggs beaten smooth, and enough flour to make a stiff batter; season the batter with salt and pepper, and drop it by the teaspoonful into smoking hot fat; as soon as the mock oysters thus formed are light brown, take them out of the fat with a skimmer, and lay them on brown paper for a moment to free them from grease; serve them on a napkin.

MOCK TURTLE SOUP

The only thing that is not plain here is the mock turtle soup. This is made from a calf's head. Boil the head, well covered with water, and cut the meat in two inch squares. Put three ounces of butter, rubbed with three tablespoonfuls of flour, in a pot to brown, and when well colored stir in gradually the liquor in which the head was boiled, and the square pieces, with some mace, cloves, sweet marjoram or other sweet herbs, pepper and salt; let it simmer an hour or two; add one and one-half gills of wine, and just before serving add some lemon juice.

MOLASSES AND LEMON PUDDING

Two cups of flour, one heaping teaspoonful baking powder, one-half cup lard or butter and a little salt, peel of two lemons, and molasses to suit the taste, are the ingredients required. Sift the baking powder and salt with the flour, then rub in the lard or butter and mix with water. Roll out one-fourth thick. Boil the lemons until the peel is tender, and cut it in small pieces. Grease a mould and line it with the paste, then put a layer of molasses with some lemon peel laid on, then a layer of paste and another of molasses and peel and so on until all is used, having paste for the top. Steam three hours.

If preferred, instead of boiling the lemons, the peel can be grated over each layer of molasses.

MOLASSES CAKE

Take two cups of molasses and one-half cup of shortening, and add as much flour as you can stir in; then add two cups of boiling water, in which you have dissolved one large teaspoonful of saleratus.

MOLASSES CAKE

Two cups of buttermilk, one cup of molasses, one teaspoonful of soda, a little salt, flour enough to make a batter not so thick but what it will run. I sometimes vary this with ginger or caraway seed.

MOLASSES CANDY

One large cup molasses, one-half cup of sugar, little vinegar, little butter. When done stir in a little soda.

MOLASSES CANDY

Two cups of molasses (I use the best New Orleans), one cup of sugar, a heaping teaspoonful of butter, and a scant teaspoonful of soda. Rub the kettle with the butter, pour in the molasses and sugar, and boil till it is brittle when a little is dropped into cold water; remove from the fire, sift the soda into it and stir till well mixed, pour into buttered tins, and cool just enough to enable you to handle it, and pull until very light and white. This is very nice and brittle.

MOLASSES COOKIES

One cup molasses, three tablespoonfuls each of water and shortening, spice to taste, ginger or cinnamon, one-half teaspoonful each of salt and soda, flour to roll, and bake in a quick oven.

MOLASSES COOKIES

Two cups of molasses, two teaspoonfuls of saleratus dissolved in it, three-fourths of a cup of shortening (lard, butter or beef fat), one teaspoonful of ginger, one of salt (less salt if butter is used), one-half cup of water. Cut the lard into a cup of flour, add the spice and salt and mix with the molasses. Then put in the water and add flour enough to roll out. Cut with a biscuit cutter and bake in a quick oven.

MOLASSES COOKIES (VERY NICE)

One cup of molasses, two-thirds cup of lard or butter, one-fourth cup of sweet milk, dissolve one teaspoonful of soda in the milk, a little salt, one teaspoonful of ginger, flour enough to roll.

MOLASSES GINGERBREAD

Two cups of molasses; one cup of boiling water; a piece of butter the size of a hen's egg; two teaspoonfuls of saleratus; one teaspoonful of ginger; make it stiff enough to roll in thin sheets.

MOLES

If you happen to have a big, black, ugly mole on your face, rub on castor oil, the oftener the better, and it will go off entirely.

MOROCCO LEATHER

The beauty of morocco leather may be quite restored by varnishing with the white of an egg.

MOSQUITOES

Try a camphor-box, hung up in a room, to drive away mosquitoes.

MOTH PROTECTION

Failing a cedar box, the best way to keep moths from woolen goods is to carefully wrap each article in whole newspapers, so that no moth or bug can in any possible way get to them. If this is done so early in the spring that none are already in possession, there will be no trouble from moths. To destroy moths in carpets, lay a wet sheet over the carpet, and then rub a hot flat iron over it. The water is converted into steam, which destroys the grub.

MOTHER'S COOKIES

Two cups of cream, one heaping teaspoonful of soda, and one even teaspoonful of salt, two cups of sugar (we use white), one egg, and flour enough to roll; when nearly the thickness desired sprinkle on sugar and roll once over.

MOTHER'S COOKIES

One and one-half cups of white sugar; the whites of two eggs; one cup of thick sour cream; one-half teaspoonful saleratus; nutmeg or spice to your taste.

MOULD PREVENTION

Put a few drops of glycerin into fruit jars the last thing before sealing them to prevent mould.

MOUNT PLEASANT CAKE

Two and a half cups sugar, five cups flour, one cup butter, one cup sour milk, one teaspoon yeast powder, four eggs. Mace, citron and currants to taste.

MRS. LINCOLN'S TEA-CAKES

The recipe for tea cakes referred to in the description of the tea-party at the "Anchorage" is as follows: Two and one-half cups St. Louis flour, one-half teaspoonful soda, one teaspoonful of cream tarter, one-half cup sugar, one-half teaspoonful salt, one egg, one cup milk, one tablespoonful butter melted. Mix in order given and bake in gem pans or cups. Add one cup of berries and this recipe makes a delicious berry cake.

MRS. ROBBIN'S PUDDING

One cupful of suet chopped fine, one cupful of syrup, one cupful of milk, one cupful of currants, one teaspoonful of each kind of spice.

Put into a tin pail covered tightly and then into a pot of boiling water and boil two hours. Sauce: One cupful of sugar, a half of butter, the juice of one lemon, half a nutmeg stirred with flour and water until boiled. Serve hot.

MUCILAGE

One part of salicylic acid dissolved in twenty parts alcohol and mixed with three parts each of soft soap and glycerin makes an excellent mucilage.

MUD REMOVAL

Traces of mud may be removed from black dresses by rubbing the stains with raw potato.

MUD STAINS

Potato water will remove mud stains from nearly every kind of cloth garment.

MUFFINS

Two quarts of sifted flour, one-half teacupful of sugar, one-half teacupful of butter, one-half cup of yeast, two eggs, a little salt, and one quart of sweet milk; let this rise all night after mixing thoroughly. Bake in muffin rings in a quick oven.

MUFFINS

For tea, make a sponge about eleven o'clock, by dissolving a yeast cake in a little warm water and flour. At two, add one pint of milk; two eggs; a quart of flour and a tablespoonful of butter. Warm the milk enough to melt the butter; mix thoroughly and keep in a warm place to rise. Bake in rings.

MUMPS

Subscriber, the following is an excellent remedy for mumps, and will prevent the disease settling in other parts of the body: Cook one quart of white navy-beans until soft and dry, mash them, and apply as a poultice to the affected parts. The swelling will soon diminish. Mrs. Pearle M. Brown.

MUSHROOM SAUCE

Put the trimmings of the beef on to boil in a quart of cold water to use for the gravy, put one tablespoonful of butter in an omelet pan, when very brown add one tablespoonful of flour, pour the water from the trimmings into the baking pan, first taking off all the grease, then add the water, a little at a time, to the butter and flour, stirring till smooth, season to taste with salt, pepper and a little lemon juice or horseradish, add half a can of chopped mushrooms.

MUSLIN WASHING

Muslin dresses should be washed in a good cold soapsuds, and rinsed in clear cold water. If the muslin is green, add a wineglass of vinegar to the water in which it is rinsed; if lilac, use ammonia in the same quantity. For black, or black-and-white muslins, use a small quantity of sugar of lead.

MUSTARD PICKLES

Equal quantities of small cucumbers, the largest ones sliced, green tomatoes sliced, cauliflower picked into flowerets, and small button onions. Keep them covered with strongly salted water for 24 hours. In the morning scald the brine and dissolve in it a bit of alum the size of a nutmeg. Pour the boiling brine over the pickles. When cold drain thoroughly and prepare as much vinegar as there were quarts of brine. To one quart of vinegar use one cup of brown sugar, half a cup of flour, and one-fourth of a pound of ground mustard. Boil the sugar and vinegar. Mix the flour and mustard, and stir the boiling vinegar into it, and when smooth pour it over the pickles.

MUTTON CHOPS

Should be taken from the loin, from one-half to three-quarters of an inch thick. They should not be put on the gridiron until everything else is ready to be served; have a clear cinder fire to broil them; if the fat falling from them should cause a blaze remove the gridiron for a moment and strew a handful of salt over the fire. They should be kept continually turned; the greater part of the chine bone should be chopped off; cut off a good deal of the fat, but do not pepper or flour the chops, and serve them immediately.

MUTTON POT-PIE

Cut from the forequarter of a sheep as much as you desire to cook. Cut this up into small pieces, put into a pot, cover with water and boil until tender. When done remove from the fire and set away in a cool place till next day; then remove the cake of fat that will have arisen to the top, after which set the pot on the fire, adding salt and pepper to taste, and, if necessary, enough hot water to cover the mutton. When boiling add small pieces of biscuit dough, and do not allow to subside till done. Put into a deep dish, first the meat, then the crust, and then the gravy over all.

MUTTON STEWS

Mutton stews must be made carefully and with little fat, and for mutton it is best to brown the meat slightly first.

MYSTERY CAKE (LOAF)

1 cup sugar, 2 cups flour, 1 cup chopped nuts, 1 cup raisins, 1 can tomato soup, 1 tablespoon shortening, 1 teaspoon cinnamon, 1 teaspoon nutmeg, 1/4 teaspoon salt, 1 teaspoon soda and 1 tablespoon lemon peel. Bake in slow oven 40 minutes.

Icing: 2 cups powdered sugar with cream cheese. Thin with milk or cream.

NANTUCKET CHOWDER

First get your fish. See to it that it is a codfish, fresh caught and weighing about five pounds. If possible, see it kick before you purchase it. At any rate, don't buy it unless its eyes are bright and its gills a bright red. Have it cleaned as for boiling, leaving the head on. Take it home. Cut it into five pieces, the head forming one; wash it clean and leave the pieces in cold water slightly salted. Take three-quarters of a pound of clean fat salt pork. See to it that the pork has been corn-fed and is pure and sweet. Cut this up into fine dice, the finer the better, and put it into a pot over a slow fire. While it is slowly trying out, cut a moderate-sized onion very fine, the finer, the better. When the pork has become a rich brown, which it will be after about twenty minutes' trying, turn in the onion, stirring it frequently; and after the onion is thoroughly cooked, which will take fifteen or twenty minutes, lay the chunks of fish on it and cover them nicely with boiling water; wet up two tablespoonfuls of flour in a half-pint of milk, working the flour very smooth, and add thereto salt and pepper to taste; when the fish has boiled fifteen minutes add the thickened milk, stirring carefully to avoid breaking the fish; Boil five minutes and serve with pickles, olives or celery, or all three. This is the only legitimate chowder. The dish usually served under that name - a mixture of potatoes, crackers, etc. - is properly a stew or fish fricassee - a palatable dish but not chowder.

NATURAL CURLING FLUID

Take equal parts of gum arabic, borax and camphor; dissolve in a quart of boiling water, a quarter of a pound of the whole; strain and bottle the preparation for use. At night apply with a small brush, and wrap the hair in papers. This is excellent and harmless for making those frizzets so popular for the fronts and bonnets.

NAVY BEANS

If you have any trouble with your navy beans ripening evenly or all at one time, try planting them "on the dark of the moon" in May, and do not cultivate after the fifteenth of July.

NECTAR

Take two pounds of raisins, chopped, and four pounds of loaf sugar, and put them into a spigot-pot; pour two gallons of boiling water upon them. The next day, when it is cold, slice two lemons into it. Let it stand five days, stirring it twice a day. Then let it stand five more days to clear; bottle it, put it into a cold cellar for ten days, and it will be fit to drink.

NERVOUS HEADACHE

Cure a nervous headache by applying hot water to the temples and back of neck.

NERVOUSNESS

A sudden attack of nervousness can often be completely controlled by simply plunging the hands into very warm water, allowing the water to reach the elbows, and holding them immersed for several minutes.

NEURALGIA

A tested remedy for neuralgia requested by a sister recently is as follows: To a teaspoonful of sweet spirits of nitre add six drops of laudanum and take the mixture; if not better in two hours, repeat the dose.

NEURALGIA

There is another simple remedy which I want to call attention to, so many suffer these days with neuralgia. I had this distressing disease, for years, and could find nothing that gave more than temporary relief until I read in a sister-paper a letter from a lady who had found help by taking a tea made of burdock-seeds! I couldn't believe it at first, but I knew the paper was dependable, so I sent for two or three cartons of the seeds - it was in winter and out of season to gather them - steeped them and drank the tea freely. That was two years ago, and I have not been troubled with neuralgia since. If I feel a twinge I steep my burdock-seeds, of which I gathered plenty the next fall.

NEURALGIA CURE

When troubled with neuralgia, apply the essence of peppermint over the pain; for intercostal neuralgia rub in oil of peppermint. This is very strong and will smart but it is a sure cure, and is better than mustard. For pleurisy apply flannel cloths wrung out of hot mustard water and change often.

NEURALGIA - NITRO-GLYCERINE

Dr. James E. Bramwell reports, in the British Medical Journal, a case of violent and persistent neuralgia, occurring in a patient 80 years of age, quickly cured, after many other remedies had failed, by drop doses, three times daily, of 0.1 percent (1 per 1000) solution of nitroglycerine.

NEVER-FAILING CAKE

Two cups of sugar, one of butter, five eggs, one cup of milk, three cups of flour, two heaping teaspoonfuls of baking-powder, and flavoring to taste. Bake in layers.

NEW SHOES HURT?

If your new shoes hurt your feet, fill them with water, let it remain a few minutes and then pour it out. The water takes the heat out of the leather, and they will not burn or press on tender places after that.

NEW SILVER POLISH

Put two-thirds of a pint of alcohol in a wide mouthed bottle, with one-third of a pint of ammonia and a tablespoonful of whitening; shake thoroughly. Wet a small sponge with this mixture, and go over your silver or brass with it as quickly as possible, rubbing it off with a soft flannel before it has a chance to dry.

NEW WOOD TASTE-REMOVAL

To remove the taste of new wood, first scald the vessel with boiling water; then dissolve pearlash, or soda in tepid water, adding a little lime, and wash the vessel thoroughly with the solution. Scald it well again with hot water and rinse with cold.

NEWSPAPER USE

Old newspapers crushed well between the hands are good to polish the stove with.

NICE BREAKFAST DISH

Remove the skins from a dozen tomatoes; cut them up in a saucepan; add a little butter, pepper and salt; when sufficiently boiled beat up five or six eggs, and just before you serve turn them into the saucepan with the tomatoes and stir one way for two minutes, allowing them time to be done thoroughly.

NICE LIGHT BISCUIT

One cup of cream; two of good sour milk or buttermilk (the milk must not be too sour or the biscuits will be bitter); one and one-half teaspoonfuls soda; mix quick; roll thin, say one inch or a little more; cut small; bake quick - much depends on skill in baking.

NICE NUT CAKES

One half cup cream; one cup sour milk; one of sugar; three eggs; cinnamon; nutmeg; salt; saleratus; flour to roll. Let them stand by the fire one-half hour before frying.

NO EGG COOKIES

One cup of butter, one of milk, two of sugar, half a teaspoonful of soda, half a teaspoonful of cinnamon or nutmeg, with flour enough to roll.

NOSE BLEED

The juice of a boiled onion with a few drops of vinegar will stop bleeding of the nose, and forms an efficacious soothing remedy for insect bites.

NOSE BLEED

For nose bleed - snuff alum, finely pulverized. This has stopped it when a doctor failed.

NOSE BLEEDING

A distinguished physician states that the best remedy for bleeding at the nose is the vigorous motion of the jaws in the act of chewing. In the case of a child he recommends placing a wad of paper in its mouth and instructing the child to chew hard. He considers it a sure cure.

NOVELTY CAKE

One egg, one cup of sugar, one-third of a cup of butter, one large half cup of milk, and one teaspoonful of baking powder in two cups of flour. This makes enough for three layers. Flavor with lemon. Scrape fine two squares of Baker's chocolate, mix with two tablespoonfuls of sugar, two tablespoonfuls of milk, set over the teakettle until the consistency of molasses, flavor or not, as you like. Take the juice of one lemon, mix stiff with powdered sugar and beaten whites of two eggs; this can be colored with strawberry juice if desired. When the cake is cold put in first a layer of chocolate and then a layer of lemon, frosting the top with the chocolate. Do not prepare the chocolate until you are ready to use it.

NUT CAKE

Two cups of sugar, one cup of butter, four eggs, one cup of cold water, three cups of flour, two teaspoonfuls of baking powder, two cups of hickory nut meats.

OAK POLISH

For oak polish, shred finely two ounces of beeswax and half an ounce of white wax; put it in a jar and cover with a pint of spirits of turpentine; let it stand twenty-four hours to dissolve; then shred half an ounce of Castile soap, and pour on it half a gill of boiling water;

when quite dissolved, add the dissolved wax and turpentine, and shake all well together into a creamy liquid. Cork the bottle securely, and it will keep good for a year's use. When used, pour the mixture on a piece of flannel, rub it well into the oak wood, and then polish it with a soft cloth.

OATMEAL

Oatmeal has become a very popular dish for breakfast, and if properly prepared will be very palatable.

We buy the meal that comes put up in packages, and like it far better than any that comes in bulk.

We do not follow the directions in cooking it; there is the failure in preparing oatmeal. You read, "boil fifteen minutes"; it should boil fully an hour; so that when it is served, instead of being hard and yellow, it is soft and white; the appearance of the dish being sufficient to tempt one's appetite.

We prefer to any patent boiler, a tightly-covered tin pail, set in a kettle of boiling water, with a tin or earthen plate upon which the pail may rest without coming in contact with the bottom of the kettle.

Put a scant cup of oatmeal into the pail, with a large teaspoonful of salt; pour upon it two and a half cups of boiling water; stir well. Let it boil an hour, stirring occasionally. Just before taking from the fire add scant half-cup of milk. When done it should be just thick enough to retain the impression of the spoon. To be eaten with sugar and cream, or butter and sugar with a little milk poured over it.

OATMEAL BREAKFAST CAKES

This is made of No. 2 oatmeal, with water enough to saturate it, and a little or no salt. Pour it into a baking tin half an inch or three-quarters deep, shake it down level, and when this is done it should be so wet that two or three spoonfuls of water should run freely on the surface. Put in a quick oven and bake twenty minutes. Eat warm. It will be light and tender.

OATMEAL CRACKERS

One teacupful of oatmeal and water enough to make a dough; mix well and quick; if it will bear to be rolled out with a rolling-pin, roll it; keep at it in the same way until it is one-quarter of an inch thick; do it quickly, or it will dry; make only dough enough for one cracker; do not brown in baking.

OATMEAL DRINK

In harvest times thin oatmeal gruel is the most nourishing and cheapest drink for the field laborer. It quenches the thirst speedily and gives more strength and endurance than beer. It has been conclusively proved by experiments that non-alcoholic drinkers utterly beat alcoholic imbibers in hard work, especially when exposed to the heat of the sun. Beer drinkers go ahead at first, but their energies soon flag, and they are much more exhausted at the end of the day. Oatmeal drink is easily and simply made by putting the meal into cold water by degrees, as it is strained through the fingers, stirring it all the while with a short stick to prevent knots until the mixture becomes homogeneous, in the proportion of a tablespoonful to a quart of water, adding a little sugar to suit the taste. Then boil thoroughly and let it stand till cold. Whey, skimmed milk, and cold tea are much better than beer, but none of these beverages equal the oatmeal drink. When oatmeal cannot be got other meal will do, but not so well.

OATMEAL GRIDDLE-CAKES

Two cups of oatmeal mush, two eggs, one tablespoonful of molasses, one teaspoonful of soda, a little salt, and flour enough to make a thin batter.

OATMEAL GRUEL

In one quart of boiling water, sprinkle two tablespoonfuls of oatmeal; let this boil forty minutes; season with salt, strain, and serve. If sugar, milk or cream is wished, it may be added.

ODOR REMOVAL

A bit of salt sprinkled on anything that is burning on the stove will take away the unpleasant odor.

ODORS OF THE FEET

Busy Mother, salicylic acid is poisonous; do not use it on the feet, as the system will take it up. Instead of trying to stop the odor by external applications, give the stomach, liver and kidneys attention, so that impurities may be thrown off in the regular way; but do not try to prevent them passing off through the pores of the feet, as that would be injurious. I knew of a case of epilepsy resulting from the use of alum in the shoes to stop the odor of the feet. The pores offer an outlet for impurities which can be thrown off in no other way. The feet should be kept very clean, and salt, soda or borax may be used in the water for bathing. A Friend.

OIL-CLOTH

Oil-cloth is ruined by the application of lye soap, as the lye eats the cloth, and, after being washed, it should be wiped perfectly dry, or the dampness will soon rot it. If laid down where the sun will shine on it much it will be apt to stick fast to the floor, unless paper is laid under it.

OLD ENGLISH CHRISTMAS POUND PUDDING

To make what is termed a pound pudding, take of raisins well stoned, currants thoroughly washed, one pound each; chop a pound of suet very finely and mix them; add a quarter of a pound of flour, or bread very finely crumbled, three ounces of sugar, one ounce and a half of grated lemon peel, a blade of mace, half a small nutmeg, one teaspoonful of ginger, half a dozen eggs well beaten; work it well together, put it into a cloth, tie it firmly, allowing room to swell, and boil not less than seven hours. It should not be suffered to stop boiling.

OLD-FASHIONED INDIAN PUDDING

Milk, one quart; Indian meal, three handfuls; one egg, molasses, butter, cinnamon, salt; stir in the sifted meal while the milk is hot, let it cool, and add the beaten egg, molasses to sweeten, butter half the size of an egg, cinnamon and salt to taste; bake three-quarters of an hour.

OLD SORES

Hopeful, try the following simple remedy for old sores: Place a quart of new milk in a clean saucepan on the stove, where it will keep warm, and put in alum enough to make it curdle; bind the curd on the sore. Continue this treatment every night until well.

OMELET SANDWICHES

Take four eggs, two tablespoonfuls of bread crumbs, and one-half ounce of chopped parsley. After beating the eggs well, add the bread crumbs, then the parsley, and two tablespoonfuls of water. Season, and fry it in small fritters, and when cold put them between brown bread and butter.

OMELET SOUFFLE

Break six eggs; separate the whites from the yolks, to the latter put four dessert spoonfuls of powdered sugar and the rind of a lemon chopped exceedingly small; mix them well. Whip the whites to a stiff froth and add the rest. Put a lump of butter into the frying pan over a slow fire, cook carefully and serve.

ONE EGG CAKE

One cup of sugar, one egg broken into a cup, fill the cup with sweet cream, pour over the sugar and beat thoroughly with egg beater, two and one-half cups flour, two teaspoonfuls of baking powder, a pinch of salt, and one teaspoonful of flavoring. Bake in a loaf.

ONE EGG COOKIES

One cup of butter, two cups of sugar, one egg, three tablespoonfuls of cream, one teaspoonful of saleratus, nutmeg or seed.

ONIONS

The unpleasant breath which eating this vegetable produces is perhaps the greatest objection to its use, but still it is a very wholesome and desirable article of food for many, and hence should be brought on the table in the most attractive form. White onions, and those grown in the South, are least odorous and pungent. Take off the outside skin, cut off both ends, and let them stand in cold water an hour, then drop them into a saucepan with two quarts of boiling water. Cover, and boil fifteen minutes. Have a kettle of boiling water on the fire ready for use, pour off the water from the onions, and add as much more - be sure the water is boiling - and boil half an hour longer. Scald a cupful of rich milk, pour off the second water from the onions, add the milk and a little graham flour to thicken it. Salt and otherwise season to taste. Boil up a few minutes and serve the onions whole; or they may be cut in halves before cooking.

ONIONS - MEDICINAL

There is great medicinal virtue in onions; eaten raw at the very beginning of an attack of cold, or of malaria. They have a decided tendency to check it, and act advantageously in kidney and stomach troubles.

ONION SOUP

Take half a pound of nice, fresh butter, put it into a large saucepan and let it melt slowly, but not brown at all. Cut up very finely ten good-sized onions, put them into the melted butter, dredge in a little flour, and let the onions stew slowly for fifteen or twenty minutes, stirring them occasionally. Then pour in a quart of boiling water, dredge in a little more flour, and mix all well together. Add a teacupful of sweet milk, and boil for fifteen minutes, stirring often. Beat up the yolks of two eggs, and after the soup is taken from the fire stir them in rapidly for a few minutes. Serve with bits of toasted bread in a tureen. Season with salt and pepper, but not till just before taking up, as the butter will nearly salt it enough.

OPENING OBSTINATE FRUIT-CANS

To open fruit-cans that are obstinate, do not try to force the covers with a knife, to the detriment of both, but lay a folded cloth wet with boiling water over the top for a few minutes, or hold it under the hot-water faucet, if you have one.

ORANGEADE

Roll and press the juice from the oranges in the same way as from lemons. It requires less sugar than lemonade. The water must be pure and cold, and there can be nothing more delicious than these two kinds of drink.

ORANGE PUDDING

Peel and slice up three oranges in a flat dish, sweeten them and let them stand. Make a corn starch pudding with the yolks of three eggs, a pint of milk and a tablespoonful of corn starch. When cold, pour over the oranges. Beat the whites of the eggs to a froth, sweeten and spread over the top.

ORANGE SHORTCAKE

Remove the peel from the oranges and cut the pulp into small bits, throwing out all seeds and tough portions; sprinkle over it sugar till it is sweet enough. Make the cake in the usual way (the short biscuit crust is as good as any), cut the crust in two when done, spread the prepared orange over it after the manner of strawberry shortcake, and serve.

ORANGE WATER

Mix with a quart of spring water the juice of six sweet oranges and that of two lemons; sweeten with capillaire or syrup. This water iced is a delicious evening drink.

ORANGES FOR SOAP

Housewives in orange-growing districts are substituting oranges for soap. The acid in them cleanses woodwork and floors beautifully.

ORMOLU

Ormolu may be cleansed with ammonia or spirits of wine.

OVERCOOKED VEGETABLES

If vegetables are cooked in a very short time, two or three minutes too long over the fire, they lose their beauty and flavor.

OYSTER OMELET

Four eggs, one small cupful of milk; butter the size of a walnut. Beat the yolks of the eggs until they are smooth like paste; pour in the milk by degrees; season to taste; beat the whites of the eggs very stiff and whip them in. Heat in a large skillet and let the butter melt in it; pour in the mixture; move the egg away from the sides of the skillet, with a knife, until the egg is "set". Then put in the oven ten minutes. Take one large cupful of oysters; put in a pan with a lump of butter, season to taste. Put the omelet on a hot plate and spread the oysters on it; serve immediately.

OYSTER STUFFING FOR ROAST TURKEY

Grate as much good stale bread as will fill the turkey, and season it well with butter rubbed into the bread; salt, pepper and a little summer savory. Moisten it slightly with oyster liquor and add as many oysters as you choose. Stuff the turkey and roast it in the usual way. Serve the thickened and strained gravy of oyster sauce with it. A turkey weighing seven or eight pounds should cook at least three hours, and a very large turkey should cook at least four.

OYSTER SOUP

Take one hundred oysters out of the liquor. To half of the liquor add an equal quantity of water. Boil it with one teaspoonful of crushed allspice, a little mace, some cayenne, pepper and salt. Let it boil twenty minutes, then strain it, put it back in the stew-pan, and add the oysters. As soon as it begins to boil, add a teacupful of cream, and a little grated cracker, rubbed in an ounce of butter. As soon as the oysters are plump, serve them.

OYSTER SOUP

Take one quart of water, one teacup of butter, one pint of milk, two teaspoonfuls of salt, four crackers, rolled fine, and a teaspoonful of pepper. Bring to full boiling heat as soon as possible, then add one quart of oysters. Let the whole come to a boiling heat quickly and remove from the fire.

PACKED BEEF

Three pounds of beef chopped fine, 1 tablespoonful salt, 1 tablespoonful of pepper, 8 tablespoonfuls rolled cracker, 2 eggs, butter the size of an egg, 1 large spoon of thyme and milk to moisten. Put in a pan and cover with water. Bake two hours.

PACKING EGGS FOR WINTER

This method is well tried: Take one pint air slacked lime, one-half pint salt and two gallons water. Have eggs well covered with the mixture.

I have put up eggs in this way in September and October and used the last of them the following May and June.

PAIN

From a boy's essay: Pain tells us that all is not right where the pain is. There are many kinds of pain, enough for everyone to have some.

PAINFUL PERIODS

Someone asked a help for painful periods; try taking a hot ginger sling the first night; and, if not relieved, take another in the morning. This remedy is simple, harmless, and has proven most effective in many cases.

PAINT STAINS

When paint stains have been gotten upon linen, apply potash which has been thinned to the consistency of paint. Roll it up for a while and then wash. If paint is wet it may be rubbed with benzene, or if hard softened with Vaseline and rubbed with benzene. Chloroform is the best agent for dried paint on clothes. Turpentine will remove it with perseverance. Use chloroform to eradicate the turpentine.

PAN PREPARATION

Before using any new gem pans or truffle tins, or any baking or frying utensil, rub them thoroughly with clean, fresh beef suet or fat, sprinkle with salt, and put into a hot oven until it burns; take out to cool off, then wash in water which a little ammonia has been poured.

PARCHED CORN PUDDING

One quart of hot milk; three cups of parched corn, pounded fine; one cup sugar; salt and season to the taste: bake two hours.

PARK STREET CAKE

One half cup of butter, one cup of milk, two cups of sugar, three cups of pastry, four eggs, one-half teaspoonful of soda, one teaspoonful cream tarter, flavor with lemon; bake in two pans. Grease the pans and then measure all the ingredients, sifting the soda and cream tartar with the flour, and separating the yolks and whites of the eggs. Pour hot water into the mixing bowl, and when the bowl is warm pour the water out, wipe and put in the butter. Rub the butter with a wooden spoon until it is like cream; add one cup of sugar gradually;

beat the other cup of sugar with the yolks of the eggs until very light, and add this to the butter. Then beat the whites stiff and dry, and let them stand while the milk and flour is added alternately, a little at a time. Add the whites of the eggs last, then flavor and bake in a moderate oven until the cake shrinks from the pan. This cake is easily made, and is particularly nice with fruit or ice-cream. It is a good family cake.

PARKER HOUSE ROLLS

The following is Miss Parloa's recipe for Parker House Rolls. These are things which must be made by rule; attempts at originality spoil them. Two quarts of flour; rub in a tablespoonful of lard and a little salt; place in a deep bread pan and make a hole in the flour, into which pour one pint of cold boiled milk and half a cup of yeast. Let the pan be covered and stand all night. In the morning stir and knead well and set in a warm place to rise; let it rise to a light sponge (ninety minutes will accomplish this) and then roll out on a board till half an inch thick. Cut oval, and fold two-thirds of it. Lay the rolls on tin sheets, let them rise an hour, and bake fifteen minutes in a quick oven.

PARKER HOUSE ROLLS

Add one tablespoonful of lard and two tablespoonfuls of sugar to a pint of milk; let the whole come to a boil, then cool it and mix with a teaspoonful of salt and five tablespoonfuls of fresh yeast; put two quarts of sifted flour into a deep bowl or bread pan; mix the above named ingredients with it, knead for fifteen minutes, and set in a warm place to rise for three hours; then form it into rolls, let them rise for half an hour, and bake them in a quick oven.

PARKER HOUSE ROLLS

One pint of new milk, scald, add one tablespoonful of sugar, cool, two quarts of flour with a little butter or lard rubbed into it, pour the milk with one-half cup of yeast into the center of the flour, let it soak in - not mixed - and in the morning mould thoroughly, raise, roll out, cut with a biscuit cutter, spread with butter, fold together, raise and bake. This makes superb biscuits.

PARSNIPS

Wash well; scrape them, and cut in two or four pieces lengthwise; boil in water with a little salt in it until tender, which will be from one-half to three-quarters of an hour; when quite done, dish up in a warm dish, with melted butter poured over them, or warm butter with a little parsley in it; or mash the parsnips and form into small cakes, roll in flour, or dip in egg and breadcrumbs, and fry a light brown; send to the table very hot. You can also brown the parsnips sliced rather thick.

PASTRY FOR PIES AND TARTS

Take three cups of sifted flour, one tablespoonful of white sugar, one tablespoonful salt, one cup of lard, and half a cup of cold water; stir with a spoon and roll out for your pies. This is for three pies, and you can enlarge it as you wish. Do not put your hands to it, now roll it out thin, if you wish it short and crispy, and not flaky and tough.

PEACH FRITTERS

Make a batter of two well-beaten eggs, half a pint of milk and a little salt; pour half this mixture on a pint of flour; beat very smooth and light and then pour in the remainder of the milk and eggs, to which is added a tablespoonful of butter or olive oil. Peel and cut the peaches in halves; dip them in the batter and fry them in boiling fat until they are a delicate brown. Serve on a hot dish and sprinkle with powdered sugar.

PEACH SHORT-CAKE

Peach short-cake is made of one pint of flour, one teaspoonful of baking powder, one saltspoonful of salt, and two tablespoonfuls of sugar passed through a sieve, and then mixed with four tablespoonfuls of butter. When thoroughly mixed, moisten with one teacupful of milk. Bake in two deep pie plates in a quick oven. Have the peaches peeled and cut in slices. As soon as the cakes are done cut them in halves, butter them, and arrange the slices of peaches between the pieces, sprinkling with sugar. Serve warm with cream.

PEANUT CANDY

To make peanut candy, take one scant pint of molasses, four quarts of peanuts, measured before they are shelled, two tablespoonfuls of vanilla, one of soda. Boil the molasses until it hardens in cold water when dropped from the spoon. Stir in the vanilla, then the soda, dry. Lastly the shelled peanuts. Turn out into shallow pans well buttered, and press it down smooth with a wooden spoon. Make into squares or oblong sticks with a knife when partly cool, so that it will break smoothly.

PEAR PICKLES

One peck of pears, three pounds of sugar, one pint of good cider vinegar; steam the pears over water until tender; then boil in the syrup, with spices, same as for peaches. I always peel the pears for pickling, but do not peaches.

PEARS IN JELLY

Peel half a dozen large pears, cut them in halves and core them, throwing them into cold water as fast as they are done, to prevent discoloration; stew them tender in water enough to cover them, with sugar in sufficient quantity to correct their acidity; as soon as they are tender drain them on a sieve, and when they are dry brush them with the yolk of egg well beaten, and dust them with powdered sugar, and arrange them prettily on a glass dish to cool completely; meantime dissolve an ounce of isinglass or gelatin in just cold water enough to cover it, put it into a pint and a half of the syrup in which the pears were stewed, boil it for five minutes, strain it over the pears, and let them stand until the jelly is firm.

PECAN PUMPKIN PIE

Prepare the pumpkin pie as usual. Before baking, mix the following ingredients together: 1/4 cup of brown sugar, 2 tablespoonfuls of flour, 1/4 teaspoon of cinnamon, 2 tablespoonfuls of chopped pecans and 2 tablespoonfuls of firm butter. Mix these all together until crumbly with a fork. Sprinkle evenly on pie and bake for a little less than an hour in a medium oven.

PEPPERMINTS

Turn half a cupful of boiling water upon two cupfuls of granulated sugar. Boil for five minutes, stir in a tablespoonful of essence of peppermint, and stir the sugar over the fire until thick, and then drop from a teaspoon upon a buttered paper, and let them harden.

PERMANGANATE OF POTASH

A solution of permanganate of potash is said to be a simple remedy for chilblains.

PHILADELPHIA ICE CREAM

Two quarts cream, if thick, add one pint milk; two cups sugar, two table-spoonfuls vanilla. This is the simplest and to many the most delicious form of ice cream. Scald the cream; melt the sugar in it, and flavor when cool. Then freeze. The cream should be very sweet and highly flavored, as both sweetness and flavor are lessened by freezing. To make it lighter and more delicate, whip the cream until you have a quart of froth, and add the froth after the cream is partially frozen. Many prefer to add the whites of eggs, beaten till foamy, but not stiff. Use two, three or four eggs to each quart of cream. The proportion of sugar should vary according to the flavor used.

PICCALILLI

Fifty small cucumbers, one large white cabbage, half a peck of green tomatoes, two quarts of small string beans, one dozen pieces of celery, three green peppers, four red peppers - seed taken out - two heads of cauliflower. Chop all quite fine and soak overnight in strong salt and water. In the morning wash well, drain thoroughly and pour over hot vinegar, spiced with cloves, cinnamon and allspice. A teacupful of grated horseradish may be added to the mixture if liked. In twenty-four hours turn off the vinegar, scald, skim and return to the pickles. Reheat three or four times if left like common pickles, or seal air-tight, while hot, at the second scalding. Pure cider vinegar should be used, and the vegetables must be fresh.

PICKLE ADVICE

Do not keep pickles in earthenware, as the glazing contains lead, and combines with the vinegar. Vinegar for pickling should be sharp. If you use copper, bell metal, or brass vessels for pickling, never allow the vinegar to cool in them, as it is then poisonous. Add a teaspoonful of alum to each three gallons of vinegar, and tie up a bag with pepper, ginger-root, spices of the different sorts in it, and you have vinegar prepared for any kind of pickling. Keep pickles only in wood or stoneware. Anything that has held grease will spoil them. Stir them occasionally, and if there are soft ones, take them out and scald the vinegar, and pour it hot over the pickles. Keep enough vinegar to cover them well. Do not boil vinegar or spice above five minutes.

PICKLED EGGS

Boil the eggs one hour, remove the shells, stick four or five cloves in each egg, pour hot vinegar over. Let stand two days before using.

PICKLED GRAPES

When grapes are not quite ripe, but dark colored, pick them from the stem and wash; put in bottles; in a dish put sugar and vinegar, and boil a few minutes; add spices to taste; boil a few minutes longer, pour over the grapes and seal up the bottles.

PICKLED GREEN PEPPERS

The peppers should be gathered quite young; the bell pepper is best for pickling. Cut one side of the pepper open so as not to injure the shell of the pepper. Then put them into boiling salt and water, changing the water every day for a week, keeping them in a warm place by the fire. Stir them several times a day. They first become yellow, and then green. When they are a fine green put them into a jar and pour cold vinegar over them, adding a small piece of alum. You may stuff the peppers as you do mangoes.

PICKLED ONIONS

Take very small onions and with a sharp knife peel them. Put them in salt and water and let them stand in the brine six days, stirring them often, and changing the salt and water every two days. See that they are closely covered. Then put the onions into jars and give them a scald in boiling salt and water. Let them stand till they are cold; then drain in a sieve, wipe them dry, and stick a clove in the top of each, and put them into wide-mouthed bottles, and adding a few blades of mace and a few slices of ginger. Fill up the bottles with the best cider vinegar, and put in the top a large spoonful of salad oil. Cork the bottles tight and seal.

PICKLED PEACHES

Nine pounds of peaches, three pounds of sugar, three quarts of vinegar. Peal the peaches; put two cloves in each peach. Put them in with the sugar and vinegar, and cook five or ten minutes. Add a little whole allspice.

PICKLED PEACHES, PEARS, ETC.

Ten pounds of fruit, four and one-half pounds of sugar, one quart of vinegar; mace, cinnamon and clove to taste. Prick each with a fork, then heat peaches in water enough to cover them. Then take them out. Add to the water, sugar, vinegar and spices in a bag. Boil until scum ceases to rise, then return fruit to syrup, and can when tender.

PICKLED PEACHES THAT WILL KEEP

Four pounds of sugar, one pint vinegar to twelve pounds of fruit;

pour sugar and vinegar together and boil; then add the fruit and let it come to a boil; the next day drain off the liquor and boil again; do this three times and your pickles are delicious; add cinnamon to the liquor and stick two or three cloves in each peach.

PICKLED PORK

When the hams have been taken off and the remainder cut into convenient-sized pieces, let each piece be well rubbed with common salt and then set to drain for twenty-four hours. Meanwhile prepare the pickle as follows: Put into four gallons of water seven pounds of common salt, two ounces of saltpetre and a pound and a half of course brown sugar. Let it boil till the scum (which must be skimmed off as fast as it rises) ceases to rise; then take it from the fire and let it stand till cold. After the pork has drained twenty-four hours, as directed, pack it closely in a clean deep tub, and pour this pickle, when perfectly cold, over it; let it stand with a heavy stone on top to keep it entirely under this pickle or brine for six weeks, taking care that the tub is kept closely covered. At the end of six weeks pour off the pickle and boil it again, adding two ounces of sugar and half an ounce of saltpetre, and when cold pour over the pork again; replace the heavy stone and keep closely covered. This pickle will keep perfectly sweet for many months.

This receipt, of course, is not sufficient for a whole barrel of pork, but for a tub. A larger amount can be made for a family that can use a barrel, by doubling or trebling the proportions here given. We think it better to make enough in October to last till just before real cold weather closes, and then replenish with a new lot to last through spring and summer. By boiling over, adding more salt, sugar and saltpetre, skimming off all the scum as fast as it rises, the foundation of this pickle will last for more than one year, and the pork will be very nice. But we much prefer to see that the pork tub or barrel is thoroughly washed, well scalded and aired, and an entirely new lot of pickle made at least once a year.

PICKLED SEED CUCUMBERS

Pare ripe cucumbers, take out the seeds, wash in cold water and wipe dry with a cloth. Cut in strips and pour cold water over them. Let them stand twenty-four hours. If the vinegar is weak, pour away part and add new. To one quart of vinegar add one and one-half pounds of sugar, one-half ounce of cinnamon buds, and the cucumbers. Boil until the cucumbers look clean. After a few days they will be ready for use, and are excellent.

PICKLED STRING BEANS

String beans make good pickles, though unless they are canned immediately after picking, they will not retain their freshness longer than a week or two. To pickle them, first remove the strings, then pour hot vinegar over them. They will be ready for use in a day or two.

PICKLING BEEF

For 100 pounds of beef pound together in a mortar till quite fine four pounds of common salt, six ounces of salprunello, six ounces of saltpetre and a pound and a half of course sugar. After all these are pounded fine, heat them over a slow fire and rub the meat thoroughly with this mixture while it is as hot as the hand can bear. Then pack the meat in an air tight cask or tub - no water to be used. The meat will be fit to cook in twelve days. Of course smaller quantities of meat can be prepared, but follow the same proportions of everything, only halving or quartering them according to the amount of meat to be cured in this way.

PIE CRUST

This is a good one - Five cups of flour, one cup of shortening, one teaspoonful of cream tarter, one-half of a teaspoonful of soda, a little salt (if all lard or cream is used), worked well into the flour, and a little saved out for the upper crust, wet with a little more than a cup of cold water; this makes five pies, and is also good for tarts.

PIE CRUST

One cup of lard and four cups of flour, using water to wet it.

Another good one is to take one cup of buttermilk, one cup of lard, four cups of flour, with just a little bit of soda. Either recipe makes four pies.

PIE CRUST - MRS. COX'S METHOD

Pour sufficient hot water upon wheat meal to make a stiff dough; roll, without kneading, to any desired thickness, from an eighth to a half inch. This makes a very tender crust, quite as much so as can be made in the ordinary way. It may be made of superfine flour, or rye meal, or a mixture of different kinds. To have the crust tender, it must not be kneaded, but rolled out with plenty of meal on the board.

PIES

Pies are wholesome or not as they are well or badly made. An apple pie can be so prepared as to be nearly or quite as simple as bread, and butter, and apple sauce. A whole meal may be made of it without injury to the health. On the other hand, it may be so prepared as to be unfit for the stomach of a rhinoceros. The model pie is in our opinion the apple pie. Peach pies are highly relished by many; but the peach loses its finest flavor by cooking, whereas the apple is improved by this process. Most of the berries in their season make good pies. So does rice and eggs, and the custard pie is not only delicious but wholesome. Mince meat pies are not to be tolerated by delicate people; though they may be eaten by men of strong digestion, who live much in the open air and do muscular work. The first point to be secured in a pie is a good crust. In general terms, this should be thin, when well baked, tender. It should not be shortened with lard, but with the best cream - or in the absence of this, good butter. Delicate fruits are soon tainted with the shortening of the crust. Many in baking pies, use too much crust. The less that can be used, the better the pie will be. The crust should be thin, the fruit good pie apples, and plenty of them, put between the crust. Where the two crusts meet on the edge of the dish, care should be taken to have the apple pressed out, so that there shall not be a wide strip of thick crust with no apples near them. An apple pie should be eaten just after it is cool. If eaten while hot, it is apt to go down only half masticated, and the effect of the heat on the tongue tends to destroy the finer sense of taste. After an apple is one day old it begins to grow stale, unless it is kept with good care. Soyer, the famous London pie-maker, thinks that if all the spoilt pies made in London on one single Sunday, were placed in a row beside a railway, it would take an express-train an hour to pass them in review. Whoever will induce bakers to improve their methods of making them, will be a public benefactor. The usual price for a piece of pie in a New York restaurant is ten cents. They could be afforded for half that price at a profit too, if there were no spoiled pies. The receipts for pie pastry which we shall give from month to month will be found excellent. They may be varied somewhat to suit individual tastes, provided only the general rules be kept in view. We commend the cream shortening as better than any other.

PIES THAT STEW OVER

Every housekeeper knows that the trouble that comes from the overflow of the contents of pies when baking. This trouble may be prevented by taking a strip of cotton cloth, about an inch and a half wide, and tying it around the pie. Wet the strip and allow half of the width to lap on the pie and the other half on the plate.

PINE TAR DISINFECTANT

Pine tar burned in a sick-room is an excellent disinfectant; it also induces sleep.

PINK COLORING

One-half ounce cochineal, one-half ounce alum, one-half ounce cream of tartar, the same of salts of tartar, one-half pint boiling water, one-half pound sugar. To the first three ingredients add the boiling water and put in a porcelain stewpan. Let it stand on the stove without boiling for twenty-five minutes. Add the salts of tarter very gradually, stirring all the time. Add the sugar. Strain and bottle. This is excellent for cakes, creams, etc. Use one or two teaspoonfuls according to the shade of pink required.

PITTSBURG GEMS

Stir together one pint of warm milk, four tablespoonfuls of home-made yeast, (or one-fourth of a pint of brewer's yeast), two tablespoonfuls of butter, one teaspoonful of salt, and wheat meal enough to make stiff as you can stir with a spoon. Let it raise about nine hours. Do not stir it but with a spoon, dip out, and fill your greased iron gem pans, about two-thirds full, and bake in the oven.

PLAIN CAKE WITHOUT MILK OR EGGS

Three cups of flour, one and one-half coffee cups of sugar, a tablespoonful of melted butter, nutmeg and seasoning to suit the taste, currants or raisins, two and a half teaspoonfuls of cream of tartar, one teaspoonful of saleratus, water, or milk if you choose. Do not make very thick. Bake with a medium fire.

PLAIN FROSTING

For this use one-half tablespoonful milk or cream, about one-half cup powdered sugar. Flavor with lemon.

Add the powdered sugar to the milk or cream till it is thick enough to spread. Lemon juice used in this will not curdle it, as there is so much sugar. Chocolate frosting may be made in this way with a square of chocolate grated and less sugar, about a third of a cup being necessary.

This may also be made with water, forming the nearly transparent icing seen on éclairs. This sort remains rather soft inside for some time.

PLASTER

One tablespoonful of ground brown mustard seed, mixed with two tablespoonfuls of lukewarm water, will make a very efficient plaster. Lay this between well-worn muslin and fold the edges, that the linen of the bed or person may not be soiled. A little molasses will prevent blistering.

PLASTER - A STICKING ONE

An excellent sticking-plaster for fresh cuts or cracked hands is made of three pounds of rosin, a quarter of a pound of beeswax, a quarter of a pound of mutton tallow. When well melted and dissolved together, remove from the fire and keep stirring till it is about as cool as it will pour. Then add about one tablespoon of spirits of turpentine; then pour the whole into a pail of cold water, and when cool enough take it out and work it as a shoemaker does his wax. When sufficiently worked roll it out in small sticks. This is equal to any plaster ever bought. Keep the hands greased to prevent it from sticking to them while working it.

PLASTER CASTS

To clean plaster casts, statuettes, bas reliefs, etc., simply make a thick paste of starch, and spread it all over the plaster article with a broad soft brush. As this paste dries it hardens and scales off, so that it can be easily be removed, carrying with it all the dust and dirt on the plaster, and leaving it as white and fresh looking as if it had just come from the manufacturer's hands.

PLASTER - MUSTARD

In making a mustard plaster no water whatever should be used, but the mustard should be mixed with the white of an egg; the result will be a plaster which will draw perfectly, but will not produce a blister even upon the skin of an infant, no matter how long it is allowed to remain upon the part.

PLASTER OF PARIS

If you need to use Plaster of Paris for stopping cracks, mix it with vinegar. Vinegar prevents it setting too quickly and makes it easy of manipulation.

PLUM PUDDING

One cup of suet; one cup of milk, one of molasses; two teaspoonfuls of ginger, one-half teaspoonful of cloves, same of nutmeg. Mix well; add flour to make a stiff batter with one teaspoonful of baking powder sifted through it. Last of all one cupful and a half of raisins, currants and citron, well floured. Put in a well-floured bag and drop into a kettle of boiling water; for the first hour, turn your bag every ten minutes, after that every half hour is often enough. Boil three hours.

PLUM PUDDING

One and one-half pound of raisins, one and one-half pound currants, half pound of bread crumbs, four ounces citron, four ounces lemon, four ounces orange peel, two ounces rinds of lemon grated, juice of one lemon, four ounces of white sugar, ten eggs, one teaspoonful each of nutmeg, ginger and cinnamon, thirty-two bitter almonds, one pint of new milk, and a small particle of salt. Mix all together gradually over night, and add a little more milk in the morning if required. Boil seven or eight hours.

POP CORN PUDDING

Two quarts of new milk; one quart of nice full popped corn; soak overnight; one egg; two-thirds of a cup of molasses; one teaspoonful of salt; spice to taste; to be baked three hours. Makes a very nice pudding.

POISON IVY

Mrs. Dora Belch sends a certain cure for ivy poisoning: Make a tea of oats and wash affected parts. Usually two or three treatments are all that is needed.

POISONOUS WOUND

Pour diluted carbolic acid at once upon every part of a poisonous wound; afterward give internal stimulants.

POLENTA

Boil one pound of Indian meal for half an hour in two quarts of hot liquor, or boiling water, salted to taste, with one ounce of fat, stirring it occasionally to prevent burning; then bake it for half an hour in a greased baking dish, and serve it either hot, or when cold, slice it and fry in smoking hot fat. The favorite Italian dish is closely allied to the hasty pudding of New England and much of the South.

For the various breads in use, as well as other compounds made from meal, many prefer the ancient Indian maize of a rich, golden color, as used in the aboriginal methods of preparation above referred to.

POLISHING BLACK MARBLE

To polish black marble, wash it with soap and warm water; when it is dry, rub it well with furniture paste or French polish, and then rub it over with an old silk handkerchief. After two or three trials the marble will become quite bright.

POLISHING BRASS

To polish brass kettles that are very much tarnished, first rub with a solution of oxalic acid, then dry and polish with rotten stone or the finest emery.

POOR MAN'S CAKE

Three cups of flour; two cups of sugar; one-half cup of butter; two eggs; two teaspoonfuls of cream tartar; one of soda; one of salt.

POOR MAN'S HAND SOAP

Put in an iron kettle five pounds of unslacked lime; five pounds of sal soda; three gallons soft water; let it soak overnight; in the morning pour off the water; then add to the water three and a half pounds of grease; boil till thick; turn in a pan and cool and then cut in bars.

PORK APPLE PIES

Make a deep pie the same as any pie of sliced apples, and cut a small piece of salt pork in small pieces and lay over the top of the apple, cover with crust or not as you wish. I usually cover them. Or it may be varied by using part molasses, add a little clove and cinnamon for spice.

PORK CHOWDER

Chop one onion very fine; boil one or two beets and one dozen potatoes; pare and slice together in a dish with the chopped onions raw; melt one large spoonful of butter and pour over the whole, together with half a cupful of warm vinegar; season with pepper and salt. Have ready to accompany this dish half a dozen slices of salt pork, cut thin and fried tender. Then, when done, take out of the frying pan and dip in batter made of three eggs well beaten, one tablespoonful of milk (sweet) and one cupful of flour mixed with half a tablespoonful of baking powder. Fry in the pork fat and serve warm.

PORK PIES

One peck of good sound apples; two pounds of salt pork, chopped fine together. Cook two hours in a saucepan; then add spice, extract lemon, raisins, sugar, molasses, 1 cup of wine. Stir well together and let it cool through before making into pies.

PORK SAUSAGES

A correspondent asks for a recipe for making pork sausages. Here is a good one.

Ingredients: Of sweet fresh pork, one-third fat to two-thirds lean; to each pound of meat, one even tablespoonful of salt, one tea-spoonful of sifted sage, a scant half teaspoonful of pepper. Chop the meat very fine, or grind it in a sausage machine or meat chopper, add the seasoning and mix thoroughly. Make cotton bags, one yard long and four inches wide, dip them in strong salt and water, dry, and fill with the sausage meat, pressing down as firmly as possible. When sausages are wanted, turn the end of the bag back, and cut off the meat in half-inch slices, and fry brown.

PORK TENDERLOINS

Cut in thin slices; stew in water till nearly done; put a little butter into a frying pan and fry them until brown; serve on butter and toast.

PORTUGUESE SWEET RICE

A Portuguese dish of sweet rice is prepared as follows: A cupful of rice is washed and boiled in a pint and a half of milk, with four tablespoonfuls of sugar and a laurel or bay leaf; when the rice is soft the bay leaf is removed, a gill of cream and the yolks of four eggs added and the rice is dished and cooled. When it is quite cold the surface is dusted with powdered sugar and cinnamon, or with burnt almond dust. The almond dust is prepared by browning peeled or blanched almonds in the oven and then pounding them to a fine powder. The use of rice is by no means confined to the semi-tropical climates we have mentioned, but the limit of our article will not permit any further description of the many dishes of which it forms the base; for there seems to be a general appreciation of its alimentary value when it is combined with flesh-forming-materials. (Miss Corson)

POTATOES, MEATS, VEGETABLES ETC

Potatoes should be put in boiling water. All meats for soups in cold water. Onions and turnips are improved by first parboiling about fifteen minutes. The test of good flour is by the water it absorbs, not by the color. In boiling fowl to ascertain when done put a skewer into the breast; if tender the fowl is done. Vegetable oysters are good with every kind of meat. Beets, peas and beans with boiled or roast meats. Carrots, parsnips, turnips, greens and cabbage are eaten with boiled meats. Mashed turnips, onions and applesauce with roast pork. Tomatoes with every kind of meat.

POTATO BALLS

Mash the potatoes; add salt, butter, cream and pepper; mix well; make into balls, roll in egg and crumbs, and fry in hot lard.

POTATO BISCUIT

Eight potatoes of medium size mashed very fine, four tablespoonfuls of butter melted, two cups of milk lukewarm, one cup of yeast, flour to make a thin batter, two tablespoonfuls of white sugar; stir all the above ingredients together except the butter, and set the sponge until light; four or five hours will be required; then add the melted butter with a little salt, and flour enough to make a soft dough; set this aside for four hours longer, roll out in a sheet three-quarters of an inch thick, cut into cakes; let them rise one hour and bake.

POTATO CAKE

Two cups mealy potatoes mashed fine, one-eighth cup sweet cream; two tablespoonfuls flour, graham or white; time, twenty minutes. Stir into the mashed potatoes the cream and flour, mixing thoroughly; beat lightly with a fork, and then make with the hand into little flat cakes, half an inch thick. Bake to a good brown, and send to the table as soon as done. The flour can be omitted if desired.

POTATO CAKES

Mashed potatoes, left from dinner, are very nice treated in this way: Make them into cakes about half an inch in thickness; put them in the cellar until next morning, laying them singly on the plate; roll them in flour, and fry in butter enough to keep them from sticking, until brown; turn and brown the other side.

POTATOES IN STEW

Potatoes combine well with stews in winter, and a stew with pieces of mutton put at the bottom of the saucepan, a layer of sliced onions placed over them, pepper and salt sprinkled on, and potatoes put last, repeated two or three times, is an excellent winter dish when it has gently simmered for about three-quarters of an hour. (Demorest's Magazine)

POTATO PUDDING

Boil four large potatoes, and pass them through a sieve; pour into them powdered loaf sugar to taste, and the yolks of two or three eggs; add a few drops of essence of lemon, then the whites of the eggs whisked to a froth; mix quickly and well; pour into a plain mould, buttered and bread crumbed, and bake for twenty minutes in a quick oven. Serve with sauce.

POTATO PUDDING

One pound (eight large) potatoes boiled and well mashed; add one-quarter pound of butter, two ounces of sugar, half a lemon chopped fine, one teacup of milk; butter the dish, and bake in a moderate oven half an hour. Two eggs may be added.

POTATO SALAD

Ten cold potatoes sliced, one tablespoonful of chopped parsley, and mixed with the French dressing.

POTATO SALAD #2

One quart of small potatoes, two tablespoonfuls chopped onions, two of chopped parsley, four of beets, and enough of any of the salad dressings, or clear vinegar, to make it slightly moist; to the latter, if used, add a little melted butter; keep in a cool place until ready to serve.

POTATO SALAD

Peel and slice cold boiled potatoes enough to fill a quart dish, salt and pepper to taste, chop two small onions very fine and mix with them. Put half a cupful of vinegar and a teaspoonful of butter in a dish and let it heat gradually. Beat the yolks of two eggs thoroughly, pour into a cup, and fill the cup with thick, sweet cream, beat well together and stir into the hot vinegar. Stir constantly till it reaches the boiling point, then pour it immediately over the potatoes and mix thoroughly.

POTATO SOUP

Wash, pare, and boil three potatoes in salted water, until very soft; put one pint of milk, one stalk of celery and one slice of onion in a double boiler; cook one tablespoonful of butter and one of corn starch, together with a little of the milk; mash the potatoes, add the milk, the corn starch and butter, and let boil one or two minutes; add one teaspoonful of salt and one saltspoonful of pepper; strain and serve hot.

POTATO SOUP

Peel and slice twelve medium sized-potatoes, cover with boiling water, cook ten minutes, drain off the water, add a quart of cold water, an onion minced and a little salt, and cook until the potatoes boil into pieces. Pass all through a colander into two quarts of good soup stock free from grease. Simmer half an hour. Boil half a cup of rice until tender and dry, put into the soup, season with pepper, salt and two tablespoonfuls of butter and serve.

POTATO SOUP

One quart of potatoes, pared and cut into small strips or blocks, a large sprig of parsley, the same of thyme or sweet marjoram, cut fine; boil three-fourths of an hour in three quarts of water, then add half a pint of cream or new milk; put a small tablespoonful of butter into a plate where it will soften, and stir into it two spoonfuls of flour, add to the soup, and boil five minutes. Drop-dumplings made with a little flour and cream, yeast and milk are an addition.

POTATO YEAST

Two large cups grated potato, one-half cup sugar, the same of salt, stir well together, pour one quart boiling water and stir briskly over the stove till it boils. When cool rise with yeast cakes, or the same. This is the best yeast I ever used, and will keep sweet a long time. If your family is large you can double the quantity.

POTTED BEEF

Take six pounds of the cheapest parts of beef, boil until the meat comes from the bone, skim all out into your chopping bowl, remove the bone and gristly pieces, chop the meat fine, and add one and one-half pints of gravy, season with salt, pepper and a small teaspoonful of powdered mace. Pack away in bowls, and when cold is very nice sliced for tea or fried in batter.

POTTED SALMON

Salmon, pounded mace, clove and pepper to taste; three bay leaves, quarter of a pound of butter. Skin the salmon, and clean it thoroughly by wiping with a cloth (water would spoil it); cut into small pieces, which rub with salt; let them remain till thoroughly drained, then lay them in a dish with other ingredients and bake. When quite done, drain them from the gravy, press into pots for use, and, when cold, pour over it clarified butter.

POULTICE-HOW TO MAKE

Dr. Brunton, in "Brain", the New London periodical, gives the following practical hints on this subject: "The common practice in making poultices of mixing the linseed meal with hot water, and applying it directly to the skin, is quite wrong; because if we do not wish to burn the patient, we must wait until a great portion of the heat has been lost. The proper method is to take a flannel bag (the size of the poultice required), to fill this with linseed poultice as hot as it can possibly be made, and to put between this and the skin a second piece of flannel, so that there shall be at least two thicknesses of flannel between the skin and the poultice itself. Above the poultice should be placed more flannel, or a piece of cotton-wool, to prevent it from getting cold. By this method we are able to apply the linseed meal boiling hot, without burning the patient, and the heat gradually diffusing through the flannel, affords a grateful sense of relief which cannot be obtained by other means. There are few ways in which such marked relief is given to abdominal pains by the application of a poultice in this manner."

PRACTICAL ANTISEPTIC SOAP

Any good soap material, to which sulphate of copper has been added, in the proportion of twelve parts of the latter to eighty-eight of the former, will make a valuable healing soap for the use of physicians, nurses and any other persons who may be exposed to blood poisoning from wounds or bruises.

PREFERENCE OF STEWS OVER STEAK

It is desirable that stews should be encouraged in winter among work-people, instead of the constant fried steaks, which do not give as much warmth or vitality to the body as the well amalgamated stew. As in all cooking, much depends upon the way of combining and carrying on the heat operation. A stew that has been cooked violently cannot well amalgamate; the meat becomes hard, the fat swims to the top, and that delicate flavor is lost which all stews ought to have, of however plain materials they may be made. There are numberless variations to be made in stews, delicate and plain, but the best teacher is your own ingenuity, when you know the principle on which stews are made. The thickening process must begin a stew, not end it, and must be most carefully executed, so as to have a good foundation to go on. There is, perhaps, no daintier dish than a brown game stew, dressed with currant jelly and some delicate canned vegetables, steamed rice or macaroni.

PREPARATION FOR BURIAL - CARE OF THE DEAD - SANITARY ━━

Human life is so fleeting that we are compelled to be among the dead, as well as among the living. Our sanitary relations to death, therefore, are of great importance. Such has been the tendency of late years to limit contagion by isolation, that it is now not uncommon for health boards to prohibit public funerals or assemblages at a church or at a house where disease has occurred, to a degree that would have heretofore been considered meddlesome or dictatorial. We accept fully the doctrine that the limitation of many diseases is greatly promoted by preventing contact or by keeping out those whose attendance is not absolutely necessary. The principle, however, has its just limitations. In these hours of deep darkness there is an outgoing for human sympathy which is not fully enough expressed by looking in a window or sending a black-edged card of condolence. That will do in many cases, but there is an immediate circle of relatives or friends whose presence we crave and whose company serves to break the tedium of desolation which is felt over a vacant chair. True, the health of the living is a first consideration; yet we ought to ask whether the preservation of the dead and the preparation for burial cannot be such as to make attendance safe. To a degree, the room in which any person has died of contagious disease is charged with the particles of contagion. These, however, are mostly dissipated readily by air and cleansing, and fortunately, belong to that low grade of life which is ephemeral and tends to lose its specificity. Certainly, with the room itself GREAT PRECAUTION SHOULD BE USED before susceptible persons, such as children, are admitted. But there is seldom need that a funeral be in the same room or in the same building or part of it in which the death has taken place. Now, with all things connected with a fatal sickness, the dead body, after due preparation had, is the least hazardous. It is a definite mass, with which we can deal by all the arts of cleanliness and render innocent as a conveyer of contagion. It is well worth while to study, in this view, some of the ancient arts of preparation, and especially the simple Jewish method, as illustrating this point. All garments were removed, and the body washed with soda or nitre wash, which acted both as a cleanser and a disinfectant. The neat and abundant bandaging was a covering from the air, while the additional use of ointment and spices served to prevent any separation of loose particles, and provide an antiseptic dressing. These spices of hydrocarbons are directly useful as neutralizing poisons. The same care was extended to the ears, the nostrils, the mouth, etc., so that every aperture was properly cleansed or plugged. The body thus became an emblem of purity, and no disease, however contagious, could be conveyed thereby. An article in the "Report of the New Jersey State Board of Health for 1879" gives in detail the best methods at present to be adopted, and enforces the value of this knowledge upon undertakers and those who have to deal with the dead. It is sometimes seemed to us that there is much in preparation feasible to be done by those who are of the immediate kin or near at hand. The proper washing is often accomplished by those who have A PERSONAL REGARD FOR THE DECEASED, and yet not so moved as to be of much grief. The use of a board or any straight resting-place is only for the purpose of securing position when the body is stiffened and cold. A table or stiff husk mattress answers a similar purpose. The habit of covering the face with a light cloth, wet with saltpetre water or weakened vinegar, is not objectionable, although it is probable that a very light oiling of the skin with Vaseline soon after washing will accomplish a similar purpose. We quote from the article above referred to some directions: All garments that have been upon the body during the sickness should be removed, not to be replaced, and the body be laid for washing on a table or cot, covered with paper or linen. The body should then be thoroughly wiped and cleansed all over with soda borax, in the proportion of a teacupful dissolved in a quart of water, or the chloride of zinc solution. If soap is used it should be Castile or carbolized soap, the greases of which do not decompose so rapidly as those of laundry and scented soaps. Anointing with Vaseline is also good. As the face and head are more especially exposed, these need the careful cleansing and washing and use of absorbents heretofore referred to. Where the hair is long it is desirable that it be partly removed;

but, if this is objected to, it also can easily and safely be washed with the zinc solution. The ancient head-dress or cap easily concealed any change of the hair, and would still be in taste, if fashionable. It is always necessary that very careful attention be paid to the proper cleansing of the hair. In case of any unusual odor of any infectious disease, the chlorinated soda, or Labarraque's solution, or the chloride of zinc solution, or a chlorine wash made by dissolving one-quarter of a pound of chloride of lime in a quart of water may be used instead or in addition. The NATIONAL BOARD OF HEALTH DIRECTS the use of a saturated solution of the chloride of zinc as a wash and the wrapping of the body in a sheet saturated with it. Dry powdered borax sprinkled over the surface after the washing and wiping is an excellent cleanser. Sawdust, well moistened with the chloride of zinc, is also recommended to be placed in the coffin. Any sore, or abrasion, or wound should be cleansed when possible, and be freely covered with copperas wash, powdered charcoal, common salt, or any of the cleansing or drying articles above named. A small bag of sawdust or fine shavings, or cotton or wool, interlaid with salt, borax, or charcoal, may properly be closely pinned about the thighs. One good authority recommends that in some cases of delay or transportation the body should be covered with sawdust, to which has been added tar or a pound of ivory black, or other crushed or powdered charcoal, so as to absorb any possible gases or to prevent escape of any fluid. Persons in attendance upon the sick, or those laying them out, do not increase their risks by such cleanliness. Indeed, those who during sickness, or in caring for the bodies after disease, are familiar with methods of cleansing and disinfection are those who themselves escape, besides protecting society. As a rule the corpse should not be placed in a tight coffin until just before burial, or, at least, it should be left so open as not to interfere with the air. Then, if for removal an airtight coffin is desirable, it can be more properly used. There is much to be said for and against the art of undertaking as at present followed. It is not always the art of the embalmer, nor is it pursued with that regard to neatness in care of the body which entitles to large rewards. The mind of the director seems to be upon the coffin, its drapery, etc., far more than upon nice details as applied to the body of the departed. We therefore gladly, as requested, draw attention to this subject as one in which the interests of public health, as well as the personal feelings of friends, is concerned. (The Independent)

PREPARING SALT BEEF FOR THE TABLE

Take that which will cut up in good slices and freshen over night; put in hot water and boil until done; then thicken and add butter the size of a butternut. This is very good and easily prepared when fresh meat is wanting. (Laura)

PREPARING SPINACH

Strip the leaves from the stems, wash them thoroughly, and boil twenty minutes in water to which salt has been added. Drain through a colander. Mix together a tablespoonful of flour, one-half cup or one cup of sour cream, and a little black pepper. Put the spinach back into the pot, stir the gravy into it thoroughly, and serve. We generally cover the spinach in the bowl with fried eggs, and think it an excellent dish.

PREPARING WHIPPED CREAM

When preparing whipped cream put in the white of one egg and whip with it. Less cream is required and the product or combination is much nicer than cream alone.

PRESERVED CITRON-MELON

Pare, core, and cut into slices some fine citron-melons. Weigh them; to six pounds of melon allow six pounds of refined sugar, the juice and grated rind of four large lemons, and a quarter pound of root ginger. Boil the slices of melon half an hour or more, till they look quite clear, and are so tender that a broom straw will pierce them. Then drain them, lay them in a pan of cold water, cover them, and let them stand all night. In the morning tie the root ginger in a thin muslin cloth, and boil it in three pints of clear water till the water is highly flavored; take out the bag of ginger, and pour the water over the pieces of sugar, which is previously broken and put in a preserving kettle. When the sugar is melted, set it over the fire, put in the grated peel of lemons, and boil and skim it till no more scum rises. Then put in the sliced citron and the juice of the lemons; boil them in the syrup till all the slices are quite transparent, and so soft that a straw will go through them, but do not break them. When done, put the slices, still warm, into jars, and gently pour over the syrup. This will be found delicious.

PRESERVED CHERRIES

Stone them; allow one pound of sugar to one pound of fruit; put a layer of the fruit in the preserving kettle, then a layer of sugar, and repeat till all are in; boil till clear. Put in bottles hot and seal them. Keep in dry sand.

PRESERVED CUCUMBERS

Take firm, ripe cucumbers, as soon as they turn yellow; pare them and take out the seeds, cut them in pieces two or three inches in length and about two in width; let them lie in weak salt and water for eight hours. Then prepare a syrup of one gallon of cider vinegar, five pounds of sugar, one ounce of mixed spices (not ground spices), boil twenty minutes, then strain. After drying the cucumbers with a soft cloth, put in the syrup, and boil till soft and transparent; skim the pieces out carefully, lay them in a colander to drain; then boil the syrup to the consistency of molasses, pour it on the cucumber, and keep in a cool place.

PRESERVED STRAWBERRIES

To two pounds of large strawberries, add two pounds of powdered sugar, and put them in a preserving kettle, over a slow fire, till the sugar is melted; then boil them precisely twenty minutes, as fast as possible; have ready a number of small jars, and put the fruit in boiling hot. Cork and seal the jars immediately, and keep them through the summer in a cold, dry cellar. The jars must be heated before the hot fruit is poured in, otherwise they will break.

PRESERVED STRAWBERRIES FOR CREAMS OR ICINGS WITHOUT BOILING

Let the fruit be gathered in the middle of a warm day, in very dry weather, strip it from the stalks directly, weigh it, turn it into a bowl or deep pan, and bruise it gently; mix with an equal weight of fine, dry sifted sugar, and put it immediately into small wide-necked bottles; cork these firmly without delay, and tie bladders over the tops. Keep them in a cool place, or the fruit will ferment. The mixture should be stirred softly and only just sufficiently to blend the sugar and the fruit. The bottles must be perfectly dry, and the bladders, after having been cleaned in the usual manner, and allowed to become nearly so, should be moistened with a little spirit on the side which is to be next to the cork.

PRESERVING EGGS

A good and old plan for preserving eggs is as follows: To each pail of water add two pints of fresh-slaked lime and one pint of common salt; mix well, fill a barrel half full of this fluid, put the eggs down in it any time after June, and they will keep for many months.

PRESERVING EGGS

To preserve eggs dip each one into melted pork lard, rubbing it into the shell with the finger; then pack it in an old fig-drum or butter-firkin, setting every egg upright with the small end downward. Eggs thus prepared in August, directly after harvest, have been eaten with relish the following January.

PRESERVING EGGS

To preserve eggs apply a solution of gum arabic to the shells and pack them in dry charcoal.

PRESERVING FOWLS' WINGS

A pail of strong copperas water was set away to cool overnight, preparatory to using in the cellar, and by some mischance a package of wings hanging overhead fell into the water with the joint ends down. In the morning they were taken out and flung into the woodshed, supposing they were ruined. Some weeks after, thinking they were dry enough to burn, they were picked up to carry to the kitchen range, but instead of being ruined, they were in the very best state of preservation - not a moth visible or a feather loose - and they lasted the best of any wings I ever used. Last year I repeated the experiment of dipping them in copperas water, and the result was splendid; and hereafter it will be my rule in preparing wings for service to dip them as soon as possible after they are taken off, and then string them on a cord and hang them up in a dry place till they are needed for use. It has often been said that some of the most useful methods of doing work and the best receipts were the result of accident instead of design. This method of preserving wings was purely accidental, and it is no waste, for the water is just as good to pour into the sink drain for a disinfectant as if the wings had not been dipped in it.

PRESERVING FRUIT ETC. BY THE FRENCH METHOD

For small fruits: To two teaspoonfuls of salicylic acid and one cup of sugar, add one quart of water.

Vegetables require three of salicylic acid, also one tablespoonful of salt, to a quart of water.

In canning corn always heat the corn and salicylic acid together until it is boiling and then put away.

I dissolve the preparation thoroughly and keep the fruit well covered.

PRESERVING STRAWBERRIES IN WINE

Put a quantity of the finest large strawberries into a gooseberry-bottle, and strew over them three large spoonfuls of fine sugar; fill up with Madeira wine or sherry.

PREVENTING COOKING ODORS

Put one or two small red peppers, or a few pieces of charcoal, into the pot where ham, cabbage, etc., are boiling, and the house will not be filled with the offensive odors.

PREVENTING FLAT IRONS FROM STICKING

Irons are apt to stick to starched articles. To prevent this, lay a little fine salt on a flat surface, and rub the iron well over it. This will make the iron smooth, and also remove smokiness.

PRICKLY HEAT REMEDY

Cream of tartar water, with a little lemon juice added, is an excellent old fashioned remedy for prickly heat. It may be drank in any quantity without harm.

PROPERLY MADE GRAPE JUICE

Steaming is considered better than stewing if best results are to be obtained. There is something worth remembering about the making of grape juice, contributed by a student of domestic science: Crush and steam the grapes, instead of crushing and stewing them, as was the old method. To the crushed fruit add one quart of water to every 16 quarts of grapes, and place the kettle containing them over a second kettle containing hot water. It is claimed that the substitution of steaming for stewing does fuller justice to the grape. After they have been rendered thoroughly tender, pour the cooked fruit into a jelly bag and let it drip over night. By morning the sediment will have settled at the bottom and the clear top can be poured off. The juice is now ready for bottling. After it has been strained into bottles (glass fruit jars may be used to as good advantage) covers and rubbers are put on and the bottles are set on a rack in the boiler, or on the shelf of the steam cooker. If you use the boiler, or a kettle, add cold water until it comes up about two inches on the bottle or jar. Bring the water gradually to the boiling point, and let the boiling continue from 30 to 60 minutes, according to the size of jar. Seal the bottles, and the juice is ready to store.

PROUD FLESH - REMOVAL OF

Pulverize loaf sugar very fine, and apply it to the part affected. This is a new and easy remedy, and said to remove it entirely, without pain. It has been practiced in England for years.

PUDDING OF FRUIT AND BREAD CRUMBS

Mix a pint of dried and pounded bread crumbs with an equal quantity of any kind of berries, or of dried and chopped sour apples. Add three eggs, half a pint of milk, three spoonfuls of fine flour, and half a teaspoonful of salt. Bake on a griddle or in an oven in muffin rings, or, when made thinner, as griddle cakes. If dried fruit is used, more milk is needed than for fresh berries. This may also be boiled for a pudding. Flour the pudding-cloth and tie tightly, as it will not swell in cooking.

PUDDING SAUCE

One egg, one tablespoonful of corn starch, and the yellow and juice of one lemon. Beat well, add one cup of sugar and butter the size of a walnut, pour on a pint of boiling water, stir constantly till it boils, and then remove from the fire.

PUDDING WITHOUT EGGS

Pare, quarter and core four or five apples, and place them in the bottom of the pudding dish; sprinkle over them four or five tablespoonfuls of sugar, a little nutmeg, five pounded crackers, and pour in slowly a quart of sweet milk, add a small piece of butter, a little salt, and a few raisins scattered among the apples if you wish. Bake an hour in an oven quick enough to brown it nicely. It is good with or without sauce.

PUDDING WITHOUT MILK OR EGGS

Soak dry bread in as little water as possible, and squeeze out all the water, add sufficient sugar to sweeten, and for a small pudding half a teacupful of chopped suet or butter, and dried fruit which has been soaked overnight, or canned or fresh fruit. Mix well together, adding a little allspice. The pudding is put into a greased tin pail, a cloth placed over it, and the cover put on. The pail is set in a kettle containing sufficient water to come half way up the pail. Boil for two hours or more for a large pudding. To be eaten with sauce.

PUFF CAKE

Two cupfuls of sugar, one of butter, one of sweet milk, three of flour, three eggs, one and one-half teaspoonfuls of yeast powder, extract of lemon. Bake quick.

PUMPKIN LOAF

With a strong spoon stir well together four pints of cornmeal and about three pints of stewed pumpkin while scalding hot; when cold add a teaspoonful of milk, a cup of hot yeast, half a cup of molasses, a teaspoonful salt, and about one and one-half cups wheat flour; mix all well in a deep baking pan, iron preferable; when light bake three hours at moderate heat; may be left over night in a moderately warm oven for a warm breakfast.

PUMPKIN PIES

Cut the squash in two, take out the seeds, pare off the rind, and boil in water until soft, then pass it through a colander, using for two pies, one teacup of squash, same quantity of sugar and of milk, two eggs beaten, two tablespoonfuls melted butter, and one teaspoonful of cinnamon. Bake with one crust. The water should be poured off before it passes through the colander.

PUMPKIN PIES

Ada wishes to know the right way to make pumpkin pies with just one crust. I suppose we all think our way is best. A poor pumpkin pie is the poorest of pies, but a good one is fit for you, Mr. Crowell, to eat, and I do not think you would refuse the second piece, even if you were not a Yankee. But the recipe. After stewing and straining through a colander or sieve, add new milk to thin it, and instead of eggs use sweet cream, say the cream from a pan of milk to six pies, and one cup of sugar, but if after tasting I think it needs more sugar, I add it. (There is a great difference in the sweetness of pumpkins.) Season with cinnamon and nutmeg. Do not get it too thick; the cream thickens when cooked, the same as eggs do. Eggs make pumpkin pies hard and flour (which some use) makes them pasty.

PUMPKIN PIES

Ada asked for a recipe for pumpkin pies. Here is one that will answer for squash or pumpkin. Peel and cut the pumpkin into pieces the size of a finger, removing the inside, and stew in just enough water to cover it, until perfectly dry and tender, then strain through a sieve or colander. Take one cup of the pulp, one cup of good rich milk, and one egg to a pie, (if your cups are just the size of mine it will just fill your pie), sweeten to taste with either sugar or molasses and season with ginger, nutmeg, cinnamon and a little salt. Bake in a quick oven, till the center rises up.

PUMPKIN PIES

One pint of well stewed and drained pumpkin, one quart of scalding hot rich milk, one and one-half cups of sugar, four eggs, one teaspoonful of salt, one tablespoonful of ginger and one of ground cinnamon. Bake in pie plate lined with good paste; do not let mixture stand after it is put together, but bake at once.

PUMPKIN PIES

For Ida: I press my cooked pumpkin through a colander. One cupful will make about two pies. To this add one egg beaten, about one-half cup of sugar, two teaspoonfuls of salt, good rich milk, sufficient to fill two good sized earthen pie plates, bake them in a pretty hot oven and a long time, bake with one crust. Your success depends largely on salt, with plenty of sugar. Do not make them too thick with pumpkin.

PUMPKIN PIES

Ada wishes good pumpkin pies with one crust. A medium sized pumpkin stewed, makes about six pies. Strain through a sieve, add a couple of eggs, a little salt, grated nutmeg, and spice, sweeten to suit the taste, thin to right thickness with milk, and bake only on one crust. Bake as fast as the plates are filled so as not to soak the crust.

PUMPKIN PIES THAT AIN'T PUMPKIN PIE

If you are fond of pumpkin pies, and have no pumpkins, have you ever tried substituting carrots? Cook and prepare them the same as you would the pumpkin, and you will find it hard to tell which is better.

PUMPKIN PUDDING

Take one pint of pumpkin that has been stewed soft and pressed through a colander; melt in half a pint of warm milk, a quarter of a pound of butter and the same quantity of sugar, stirring them well together; one pint of rich cream will be better than milk and butter; Beat eight eggs very light, and add them gradually to the other ingredients alternately with the pumpkin; then stir in a wineglass of rosewater and two glasses of wine mixed together, a large teaspoonful of powdered mace and cinnamon mixed, and a grated nutmeg. Having stirred the whole very hard, put it into a buttered dish and bake three-fourths of an hour.

PURIFYING THE AIR

To purify the air of a damp cellar strew charcoal about floor and shelves.

QUAILS ON TOAST

Brown the birds, either in salad oil or butter, mix a tablespoonful of flour among them, and brown that, then cover them with boiling water, season them highly with salt, pepper, cloves and mace, and stew them fifteen minutes; melt in a tablespoonful of butter for every two birds, and serve on toast.

QUEEN OF PUDDING

One pint fine bread crumbs, one quart sweet milk, three ounces loaf sugar, small piece of butter, yolks of four eggs, grated rind of one lemon; bake till done, then spread over a layer of preserves or jelly; whip the whites of the eggs stiff, add three ounces of pulverized sugar in which has been stirred the juice of the lemon. Pour the whites over the pudding and replace in the oven. Let it brown lightly. To be eaten cold.

QUICK PUDDING

Pour a pint of boiling milk on ten teaspoonfuls of grated bread crumbs. Let them stand ten minutes. Then add the yolks of four eggs, well beaten, six tablespoonfuls of sugar and two of butter. Season with lemon extract. Stir well; add the whites of the eggs, previously beaten to a stiff froth; pour into a buttered pudding dish, and bake quickly. To be eaten with wine sauce or cream and sugar.

QUICKLY MADE PUDDING

One pint of milk, quarter pound of butter, half a pound of sugar, quarter of a pound of flour, five eggs, rind and juice of half a lemon. Heat the milk, stir into it the quarter of a pound of butter, half a pound of sugar; when cool add gradually the flour, five eggs well beaten (omitting the whites of two), flavor with the grated rind and juice of half a lemon; beat well. Butter some small cups, pour in the mixture to rather more than half full, then bake about half an hour. Serve with stewed fruit, boiled custard or sauce.

QUINCE AND APPLE PRESERVES

For quince and apple preserves have one-third weight of apples pared, cored and quartered; equal weight of sugar and fruit. When the quince is boiled tender take it out; boil the apple in the quince water, put them in the syrup and let them boil until they look red and clear; an hour and a half is not too long. Do not boil the quince in the syrup, but put layers of the apple, when done, into jars with the quince, previously cooled tender in water, and pour the syrup over them.

QUINCE JELLY

Wipe the fruit carefully and remove all the stems and parts not fair and sound. Use the best parts of the fruit for canning and preserving, and the skins, hard parts, and cores for jelly. The seeds contain a large portion of gelatinous substance. Boil all together in enough water to cover, till the pulp is soft. Mash and drain. Use the juice only, and when boiling add an equal weight of hot sugar, and boil till it jellies in the spoon.

QUINCE MARMALADE

Rub the quinces with a cloth; cut them in quarters; stew them in a little water till they are tender enough to rub through a sieve; when strained put a pound of brown sugar to a pound of fruit; set it on the fire and let it cook slowly till thick enough to cut smooth.

QUINSY REMEDY

Make a poultice of corn meal mush; add about one tablespoon mustard and half as much cayenne pepper. Apply to affected parts as hot as one can bear and repeat. This is a tried remedy.

QUINSY SORE THROAT

If Rough and Ready, Placerville, Calif. who asks a remedy for quinsy sore throat, will steep sumac-berries and use the tea as a gargle, I know she will be gratified at the result. This simple remedy has been known to cure the worst cases.

RABBIT ON TOAST

Cut cold rabbit in pieces and fry brown with slices of bacon or ham, and half its quantity of small onions or mushrooms, and stew them until tender in hot water enough to cover; put in plenty of pepper and salt, and serve on toast. Should be stewed slowly.

RABBIT SOUP

Cut up your rabbit, and put into a soup pot, with a ham bone, a bunch of sweet herbs, a bay leaf, an onion stuck with cloves, some whole pepper, and let it simmer until the meat is tender; then cut off the meat in neat squares, and return the bones and trimmings into the soup, and let it simmer until the meat is in rags; then strain it and thicken it with butter and flour, mixed on the fire without being browned; add a pint or more of red currant shrub; season to taste; let all simmer together with the meat that was cut off. Serve very hot.

RAGOUT OF PIGEONS

First clean and wash the pigeons, then put a very little water in a kettle, and put them in; let them simmer gently until tender; then remove, keeping them hot, and if there is not enough gravy in the kettle, add a little more water; put in two ounces of butter, a little salt, pepper and sweet marjoram; let these all boil together, thicken with a little dusting of flour, then put back the pigeons and let all boil for a few minutes, so as to season them; have some toast sippets cut into diamonds, put them around the edge of a dish, and put the birds and gravy in the center.

RAILROAD CAKE

Two eggs, 1 large cup of white sugar, half a cup of sour milk, and butter the size of a butternut, two teaspoonfuls of cream tartar, and 1 of soda.

RAISED DOUGHNUTS

At noon take a bowl that will hold a good large pint; put into it two cups of sugar, then pour boiling water on until the bowl is full, add a piece of butter the size of a large egg; as soon as cool enough add one cup of yeast, putting all into a larger dish or pan; nutmeg or cassia, a little salt, and flour to knead; let them rise again; then roll and cut out before the fat is put on the heat, as it gives them a chance to rise a little before frying; set them in the oven to warm before eating.

RAISED DOUGHNUTS

One pint of warm water; one cup of yeast; two eggs; one cup of sugar; small piece of lard or butter; cinnamon; flour, to be made just as stiff as can be stirred with a spoon. When raised light, set them in a cool place, to be fried as you like them.

RAISIN PIES

Five crackers rolled; 1 cup molasses; 1 cup sugar; one-half cup of butter; 1 cup chopped raisins; 3 cups hot water; one-half cup of vinegar; spice as the same for meat pies.

RASPBERRY JAM

Raspberries, currant juice, sugar. Take one pound of sugar to one quart of raspberries, and to six pounds add one pint of currant juice; put on the fire and boil thirty minutes after it commences.

RASPBERRY JAM

To every quart of ripe raspberries allow a pound of the best loaf sugar. Put sugar and berries into a pan and let them stand two or three hours. Then boil them in a porcelain kettle, taking off the scum carefully. When no more scum rises mash them and boil them to smooth marmalade. When cold put in glass tumblers.

RASPBERRY JAM

Allow a pound of sugar to one of fruit; boil the fruit half an hour; strain one-quarter of the fruit and throw away the seeds; add the sugar, and boil the whole ten minutes.

RASPBERRY VINEGAR

Mash two quarts of raspberries, let them stand in a pan to get sour; strain the juice through a sieve, and to every pint put a pound of loaf sugar, and a pint of Beaufoy's Criotal Vinegar (or the usual white wine vinegar); let boil ten minutes, skim, and when cold, bottle.

RASPBERRY VINEGAR

Every housekeeper should endeavor to have at least a small quantity of this delightful beverage. In cases of fever it is indispensable, and will quite often soothe when nothing else will. Put two quarts of red raspberries, nice and fresh, into a jar, and pour over them a quart of good vinegar. Let it stand twenty-four hours. Strain through a flannel bag. Pour this liquid over two more quarts of fresh berries and again let it stand twenty-four hours. Strain again. Allow three-fourths of a pound of loaf or good white sugar to every pint of juice. Stir well into the liquid, put into a stone jar, cover closely, and let it stand in a kettle of boiling water to be kept boiling for an hour. Strain it, and bottle ready for use. A teaspoonful to a tumbler of water is the manner of using it.

RASPBERRY VINEGAR

Take ripe raspberries, put them in a pan, and mash them with a large wooden spoon or masher. Strain the juice through a jelly-bag, and to each pint of juice add one pound of loaf sugar and one quart of vinegar. When the sugar has dissolved place the whole over the fire in a preserving kettle, and let it boil a minute or two, and skim it. When cold bottle it, cork it well, and it will be fit for use.

RASPBERRY VINEGAR

Raspberries, sugar, vinegar. Take three quarts of fruit and one of vinegar, steep for three days, strain and simmer gently, with one pound of sugar to every pint of juice and vinegar mixed; when cold, bottle and cork very securely. A large tablespoonful of this in a glass of iced water is a most refreshing drink.

RASPBERRY VINEGAR

For raspberry vinegar, to seven pints of berries add one quart of vinegar. Let them stand forty-eight hours; then strain, and to every pint of juice allow a pound of sugar; boil fifteen minutes and bottle for use. This is a pleasant drink for the sick.

RAT ELIMINATION

A correspondent of the Chambers' Journal says that chloride of lime will drive rats away. He first made this discovery on board ship, and says also: "On my return to England I took a house and furnished it. After being in it a short time I found that it was infested with rats. They would get through every part on the ground floor. On examination I discovered that a drain ran under the house, emptying into the harbor. I here again used the chloride of lime freely, and in less than a week every rat had taken its departure. I have recommended this remedy to many ship masters and friends on shore; and in all cases it has proved a success. I have occupied my present residence for five years, and we have neither rat nor mouse on the premise. I attribute this to the free use of the above mixture, which is also effective as a deodorizer and disinfectant.

RAW BEEF

Raw beef chopped fine and served with pepper, salt and vinegar, is excellent, but do not add the seasoning until it is taken to the invalid.

RED AND WHITE CAKE

Ora asks for a cake shaded with red instead of spices. Any cake recipe may be used, reserving half the quantity and using a few teaspoonfuls of cochineal coloring to give the requisite color. The cochineal may be obtained at the druggist and is said to be harmless. It is used in coloring candies.

RED APPLE JELLY

Pare, core, and slice two dozen large, juicy apples; put them into an enameled preserving-kettle with just enough water to cover them; simmer slowly until the liquor is almost a syrup; put all into a flannel bag; drain the juice from the pulp; put with it two-thirds its weight of fine clarified sugar, boil and skim it, and add a pint of red currant jelly. Boil it until it will jelly in cold water. Strain it through a jelly bag again, into jars or tumblers, and when cold cover with brandied paper and air-tight covers. If you wish a mould for the table, warm the jelly, and pour it into a mould washed with white of egg, let it get cold, and turn it out.

RED BRICK FLOORS - CLEANING

To clean red brick floors, rub them with a brick moistened with a little warm milk and water, and wipe them dry with a soft cloth.

RED MAYONNAISE

To give bright color to mayonnaise, lobster coral pounded to a powder and rubbed through a sieve, then thoroughly blended, or juice from boiled beets.

REMOVING A GLASS STOPPER

To remove a glass stopper that has become fast, put a drop of sweet oil or glycerin in the crevice about the stopper. In an hour or so the stopper may be easily removed.

REMOVING GREASE SPOTS FROM SILK

Place some coarse brown paper - the soft kind - on both sides of the spot, then press carefully with a hot iron; change the paper often, as it absorbs the grease. If the goods are so rich or delicate that the iron is likely to injure them, try friction by using raw cotton - rub the spots off, changing the cotton often. If the cashmere or cassimere is soiled or stained in many places, rip the article and wash it in tepid water softened with pulverized borax. It can be made to look as good as new.

REMOVING INK STAINS

Ink stains may be removed from white articles by means of a little salt of lemons, diluted muriatic acid, oxalic acid, or tartaric acid, and hot water; or by means of a little solution of chloride of lime or chlorine.

When the stain is caused by ink manufactured with logwood, a red mark remains, which may be removed by the application of a little chloride of lime. All strong acids and alkalis tend to injure the fabric. For this reason the spots should be well rinsed in cold water immediately after the stains are removed.

REMOVING SHINE FROM BLACK SILK

Lay the silk upon a table, and with a sponge wet with cider vinegar rub the shiny places until they disappear. Then hang up in a shady place until dry, and the silk will look almost as good as new. The same treatment may be used upon fine black diagonal.

REMOVING WAX STAINS FROM CLOTH

Lay over the stains two thicknesses of blotting paper, and apply for a moment the pressure of a moderately-hot iron. The stains will be instantaneously and entirely removed.

RENEWING CRAPE

Two of the sisters inquire for a recipe for renewing crape; here is a reliable one. I have tried it. Heat skim milk and water, dissolve in half a pint of it a piece of glue an inch square, rinse the crape in vinegar to clean it, then, to stiffen it, put it in the mixed glue and milk, wring it out, then clap it like fine muslin till dry, smooth it with a hot iron, laying a paper over it while ironing. Or dip in gin and clap dry, ironing as above.

RENOVATING CRAPE

Crape may be renovated by thoroughly brushing all dust from the material, sprinkling with alcohol, and rolling in newspaper, commencing with the paper and crape together, so that the paper may be between every portion of the material. Allow it to remain so until dry.

RESTORING COLORS IN CARPETS

To restore the colors in carpets spread on them a thin layer of hardwood sawdust, well dampened with a solution of common salt, and allow it to dry before sweeping it up.

RHEUMATISM

There is nothing better for rheumatism than the following chloroform liniment. It is also excellent for sprains. Shake the bottle well before applying, and rub in thoroughly. Put into a bottle one ounce sweet oil, one-half ounce oil of sassafras and four ounces aqua ammonia. Shake these ingredients until perfectly mixed, add one ounce laudanum, two ounces tincture of arnica and one-half ounce chloroform; shake again and it is ready for use. Keep well stopped, using a rubber stopper if you have one.

RHEUMATISM

For rheumatism try taking three to four drops of oil of wintergreen on a cube of loaf sugar, three times a day. It is pleasant to take and has made some marvelous cures.

RHEUMATISM (OR GRIP)

Cayenne pepper, salt and lard mixed thoroughly, and applied to the affected parts will cure rheumatism or grip.

RHEUMATISM RELIEF

We have used Oil of Wintergreen for rheumatism, and it is "just the thing". Take ten drops on sugar; get the oil, not the essence. In severe cases take it three times a day.

RHEUMATISM REMEDY

When you make your cucumber pickles, save the juice of your cucumbers and to one quart of juice add one-half cup of fine salt; bottle up tight, and when you feel the rheumatism, bathe often and rub well. I have used it and know it is good. (M.C.C., Vermont)

RHUBARB DUMPLINGS

Wipe your rhubarb and cut as for sauce. Make up a soft dough as for cream tartar biscuits; one quart of flour, one teaspoonful of soda, two of cream tartar, a little salt; mix with water or milk, just which you have the most of, and into the dough stir the rhubarb as you would plums into cake; steam one hour and a half. Eat hot with sweet sauce. A pint bowl full of cut rhubarb is enough for a quart of flour.

RHUBARB JELLY

Prepare as for sauce, put into a preserving kettle with a very little water (just enough to keep from burning at first), and cook until soft. Press through a sieve and then strain through a jelly bag. To every pint of the juice allow one and one-half pounds of granulated sugar. Boil the juice ten minutes, skim, add the sugar and boil ten minutes longer. Test by dropping a very little in a cup of cold water, and if it immediately falls to the bottom it is done. If not firm, stand in the sun, same as strawberry jelly. The jelly should be made as soon as the berries or the rhubarb is cut, and it is best not to attempt to make it in damp or cloudy weather.

RHUBARB PIE

Chop the rhubarb fine, take one and one-half cups sugar, two large spoonfuls of flour, one egg and the yolk of another, flavor with lemon, beat it well, and bake with one crust. When cool, frost it. Like any rhubarb pie, better for having the rhubarb chopped.

RHUBARB PIES

Wipe as for sauce, line a deep plate with good crust, rolled very thin, and cut rhubarb in as you sometimes do apples. Add one cup of white sugar to a pie; three tablespoons full of water, two of flour sprinkled over the top; cover very tight - tucking in the edges to keep in the juice - and bake brown. Eat for tea or the next morning. Rhubarb pie over one day old is poor eating. White sugar is very much better to use with rhubarb than brown, as it makes a richer syrup and gives a different flavor. By cutting your rhubarb and putting boiling water to it, and letting it cook about five minutes, and then pouring off the water and filling your pie with the rhubarb thus deprived of half its acidity you need use only a large half cup of sugar. Many prepare it so, but I think it makes the pie flat and takes away the good flavor.

RHUBARB SAUCE

Wipe the stalks very carefully with a damp cloth, and then with a dry one. Never peel it. It destroys the flavor to remove the peeling, and spoils the color. Cut into pieces about half to three-quarters of an inch long. Put into a porcelain kettle or a new, bright tin, not an old black one; add as much white sugar as your judgment dictates; cover with boiling water; put a plate tightly over the dish and cook until quite soft, never touching it, as it mashes it all up. When done (if cooked in a porcelain kettle), set in a cool place, undisturbed, till tea time, then slide it carefully into your glass dish, and you have a nice looking sauce with a clear pink jelly-like syrup, making it look very different from the mass of little strings, usually called rhubarb sauce. If cooked in a new tin, it must be slid out into a bowl or pudding-dish as carefully as possible and not transferred to your glass dish until cold.

RIBBON CAKE

Two eggs, one cup sugar, one-half cup butter, two teaspoonfuls baking powder, one cup milk, salt, and flavor to taste; flour till it will drop from a spoon easily. Cover two washing pie pans with this mixture. Add to the remainder chopped citron, currants and spice to suit and fill the third pan. When baked put the layers together with currant jelly, the dark one in the middle. Save out the white of one egg to frost it and add coconut to the frosting. Makes a handsome, nice and economical cake. (Mrs. Cleasby)

RICE AND APPLE PUDDING

Boil a cupful of well-washed rice fifteen minutes in water, adding a pinch of salt. Drain on a sieve until quite dry. Put part of the rice on the bottom and along the side of a pudding mould or tin pail, peel and quarter six apples and place in the centre of rice with half a cup of sugar and a little chopped lemon peel. Cover the fruit with the rice, tie down and steam one hour. Serve with sweetened cream, lemon sauce or sweetened melted butter.

RICE CUPS

Take half a pound of the best rice; cook until thoroughly done; turn into cups; when cold, place on a dish and serve with milk, a little granulated sugar, some grated nutmeg, and a tablespoonful of any kind of jelly or preserved fruits, such as blackberries.

RICE DISH OF ITALY

The rice dishes of Italy are popular and delicious, so unlike our own well-known ones, that we urge a trial of their excellence upon our readers. Chief among them rank the rizotto of Milan. The rizotto is made by par-boiling well-washed rice in boiling water for five minutes, draining and drying it on a cloth, frying it light brown with a little chopped onion and butter, and then stewing it until tender in enough highly-seasoned broth to well cover it; it has to be watched carefully and the saucepan shaken as the rice absorbs the broth, so that it shall not burn; when the rice is done it is put into a buttered mould with shreds of cold chicken, tongue or ham, well shaken down, dusted with grated cheese and browned in the oven. Slices of mushroom or a little tomato sauce are used as variations from the chicken or tongue.

RICE DISH OF PORTUGAL

A matelote of fish with rice is well worth a trial. Some highly flavored fish, such as eels, is fried brown in oil or bacon fat, with a clove of garlic, a tablespoonful of saffron, and plenty of red pepper and salt;

then rice, partly boiled and dried, is added and browned, enough red wine is poured over these ingredients to cover them, and they are allowed to simmer gently until the rice is tender, the saucepan being shaken to prevent the burning of the rice.

RICE ENTREE

Stew a cupful of rice until well done. Add a small cupful of milk, two eggs (well beaten), and pepper and salt to taste. Pour into a shallow pan, sprinkle grated cheese thickly over the top, and bake until the top is nicely browned.

RICE GRIDDLE-CAKES

One cup cold boiled rice, one cup sour milk, or buttermilk, one cup sifted graham flour, one egg, well beaten, one teaspoonful soda, dissolved in boiling water. Moisten the rice with the milk, and mix them well together; if there are lumps remaining, mash fine with a spoon, or fork, which is better. Stir in the graham flour and beaten egg, forming a thin fritter batter; then the dissolved soda, and beat well. Bake in small thin cakes to a good brown; the griddle must be clean and well oiled.

RICE GRIDDLE CAKES

Cook a half teacupful of whole rice till every grain is dissolved and like jelly. Warm half a pint of rich milk, put in half a teaspoonful of salt, stir the rice into the milk till it is smoothly mixed. Beat three eggs, whites and yolks separately, till very light, and pour into the rice and milk the last thing. Bake on a hot greased griddle till brown and light.

RICE PIE

Take cold rice, cooked in milk; add sufficient cream to make quite thin; mash it with a wooden or silver spoon till free from lumps. Beat up four eggs very light - yolks and whites separately; sweeten to suit your taste, and pour in the eggs - the whites last; stir well; cover a deep custard or pumpkin pie plate with pastry, pour in the rice and bake, but not long enough to make the custard watery. Rice pie should be made thick, and eaten when fresh, but not till after its cold. Children are fond of it, and may be allowed as much as they wish.

RICE PUDDING

One and one-half pints of milk, one half cup of rice, one cup of sugar, and a little salt and nutmeg. Bake three hours in a slow oven.

RICE PUDDING

Four tablespoonfuls of rice; one quart of sweet milk; boil until tender, and the milk is absorbed; then stir in the yolks of four eggs, well beaten, and three tablespoonfuls of sugar, with the grated rind of one lemon. To the whites of the eggs, well beaten, add eight tablespoons of powdered sugar, with the juice of the lemon; lay it over the pudding and return to the oven until slightly browned; serve cold.

RICE PUDDING

Take one cup of rice, boil until done, and evaporate water from it with gentle heat until dry; stir together three pints of milk and one cup of white sugar; add two eggs, well beaten, reserving white of one egg for frosting; add two table-spoonfuls of melted butter, and salt to suit the taste; also add one cup of raisins; after baking, frost with the reserved white of egg, beaten with one tablespoonful of powdered sugar.

RICE WAFFLES

Beat three eggs very light, stir them into one and one-half pints of flour; mix with the flour one quart of milk and then add one pint of boiled rice, with a tablespoonful of butter stirred in while the rice is hot. Add a tablespoonful of good yeast and salt to your taste.

RICH CHRISTMAS PUDDING

One pound of raisins stoned, one pound of currants, half a pound of beef suet, quarter of a pound of sugar, two spoonfuls of flour, three eggs, a cup of sweetmeats, and a wine-glass of brandy. Mix well, and boil in a mould for eight hours.

RICH GRAVY FOR ROAST FOWL

Cut small one pound of gravy beef, slice two onions, and put them in a stew-pan with a quart of water, and some whole black pepper, a small carrot, and a bunch of sweet herbs; simmer till reduced down to one pint; strain the gravy and pour it into another stew-pan, upon one-quarter pound of butter browned with two tablespoonfuls of flour. Stir and boil up.

RIGHT WAY TO COOK STEAKS

Broil steak without salting. Salt draws the juice in cooking. It is desirable to keep this in if possible. Cook over a hot fire, turning frequently, searing on both sides. Place on a platter. Salt and pepper to taste.

RINGROUNDS

Try this cure for ringrounds. Wet the part affected with vinegar in which plenty of gunpowder has been stirred, repeating the operation several times a day. Painting with iodine is also an effectual remedy. Fresh butter or lard, mixed with gunpowder, is recommended also, and Vaseline, used alone, is said to be excellent.

RIPE BERRY PIES

Place the under crust upon a deep plate, and the upper one - cut just the right size - on a flat tin or sheet-iron; prick to prevent blistering, and bake. Fill the deep dish while hot with berries, and cover with the flat crust. If the fruit is rather hard, replace in the oven till heated, or slightly baked; if quite ripe, the crust will steam them sufficiently. Raspberry and blackberry pies may be made in the same manner. The flavor of these delicious berries, when ripe, is greatly injured by cooking; and they are also changed to a mass of little else than seeds and juice.

RIPE CUCUMBER PICKLES

Take large yellow cucumbers, pare them thin, take out the cores, and soak in salt water two days, then pour over them boiling water and let them stand overnight. Prepare the pickle thus: For each quart of sharp vinegar take one pint of hot water, two cups of sugar, one tablespoonful of cloves, cinnamon, allspice and nutmeg tied in a bag, and add a handful of ripe grapes or raisins.

RIPE GOOSEBERRY PUDDING

Scald a pint of ripe gooseberries in very little water; when tender mash them in the liquor in which they were boiled; pulp them through a sieve, and add to them the beaten yolks of four eggs, a quarter of a pound of blanched sweet almonds, lightly chopped. Mix all very well together, and bake it in a pie-dish edged with a rim of puff-paste. Half an hour's baking will do it. Serve with cream.

RISSOLES

Mince beef or veal a la mode, extremely fine; grate into it a little boiled ham. Mix well together with white sauce flavored with mushrooms. Make of beef drippings a very thin paste, roll into small squares, enclose the minced meat, forming small balls; fry them in drippings to a light brown color. The same mince may be cemented with egg and bread crumbs, and fried without the pastry.

RIZ A LA IMPERATRICE

Boil three tablespoonfuls of rice into a pint of milk, with sugar and vanilla to taste; when done put in a basin to get cold; then make a custard with a gill of milk and the yolks of four eggs; when cold mix it with the rice; whip to a froth a gill of cream, with some sugar and a pinch of gelatin dissolved in a little water; mix this lightly with the rice and custard, fill a mould with the mixture and set it on ice; when moderately iced turn it out and serve.

RIZOTTO

Rizotto is prepared with sausages in the north of Italy in a very appetizing dish; the sausages are twisted without breaking the skin in inch pieces, and fried brown; the rice is washed, boiled for five minutes in boiling water, drained and dried, and then browned in the sausage fat with a chopped onion; last of all these ingredients are stewed in highly-seasoned broth until the rice is tender and has absorbed all the broth, enough being used to well cover it when set to stew.

ROAST BEEF PIE

Cut cold roast beef or beef steak into thin slices, line a deep dish on the sides with paste; lay some of the meat on the bottom, sprinkle it with salt, pepper, a pinch of ground cloves, small bits of butter, and a few slices of tomatoes, then add another layer of meat and so on, until the dish is full, cover with crust, and bake one-half hour.

ROAST CANVAS-BACK DUCKS

Having trussed the ducks, put into each a thick piece of soft bread that has been soaked in port wine. Place in quick oven and bake an hour. Before they go to table squeeze over each the juice of a lemon or orange, and serve up very hot with their own gravy about them. Eat with currant jelly. Have ready, also, a gravy made by stewing slowly in a saucepan the giblets of the ducks in butter rolled in flour, and with as little water as possible. Serve up the additional gravy in a bowl.

ROAST CHICKEN

Dress it; sprinkle a little salt and flour over it; fill the sauce pan with water, and cover the whole with another sauce pan. Set in the oven till done, when it will be found to be delicious.

ROAST GOOSE AND APPLE SAUCE

Cover the breast of the goose with paper, and roast it from one to two hours, according to its size, in a moderate oven; place it on a hot dish, pour some rich brown gravy over it, and send the following sauce in a boat: Pare one dozen apples, place them in a stewpan with a pinch of sugar and a pinch of salt, one pint of stock broth; let simmer until the apples are cooked, pass the sauce through a fine hair sieve, bring to a boil, take off the scum, and serve very hot.

ROAST MEAT

Put the meat rack into a baking pan; wipe the meat with a wet towel; lay it on the rack; then sprinkle well (on all sides) with salt, pepper and flour, letting the bottom of the pan to get well covered with the seasoning. Now put into a very hot oven for a few minutes, and when the flour begins to become a dark brown turn in hot water enough to cover the bottom of the pan; close the oven door, and let the meat get well browned, but not scorched, on one side; then baste with the gravy from the pan, dredge with flour, and brown again. Now turn the meat over, baste with gravy, dredge with salt, pepper and flour, and brown this side. A piece of beef weighing six pounds will require forty minutes, if it is desired rare, twenty minutes longer if well done. Mutton the same time. Lamb one hour and ten minutes. Veal two and a half hours. Pork three hours. Put the meat on a large hot dish; take the rack from the pan; skim all the fat from the gravy; add half a cup of boiling water, if there is about that amount in the pan; mix one teaspoonful of flour with cold water enough to make a thin paste; stir into this the boiling gravy, and season with salt and pepper; strain and serve. Remember that you must keep adding water to the pan all the time the meat is roasting, as the bottom of the pan should be covered all the time; and yet if there is too much water in the pan at once it steams the meat. Never roast meat without having a rack in the pan, because if the meat is put into the water it becomes soggy, and has no good flavor. Putting salt on fresh meat draws out the juices, and it would not be well to use it if the flour was not also used; but the flour makes a paste which keeps all the juices in the meat, and also helps to enrich and brown it; so that by using both salt and flour we get a rich, well seasoned piece of meat, which we could not by either alone. A very poor piece of meat may be greatly improved by constant basting. Beef requires that it be cooked either very little or a great deal to be good. Between the two extremes it is always unhealthy, unless, of course, the pieces are choice, like the tenderloin and sirloin. The choicest and most expensive parts of the beef are the tenderloin, the sirloin, the five ribs called the fore rib from the fore quarter, and the middle ribs. All the cheap parts of the beef are good for stews and soups, and this is the most economical mode of cooking all meats, as in this way nothing is lost. The cheapest parts of the beef are the neck, the flank, the skin and the liver. Good ox beef has a fine grain, yellowish-white fat and bright red color. Cow beef has white fat, and the color is a paler red than ox beef. It is not rich and juicy like ox beef. Mutton and lamb should have the fat white and the meat firm. The meat should be dark. Veal should be firm to the touch, and at least three months old before being killed. The fore quarters of the last three mentioned meats are always the cheapest. Steaks are cut from the sirloin, the tenderloin, the rump and round. The most economical is the round steak, and when the beef is large and tender and the steak cut from the top of the round, it is a very delicious piece of meat.

ROASTING A TURKEY

Prepare a stuffing of pork sausage meat, one beaten egg, and a few crumbs of bread; or if sausages are to be served with the turkey, stuffing as for fillet of veal; in either, a little shred shallot is an improvement. Stuff the bird under the breast; dredge it with flour, and put it down to a clear, brisk fire; at a moderate distance the first half hour, but afterwards nearer. Baste with butter; and when the turkey is plumped up, and the steam draws toward the fire, it will be nearly done; then dredge it lightly with flour, and baste it with a little more butter, first melting it in the basting ladle. Serve with gravy in the dish, and bread sauce in a tureen. It may be garnished with sausages, or with fried forcemeat, if veal stuffing is used. Sometimes the gizzard and liver are dipped into the yolk of an egg, sprinkled with salt and Cayenne, and then put under the pinions, before the bird is put to the fire. Chestnuts, stewed in gravy, are likewise eaten with turkey. A very large turkey will require three hours' roasting; one of eight or ten pounds, two hours; and a small one, an hour and a half. Roasted chestnuts, grated or sliced, and green truffles, sliced, are excellent additions to the stuffing for turkeys.

ROCK CREAM

This will be found very ornamental as well as a delicious dish for the supper-table. Boil a teacupful of the best rice till quite soft in new milk, sweeten it with powdered loaf sugar, and pile it up on a dish. Lay on it in different places square lumps of either currant jelly or preserved fruit of any kind: beat up the whites of five eggs to a stiff froth, with a little powdered sugar, and flavor with either orange-flower water or vanilla. Add to this, when beaten very stiff, about a tablespoonful of rich cream, and drop it over the rice, giving it the form of a rock of snow.

ROLL JELLY CAKE

Jennie E. asks for a recipe for roll jelly cake. I wish to give her one which I know to be very good. One cup of sugar, one cup of flour, three eggs, two teaspoonfuls of cream of tartar, one teaspoonful of soda, bake in a square tin. After it is baked spread with jelly and roll up.

ROLLS

Take six cups of flour, two eggs, a half cup of yeast, one-fourth cup of sugar, a small piece of butter and a little nutmeg. Mix with warm water and let it rise over night; knead and set in a cool place until afternoon, then shape into rolls and let them rise. Bake in moderate oven. When done, glaze them with a little milk in which a tablespoonful of brown sugar has been dissolved and set back in the oven for a few minutes.

ROOT BEER

Root beer is made by infusing herbs and bruised roots in boiling water. Burdock, yellow dock, sarsaparilla, sassafras, dandelion, spikenard, hops, coltsfoot, nettles, wintergreen, wild cherry, black alder, prickly ash, birch bark, ginger root, spruce twigs, and coriander and aniseed are all used. An experienced housekeeper says to take half an ounce each of the bruised ginger, sassafras, yellow dock, sarsaparilla and wintergreen, and a quarter of an ounce each of wild cherry bark, dandelion root, coriander seed and hops. Simmer these for an hour in a gallon or more of water, and add enough more boiling water to make four or five gallons. When lukewarm strain the liquor off, add about three pounds of brown sugar, or sweeten to taste with molasses, and put in an ounce of cream tartar and half a teacup of yeast. Let the mixture work for twenty-four hours, then skim, strain and bottle. Soak new corks in boiling water, pound and tie them down close, and lay the bottles on the side in a cool place. It will be ready for use in twenty-four hours, and is excellent in the spring for purifying the blood.

RULE FOR SALTING MEAT

As it is now the season for salting meat I will give a recipe that we have tested for several years, for beef: Let the beef get cold; cut up in pieces to suit your convenience, then pack it in a tight vessel as tight as possible - we usually pound it down as solid as possible - without any salt; take cold water and stir in salt until the brine is strong enough to bear an egg or potato; add one pound of sugar for each 100 pounds of beef; pour it over the beef; Put on a weight so that the beef cannot float; it will keep until spring if not eaten before that time; what you wish to dry roll and pack in the bottom of the vessel.

RUSSET SHOE CLEANING

Russet shoes may be kept clean and shining by rubbing them with a slice of banana and polishing with a cloth.

RUSSIAN SAUCE FOR COLD MEATS

Four spoons grated horseradish, two spoons mode mustard, one spoon salt, one spoon sugar, vinegar enough to cover all. This will keep some months.

RUSSIAN TEA

Ice, sugar, and slices of lemons, over which the tea is poured in the goblets in which it is served, makes this most delightful of drinks. The lemon prevents the headache and sleeplessness that tea induces in some persons.

RUST, GRASS AND MILDEW STAIN REMOVER

To take rust, grass stain or mildew out of clothes try this: Put salt on the spots, then wet with lemon juice, rub well, then wet and let stand overnight, repeat until it is all removed; lay on the grass at night so the dew will fall on it.

RUST PREVENTION

To prevent the rusting of steel instruments, take equal parts of carbolic acid and olive oil, and smear over the surface.

RUST REMOVAL

To take the rust out of steel rub it with sweet oil; in a day or two rub with finely powdered unslaked lime until the rust all disappears, then oil again, roll in woolen and put the article in a dry place, especially if it is table cutlery.

RUST REMOVAL

If Emma O. Hirschey will saturate the rusty spot with lemon juice and place in the sun, she will be successful in removing the stain. It may be necessary to repeat the operation, but it will guarantee success.

RUSTING STEEL

To take the rust out of steel, rub the steel with sweet oil, in a day or two rub with finely powdered unslaked lime until the rust all disappears, then oil again, roll in woolen, and put in a dry place, especially if it be table cutlery.

RYE AND INDIAN BREAD

One and one-half cups of Indian meal, one and one-half cups of rye meal, two cups of sour milk and one cup of sweet milk, salt and molasses to taste, and two teaspoonfuls of saleratus. Steam three hours, and bake in the oven for half an hour.

RYE DROP CAKES

One cup of sour milk, or buttermilk, three tablespoonfuls of sugar, if buttermilk is not used, put one tablespoonful of melted butter in with the sour milk, one well beaten egg, one even teaspoonful of soda, and one of cinnamon. Make a stiff batter by the addition of rye flour. This is to be dropped by   large spoonfuls into boiling lard. Serve warm.

RYE MUFFINS

A good rule for rye muffins is as follows: One cup of flour, two of rye meal, one pint sweet milk, one tablespoonful of sugar and a little salt, two teaspoonfuls cream tartar, one of soda; mix so that it will drop readily from the spoon into muffin rings or roll-pans.

SADDLE OF LAMB

Time, a quarter of an hour to the pound; one hour and a half to two hours. Cover the joint with buttered paper to prevent the fat catching, and roast it at a brisk fire, constantly basting it, at first with very little butter, then with its own drippings. Mint sauce.

SAGO IN SOUP

To one quart of boiling stock, with a little salt, add one teaspoonful of large sago; leave it to boil ten minutes, stirring it occasionally;

when the sago is cooked sufficiently, it will appear floating in small transparent balls. If more than the above quantity of sago is used, the stock becomes too thick, which prevents the sago being kept separate in boiling.

SALMON SALAD

Flake cold boiled salmon with a silver fork, or better still with the fingers, to discover the presence of bones; if canned salmon is used, and that by the way makes a very good salad, pour off all the oil and pick to pieces with the fingers, removing all bone; mix one saltspoonful of salt and one-half saltspoonful of pepper in the salad spoon, then fill the spoon three times with oil and once with vinegar and toss all lightly together; pour over the salmon; mix well and set on the ice. When you wish to serve it line the salad bowl with crisp, fresh lettuce; lay on this the salmon and cover with a mayonnaise dressing, or, if preferred, a boiled dressing.

SALSIFY OR OYSTER PLANT WITH EGG SAUCE

Scrape and cut the salsify into rings one-fourth of an inch thick and lay it in vinegar and water to prevent from turning black. When all is ready put it in boiling salted water, and boil one hour. To make the sauce, melt two tablespoonfuls butter in a saucepan and stir into it one tablespoonful flour and one-fourth teaspoonful salt. Then pour in slowly one cup and a half of scalded milk. Boil one minute and add two hard boiled eggs chopped fine. Stir well and boil three minutes more. Strain the salsify and turn it into a vegetable dish. Pour the sauce over it and serve.

SALT OR MILK-RISING BREAD

Take one cup of sweet milk, two of boiling water, and a teaspoonful of salt; while hot stir in enough cornmeal to make a thin batter; let it stand till cool; add enough flour to thicken well and set in a warm place, beating it up occasionally to make it rise better; after this yeast has risen sufficiently add more flour and knead into loaves; place them in pans to rise again, and bake; in making up the second time put a little more salt in, as the quantity put in the yeast is scarcely sufficient to season the bread.

SALT PORK

Try pouring boiling water over your sliced salt pork to be fried for breakfast; let stand overnight, drain and fry. You will find it much nicer than when cooked in the usual manner.

SALT PORK AND APPLES

Cut half a pound of nicely cured pork in slices quarter of an inch thick, fry them slowly until brown in deep frying-pan, and take them up on a hot dish. Meantime wash, wipe, and slice six sour apples, and when the pork is taken up put them into the frying-pan to cook until they are tender, but not broken. Lay them on a dish with the pork and serve them hot.

SALT-RISING BREAD

Put one tablespoonful of salt and the same of white sugar in a stone jar; pour upon it one quart of boiling water; when cool, so as not to scald, stir in flour until thick as fritters; place in a kettle of hot water. Be particular to keep the same temperature; the water in the kettle must remain just hot enough for you to dip your hand in without scalding it. I always put a tin or earthen plate in the kettle so that the jar will not rest on the bottom; let it rise very light; if it is kept at the right temperature it will rise in five hours; when light proceed as you would had you made a sponge with yeast.

The manipulation of the dough and good yeast are the principal parts of good bread making; you cannot knead too much; you ought to mould each loaf thoroughly, using as little flour as possible.

SALT RISING BREAD

To 1 pint hot water put ½ teaspoon salt, and when the water has sufficiently cooled to not scald flour, add enough to make a very soft batter. Stir thoroughly and place in a kettle of warm water (or warming oven) and keep the temperature even until the batter is very light, then add flour to make a soft dough. Mix thoroughly and lightly and put again in a warm place to rise. Then mould into loaves and bake in a moderate oven when light. It is an improvement to add two potatoes, well sifted, when the water and flour are added.

SALTED CORN

Gather perfect ears for table use; scald and cut off as for dried corn. Then strew in a large stone jar or wooden keg a layer of corn and a layer of salt. The brine formed of the juice of the corn will thoroughly preserve it, and very little soaking will be required to freshen it for the table. Various air tight processes are resorted to, and some of them answer nicely; yet I have never seen any answer quite as well as the packing of young, tender ears into a barrel of boiled brine and carefully headed to exclude the light.

SALTING BEEF FOR FAMILY USE

For one hundred pounds of beef take eight pounds of salt, four pounds of brown sugar, make a brine, boil and skim, add two ounces of soda, two ounces of saltpetre, one-half ounce of cayenne pepper, let it cool, then pour over the beef, packed firmly in a barrel. Let the brine cover the meat.

SALTING DOWN CUCUMBERS FOR PICKLES

Leave half an inch stem on cucumbers, wash them in cold water; immediately pack with salt in layers; salt next to wood; one barrel of salt to five of cucumbers. Fill barrel full, putting salt on top; cut a white board so as to fit inside of barrel; bore half a dozen holes, half inch, through; place it on pickles with a stone on, which should weigh at least twenty-five pounds, so as to keep pickles always in brine. Take off all scum which rises. Keep the barrels in the shade, and in four weeks take off stone, and fill to top, as they will settle some. Put more salt on, then head up, and they are ready for market.

It is best to have two sizes of pickles. (Country Gentleman)

SALTING HAMS

Pack them close in a cask; to one hundred pounds, ten pounds of salt, one-fourth pound saltpetre, and one quart of molasses; dissolve these in sufficient water to cover the hams, and let them stay five weeks. Smoke to taste.

SALTS

When taking salts, try one-third teaspoonful of powdered ginger, or half a teaspoonful of peppermint with the dose. It will act more quickly, and bloating will be prevented.

SAMP

There is not, in the annals of the edibles, a more delicious vegetable substance than this, which is simply corn in its primitive state, divested of the outer hull, and cracked for use. The original method of having it beaten in a mortar was better than the new-fangled processes of preparing it. Of course it must be thoroughly boiled and richly seasoned.

SAMP - CORN

0. The original samp was made of whole grains shelled and thrown into a weak decoction of boiling lye made clean with wood ashes. Only a few minutes were required to crack and loosen the hulls, which peeled off the instant the grains were thrown into clean, cold water, leaving the kernels white as snow and sweeter than the samp which had been run through the water mill. It is very healthy and susceptible of wonderful transformations in the preparation, either as a vegetable or dessert, or served with milk and sugar, as a dainty breakfast dish.

SARATOGA POTATOES

Take white peachblow potatoes, peel and slice very thin with potato slicer; let them stand in cold salt and water for half an hour; dry them with a napkin and fry in boiling hot lard, taking out as soon as they rattle against the spoon; salt while hot.

SARDINE DRESSING

Pound in a mortar until perfectly smooth the yolks of four hard boiled eggs and three sardines freed of bones. Add this to either mayonnaise or cream dressing and you have an excellent fish dressing.

SARDINE SALAD

Arrange about a pint of any cold cooked fish, previously shredded and freed from bones, on a bed of crisp lettuce leaves. Cover the fish with a sardine dressing; over this arrange six sardines split, having the ends meet at the centre. Around the dish place thin slices of lemon and a wreath of parsley or young lettuce leaves.

"SATISFYING" SUPPER DISH

Toast common crackers in the oven until a delicate brown, heat and season well a can of corn. Put crackers and corn on the table in separate dishes and put the corn over crackers as you serve the individual.

SAUCE FOR A FOWL

Stew the neck and the gizzard, with a small piece of lemon peel, in about a cupful of water; then bruise the liver of the fowl with some of the liquor; melt a little good butter, and mix the liver with the gravy from the neck and gizzard with it; let boil a minute or two, and pour into the same tureen.

SAUERKRAUT

Next time you cook sauerkraut put in plenty of water, enough pork to season, and add dumplings of rich biscuit dough rolled thin; thus you will have a toothsome dish.

SAUSAGE ROLLS (A nice supper dish)

Cream together one-half cup butter, one-half cup lard; and add one and one-half cups flour and a little salt. Moisten with sufficient water to make a very stiff paste. Roll out about an eighth of an inch thick and cut into pieces about six inches long and five inches wide. Skin the sausage and put one into each piece of paste. Fold over and wet the edges with water to stick them together, trimming them neatly. Bake thirty minutes. Serve cold.

SAUSAGES

For 25 lbs. of meat chopped fine, use 10 oz. of salt, 2 ½ oz. of pepper, and 2 oz. of sage. These ingredients should be finely powdered and thoroughly mixed with the meat.

SAUSAGES

No. 1: For twenty pounds of meat, use ten ounces of salt, two ounces of sage, one large spoonful of pepper, the same of ginger; cut the meat into strips for the machine, add the seasoning, then grind, and it will be well mixed.

No. 2: For fifty pounds of meat, lean and fat mixed, measure three teacupfuls of salt, four of sage, or two of sage and two of summer savory, two-thirds cup of black pepper, one-half cup of cloves. It is better to try a little by frying to see if it is seasoned to taste. This rule will not make it highly seasoned. With care it can be kept for a year.

SAUSAGE SEASONING

For twenty pounds of meat take ten ounces of salt; three ounces of sage, powdered; a wine glass of black pepper; great spoonful of ginger.

SCALLOPED OYSTERS

Butter a baking dish; fill it with alternate layers of rolled crackers and oysters; over each layer of oysters spread bits of butter and dash pepper - not salt, as it will shrivel them. Heat the liquor of the oysters, add to it one teacupful of cream, season to taste and pour over the oysters. Set in a moderate oven and bake nearly an hour. A famous dish in our state. (Kitty - Maryland)

SCALLOPED OYSTERS

Butter an earthen pudding dish, and fill with alternate layers of crushed crackers and oysters - the first layer should be the crushed crackers - wet them with a mixture of the oyster liquid and milk. Then a layer of oysters, which sprinkle with salt, pepper, and a small bit of butter the size of walnuts. Let the top layer be crumbs, and add a beaten egg to milk to pour over it, and put bits of butter quite quickly over it. Bake about one hour.

SCALLOPED OYSTERS

The scalloped oysters will cost thirty cents. Pound crackers fine, then butter deep dish, put in alternate layers of the crumbs and oysters, having a layer of crumbs on the top. Season them with salt and pepper and some bits of butter. Moisten the whole with milk and one egg. Bake till brown.

SCARLET FEVER

An eminent physician says he cures ninety-nine out of every one hundred cases of scarlet fever by giving the patient warm lemonade with gum-arabic dissolved in it. A cloth wrung out in hot water and laid upon the stomach should be removed as soon as it becomes cool.

SCARLET FEVER

I want to give you a remedy for that much-dreaded scarlet fever, which I know through thorough testing, will cure as well as prevent others taking the disease. Put in a four ounce bottle one grain each of sulphate of zinc and digitalis or foxglove, in powder form; add a teaspoonful of sugar and two spoonfuls of cold water, shake well to dissolve, fill up the bottle with cold water and the mixture is ready for use. The dose for an adult is one teaspoonful every hour. This is harmless and may be given even with the doctor's medicine with

334

perfect safety. With this remedy in the house I would rather my children would have scarlet fever than measles. I get the zinc and digitalis put up in one-grain powders, then I can mix the remedy myself at any time. It is said to be as good for smallpox as for scarlet fever, but I have not tried it in such cases, and cannot speak from experience.

SCARS

Place the ends of two or three fingers on a scar, if it be a small one and on the margin if it be large, and vibrate the surface on the tissue beneath. The surface itself is not to be subjected to any friction; all the motion must be between the integument and the deeper parts. The location of the vibratile motion should be changed every ten of fifteen seconds until the whole scar has been treated, if it be of moderate size. In the course of two or three weeks of faithful treatment the surfaces of the scar of moderate size become more movable, and will begin to form wrinkles, like true skin, when pressed from side to side. All these changes are due to improved nutrition, consequent or better blood circulation; the development of entirely new sets of blood vessels in the cicatricial tissue.

SCORCHED LINEN

When linen has been scorched use the following remedy: Add a quart of vinegar, the juice of half a dozen large onions, about an ounce of soap rasped down, a fourth of a pound of fuller's earth, an ounce of lime and one ounce of pearl ash. Boil the whole until it is pretty thick, and spread some of it upon the scorched part. Allow it to remain until dry, then scrape it off and wash. Two or three applications will restore the linen, unless so much scorched that the fibre is destroyed.

SCOTCH BARLEY BROTH

Take the middle cut of a neck of mutton, put it on to boil, with a quart of water to each pound of meat; put in, while the water is cold, a breakfast cupful of pearl barley; cut up into dice, quite small, turnips, carrots, green onions, or a little leek and cauliflower, in a quantity double that of barley; when the soup is boiling add these, and a few blades of parsley when half-done; let the broth boil two hours; then serve the meat with some of the broth as gravy.

SCOTCH HOTCH-POTCH

Take four pounds, neck and breast of mutton, the latter cut into neat square pieces. Cut into dice, very small, turnips, carrots, onions, cauliflower, and a very little cabbage, in a quantity to fill a quart bowl, put these on together with two quarts of cold water, boil gently for two hours, add a few peas and some blades of parsley. When ready, serve in a tureen, the meat with the rest after seasoning to taste.

SCOTCH PIE

Take pieces of biscuit dough the size of a teacup, and roll into it butter the size of an egg; then roll out a crust for a deep pie plate. Take one cup good milk; two or three spoonfuls of sugar; one spoonful of flour; one of butter cut small; a little cinnamon or nutmeg; cover with another crust, and bake slowly half an hour. Good warm or cold. Jennie.

SCOURING POWDER

Mix equal parts of fine sand, brick dust and wood ashes together and use to scour steel knives and tinware.

SCRAP-BOOK PASTE

Remember that a fine paste for scrap-books can be made from alum-water - a teaspoonful and a half of powdered alum dissolved in enough cold water to make a pint of paste. Pour the water when the alum is all dissolved, on to flour enough to thicken it as thick as common paste, bring it to a boil, stirring all the time, and when it is done add a few drops of oil of cloves. The alum prevents fermentation, and the oil of cloves will prevent or destroy all vegetable mold.

SCURVY

Water cress contains much sulphur and is one of the best remedies for scurvy known. It should be eaten raw with salt.

SEASONING SAUSAGE

For twelve pounds of meat before grinding take a small teacupful of salt, one cup of powdered sage, six even teaspoonfuls of black pepper and a tablespoonful of ginger. Sprinkle over the meat, then mince. Pack as compactly as possible into stone jars; over the top pour melted lard to the depth of one inch. When wanted scrape off the lard and take out the sausage, but be careful always to melt the lard and pour it over the sausage at once.

SERVING ORANGE JELLY

To serve orange jelly, take six handsome oranges (not very large), cut off smoothly a small piece at the top; take out carefully all the inside with a spoon or sharp knife. When the jelly has cooled a little, pour it into the oranges as into cups and set on the ice to harden.

SEWING ON BUTTONS

If the housewife sews on buttons like tailors do, they will stay on and the work will not be harder, either. Tailors double the thread used to sew on buttons, but make a knot, hold the knot in their teeth while they twist the thread, then wax it, and that keeps it twisted. Next they put a pin across the button, and after the buttons are sewed on they remove the pin and wind the thread around under the button several times, making a kind of stem. This makes it more easy to button the garment. The buttons on children's waists should be sewed on in this same way, so that more than one garment can be buttoned to the same waist.

SHABBY WASTE-PAPER BASKETS

To beautify a shabby waste-paper basket that is not broken, cover it with gold or bronze paint and ornament it to suit your fancy. If you wish to make it really fine, cover it with a coat of mucilage and then, while it is still damp, sprinkle rice or sago or barley over it; when it is quite dry, guild or bronze it. Small baskets may be treated and shabby picture frames made "as good as new" in the same way.

SHELLAC

For finishing a bracket shelf or other article made of close grained wood, there is scarcely anything better than shellac, and it is easily made ready. Purchase the bleached, break in small pieces and fill a small bottle to one-fourth its height, and fill up with alcohol. It will be ready for use the next day. Apply with a sponge or piece of cotton. It dries so rapidly several coats can be applied in a short time.

SHORT DOUGHNUTS

Two eggs; two cups milk; one cup sugar; small piece of butter; one small teaspoonful cream tartar; one of soda; salt; nutmeg; flour enough to mould and roll; but not hard.

SHOULDER OF LAMB STUFFED

A shoulder of lamb, forcemeat, seasoning, a few slices of bacon, two onions, a quart of good stock, a bunch of herbs, pease. Take the blade bone out, and fill the place up with forcemeat and sew it up. Put into a stewpan a few pieces of fat bacon, herbs, onions, stock and seasoning, then put in the shoulder and stew very gently for rather more than two hours. Glaze and serve with green pease around it.

SICK HEADACHE

I am making a tea of balm, for sick headache, and it is certainly the finest remedy ever known for that distressing complaint - I take a generous tablespoonful of the leaves, pour over them a half pint of boiling water, cover closely, let stand twenty to thirty minutes, strain and give to the patient to drink.

SICK-ROOM ODORS

Try removing odors from a sick-room by sprinkling coarse ground coffee on a shovelful of burning coals, thrusting this into all corners of the room; or, put some ground coffee in a saucer, place in the center a small piece of camphor-gum and ignite this. As the gum burns, allow sufficient coffee to be consumed with it. The perfume is very pleasant and healthful.

SICK STOMACH DRINK

The following drink for relieving sickness of the stomach was introduced by Dr. Halahan, and is said to be very palatable and agreeable: Beat up one egg very well, say for twenty minutes, then add fresh milk, one pint; water, one pint; sugar to make it palatable; boil, and let it cool; drink when cold. If it becomes curds and whey it is useless.

SILK ARTICLES

Silk articles should not be kept folded in white paper as the chloride of lime used in bleaching the paper will impair the color of the silk.

SILKY HAIR

Dry salt applied every day and brushed into the roots will make the hair silky and cause it to grow. Do not continue but a year, or two at the longest, as it is a strong tonic.

SILVER CAKE

Scald in a bowl of boiling water two ounces of shelled bitter almonds. As you peel off the skins throw each almond into a bowl of ice cold water. When all are blanched, take them out, and wipe them dry on a clean napkin. Put them, one at a time, into a very clean marble mortar, and pound each one separately to a smooth paste, adding, as you pound them, a few drops of strong rosewater, till you have used up a large wine-glass full. As you remove the pounded almonds from the water, lay them lightly and loosely on a plate. When all are done, put them into a very cool place. In a deep earthen pan cut up a pound of fresh butter into a pound of powdered sugar, and with a wooden paddle stir the butter and sugar together till perfectly light. In another pan sift three-quarters of a pound of fine flour, and in a broad, shallow pan beat with small rods the whites only of eighteen eggs, till they are stiff enough to stand alone. Then gradually and alternately, stir into the pan of beaten butter and sugar the flour, the beaten whites of eggs, and the pounded almonds. Give the whole a hard stirring at the last. Transfer it to square tin pans greased with the same butter, and bake it well. When cool, cut into square cakes, and send it to the table on china plates, piled alternately with pieces of golden cake, handsomely arranged. If you ice silver cake, flavor the icing with strong rosewater.

SILVER CAKE

Two cups of sugar, the whites of eight eggs, one-half cup of butter, one cup of milk, three cups of flour, one teaspoonful of soda , and two teaspoonfuls of cream of tartar.

SILVER CAKE

The same as gold cake, using the whites in place of golds of eggs and one-fourth cup of milk.

SILVER CASE

A very pretty case for silver in daily use is made as follows: Take a piece of ticking thirty inches wide and the length of your cupboard; the length to be taken lengthwise of the goods. Turn up one-third for the pocket; stitch it at convenient intervals to the back, making pockets from two to three inches wide and ten inched deep. Bind with braid, and work the strips in any fancy stitch and colors to taste. This is to be tacked between two shelves on the back of the cupboard. For silver to be put away, make the case ten inches wider for a flap at the top, and with a pointed end flap with strings to tie around. For this the division pockets should be narrow, to hold only one spoon, knife or fork. The silver is thus prevented from being scratched, as when you put away in a box.

SILVER CLEANING

To clean silver, first wash to remove all the grease from the silver, then rub with a woolen cloth wet with ammonia and whiting, and polish on the chased and filigree parts with a tooth brush. The whiting is wet with ammonia and made into cakes or boxes, and agents are around selling it for fifty cents a box, that the probability is, cost them ten cents. It is nice to clean glass windows and all kinds of glass ware.

SILVER ORNAMENT CLEANING

To clean frosted (dead) silver ornaments, dissolve a lump of soda in a saucepan of boiling water and place them in it, and leave for a few moments; then add a small piece of yellow soap and rub the articles with a soft toothbrush; when taken out of the water place them in a hot oven, on a brick, until the desired effect is produced.

SILVER PROTECTION

Those who are not so fortunate to have velvet-lined cases for their silver spoons and forks, can protect them in this manner: Take a strip of the heaviest Canton flannel, wide enough so that after laying the spoons and forks on it, the cloth can be folded over them. Then stitch a band of the material to the upper part of it, and fasten, leaving spaces or loops through which to slip the silver.

SIMPLE BEVERAGES FROM FRUIT

The juices of various fruits may be used with water and sugar for making most delicious and wholesome beverages. Put a gallon of water on to boil, cut up one pound of tart apples, each one into quarters, and put them into the water, and boil them until they can be pulped; pass the liquor through a cullender, boil it up again with half a pound of sugar, skim, and bottle for use, taking care not to cork the bottle, and leaving it in a cool place. The apples may be eaten with sugar as a sauce.

SIMPLE DESSERT ━━━━━━━━━━━━━━━━━━━━━━━━━━━━━

Boil half a cup of rice in a pint of salted water. When it has cooked fifteen minutes pour off the water and let the rice steam twenty minutes in the top of the double boiler. Never use a spoon to stir boiled rice if you wish to have kernels distinct. If necessary to touch at all use a fork for the purpose.

The time given to cook the rice is the longest necessary. Try it, and if done before, remove, or it will grow pasty. The time required varies with the seasons, as the drought is supposed to affect it in this way.

Cold rice can be used for this instead of hot, but it is not so nice for dessert, as it is apt to be rather pasty. Make a border on a platter of the rice, put strawberry preserve, or any other sort if preferred, inside, and pile whipped cream on top.

Cream to be whipped stiff enough to stand on hot mixtures such as chocolate, etc., should be good, thick country cream, and should be whipped with the egg beater, which makes it stiffer. It can be sweetened before or after whipping as you choose. The whipped cream of the restaurants is like a charlotte russe mixture, stiffened with a little gelatin usually.

Garnish with bits of jam or candied fruits if you wish to add color. Cherries or green-gages are pretty for this purpose, though simply the jam makes a very tempting-looking dish, as "the class" enthusiastically testified on looking at it. They waxed still more enthusiastic on testing it in the most practical way, that is, with their own spoons, and very few of the "samples" handed about were returned to the waiters.

SIMPLE REMEDIES ━━━━━━━━━━━━━━━━━━━━━━━━━━━

Make onion poultices in case of colds, and see how quickly the trouble is relieved. If baby has a cankered mouth wash several times a day with a solution of boric acid or alum. For fainting spells take three drops of camphor in one-fourth glass of warm water. These simple remedies are all tried and true.

SKELETON LEAVES

They should not be picked when young and tender; June and July are generally the best months to gather them for the purpose; the edges of the leaves should be perfect, also the ribs and veins, which can be ascertained by holding them up to the light. Some of the yellow Autumnal leaves, and dark tinted also with the seed vessels of different plants, can be used with good effect on the grouping.

SKELETONS

Two eggs, three tablespoonfuls of sugar, and one tablespoonful of butter. Flour to make very stiff, roll very thin, and cut in fancy shape.

SKILLET CLEANING

You can clean your skillets, and make them smooth, like new, by placing them on the coals of a wood-fire and burning them, then scraping with an old knife or stick.

SLATE FLOORS - POLISHING

To polish slate floors, use a smooth flat piece of pumice stone, then polish with rotten stone. Washing well with soap and water once a week is usually enough to keep the slates clean, but by adopting the above method, not only do the slates become polished, but any stains are taken out.

SLEEPLESSNESS CURE

If you are suffering from sleeplessness try this very simple and harmless cure. Take a common towel, double it four times and dip in cold water and pin it around the waist with a dry towel on the outside. For croup or sore throat put the towels around the neck and they will give almost instant relief.

SMALL POX REMEDY

The following will cure not only small pox but also scarlet fever. It is harmless when taken by a person in health: Sulphate of zinc, one grain, fox-glove (digitalis), one grain, half a teaspoon of sugar, mix with two tablespoonfuls of water. When thoroughly mixed, add four ounces of water. Take a spoonful every hour. Either disease will disappear in twelve hours. For a child, smaller doses, according to age. If countries would compel their physicians to use this, there would be no need of pest houses.

SMALL SPONGE CAKES

Put six whole eggs into an earthen pan with half a pound of sugar, upon which you have previously rubbed the rind of a lemon; stand the pan in very hot water, keeping its contents well mixed until becoming rather warm, when take it from the water, continuing to whisk until quite cold and thickish; stir in gently half a pound of sifted flour; have ready buttered, and dusted with sugar, about a dozen small sponge cake tins, put a tablespoonful of the mixture into each, shake sugar over, and bake them, in a moderate oven.

SMOKING LAMP

To prevent a lamp from smoking soak the wick in vinegar and dry it thoroughly before you use it.

SMOTHERED CRAB APPLES

Pour two cupfuls of boiling water over half a box of gelatin, stir until dissolved, then add a spoonful of vanilla and one cupful of sugar. When cool stir in the whites of three eggs beaten stiff. In a deep dish have a quantity of preserved crab apples placed, and pour the gelatin custard over. Keep on ice until ready to serve.

SNAILS

Try sprinkling a little salt on those troublesome snails; you will soon be rid of them.

SNOW BALL CAKE

One cup of sugar, half cup of butter, half a cup of sweet milk, 2 cups of flour, the whites of three eggs, one teaspoonful of cream of tartar, half a teaspoonful of soda, flavor with lemon.

SNOW-BALL PUDDING

Two teacups rice, wash and boil until tender. Pare and core (leaving apples whole) 12 large sour apples. Fill the apples with the rice and put it around outside. Tie each one into a separate cloth and drop in boiling water. Serve while hot with cream and sugar or any sauce desired.

SNOW BALLS

One cup of sugar; two eggs; four table spoonfuls of milk; one teaspoonful of cream tartar; one of soda, if the milk is sour; spice to your taste; mix them hard enough to roll out; cut with small cake cutter, and fry in hot lard; then dip them in the white of an egg, and roll in powdered white sugar till white.

SNOW CUSTARD

One-half box of Cox's gelatin; pour over it one pint of boiling water, stir until all is dissolved; add two cups of sugar and the juice of two lemons; when nearly cool add the whites of three eggs; beat all 45 minutes, and pour into a dish to harden.

Sauce: Take the yolks of the three eggs, one pint of milk, sweeten to taste; set in a vessel of hot water, and stir constantly till done. When nearly cool add a little salt, and flavor with vanilla or lemon.

SNOW PIE

Two tablespoonfuls of corn starch, wet the starch in cold water, as for making starch, pour on one pint of boiling water until it gets as thick as jelly, add one cup of sugar, keeping it on the stove till it comes to a boil, stirring all the time, then add the white of one egg, well beaten, and one tablespoonful of lemon; bake the pie crust first as for jelly pies, put the above mixture in and set in a cool place, as it does not stay good for long.

SNOW PUDDING

Take a little more than a third of a package of Cox's gelatin; pour a pint of cold water over it, and let it stand ten minutes; add the juice of one lemon and one cup of white sugar (sweeten and flavor to taste); add a pint of boiling water; stir and beat till worked up to a light froth, adding to it the well-beaten white of the eggs that are used for the soft custard. Do not commence to beat the gelatin till nearly cold; when well frothed up, put it into a mould in a cold place. Have a nice soft custard to pour round it when taken from the mould. It is very nice and a pretty dessert.

SNOW PUDDING

Snow pudding is very nice and should be eaten cold. Pour on to three tablespoonfuls of corn starch dissolved in a little cold water, one pint of boiling water, and the whites of three eggs beaten to a froth; pour into a three pint earthen dish and put into a steamer and steam ten minutes.

Sauce: Beat the yolks of three eggs, add one cup of sugar, one of milk, a piece of butter the size of a walnut; boil a little.

SODA BISCUIT

Two quarts of flour, a teaspoonful of salt, two teaspoonfuls of cream of tartar, mixed together and sifted; a small tablespoonful of butter and one tablespoonful of lard rubbed into the flour; one quart of milk with a teaspoonful of soda dissolved in it. Roll thin and cut with a cake cutter.

SOFT COOKIES

Two cups thin cream; two cups of sugar; three eggs; caraway; flour, sufficient to make as thick as pan-cakes; two even teaspoonfuls of saleratus; drop with a spoon on buttered tins, and bake fifteen or twenty minutes.

SOFT GINGERBREAD

Two cupfuls molasses, one of shortening (either butter or drippings), one cup of boiling water, one tablespoonful of ginger, one of soda, flour to thicken.

SOFT GINGERBREAD

One cup of cream, one cup of molasses, one teaspoonful of ginger, one of saleratus, dissolved in hot water, and a little salt.

SOFT GINGERBREAD

Soft gingerbread, if eaten while fresh and warm, may well take the place of more expensive cake. One egg, one cup of molasses, one-third of a cup of melted butter, one-half cup of sweet milk, one teaspoonful of soda, one teaspoonful of ginger, two and one-half cups of flour, and a little salt, dissolve the soda in very little hot water. Bake in a buttered tin.

SOFT GINGERBREAD

One cup of molasses, 1 of sugar, 1 of butter, 1 of sour milk, 1 teaspoonful of saleratus, and a little salt. Bake in a quick oven.

SOFT GINGERBREAD

Take one cup of molasses, one teaspoonful of soda, one tablespoonful of ginger, half a teaspoonful of salt, one-third to one-half cup of butter or drippings (softened), one cup of milk and three cups of pastry flour. Bake in shallow pans in a moderate oven about thirty minutes.

SOFT GINGER CAKE

One-half cup each of sugar and shortening, two cups of molasses, one cup sweet milk, one tablespoonful ginger, teaspoonful each of salt (unless butter is used for shortening) and soda, one egg, one-half cup chopped raisins or currants, flour to make a stiff batter, and bake in a moderate oven forty-five to fifty minutes.

347

SOFTENING THE HANDS

After cleansing the hands with soap, rub them well with oatmeal while wet.

SOOT WATER FERTILIZER

Soot water is the best fertilizer for pot plants. Put a pound of soot in a piece of cloth and tie it securely. Then drop the bag into a large pan of rain water and let it soak for twenty-four hours. Use the water moderately once or twice a week.

SORE EYES

For sore eyes, dissolve salt and honey together. Wash the eyes in this solution and at night apply a cloth wet with it to the affected parts.

SORE MOUTH - AN EXCELLENT WASH FOR

Take plantain, honeysuckle, sage and rosemary, equal parts, and boil them in sour wine; add thereto a little honey and alum. Wash the mouth with this as often as necessary.

SORE THROAT

Chop onions fine, sprinkle with salt and pepper. Place between thin cloths and bind on throat at night.

SORE THROAT

Place some sulphur in a hot pan, cover it with a tin funnel, put the patient's mouth over the end and inhale the odor.

SORE THROAT GARGLE

Take one teaspoon of cayenne pepper, one teaspoon of salt, one teaspoon of vinegar, and one-half pint of boiling water poured over these, then settle. Gargle the throat every half hour, swallowing some.

SOUP

The value of good soup for food cannot be overestimated. In times of scarcity and distress, when the question has arisen of how to feed the largest number of persons on the least quantity of food, the ailment chosen has always been soup. There are two reasons for this: First, by the addition of water to ingredients used to secure the aid of this important agent in distributing nutrition equally throughout the blood, to await final absorption; and second, we gain that sense of repletion so necessary to the satisfaction of hunger, the facts being acknowledged that the sensation we call hunger is often allayed by the presence of even innutritious substances in the stomach. Good soup is literally the juice of any ingredient from which it is made - the extract of the meat, grains or vegetables composing it. The most economical of soups eaten with bread will invariably satisfy the hunger of the hardest worker. Many soups are better on the day after they are made, provided that they are not warmed too quickly, or left too long over the fire after they have become hot.

SOUP

For soup, take mutton bones cracked; two pounds lean veal from the knuckles, bones broken and meat cut up; two tablespoonfuls of butter rubbed in flour, half cup of raw rice, half cup of milk, one onion chopped, three eggs, minced parsley, salt, pepper, three quarts water; put bones, meat, onion and rice on in the cold water, and cook slowly three hours; strain, rubbing the rice and onion to a pulp through a coarse sieve; season, boil up, skim and stir in parsley and butter; heat the milk, pour upon the beaten eggs, and add to the soup stirring in well; let it almost boil; take from the fire and serve.

SOUP BALLS

Take one pint of sweet milk; when boiling hot stir in dry flour until it is stiff. When cool add one egg and enough flour to allow you to form it into balls; add a pinch of salt. About ten minutes before serving your soup drop the balls in, they will be very light and will not fall after being lifted. (J.A.W.)

SOUP WITHOUT MEAT

To one quart of water add three potatoes, three onions, three turnips, two carrots, a tablespoonful of rice or barley, and salt to taste. Boil it down to one pint, then add a little parsley, chopped fine, about ten minutes before it is to be taken off the fire.

SOUR SPONGE

Lemon juice well rubbed in will sweeten a sour sponge.

SOUSED TRIPE

Cut in pieces the right size to serve at table, put in a deep dish with bits of butter laid over the top, and set in a hot oven one-half to three-quarters of an hour.

SOUTHERN POTATOES

Peel and boil Irish potatoes until tender; when done, drain, mash, season with salt, pepper and a little butter. Mince a large onion very fine and mix well through the potatoes. Put into the oven and brown.

SPANISH RICE DISHES

The rice dishes of Spain are more highly flavored with garlic than those of Italy, but the native palate calls for abundance of this pungent bulb. The rice is washed, boiled and browned in butter, a little garlic being substituted for the onion; then two large ripe tomatoes, a spoonful of grated cheese and plenty of Spanish red pepper or pimiento is added, and the rice simmered until tender in a little broth, sometimes it is served with slices of ham, bacon, sausage, smoked salmon or dried fish, any one of these stewed with the rice. Polle con arroz is made in the same way, morsels of fowl being substituted for the meat, and the seasoning being varied with warm spices.

SPANISH WHITING

Spanish whiting is a good polish for tinware, also for copper, silver, and tea-stained or old looking chinaware, such as cups, saucers and plates that have been tinged or darkened in any way. Dampen a cloth, dip it in the powder, and rub thoroughly, wash off, and your dishes will look like new.

SPICE CAKE

Take 1 ½ cups of molasses, sugar and butter, half a cup of milk, 4 eggs, 1 teaspoonful of soda, 1 teaspoonful each of cinnamon, cloves, nutmeg and mace, 1 cupful each of currants and raisins, five cupfuls of flour sifted before measuring. Frost with 1 cup of sugar allowed to each cake; put into bright tin dish and add 5 tablespoonfuls of sweet milk, stir and boil from 3 to 5 minutes; when nearly cold spread on cake; put in a cool but not damp place, as too much moisture spoils the frosting.

SPICE CAKE

Dark part: Two cups of brown sugar, one of butter, one of molasses and one of milk, yolks of eight eggs and one whole one, one teaspoonful each of cloves, cinnamon and nutmeg, one of cream of tartar, half a one of soda. Beat the yolks light, cream butter and sugar. Add eggs, molasses and other ingredients, flour enough to make rather a stiff batter. Put in the pan alternately a layer of dark and white, ending with the dark. Bake one and one-half hours.

SPICE CAKE

One cup of sugar, one-half cup of molasses, one-half cup of butter, one-half cup of sour milk, two and one-half cups of flour, one teaspoonful of soda, the yolks of four eggs, and one teaspoonful each of cloves, allspice, cinnamon and nutmeg.

SPICED BERRIES

Five quarts of berries, one quart of vinegar, three pounds of sugar, one tablespoonful of cloves, one and one-half tablespoonfuls of cinnamon, one tablespoonful of allspice; put the spices in a bag and boil the berries down pretty thick.

SPICED PLUMS

One pint vinegar, three pounds sugar, seven pounds of plums, a large tablespoonful clove and one of allspice.

SPICED ROUND OF CORNED BEEF

Take a strong twine string and tie it tightly around the round to keep it in good shape, then stick it well with cloves on both sides, squeezing them in as far as possible; rub into also three tablespoonfuls of powdered salt, and then with plenty of fine salt; lay it in a large wooden tray or round vessel that is tight, and every other day turn it well into the brine that drips from it; in ten days, if properly attended to, it will be fit for use.

SPIDER CAKE

Mrs. Parloa's breakfast "spider" cake is made of one and two-thirds of a cup of yellow cornmeal, one-third of a cup of flour, one-quarter of a cup of sugar, a teaspoonful of salt, two well beaten eggs, a cup of sour milk and a cup of sweet milk, into which a scant teaspoonful of soda is stirred. This mixture is beaten vigorously and poured into a hot spider, greased on the bottom and sides with a piece of butter, half the size of an egg. After the cake has been put in the spider a cup of sweet milk is poured in the center, and the whole is baked half an hour.

SPIKENARD-ROOT TEA

I do wish that every expectant mother of our circle would try that tea made of spikenard-root say for two months before the arrival of the wee stranger. I consider it the greatest boon in the world, and I have had plenty of experience. Never an opportunity is lost to tell other mothers about it, believe me - sometimes I am almost tempted to start out on a lecture tour! Just try it, sisters. A mother.

SPINACH

Wash carefully in plenty of cold salt and water, put into a saucepan that will just hold it, put in some salt, and pour over it a pint of boiling water. Cover close, and let it cook slowly twenty minutes. Drain off all the water, and pour over it a gill of scalded cream or a little butter, and it is ready for the table.

SPONGE CAKE

One cup of white sugar; two eggs; one-half cup of cream; one and one-half cup flour; one teaspoonful cream tartar; one-half teaspoonful soda; a little salt; a little lemon or rose water to flavor; bake quick.

SPONGE CAKE

One and one-half cups of white powdered sugar; one and a quarter cups of flour; three eggs; half a cupful of sweet cream; one teaspoonful cream tartar; half a teaspoonful of soda; one teaspoonful of extract of lemon. Bake quick.

SPONGE CAKE

Four eggs, beaten to a froth, with one cup of white sugar; one cup of sifted flour; one bit of salt; don't have oven too hot; do not remove it from the oven too quick, as the secret of sponge cake is in the baking.

SPONGE CAKE

Two eggs, well beaten, one cup of sugar, one and one-half cups of flour, four table-spoonfuls of milk, one tea-spoonful of cream of tartar, one-half tea-spoonful of extract of lemon, salt. E.S.

SPONGE CAKE

Ladies who object to making sponge cake, because beating all the whites of the eggs is tiresome, will find here a rule which obviates that trouble. To three-fourths of a cup of flour, add one teaspoonful of yeast powder. Mix thoroughly with it one cup of sugar. Break into the flour and sugar three eggs, and also add one-half teaspoonful of extract of lemon. Beat all together quickly, remembering not to stir the cake, but beat one way. As soon as small bubbles rise on top, pour into a pan, and bake immediately in a quick oven. This cake will require thirty-five minutes for baking.

SPONGE GINGERBREAD

One cup of sour milk, one cup of molasses, one-half cup of butter, two eggs, one and one-half teaspoonfuls of saleratus, one tablespoonful of ginger, flour to make it as thick as pound cake. Put the butter, molasses and ginger together and make them quite warm, then add the milk, flour and saleratus and bake as soon as possible. I think I never have known the above recipe to fail. Instead of butter, nice fat may be used, even the fat that fries out of sausage.

SPONGE GINGERBREAD

Three eggs; one cup of molasses; one-half cup of sugar; one cup of sour cream; one teaspoonful of soda; a little salt; a teaspoonful of ginger; and three cups of flour. This will make two loaves.

SPRAIN - CURE FOR

Take one tablespoonful of honey, the same of salt, and the white of one egg; beat all well together for at least one hour - or two would be better. Let it stand for an hour. Then anoint the sprained place freely; keep well rolled up with a good bandage.

SPRAIN OR BRUISE

Place plantain-leaves between two folds of muslin, press with a warm iron, and apply to the sprain or bruise, changing as often as they become dry.

SPRAINS - SEVERE

The white of an egg, a tablespoonful of vinegar and a tablespoonful of spirits of turpentine. Mix in a bottle, shake thoroughly, and bathe the sprain as soon as possible after the accident.

SPRING DRINK

Rhubarb, in the same quantities, and done in the same way as apples, adding more sugar, is very cooling.

SPRING LAMB

Ten minutes to a pound will be sufficient for the forequarters; fifteen will be needed for the hindquarter, unless preferred rare, in which case twelve will be enough. Lay in the dripping pan, dash a cup of boiling water over it, and baste after the first twenty minutes, dredging with flour ten minutes before it is done. Where mint sauce is used the gravy need not be sent to the table, but can be made and set aside for use, either with the cold meat or in a mince ragout.

SPOT REMOVER

Warm water in which a teaspoonful of soda, and a tablespoonful of Epsom salts have been dissolved, will lighten moth and liver spots; after using, rub in cold cream.

SPRUCE BEER

As the season is here when pleasant summer drinks, free from alcoholic influence, are frequently brewed by the housewife, or the well brought-up daughters, who are taught a little of everything in the way of household duties - we append the following receipts, which are claimed to be excellent:

1. Take three gallons of water, of blood warmth, three pints of molasses, a tablespoonful of essence of spruce, and the like quantity of ginger - mix well together, with a gill of yeast; let stand overnight, and bottle in the morning. It will be in good condition to drink in twenty-four hours. It is a palatable, wholesome beverage.
2. Those who prefer mead have only to substitute honey for

the molasses named above, and for one-third the ginger use allspice. Half the quantity of yeast will be sufficient, and the bottling should occur the second day instead of the next morning. It will be fit to drink in four days after being bottled, and will keep for many weeks. A small quantity of alcohol is formed during the fermentation, and this prevents the acetous fermentation so common to spruce beer. The essence of spruce is of course left out in the making of mead. The alcohol formed from the fermentation of honey, resemble that found in metheglin, while the alcohol from the fermentation of molasses is rum. Those who imagine that they can make either spruce beer or mead without forming any alcohol are mistaken.

3. Prepare a five or ten gallon keg, in proportion to the size of the family - draw a piece of coarse book-muslin over the end of the faucet that is inserted into the keg, to prevent its choking, a good tight bung, and near to that a gimlet hole, with a peg to fit it tight.

4. Receipt for five gallons. One quart of sound corn, put into the keg, with half a gallon of molasses; then fill with cold water to within two inches of the bung. Shake well, and in two or three days it will be fit for use. Bung tight.

If you want spruce flavor, add one teaspoonful of essence of spruce - lemon, if lemon is preferred - ginger, or any flavor you prefer. The corn will last to make five or six brewings; when it is exhausted, renew it. When the beer passes from the vinous to the acetous fermentation, it can be corrected by adding a little more molasses and water. This is a simple cheap beverage, costing about three cents a gallon. After the beer becomes ripe, it ought to be kept in a cool place, to prevent it from becoming sour before it is exhausted.

SPRUCE BEER ━━━━━━━━━━━━━━━━━━━━━━━━━━━━━━

Allow an ounce of hops and a spoonful of ginger to the gallon of water. When well boiled, strain it, and put in a pint of molasses, and half an ounce or less of the essence of spruce; when cool, add a teacupful of yeast, and put into a clean, tight cask and then let it ferment for a day or two, then bottle it for use. You can boil the sprigs of spruce-fir in place of the essence.

SPRUCE BEER

Hops, two ounces; sassafras, in chips, two ounces; water, ten gallons. Boil half an hour, strain and add brown sugar, seven pounds; essence of spruce, one ounce, pimento ground, one-half ounce: put the whole in a cask and let cool; then add one pint of yeast, let stand twenty-four hours, fine and bottle it.

SQUASH AND RICE SOUP

Pare and slice a quart of summer or winter squash, and boil it tender in two quarts of broth or water, with two large onions peeled and sliced, six cloves, ten peppercorns, or a quarter of a saltspoonful of ground pepper, and two sprigs of parsley or celery. In the meantime put half a teacupful of well-washed rice in two quarts of boiling water with a teaspoonful of salt, and boil it until the grains begin to crack, which will be in about half an hour; then drain in a colander. As soon as the vegetables are tender rub them through a sieve with a potato masher, put them into the soup kettle again with the liquor in which they were boiled, and the rice; see if the soup is seasoned palatably, adding enough broth or water to make three quarts of soup, and serve it as soon as it is hot.

SQUASH BISCUIT

Take 1 cup of sifted boiled squash, 3 cups of sifted flour, 1 tablespoonful of sugar, 2 teaspoonfuls of cream tartar, 1 teaspoonful of soda and 1 of butter; mix the squash and flour well together, then dissolve the soda in a little hot water, and fill the cup with milk, stirring the soda well into it. Pour the milk over the flour and stir it in well, adding more milk if needed, to form a stiff batter. I have the gem pans piping hot, and put in the batter, nearly filling the pans, and bake in a quick oven. Eaten warm with butter and maple syrup they are delicious.

SQUEEZING LEMONS

More juice can be extracted from a lemon by heating it slightly than if it be squeezed cold.

SQUIRREL ON TOAST

Mince the meat of a cold squirrel very fine, chop an equal quantity of onions and mushrooms, and stew them until tender with a tablespoonful of butter, a cupful of cold gravy and a little salt and pepper. When the vegetables are tender put in the mince; let it boil up once, and serve it immediately on toast.

SQUIRREL SOUP

Cut up two young squirrels and put them in a pot with five quarts of cold water; season with salt and pepper. Boil until the meat is well done, then remove it from the liquor and cut up in very small pieces. Put in the soup one-fourth pound of butter mixed with a little flour, and pint of cream; milk will do, but it is not as good. Throw in the cut meat, and just before you serve, add the beaten yolks of two eggs and a little parsley.

STARCH FOR CLOTHES

For starch that will not stick, turn white, or freeze out of the clothes, try this: Put starch in a granite dish, add a tablespoonful each of kerosene and salt and a little cold blue-water, stir until smooth, then add boiling water and stir until well cooked. Thin to the proper consistency while hot.

STEAMED INDIAN PUDDING

Two cups of Indian meal; one-half cup of molasses; two cups of milk; a handful of flour; a little saleratus; a cup of dried apples soaked and chopped; spice to taste; mix thin, and steam two hours.

STEAMED PUDDING

One cupful chopped suet or a half-cupful butter, one cupful sweet milk, two-thirds cupful molasses, a teaspoonful of salt, if you use suet; if butter, not any salt will be needed; a teaspoonful soda, a cupful chopped raisins, three cupfuls flour; steam three hours. Sauce: Stir a tablespoonful of flour into two tablespoonfuls of melted butter till smooth; add a cupful and a half of boiling water and let it cook awhile; add a half cupful of sugar and two tablespoonfuls of vinegar, nutmeg and lemon; boil up and serve.

STEAMED PUDDING

A cupful of suet chopped fine, a cupful of sour milk, the same of molasses and fruit, four cupfuls of flour, a teaspoonful and a half of soda, a teaspoonful each of salt, cinnamon and cloves; steam three hours and serve with sour sauce, or with butter.

STEAMED PUDDING

One cup of new milk; one cup of molasses; one cup of finely chopped suet; one cup of raisins or currants; one-half teaspoonful of soda; a little salt, and flour to make it like soft gingerbread; steam three hours; eat with sauce.

STEAMED PUDDING

One cup of molasses; one and one-half pints of lukewarm water; one large teaspoonful of soda; a little salt; flour enough to make as stiff as possible; steam two hours and one-half. To be eaten with sweet sauce.

STEAMED PUDDING

Take two cups of sour milk; one-half cup of sour cream; one-half cup of sugar or molasses; one cup of raisins (or dried berries); one teaspoonful of saleratus; spice to your taste, and add a little salt; stir in flour until it is as thick as common gingerbread; steam one hour and a half. To be eaten with sour sauce or sweetened cream.

STEEL KNIFE CLEANING

Steel knives may be cleaned and brightened by rubbing with a raw potato, cut in two, and rubbed in brick dust.

STEEL KNIFE PROTECTION

Steel knives which are not in general use may be kept from rusting if they are dipped in a strong solution of soda - one part water to four of soda - then wipe them dry, roll them in flannel, and keep them in a dry place; or the steel may be covered well with mutton tallow, then wrapped in paper and then put away.

STEWED CORN

Cut the corn from the cobs; boil the cobs for ten or fifteen minutes; then take them out and put the corn into the same water. When it is tender put into a quart of corn a pint of milk and three well beaten eggs, with butter, salt and pepper to taste.

STEWED PEARS

If small and ripe, cut out the blossom end without paring or coring. Put into a saucepan with water enough to cover them, and stew until tender, add one cup of sugar for every quart of pears, and stew all together for ten minutes; take out the pears and lay them in a covered bowl to keep warm; add to the syrup a little ginger and a few clove; boil fifteen minutes longer and pour over the fruit hot.

STEWED POTATOES

Peel and cut into small, uniform pieces as many potatoes as may be needed. Have ready enough boiling water (slightly salted) to cover them; boil until done. Skim them out of the water into a dish and pour milk gravy over them (made of a pint of boiled milk, into which has been stirred a tablespoonful of flour previously dissolved in a little cold milk). Cold boiled potatoes can be served in the same way.

STEWED RABBIT

Cut the rabbit up in nice-sized pieces, wash well and dry. Then fry nice brown. Take two large onions, slice very thin, and fry also, and dredge with flour. Put all in a saucepan with pepper, salt and some good stock or water, with herbs, mixed, carrot and turnip, but, if possible, the stock, as only the onions are served with it. Let it stew gently two hours, adding a little catsup ten minutes before serving. Stir all together.

STEWED SHOULDER OF MUTTON

The shoulder must not be too fat. Bone it, tie it with a cloth, and boil for two hours and a half; then take it up, put a little cold butter over it and strew it thickly with bread-crumbs, parsley, thyme pepper, and salt, all properly mixed. Let it remain in the oven half an hour, so as to brown it perfectly. Serve with lumps of currant jelly on the top and gravy or spice round the dish.

STEWED TRIPE

See that the tripe is washed very white; cut up in pieces, and put them in a stew-pan with two quarts of water, and pepper and salt to taste. Let boil until quite tender, which will take about two hours and a half, or perhaps longer. Have some white onions boiled until quite tender; then turn them out in a colander to drain; then mash them, putting them back into your sauce-pan (which you have previously wiped out) with a piece of butter, two tablespoonfuls of cream or milk, a grating of nutmeg and a little salt. Sprinkle in a little flour, set the pan on the fire, keeping it well covered, and give it one boil. Place at the bottom of a dish two slices of buttered toast, cut in pieces, and put the tripe over it.

STOCK

When one has only materials enough for a little stock, it still pays to make it. It is very easy to cover the findings from steak, chops or chicken, one or all three, with cold water, and allow this to simmer two or three hours. If the result is not more than a cupful of stock, even that will materially add in nourishment and flavor to a can of soup or in the preparation of stews, gravies and vegetables.

STOMACH SICKNESS

In case of sickness at the stomach, make a paste of a generous teaspoonful of ground mustard, and half-teaspoonful each of ginger, cinnamon and cloves; moisten with vinegar, spread on a thin cloth, fold one end of the cloth over the paste, and apply to the stomach. This will nearly always settle the sickness. In case of diarrhea or inflammation, the same pack, wet with any kind of liquor, gives great relief.

STOP THE CRACKS

There is a timely and valuable suggestion. A very complete filling for open cracks in floors may be made by thoroughly soaking newspapers in paste made in one pound of ordinary flour, three quarts of water and a tablespoonful of alum. These ingredients should be thoroughly boiled and mixed, the final mixture to be about as thick as putty, and it will then harden like papier mache, and may also be used for molds for various purposes.

I use an old crock or pail, tear the paper into small bits, cover with hot water and keep warm; this will digest the paper, making a smooth body, not too thin. To one gallon I add one-half cup alum and a flour paste, one cup of flour as thick as can be made and stirred in. The alum keeps insects out. I use this in many places, sometimes add a little cement to stop rats. Make as dry as you can work.

For fine work it may take a week to digest the paper. This filling can be used in many ways. An old summer kitchen with broad cracks was filled. When hard was covered with cloth tacked on, papered over with a pretty wallpaper and was a thing of beauty. ("Michigan Woman")

STOVE CARE

To keep stoves from rusting, while standing away through the warm weather, grease them well with mutton-tallow, and before putting them up in the autumn, put them in the yard and build a fire in them, which will burn off the tallow. Wash them with soapsuds and then polish them. This is troublesome but effectual.

STOVE PIPE RUST

A little raw linseed oil rubbed upon a stove pipe will stop rust; cover the place with stove polish and the pipe will look as good as new.

STOVE POLISH

Mix your stove-polish with soap-suds to the consistency of thick cream and add a teaspoonful of sugar. This will stick and make the stove shine like new dollars, no matter how white it was when you started.

STOVE POLISH

Put into a bottle one tablespoonful each of powdered alum and brown sugar, two tablespoonfuls of good, dry stove-blacking and one pint of vinegar. Shake the bottle well before using, and apply the liquid with a cloth, when the stove is slightly warm, polishing with a woolen rag. I find this does not burn as readily as does clear blacking. Black the stove twice a week, and "between times" rub it well with a newspaper, and it will always look clean and bright.

STOVE POLISH

A teaspoonful of brown sugar added to the prepared stove polish will make it stick better.

STRAWBERRIES STEWED FOR TARTS

Make a syrup of one pound of sugar and a teacup of water; add a little white of eggs; let it boil, and skim it until only the foam arises; then put in a quart of berries free from stems and hulls; let them boil till they look clear and the syrup is quite thick. Finish with fine puff paste.

STRAWBERRY CREAM

One quart of fresh strawberries, one pint of cream, one cup of sugar, half cup of boiling water, half cup of cold water, half package of gelatin. Soak the gelatin two hours in the cold water, mash the berries and sugar together and let them stand one hour, strain the juice from the berries as free from seeds as possible; dissolve the gelatin by adding the boiling water, and strain it on the juice; whip the cream to a froth in a basin, which should be set in a pan of ice water; beat until as thick as soft custard, then add to fruit juice, stir well, and put in moulds to harden; serve with cream and sugar.

STRAWBERRY JELLY

Express the juice from the fruit through a cloth, strain it clear, weigh and stir to it an equal proportion of the finest sugar, dried and reduced to a powder; when this is dissolved, place the preserving pan over a very clear fire, and stir the jelly often until it boils; clear it carefully from scum, and boil it quickly from fifteen to twenty minutes. This receipt is for a moderate quantity of the preserve; a very small portion will require much less time.

STRAWBERRY JELLY

Crush the fruit and strain through a coarse linen bag. To a pint of juice allow one pound of granulated sugar. Boil the juice ten minutes, skimming as necessary, then add the sugar and boil ten minutes longer. Pour hot into glasses and stand in the sun - protecting from insects - the sunny part of two days.

STRAWBERRY PUDDING

Cream, a cup of sugar and a tablespoonful of butter; add the beaten yolks of five eggs and two cups of fine bread-crumbs soaked in a quart of sweet milk. Flavor with lemon or vanilla. Pour into a deep pudding dish and bake until the custard is "set". Roll a pint of nice strawberries in powdered sugar, spread over the pudding and cover with a meringue made of the beaten whites and three tablespoonfuls of powdered sugar. Return to the oven until the top is delicately browned.

STRAWBERRY-WATER ICE

Strain the strawberries through a hair-sieve over a pan or basin; add to the juice clarified sugar-water and lemon juice to the taste.

STRING BEANS

Gather them while young enough to break crispy; break off both ends; and string them; break in halves and boil in water with a little salt, until tender; drain free from water, and season with butter.

STUFFED CORN BEEF

Take a piece of well corned rump or round, nine or ten pounds; make several deep cuts in it; fill with a stuffing of a handful of soaked bread, squeezed dry, a little fat or butter, a good pinch of cloves, allspice, pepper, a little finely chopped onion, and a little marjoram or thyme; then tie it up tightly in a cloth and saturate it with vinegar; boil about three hours.

STUFFED TOMATOES

Choose a dozen large, round tomatoes, cut them off smooth at the stem end, take out the seed and pulp; take a pound of lean steak and two slices of bacon, chop them fine with the inside of the tomatoes, season with finely chopped onions fried, a dessertspoonful of salt, half a teaspoonful of white pepper, as much cayenne pepper as you can take on the end of a knife, and a tablespoonful of finely-chopped parsley; add four rolled crackers and, if too thick, thin with stock, water or cold gravy. Fill the tomatoes with this, force meat, packing tight; sift cracker crumbs over the top and bake for an hour in a moderate oven.

STUFFING FOR TURKEYS, FOWL AND VEAL

Chop finely, half a pound of suet, and with it mix the same quantity of bread crumbs, a large spoonful of chopped parsley, nearly a teaspoonful of thyme and marjoram, mixed, one-eighth of a nutmeg, some grated lemon peel, salt and pepper; and bind the whole with two eggs. A teaspoonful of finely-shred shallot, or onion, may be added at pleasure.

STUTTERING

Try the following remedy for stuttering: When you talk, keep your thumb and forefinger in motion, by opening and closing as you would do if you were making "shadow pictures" of duck or chicken in the act of quacking or cackling. Keep them constantly in motion, and rather rapidly. This simple plan has been tried with success. Please let us know if it helps you. Rosalia.

SUBSTITUTE FOR ROOT BEER

A good substitute for root beer may be more easily made by using the oils or essences instead of the roots and bark. For instance, put an ounce each of the essence of spruce and sassafras, and half an ounce of the essence of wintergreen in two quarts of boiling water. Put in two pounds of sugar and enough more boiling water to make three gallons, and when lukewarm add two beaten eggs, and half a cup of yeast. Mix well and strain; let it stand two or three days, then bottle and cork, or put into a keg.

SUCCOTASH

For succotash, take a quart of shelled beans before they get hard and put them in cold water; put over the fire and let them come to a boil, then throw in the colander, letting the water runoff; put them again into cold water, with a small lump of soda, and let them boil up a minute or two; empty them again into the colander; then put them into fresh water, a little more than enough to cover them. Let them simmer or boil an hour or more. Cut the corn from eight ears of corn, and scraping the pulp off, which adheres to the cob, add the corn to the boiling beans, and let them boil together half an hour, or according to age of the corn. As the water becomes used up, be careful it does not burn at the bottom, as the richness of the dish depends much upon retaining all the water the vegetables have been boiled in. Changing the water twice takes away a quality of the beans which make them harmful to some people. Add butter and salt to taste.

SUCCOTASH

Take a pint of shelled lima beans (green), wash, cover with hot water, let stand five minutes, pour off, place over fire in hot water and boil fifteen minutes, have ready corn from six ears, and add to the beans; boil half an hour, add salt, pepper and two tablespoonfuls of butter. Be careful in cutting down the corn not to cut too deep; better not cut deep enough and then scrape; after corn is added watch carefully to keep it from scorching.

SUCCOTASH

Cut the grain from ten full-grown tender ears of corn, mix them with one quart of shelled Lima beans, boil them until tender in plenty of well-salted water, boiling, and then drain them in a colander; meantime beat two eggs smooth, put them in a saucepan with the succotash and two tablespoonfuls of butter, season it to taste with salt and pepper, and heat it thoroughly; serve in a covered dish. A cup of sweet cream is sometimes used instead of the eggs and butter: or a small piece of salt pork or bacon is boiled in the succotash.

SUCKING PIG BAKED

Place in a dish in which it is to be baked (after preparing it exactly in the same way as for roasting), and lay thickly on it white of an egg, which has been slightly beaten. It will require no further attention. Send it with a quarter of a pound of butter for basting.

SUET PUDDING

One pint of milk, one pint of syrup, half pound of raisins, half pound of currants, half pound of suet; add prepared flour as stiff as pound cake. Spice to suit taste.

SUET PUDDING

1 cup full of molasses, 1 cup full of suet cut fine, 1 cup full of milk, 1 teaspoon of soda, 1 teaspoon of salt, 1 teaspoon of cinnamon, ½ teaspoon of cloves, 1 teaspoon of ginger, flour. Steam 2 hours.

SUET PUDDING

Take one teacupful of chopped beef suet, one of molasses, one of milk, two of raisins, and three and a half of flour; one teaspoonful of soda, one of cream tartar and one of salt. Mix all carefully; give a good beat up; tie tight in a well floured cloth, leaving room for it to swell; put it into hot water, and boil hard for three hours, occasionally turning it over. For the sauce take one pound of brown sugar and ½ pound of butter; mix them and stew about ten minutes, stirring all the time; take it off and let it cool; then stir in two eggs which have been beaten; put it back on the fire; and stir it all the time; let it stew about five minutes; take it off and set it aside to cool, then stir in a wineglass of wine and a grated nutmeg; warm it up in time for your pudding. This is a No. 1 sauce for any kind of a pudding.

SUGAR CANDY

Six cups white sugar, one-half cup butter, two tablespoonfuls vinegar, one-half teaspoonful soda, one cup cold water, vanilla flavoring. Pour water and vinegar upon the sugar and let them stand, without stirring, until the sugar is melted. Set over the fire and boil fast until it "ropes". Put in the butter; boil hard two minutes longer, add the dry soda, stir it in and take at once from the fire. Flavor when it ceases to effervesce. Turn out on greased dishes and pull with the tips of your fingers until it is white.

SUGAR CORN STEW

Take any of the sweet varieties which have been previously dried in the sun for winter use, soak it over night, and stew until the grains expand to their former size. Season with butter, pepper, salt and a little more sugar if desirable and serve as a vegetable.

SUGAR GINGERBREAD

One cup of butter; two cups of sugar; two eggs; two teaspoonfuls of cream of tartar; one teaspoonful of saleratus; one teaspoon ginger; one-third of a cup of sweet milk; flour enough to roll out thin; bake quick.

SUGAR SNAPS

One cup butter, two cups sugar, four cups flour, one egg, half cup water, and a half teaspoon soda, with twice as much cream of tartar; roll very thin.

SUGAR SNAPS

One cup of butter, two cups of sugar, three eggs, one teaspoonful of soda, one tablespoonful of ginger, flour to roll.

SUMMER DRINK

Cold water is a luxury which would be irreplaceable if denied us, but there are occasions when it's too free use proves injurious, and when other harmless liquids may be substituted for it with benefit. For persons working in harvest fields or exposed for a length of time to the heat of the sun, a cool, unintoxicating drink, but one slightly stimulating in its effect is to be preferred. Oatmeal water is recommended as being highly nutritious.

SUMMER DRINK

Six quarts boiling water poured upon one pint of molasses; let it stand until about milk warm, then add one pint of good yeast, and two tablespoonfuls of checkerberry or any other essence. It will work in a few hours. Bottle and stand it upon ice, and you will have a drink good enough for anyone. Yours &c., Jennie.

SUMMER SQUASH

Gather the summer squashes when young and tender. If the scallop, the seeds will do no harm. Cut it in quarters, and boil in a bag until tender. Squeeze out all the water, and season with salt and butter; pepper can be added at the table.

SUNSTROKE - TREATMENT OF

The new treatment of this terrible complaint by heat is being received with favor. Recently, Dr. F. G. Herron, one of the city physicians of Cincinnati, Ohio, tried it in two cases with success. Instead of cold water he applied warm water to the head, in cloths, the water as hot as the skin could bear without injury. The effect was very striking, restoring the patient to consciousness very soon. Then, as a stimulant, he administered Liquor Ammoniac Acetates. In this city it was tried in a number of cases, with it is said, excellent results.

SUPERFLUOUS HAIR

Try peroxide of hydrogen for superfluous hair; it lightens it, and is said to kill the roots in time.

SUPERIOR CUCUMBER PICKLES

To every five gallons of strong vinegar add a pint of pure alcohol, a lump of alum the size of a small walnut, and a handful each of ground or pounded pepper, cloves, cinnamon and allspice. Pepper alone may be used if preferred, or the spices can be omitted altogether, but they add greatly to the flavor of the pickles. A few pieces of horseradish are also an improvement. The alum must not be omitted, as it hardens the pickles. Put the cucumbers right in the barrel, keg or crock containing the prepared vinegar each day, as they are gathered. If necessary to wash them do not rub them. Lay a board on them with sufficient weight to keep the pickles under the vinegar, and allow no scum to form. Cucumbers should be cut late in the evening, or early in the morning, and handled carefully. We always follow the above mode, and many have declared our pickles the best they ever tasted.

SUPERIOR DOUGHNUTS

Take two cups sugar; one and one-half cups sweet milk; five eggs; three spoonfuls of butter; three teaspoonfuls of baking powder; salt and flavor to suit the taste. Mix as soft as possible, roll out, cut in proper sizes and drop into hot lard; when removed from lard and partly cooled dip in powdered sugar.

SUPERIOR OMELET

Beat six eggs very light, the whites to a stiff froth that will stand alone, the yolks to a smooth thick batter. Add to the yolks a small cupful of milk, pepper and salt to season properly. Lastly stir in the whites lightly; have ready in a hot frying pan a good lump of butter, when it hisses pour in your mixture and set over a clear fire, do not stir it but contrive as the eggs set to slip a broad-bladed knife under the omelet to guard against burning at the bottom. It should cook in eight or ten minutes at the most. When done lay a hot plate bottom upwards on the pan, turn it over and bring the browned side up. To be eaten hot.

SWAMPSCOTT BUNS

Buns are easily made and are excellent when this recipe is followed: Take one cup of yeast, one cup of sugar, one cup of butter, three cups of sweet milk; mix at night, omitting the butter and sugar; make a very soft sponge, let it stand till morning and then add the butter and a pinch of soda and the sugar; let it rise again until it is very light, then knead lightly and put into the tins. When light enough bake in a moderate oven till the top is dark brown; while hot rub over the top with a little bit of butter, this makes the crust tender and smooth. If you choose you can add English currants, and when brought to the table warm they are said to resemble the wonderful tea cakes of Mrs. Southey, which Shelley, having once tasting them, wished his wife to serve for supper ever after.

SWEDISH ROLLS

One pint of milk, which has been boiled and set to cool until it is lukewarm; one-half cup of butter creamed with one-quarter cup of sugar; add to this the whites of two eggs beaten stiff: stir the butter, sugar and egg into the milk , add one-half a cake of compressed yeast, dissolved in a little lukewarm water; stir in seven or eight cups of flour, making it just stiff enough to work easily with the hands; knead until it is smooth and well mixed together, and set away to rise; when well risen and ready to shape, roll out until the dough is one-half an inch thick; spread with sugar, spice, grated lemon and currants, and roll up like a jellyroll; cut in inch slices, rise again and bake. If you prefer a plain roll, you can have the White Mountain roll by using the first part of the receipt; then when the dough is risen, simply shape into rolls, rise and bake.

SWEEPING DUSTY CARPETS

When you have dusty carpets to sweep, take a pan of water and pour in a little coal oil. Dip the broom in this frequently, shaking off all the water possible.

SWEET APPLE CAKES

Five cups of sour milk; five cups of corn meal; two and a half spoonfuls of soda; half a cup of molasses; a teaspoonful of salt, and about two quarts of sliced sweet apples. It requires a very hot oven, and a good deal of baking.

SWEET CORN, TO DRY

Have tried putting down sweet corn with salt, and would say to all, do not do it, for when you have washed or cooked it enough to get the salt out there is no goodness in it. I think there is no better way than to take it when just right for eating, first thing in the morning, cut from the cob with a sharp knife, then scrape the cob, being careful not to cut into it at all, or it will spoil the corn by making it taste hard and unpleasant; put on tins and plates in a pretty hot oven, stirring often at first, and as it dries having less fire. By night mine is almost dry enough, and by the next day can be put in bags and hung up for winter use. In winter take what is needed for use, wash in two or three waters, put to soak in clean water, and when soft enough cook fifteen minutes in same water, and put in cream or milk, and season. It needs to soak four or five hours, or in cold weather can soak all night.

SWEET CORN, TO PRESERVE

Boil the corn on the ear from three to five minutes, then slice off, being careful not to cut too close to the cob, pack down in a stone jar, allowing three pints of corn to one pint of salt, put in layers. When wanted for use, soak overnight to freshen. Corn put up in this way late in the season, will keep nice and fresh all winter.

SWEET FLAG CANDY

This sweetmeat is made from the roots of the sweet flag by washing and slicing them fine, then placing them in a porcelain kettle with enough cold water to cover them, and slowly heating it over the stove or fire until the water boils. If the candy is to be used rather as a sweetmeat than a medicine, the roots should be treated four or five times this way, each time pouring off the water. To each two cupfuls of the boiled roots add a cupful and a half of white sugar, then water sufficient to cover them, and allow the whole to simmer slowly on the stove till the water has quite boiled away. The candy is then to be emptied out on buttered plates, and stirred frequently till dry.

SWEET PEACH PICKLES

To a pint of vinegar add one cup of sugar, with clove or other spices as liked. Pare a sufficient number of peaches to be covered by the vinegar, put them in a granite preserving-kettle, let come to a boil, pour into fruit jars and seal. Jessie.

SWEET PICKLE

Take green tomatoes and slice them thin and soak in weak salt water

12 hours. Take them out and put them into weak vinegar and soak 12 hours more. Then take good vinegar and one pound of sugar to every quart of vinegar. Put in your tomatoes and boil until soft, then take them out and put spice such as you like into the liquor and boil until thick, then pour it hot on the tomatoes. If your spice is ground tie it up in a rag. (One ounce of spice to a gallon of vinegar.)

SWEET PICKLED CUCUMBERS

Peel the cucumbers, steam as soft as liked and let stand overnight in a weak brine. In the morning drain and put on vinegar enough to cover and let stand overnight; again in the morning drain. Take to one pint of vinegar, three pounds of sugar and one ounce of cassia buds. I have kept them two years, and the last were just as good as the first. Do not use cloves or cinnamon in sweet pickles.

SWEET PICKLES

Take ripe cucumbers, pare them and cut out the seeds, cut in strips and soak in weak brine twenty-four hours; then put them in vinegar and water and soak twenty-four hours; then put them in sweetened vinegar the same as for any sweet pickles, and cook until tender. I take to a quart of vinegar three pounds of coffee sugar, a teaspoonful of ground cinnamon tied in a cloth, also a few whole cloves, and boil all together.

SWEET PICKLES

Eight pounds of fruit, four pounds of best brown sugar, one quart of vinegar, and one cup of mixed whole spices, stick of cinnamon, cassia buds, allspice and cloves; less of the latter than the former. Tie the spices in a bag and boil with the vinegar and sugar. Skim well; then add the fruit. Cook ten minutes, or till scalded and tender. Skim out the fruit and put into stone jars. Boil the syrup five minutes longer and pour over the fruit. The next day pour off the syrup and boil down again, and do this for three mornings. Keep the bag of spices in the syrup.

SWEET SPICED CRAB APPLES

Select large ones, cut out the blows. One pint of vinegar, one-half pint of water, five pounds of sugar, one tablespoonful each of whole cloves, stick cinnamon, whole allspice, and one-half teacup of mustard seed. Cook the syrup a few minutes. Put in a few apples at a time, skim out as soon as soft into a jar, then turn the syrup over all. For one peck of apples. I also can crab apples as I do strawberries, or preserve them whole, pound for pound.

SYRUP OF CURRANTS

Pick ripe currants, and put them into a stew pan over the fire, so that they get hot and burst; press them through a sieve, and set the liquid in a cool cellar for thirty-six hours; then strain it through cloths, sweeten with loaf sugar, and bottle for use. The juice of cherries and raspberries may be prepared as above. The syrup, mixed with spring water, makes a refreshing summer drink.

TABLE LINEN

Table linen should not be stretched, but ironed when quite damp with hot irons until dry; if not damp enough when ironed, it will be too limp.

TABLE LINENS

Tepid water with a little borax dissolved in it is good to wash colored table linens in. Nice tablecloths and napkins should not be allowed to become much soiled, so that they will require vigorous rubbing with soap or in hot water.

TABLE SALT

A little corn starch, or even flour, sifted into table salt will keep it from collecting dampness, even in moist weather.

TAKING INK SPOTS OUT OF LINEN

Dip the ink spots in melted tallow; rub until the tallow comes out, and the ink will come out with it.

TAKING RUST OFF OF STEEL

Cover the steel well with sweet oil, and let it remain there for two or three days; then use unslacked lime finely powdered, and rub with it until all the rust disappears.

TANNING A LAMB-SKIN WITH THE WOOL ON

Make a strong soap-suds, using hot water; when it is cold, wash the skin in it, carefully squeezing it between the hands to get the dirt out of the wool; then wash the soap out with clean cold water; next, dissolve alum and salt, of each half a pound in a little hot water, which put into a tub of cold water sufficient to cover the skin, and let it soak in it over night or twelve hours; now hang the skin over a pole to drain; when well drained spread or stretch carefully on a board to dry. It need not be tacked if drawn out several times with the hand while drying. When yet a little damp, sprinkle pulverized saltpetre and alum (an ounce each mixed together) on the flesh side, rubbing it in well. It is now to hang in the shade two or three days, the flesh side in, until perfectly dry. When entirely dry, scrape the flesh side with a blunt knife to remove any scraps of flesh. Trim off all projecting points, and rub the flesh side with pumice or rotten stone, and with the hands. Prepared in this way, it is white and beautiful, suitable for a door mat, and also nice for the feet in a sleigh or wagon in cold weather.

TANNING SKINS

An old trapper gives the following process for tanning skins with the fur on. Take two parts each of alum and salt, and one part saltpetre, all well pulverized. When the flesh side of the skin has been cleaned of fatty and other adhering matter, sprinkle it freely, enough to make it white, with the mixture. Fold in the edges and roll up the skin. Let it remain for three or four days; then wash, first with clear water and then with soap and water. It should be pulled in various directions as it is drying, to make it soft and pliable.

TANNING SKINS

An excellent plan for tanning any kind of skins with the fur on is to proceed as follows: Cut off all the useless parts, soak the skins in order to soften it, then remove the fatty matter from the inside and soak the skin in warm water for an hour. Next mix equal parts of borax, saltpetre and Glauber salts (sulphate of soda), in the proportion of about ½ ounce of each for each skin, with sufficient water to make a thin paste. Spread this mixture with a brush over the inside of the skin, applying more on the thicker parts than on the thinner; double the skin together, flesh side inwards, and place in a cool place. After standing 24 hours, wash the skin clean, and apply, in the same manner as before, a mixture of 1 ounce of salsoda, 1/4 ounce of borax and 2 ounces of hard white soap, melted slowly together without being allowed to boil, fold together again and put away in a warm place for 24 hours. After this, dissolve 2 ounces saleratus, in sufficient hot rain water to saturate the skin; when cool enough not to scald the hands soak the skin in it for 12 hours: then wring it out and hang it up to dry. When dry repeat this soaking and drying two or three times, till the skin is sufficiently soft. Lastly, smooth the inside with fine sandpaper and pumice stone.

TAPIOCA CREAM

Three tablespoonfuls of tapioca soaked overnight in water to cover. In the morning take a pail and set in a kettle of boiling water, into that put your tapioca and three pints of milk, let boil slowly- half an hour, then add the yolks of three eggs and three-fourths cup of sugar, let it cook a few minutes and pour into your dish, then add the whites of the eggs beaten to a froth, and beat all together. Flavor with lemon or vanilla.

TAPIOCA CREAM

Soak two spoonfuls tapioca for two hours. Boil one quart milk, add the tapioca, put in the yolks of three eggs, well beaten, with a cup and a half of sugar; let this just boil up, and set away to cool. Beat the whites of the eggs to a stiff froth, and add on top as for boiled custard.

TAPIOCA CREAMS

Cover three tablespoonfuls of tapioca with water and let it stand overnight; in the morning pour off the water, if any, and put the tapioca into one quart of new milk over the fire. When it boils stir in the yolks of three eggs well beaten, one cup of sugar, a little salt, and continue stirring until it begins to thicken, then pour it over one pint of strawberries. Make a frosting of the whites of the eggs, with three teaspoonfuls of sugar, and spread over the top; brown it in the oven. To be eaten cold or nearly so. It is delicious! Try it.

TAPIOCA PUDDING

Take one and one-half cups of tapioca and soak overnight; three eggs beaten thoroughly, and reserving the white of one for the frosting; one cup of white sugar; one teaspoonful of butter; one and one-half pints of milk; a little salt and nutmeg. Bake until well done. Frost same as directed for lemon pie, and return to oven until brown.

TAPIOCA PUDDING

Three-fourths of a cup of tapioca, three pints of milk. Boil the tapioca with a portion of the milk and the yolks of four eggs, until soft; pour into a pan, and add the whites of three eggs, with the rest of the milk, and two tablespoonfuls of sugar.

Butter a dish, sprinkle the bottom with finely minced candied peel, and a very little shred suet, then a thin layer of light bread, and so on until the dish is full. For a pint dish make a liquid custard of one egg and one-half pint of milk, sweeten, pour over the pudding, and bake as slowly as possible for two hours.

TAPIOCA PUDDING

(With preserved apples, peaches, etc.)

Prepare one teacup of tapioca with 3 cups of lukewarm water and soaked 5 or 6 hours in a warm place. Sweeten to taste, add 1 well beaten egg and one teaspoonful of salt. Place in an earthen baking dish alternately with the fruit, the first and last layers being tapioca. Bake one hour. Serve with cream.

TAPIOCA PUDDING

Soak a teacup of tapioca in three and one-half cups of boiling water, and two spoonfuls of white sugar. Keep it in a warm place for three hours. Fill a two quart pudding-dish two-thirds full of rich, ripe, tart apples, peeled and quartered. Pour the tapioca over the apples and add half a teacup of cold milk to brown the tapioca. Bake an hour.

TAPIOCA PUDDING

A small teacup of tapioca, one quart of milk, six eggs, a piece of butter the size of a chestnut, a teacup of sugar, a teaspoonful of salt; rose water, essence of lemon, or nutmeg as you prefer. The lump tapioca is the best, and if it is white it should not be washed, as the powder, which is the best part, will be washed away. Pick it over very carefully, soak it overnight in a part of the milk. If you have omitted to do this, and need the pudding for dinner, it will soak in water in two or three hours; put barely enough to swell it thoroughly, boil it in the milk, stirring it often; beat the eggs some time with the sugar in them; stir them and all the other ingredients into the milk while it is yet hot. If the pudding is put immediately in the oven, it will bake in three-quarters of an hour, or a little less. Three eggs to a quart of milk will make a very good tapioca or sago pudding. Tapioca is very nice soaked in water, and boiled in milk, (about a pint to a coffee cup of tapioca), with grated lemon peel or a little essence of lemon, and eaten with cream and sugar.

TAPIOCA PUDDING WITH PEACHES

This choice rule is given in the "Cook": Wash half a pint of small tapioca; put it in a double boiler, add a liberal quart of boiling water and boil half an hour. Peel and halve a dozen peaches, put them in a pan, add a quarter of a pound of powdered sugar, a saltspoonful of mixed ground spice, four ounces of butter and the grated rind of a lemon. Pour the tapioca over the fruit, bake to a delicate brown and serve, hot or cold, with cream or wine sauce.

TAR STAINS

Wet tar stains with turpentine. Then wash out.

TARNISHED BRASS RESTORATION

Vinegar and salt, or oxalic acid, will restore badly tarnished brass. After rubbing with this, wash the brass thoroughly with soap and water and polish with rotten stone and oil.

TEA

Everybody knows how to make tea; but everybody does not know how to make it well. Tea, like coffee, goes much further if you warm the leaves a little first; then, if the water be hard either for tea or coffee, add a little carbonate of soda. Make the pot hot, and use only boiling water either to make it or replenish the pot. If any tea is left, pour it off into an earthen jug; do not leave the cold tea on the leaves.

TEA BISCUIT

One quart of sifted flour, two tablespoonfuls of lard, one pint of milk and water mixed, a half teaspoonful of salt, three teaspoonfuls of baking powder; mix the flour, salt and powder together, then rub in well the lard; add the milk and water; knead until smooth; cut in round cakes and bake in a quick oven.

TEA CAKE

One cup sugar, one cup morning's milk, three cups flour, one-half cup butter, one teaspoon yeast powder, one-half teaspoon soda, spice or flavor to taste.

TEA ICE CREAM

To a pint of sweetened cream add a cup of strong tea and freeze.

TEA MAKING

A teapot should be scrupulously cleaned and freshly scalded before the tea is put into it, and that the water used for tea-making should be freshly boiled and be actually boiling when used.

TEA MUFFINS

1 cup of milk, butter the size of an egg, 1 tablespoonful of sugar, 2 eggs, 1 teaspoonful cream of tartar stirred into the flour, ½ teaspoonful of soda in a tablespoonful of hot water, and about one pint of flour, or enough to make a batter stiffer than usual for cake. Drop it into well-greased muffin pans or rings, and bake in a hot oven fifteen minutes. First mix the butter, sugar, and eggs together; then add the milk, then flour, and the soda last.

TEA OR COFFEE POT WASHING

Never wash a tea or coffee pot in soap-suds as it sets the stains. When discolored boil a teaspoonful of soda in them an hour and wash clean.

TEMPER

Keep your temper, whatever else you may give away.

TENDER CRUSTS

If your oven is browning your bread too quickly, take a large dripping-pan, fill with cold water and set it on the grate iron. This prevents burning and makes the crusts tender.

TENDERFOOT

The following is said to be good for corns: One tablespoonful turpentine, two tablespoonfuls olive-oil. Mix thoroughly and apply night and morning.

When the skin cracks between the toes, wash with a solution of phenol, then dust with plain powdered chalk. The chalk which is used for writing on blackboards is the kind to use.

Paint the enlarged joint with tincture of iodine, or apply squares of the French "paper cure", a paper plaster which gives great relief.

A hot foot bath every night brings foot comfort, and a wash-cloth wrung out of cold water and applied to the enlarged joint, will reduce the inflammation. A small quantity of absorbent cotton placed between the toes will also give some relief.

TETTER REMEDY

To one-half cup of pure apple vinegar add two tablespoonfuls of salt; apply hot as possible.

THANKSGIVING

I think Thanksgiving Day should be abolished. (T. Gobbler)

THICK BLOOD

Thick blood causes colds and countless other diseases. Keep the lungs active by deep breathing, the skin by baths and friction, the kidneys by free draughts of warm water, the bowels by correct eating and the blood will be pure.

THIRST - QUENCHING

A celebrated military surgeon recommends, for quenching thirst and sustaining strength, oat-meal water as superior to any other drink. Boil a quarter pound of the meal in two or three quarts of water, add one and one-half ounces of sugar, if sweetening is desired; use cold in summer and warm in winter, shaking before taking. If supper is to be missed, or extra demand made upon the system, as some day in harvest time, the proportion of meal may be advantageously increased to half or three-quarters of a pound.

THIRST QUENCHER

A feverish thirst that cannot be quenched by water may be thus allayed: Throw a slice of bread upon burning coals, and when it is aflame throw it into a tumbler of water and drink the water. This remedy has been tested and proven good.

THREAD DRAWING

Thread drawing for hemstitching may be made easier by taking a lather brush and soap, and lathering well the parts where the threads are to be drawn. Let the linen dry, and the threads will come out easily, even in the finest linen.

THREADING NEEDLES

Hold your needle over something white if you have trouble in threading it.

TINNY TASTE REMOVAL

Soaking canned goods in ice water for an hour before eating them will remove any tinny taste that may be noticed in them.

TOBACCO SMOKE

Place a pail of water containing a handful of hay in a room where there has been smoking. It will absorb the odor of tobacco.

TOBACCO-STEMS

Old tobacco-stems are "the best ever" to put in hens' nests early in spring, to drive vermin away before sitting time.

TOMATO CANNING

In canning tomatoes in glass jars, if you will either put a little salt in when cooking or on the top after filling the jar - say a tablespoonful - you will find them to keep much better, and taste more like fresh tomatoes when opened.

TOMATO CATSUP

Cook one bushel of ripe tomatoes until soft, strain out all the seeds and skins, add two gallons of cider vinegar, one pint of salt, one-fourth pound each of whole cloves and allspice, one tablespoonful of pepper, one pod of red pepper, and five heads of garlic. Boil until reduced to one-half the quantity, strain and bottle.

TOMATO CATSUP

One gallon of ripe tomatoes, stewed and strained; Then add four tablespoonfuls salt, four tablespoonfuls of ground black pepper, three tablespoonfuls of ground mustard, half a tablespoonful of allspice, half a tablespoonful of cloves. Boil slowly three or four hours, with a pint of vinegar. Cork and seal.

TOMATO CATSUP

Wash and wipe (this is to prevent the addition of any liquid) one bushel of just ripe tomatoes, cut into pieces and put over the fire to heat. When cooked sufficiently to strain put through a fine sieve. Allow two ounces each of whole black pepper, cloves and allspice - then tie in a thin muslin bag -add one ounce each of ground mace and cinnamon, a teaspoonful of cayenne pepper and a cupful and a half of salt, stirring the ground spice into the tomatoes. Boil until reduced a little more than one-third. I cannot specify the time required to boil down, because it varies with the quality of the tomatoes. When cold bottle and tie down the corks.

TOMATO RAREBIT

2 tablespoonsfull of butter, 2 tablespoonsfull of flour. Stir until well blended, then pour on 3/4 cup of milk or cream, bring to boiling point. Add 3/4 cupful of stewed and strained tomatoes mixed with 1/8 of a teaspoon of soda. Then add 1 cupful of finely cut cheese, two eggs slightly beaten, ½ teaspoon of salt, ½ teaspoon mustard and a few grains of cayenne. Serve on crackers as soon as cheese is melted.

TOMATO SALAD

Ripe tomatoes peeled and very cold, cut in thin slices; arrange on a flat dish; put a teaspoonful of mayonnaise dressing in the centre of each slice and arrange a border of parsley around the dish; also a sprig here and there, and you will have something dainty and inviting.

TOMATO SOUP

Three pounds of beef, one quart canned tomatoes, one gallon water. Let the meat and water boil for two hours, or until the liquid is reduced to little more than two quarts. Then stir in the tomatoes, and stew all slowly for three-quarters of an hour longer. Season to taste, strain and serve.

TOMATO STEW

Two cupfuls of cold chopped meats - two kinds may be used, as veal and ham, or beef and pork - one small onion, chopped fine, one cupful cold stewed tomatoes. Brown a lump of butter in your skillet; rub two scant tablespoonfuls flour into this; add a few drops at a time, half a pint of cold water; then your tomatoes and onion; season well. Boil five minutes; add the meat; simmer ten minutes and serve hot on a meat platter garnished with bits of toast.

TOMATOES FOR SUPPER

Six eggs, one teaspoonful of mustard, olive oil, salt, cayenne pepper, tomatoes, vinegar. For half a dozen persons take six eggs, boil four of them hard, dissolve the yolks with vinegar and the mustard, and mash as smooth as possible; add the two remaining eggs (raw), yolks and white, stir well, then add oil to make altogether sauce sufficient to cover the tomatoes well; add the salt and pepper and beat thoroughly until it thickens; skin and cut the tomatoes the fourth of an inch thick and place on ice an hour before they are to be used, then pour the sauce over. Though a little troublesome to prepare, yet, if once eaten by persons who are blessed with palates to enjoy good things, they will be pronounced to be superior to any other mode of preparation.

TONSILLITIS

If Sister Place will put a teaspoonful of alum in a glass of water, a teaspoonful of salt in another glass of water, and gargle the throat every half hour, first with the salt and then with the alum-solution, she will find a cure for tonsillitis. I do not know whether I obtained this from Hearth and Home or from one of its sister-papers, but it is a speedy cure and I am glad to pass it on. Mrs. R. E. Dunn, Brockville, Ont.

TONSILLITIS

In return for much useful information I have received from The Blade, I wish to say to those afflicted with tonsillitis, that a cure can be quickly effected by placing a piece of porous plaster about as large as a silver dollar over the tonsils as soon as there are any symptoms of the disease. I have been subject to this trouble for years, usually having one or two attacks every winter, but have had none since I began using this treatment.

TONSILLITIS REMEDY

A tried remedy - or perhaps I should say preventive - for tonsillitis is lemon juice, used as soon as the throat becomes sore. Have known it to cure sore throat when it was cankered. A very cheap remedy and a good one. Ohio Sister.

TOOTHACHE

To cure toothache, saturate a bit of cotton in vinegar that has been boiled, and apply to the tooth.

TOOTHACHE CURE

Cayenne pepper, four ounces; rectified spirits, twelve fluid ounces. Macerate for seven days, then strain.

TOOTHACHE DROPS

Chloroform, one ounce; spirits of camphor, one ounce; oil of cloves, half drachm; mix and keep in a tightly corked bottle and apply by dropping on a bit of cotton batting and lay on the teeth, and rub a little on the face if that is painful. It will give instant relief.

TOOTHACHE DROPS

Opium, ten grains; camphor, ten grains; oil of cloves, one drachm; kajeput, one drachm. Alcohol sufficient to make a thin liquid.

TOPPING

If a little sausage is left over from breakfast, it will add flavor if broken up fine and mixed with bread crumbs to put on top of baked macaroni or scalloped potatoes or baked beans.

TOSSED POTATOES

Boil some potatoes in their skins, peel them and cut in small pieces; toss them over the fire in a mixture of cream, butter rolled in flour, pepper and salt, till they are hot and well covered with the sauce.

TOUGH FOWL

A spoonful of vinegar added to the water in which a tough fowl, or meat, is boiled will render it tender.

TRIPE a'la BORDELAISE

Cut two pounds of tripe into strips the length and width of a finger. Put two tablespoonfuls of butter into a hot saucepan, with half an onion chopped fine, and a tablespoonful of chopped parsley. When the butter is piping hot turn in the tripe, and cook until brown, seasoning it with salt and pepper to taste.

TROUBLESOME COUGH

Take an ounce of licorice, a quarter of a pound of raisins, a teaspoonful of flaxseed and two quarts of water. Boil slowly until reduced to one quart, then add a quarter of a pound of finely powdered rock candy and the juice of one lemon. Drink half a pint of this when going to bed, and a little more when the cough is troublesome.

TROY PUDDING

Two-thirds of a cup of pork or suet chopped fine, two-thirds cup of molasses, one cup of sour milk, one teaspoonful of saleratus, four cups of flour, three cups of any kind of berries or chopped apples. Steam three hours. Sauce - Butter, sugar, a little boiled cider, flour and water. Indian meal may be substituted for part of the flour with economy.

TUBERCULOSIS

I have been greatly helped by the "warm strippings from the cow" recommended for tuberculosis, and am very grateful to the one who sent this simple remedy to our paper, and to the good physician who originated the idea. Since I began taking the strippings I have gained steadily, and feel certain of a cure.

TUBERCULOSIS - LEMON-CURE

The following is the lemon-cure asked for: Boil nice fresh lemons as you would eggs, and eat one or two before each meal; scrape out the juice and pulp from the inside and eat with sugar. This is said to be very effective if taken in the early stages of the disease.

TUBS AND IRONING BOARDS

Tubs and ironing boards should be kept in a cold place, and there is no objection to a little dampness.

TURNIPS

Turnips boiled like beets, with their jackets on, are of better flavor and less watery. A small bit of sugar added while the vegetable is boiling corrects the bitterness often found in them.

TURPENTINE

A useful article. Turpentine has almost as many uses in the house as borax. It is good for rheumatism, and, mixed with camphor oil and rubbed on the chest, one of the best remedies for bronchial colds. It is an excellent preventive against moths, although naphtha is preferable, the odor leaving much sooner; it will drive away ants and roaches if sprinkled about the shelves and closets; a spoonful of it to a pail of warm water cleans paint excellently and a little in the boiler on washing day whitens the clothes.

TWELVE WAYS OF COOKING POTATOES

1. To Boil Potatoes - To boil, potatoes should be pared; if boiled with skins on, they will taste strong (at least I never saw any that did not). Pare, wash and throw them into a pan of cold water; then put them on to boil in a clean kettle with water sufficient to cover them, and sprinkle over a little salt; let them boil slowly, uncovered, till you can press a fork through them; pour off the water, and put them where they will keep hot till wanted (they are better if eaten immediately). When done in this way they will be dry and mealy. They should never be covered to keep them hot. They will be sweet boiled this way.

2. Another Way - Wash them clean, and put them in a pot or kettle, with water just enough to cover them. Shortly after the water has come to a boil, pour it off, and replace it with cold water, in which throw a handful of salt. The cold water sends the heat from the surface to the heart, and makes the potatoes mealy. The moment they are done, pour off the water, and let them stand on the fire ten or fifteen minutes to dry. Potatoes either boiled or roasted, should never be covered to keep them hot.

3. To Boil New Potatoes - Put them in cold water, scrape off the skins, wash them and drop into boiling water. When soft, dress with cream and melted butter.

4. Stewed Potatoes - Slice thin, and boil in water till tender; pour off the water, and put in some butter, salt, pepper, and rich cream and a dust of flour. Before taking up, stir in the beaten yolk of an egg with some chopped parsley.
5. Fried Potatoes - Cut cold potatoes in thin slices; drop into boiling fat until a nice brown. Sprinkle with salt, and serve hot.
6. Roasted Potatoes Clean thoroughly; nick a small piece of the skin, and put in a hot oven. A little butter is sometimes rubbed over the skins to make them crisp.
7. To Mash Potatoes - Boil the potatoes as above; peel them, remove all the eyes and lumps; beat them up with butter and salt, until they are quite smooth; force them into a mold which has been previously floured; turn into a tureen; brown them before the fire, turning gently so as not to injure the shape, and when of a nice color send to table. They are sometimes coated with white of egg.
8. Mash some floury potatoes quite smooth, season with pepper and salt, add fresh butter until sufficiently moist; make into balls, roll them in vermicelli crumbled or bread crumbs; in the latter case they may be brushed with the yolk of an egg; fry a nice brown. Serve on a napkin, or round a dish of mashed potatoes which has not been molded.
9. To Boil Sweet Potatoes - They should be as near one size as possible. Cook with the skins on; try them with a fork to see if they are done through before taking from the fire, and peel them before sending to the table.
10. To Bake Or Roast Sweet Potatoes - Wash them clean, and wipe them dry; place them in a quick oven, in the hot ashes of a wood fire, or in a Dutch oven. They will take from half an hour, to an hour, according to size.
11. Another Way - Peel them, slice in large slices, and put into a baking dish, with plenty of butter, a little water, and some sugar; and serve in the dish in which they are cooked.
12. To Fry Sweet Potatoes - Take cold boiled potatoes, slice them lengthwise, and fry in hot lard.

TYING A SHOESTRING

Proceed exactly as if you were going to tie an ordinary bow knot; but before drawing it up, pass the right-hand loop through the knot, then give a steady and simultaneous pull on both loops, and your shoestring will be tied fast. When you wish to untie it pull the right hand string, and you will have no difficulty.

UNION CAKE

One cup of butter, two of sugar, three of flour, one of milk, one-half cup of corn starch, four eggs, two teaspoonfuls extract of lemon, one of cream tarter, one-half teaspoonful of soda.

UMBRELLAS

Always dry an umbrella with the handle down to prevent rotting the silk.

VANILLA ICE CREAM

Boil, in a double boiler, one quart of milk. Mix four tablespoonfuls of flour, one-half a teaspoon of salt and one cup of sugar; add the yolks of four eggs and beat well; pour over them the boiling milk and cook in the double boiler for twenty minutes, stirring quite often. Add the whites of the eggs, beaten stiff, another cup of sugar and one pint of cream. Take from the fire, flavor with vanilla to taste, set away to cool and when cold freeze.

VANILLA TAFFY

Two cups water, one cup sugar, 1/3 cup molasses, two tablespoonfuls vinegar, butter size of an egg; when nearly done, add one-half teaspoonful of vanilla.

VARICOSE ULCER

In my experience, the varicose ulcer came from a bruise on the ankle, when the veins were badly broken. I obtained relief in this way: Lie down on a sofa, with the foot on pillows piled high at the head, your own head at the foot and not raised at all, so that the heart is much lower than the ankle. Bathe the ulcer twice a day with water hot as can be borne; use a folded cloth taken from hot water and pressed on the affected part, dipping it again when cool. This should be kept up for half an hour, putting in hot water as fast as it cools. Then cover the sore with a clean, white cloth, and bind with red flannel, cut in strips nearly two inches in width, from the toe to the knee. If this treatment is continued for ten days without using the foot, I am sure the cure will be effected.

VARIETY CAKE

One cup of sugar, one-half cup of butter, three eggs, one-half cup of sweet milk, one heaping teaspoonful of baking powder and two cups of flour. Divide this into three parts, baking two of them in long pie tins. To the third part add one scant teaspoonful of cinnamon, one-half teaspoon of cloves, and a little nutmeg, and two-thirds cup of raisins, seeded, chopped and dredged. Bake this in the same sized tin, and put all three together with frosting, the fruit layer in the center, and frost over the top. This makes a nice and very pretty cake.

VARNISHED PAINT CLEANER

For varnished paints save some tea leaves for a few days; then steep them in a tin pail for half an hour; strain through a sieve and use the tea for cleaning the paint. The tea acts as a strong detergent, and makes the paint nearly equal to new in appearance; it will not due to wash unvarnished paint with it.

VASELINE AND EGGS

According to Mittheilungen uber Lanawirthschaft, Vaseline is a good preservative for eggs. The eggs should be thoroughly washed and rubbed in with Vaseline previously melted with three-tenths percent of salicylic acid. The operation should be performed twice, the latter one month after the former. On boiling the skin of Vaseline easily separates from the eggs. Eggs thus treated are said to keep perfectly fresh for a year.

VEAL CAKE

Butter your mould, then put in a layer of veal and ham, cut in thin slices, season it with cayenne, salt and a little beaten mace, some parsley, some eggs boiled hard and cut in slices; press it down and bake it. Make a little veal gravy with a few shreds of isinglass; strain it, and add a small quantity of catsup, pour it over hot, when cold turn out.

VEAL CUTLETS

Cut in large squares, dip each square in raw egg, then in flour; season with salt and pepper; fry in butter, and when ready to serve pour over a gravy made of one pint of water, two tablespoonfuls of browned flour mixed with a little cold water, small piece of butter, pepper and salt.

VEAL CUTLETS

Let the cutlets be thin and not too large; beat them lightly, then season with salt, pepper and a little grated nutmeg or sweet marjoram; let them lie for a time so that the seasoning may penetrate; have ready a frying pan covered with hot lard; beat a couple of eggs in one dish, and put some flour in another; take the cutlets one at a time and dip first into the egg, then into the flour, and put directly into the hot fat; lay them in till the pan is covered, and do not attempt to turn till one side is of a delicate brown; take up on a platter and keep hot till served; pour most of the fat from the pan, put in some flour, and let it brown over the fire; then add some boiling water, stir well, add some pepper and salt, let it boil up and send to the table in a gravy-boat.

VEAL FOR TEA

One pound veal, 2 slices salt pork - both well chopped together and mixed with 2 cups of bread crumbs. Put in a deep baking dish, season with pepper and salt, and pour over it 2 eggs well beaten and 12 pint milk. To be eaten cold.

VEAL LOAF

Take six pounds of veal chopped fine, 9 large crackers rolled to a powder, 3 teaspoonfuls powdered sage, 3 of pepper, 2 even tablespoonfuls of salt, 6 of sweet cream, 1 cup of butter and 5 eggs. Mix thoroughly and pack in pan and bake two hours.

VEAL PIE

Cut the veal into small pieces, boil an hour or longer, if necessary, to make tender; season with salt and pepper, and a small piece of butter. Line the sides of a deep pudding dish or bake pan with rich shortcake crust, put the meat in and fill with gravy. Shake in a very little flour and cover with a not too thick crust, leaving a hole in the center. Bake about one hour.

VEAL ROLLS

Cut thin slices of veal and spread on them a fine seasoning of a very few crumbs, a little chopped bacon, parsley and shallot, some mushrooms stewed and minced, pepper, salt and a small piece of pounded mace. This stuffing may either fill up the roll like a sausage or be rolled with the meat. In either case tie it up very tight, and stew very slowly in a gravy. Serve it when tender, after skimming it nicely.

VEAL SOUP

Take a knuckle of veal, put it in a pot, with four quarts of water, and add a teaspoonful of salt to each quart. Pare and slice three onions, four turnips, two carrots, a bunch of sweet herbs, and a small portion of celery. Let the veal boil one hour, then add the above vegetables. When they are tender, strain the soup. Put it in the pot they were boiled in, thicken the soup with some flour mixed smoothly with a little water, and add a little parsley finely chopped.

Make some dumplings of a teaspoonful of butter, to two of flour, and milk and water enough to make a very soft dough. Drop them into the boiling soup. They should be about as large as a walnut when they are put in. Dish the meat with the vegetables around it. Drawn butter may be served with it, or any other meat sauce.

VEAL STEAKS

Cut thin, season with salt, pepper and sweet marjoram, broil over hot coals, turning frequently; do not let one side remain over the fire till done, or it will be hard and dry; if turned frequently it will be juicy and tender; take up in a hot dish in which there is a little boiling water, with a lump of butter and a little lemon juice or catsup.

VEAL STEW

Veal stews are delicious simmered in their own gravy or with the addition of a slice or two of lemon and a tin of green peas when the stew is nearly done. Mashed potatoes fit well with veal stews.

VEGETABLE SALADS

All kinds may be made by using cold boiled pease, string beans, cauliflower, asparagus tops, beets or celery, cutting not too small and using any of the salad dressings, according to taste. Nothing need be wasted.

VEGETABLE SOUP

Pass through a sieve all the vegetables used to make vegetable stock, melt a piece of butter in a saucepan, add a little flour to it, mix it well, then add the vegetable pulp; stir well, and moisten with as much stock as may be necessary; let the soup boil, stir into it, off the fire, the yolks of two eggs, beaten up with a little water and then strained. Serve with pieces of toasted bread, fried in butter.

VEGETABLE SOUP

Purchase a small piece of shin, with some meat upon it - a piece costs 15 cents - put into the vessel that you make the soup in, four quarts of water, with salt, boil three or four hours, then add half a teacupful of rice, one carrot grated, one turnip cut in pieces, one leek, cut up a stalk of celery, a little pepper; just before serving for the table, take out the shin, removing the meat, which you cut in small pieces, put the meat into the tureen and pour the soup over it; send to the table to be eaten with catsup or spiced sauces. Yankee.

VEGETABLE STEWS

Very appetizing vegetable stews may be made of vegetables alone, beginning always with the foundation gravy. Drippings can very well be used, or finely chopped suet. For stews mix onion with turnip and carrot, add pepper and salt; mix carrots with potatoes and chopped parsley, parsnips and carrots, cabbage and a few whole onions, and employ your ingenuity how to vary for a family. A small piece of meat is sufficient with vegetable stews, or no meat at all is needed. You will be astonished what heat these vegetable stews supply.

VELVET

Velvet wears better if brushed with a hat brush, by pressing down into the nap and then turning the brush as on an axis, to flirt out the lint. Do not brush backward or forward.

VENISON STEAKS ON TOAST

Cut four good steaks through a leg of venison, bone and all. Season one hour before cooking with salt, pepper, one onion finely chopped and a few drops of vinegar. Have some clean melted butter in a frying-pan, put your steaks in and set over a strong fire. As soon as they are cooked on one side turn them over. When they are cooked (rare) on both sides, take the butter out of the pan, then put in the pan a spoonful of flour and let it simmer for five minutes, turning your steak every minute; then add a pint of claret, the juice from a can of mushrooms and afterward the mushrooms chopped fine;

let simmer again for ten minutes. Serve hot on toast, and pour the sauce on the top of the steaks.

VERMIN

Try sassafras-oil for vermin on children's heads. Two or three applications, at most, will be needed; apply once a day.

VERMIN ON CHILDREN'S HEADS

I wish to give you a sure, harmless remedy for vermin on children's heads - flaxseed-tea, used as a wash. A single application usually does the work, but may be repeated if necessary. The seed is inexpensive.

VERY NICE CAKE

Five eggs, two cups of butter, three of sugar, one cup of new milk, one teaspoonful of soda, two teaspoonfuls of cream of tartar, five cups of flour, four cups of chopped raisins, all kinds of spice.

VICTORIA FRITTERS

Cut a loaf of bakers bread into slices an inch thick; cut the slices in the centre, trimming off the crust, and place on a flat dish; take a quart of rich milk, one saltspoonful of salt, eight beaten eggs; stir the whole together and pour over the bread several hours before dinner, that it may be equally moistened; fry in hot butter a delicate brown and eat with sweet sauce.

VILLAGE CAKE

One teacupful of sugar, two eggs, half a cupful of butter, one teaspoonful of yeast-powder, one cupful of cold water and two of flour. Flavor with lemon. The above quantity will make a loaf for a long tin.

VINEGAR AND SALT CLEANER

Vinegar and salt will clean the black crust off sheet-iron frying-pans, but they should be thoroughly scoured afterward with sapolio.

VINEGAR COOKIES

One cup of molasses, one-half cup of sugar, one tablespoonful of ginger, one tablespoonful vinegar, two teaspoonfuls of soda, one egg and a pinch of salt. Bring the molasses to a boil, add soda and pour on the egg and sugar, beating together while foaming, add vinegar and ginger, then flour to roll thin.

VINEGAR PIE

One-half cup of water, one-half cup of molasses, one cracker, a little salt and nutmeg and one tablespoonful of vinegar.

VIRGINIA BATTER-BREAD

This is one of the most palatable preparations of corn meal. Mix together six tablespoonfuls of flour, three tablespoonfuls of Indian meal, one saltspoonful of salt, and four eggs beaten to a froth; then quickly add to these milk enough to make a thin batter, and bake the whole immediately in small buttered moulds, in a quick oven.

VIRGINIA BEATEN BISCUIT

Two quarts of flour, a large tablespoonful of lard, one of salt; mix with sweet milk or water, either, but milk makes them brown nicer; make quite stiff, and then beat the dough till it puffs and breaks. It is not beating hard that makes the biscuits nice, but the regularity of the motion. Beating hard, the old cooks say, "kill" the dough.

VOMITING - TO STOP

A cloth wet in essence of peppermint, laid across the stomach is good. A plaster, made of pulverized cloves, ginger and Indian meal, applied to the stomach, is also good. A pill of cayenne pepper will sometimes stop it very soon.

WAFERS

One quart of flour, four ounces of lard or butter, a little salt, mix with cold water; pound with a rolling pin twenty minutes, to be rolled out very thin and cut with a doughnut cutter. To be eaten with jelly.

WALNUT FURNITURE

When oiled walnut furniture begins to grow dingy, it can be made to look as fresh as new by re-oiling. Linseed or even olive oil can be used, but pure, good kerosene oil is much the best. Rub it well with a soft woolen rag, and polish with clean, dry flannel.

WARMING UP COLD BEEFSTEAK

Put a fine minced onion in a stew-pan, add half a dozen cloves and as many peppercorns, pour on a coffee-cup of boiling water, and add three tablespoons butter. Let it simmer ten minutes. Then cut up the meat in pieces an inch square, and let it simmer in this gravy about five minutes. Three large tomatoes stewed with the onion improves this.

WARTS

To the mother who asked how to remove large warts from her daughter's hand without leaving a scar, I recommend lemon-juice, having given this simple remedy a thorough test. Saturate the warts with the juice once or twice a day for three days or four, or possibly a week. The juice of one lemon will be sufficient, usually; press it out and put it into a small vial, place the mouth over the wart and tip it up. Application may, of course, be made in some other way, but this is my method. The warts diminish gradually and finally disappear altogether, without pain and leaving no scar. Another simple remedy which a friend has tried successfully is potato-water or rubbing the juice from a raw potato on, still another is salt water, and another equally efficacious application is castor-oil. Lemon-juice I have personally tried, the others are recommended by friends.

WARTS

J. W. Murphy, the following is a tried and true remedy for warts: Simply paint them with iodine three or four times daily, touching each carefully with a tiny brush or a bit of cotton batting tied to a toothpick. In three or four weeks they will have entirely disappeared.

WARTS

I have read many remedies for warts, and wish to ask whether any one has tried castor-oil? Just put a drop on the wart at any time it is convenient, and a cure is sure to be effected in a short time.

WARTS — PAINLESS CURE FOR

Drop a little vinegar on the wart and cover immediately with cooking soda, or saleratus; put on as much soda as you can pile on and let it remain for ten minutes; repeat several times a day, and in three days the wart will be gone. A good remedy for corns also.

WARTS - REMOVING WITHOUT PAIN

S.E.B., Osage Mission, Kas., says: "Cover the warts thickly with saleratus and wet the saleratus with strong vinegar once or twice each day for a week, or until the warts begin to get sore; then they will come off like a dry scab."

WARTS - REMOVING WITHOUT PAIN

A lady subscriber, of Dayton, Ohio, writes that she has removed nearly two dozen warts from her hands by applying common baking soda two or three times daily. Mix soda with pure rain water to the consistency of cream, and let it dry on the wart.

WARTS - REMOVING WITHOUT PAIN

J.G.T., of Cromwell, Ct. says that alum will remove warts. Carry a lump in your pocket, moisten it, and rub the wart briskly with it several times a day.

WARTS - REMOVING WITHOUT PAIN

E.V.H., LosAnimas, Col., W.C.A., of Sylvania, Ohio, says that the common milkweed (Asclepias cornuti) is a painless remedy for warts.

Apply the milky juice of the plant to the wart three or four times daily, paring off the top of the wart as it becomes dead.

WARTS - TO CURE

To cure warts rub with a strong solution of potash till they disappear, or wet gum ammoniac and rub it on the excrescences at night.

WARTS - TO TAKE OFF

To take off warts, moisten each well with warm water, rub for two or three minutes with common table salt, leave a coating of salt on for five minutes, then remove it. Do this several times a day, and generally at the end of a week the warts will be gone without leaving a scar.

WASHING COLORED MUSLIN

Colored muslins should be washed in a lather of cold water. Never put them in warm water, not even to rinse them. If the muslin should be green, add a little vinegar to the water; if lilac, a little ammonia, and if black, a little salt.

WASHING DISHES

Half the battle in washing dishes is in keeping the dish cloths and towels perfectly clean. They should be washed and dried after using, and at least once a week - oftener in warm weather - should be washed in ammonia water, well rinsed and dried in the sun.

WASHING FLUID

One of the best washing fluids ever made is composed as follows: Add one pound of unslacked lime to three gallons of soft boiling water; settle and pour off. Add three pounds of washing soda and mix with this lime water. When dissolved use half a cup full to each pailful of water.

WASHING LINEN

A little pipe clay, dissolved in the water used for washing linen, will clean it thoroughly, with half the amount of soap and a great diminution of labor. The article will be greatly improved in color, and the texture will be benefitted.

WASHING MADE EASY

I soak my clothes overnight; in the morning I fill my wash boiler half full of water, and place it on the stove to heat, throwing in a handful of soft soap, or about two ounces of hard; I then wring out the soaked clothes, soap the dirty parts, and by this time the water is hot; put them in and let them boil fifteen minutes, stirring often; I now take out, and put them in cold water, wash out the suds; if any dirt remains, give it a few rubs and it is gone; I rinse them well in plenty of water, and my clothes are as white and clean as those that have gone through the long process of rubbing. I have washed my clothes this way for ten years, and they have never turned yellow.

WASHING PREPARATION

A good washing preparation is the following: To one boiler of cold water, one heaping teaspoon of borax, two each of ammonia and kerosene, plenty of soap shaved fine and dissolved in hot water. Put in the clothes while the water is cold and boil fifteen minutes. You will find this a saving of labor.

WASHING SILK ARTICLES

To wash silk articles use tepid water with a suds of white Castile soap. Do not rub or wring them. Handle them as you would nice laces in washing. Rinse in clean cold water, and press the water out by placing them in a clean dry towel or cloth under a heavy weight. When they are entirely dry rub them lightly with a piece of flannel to give them a nice finish. Of course some delicate shades are not intended to be washed any more than a daintily colored silk dress.

WASHING SOAP

Two pounds bar soap, (made from the Saponifier) and ten ounces borax. Shave the soap fine. Put that and the borax in one quart of water and simmer until well mixed. One-fourth of a pound of this is sufficient to do a washing for six persons.

I have used this soap with the Union Washing Machine and Wringer, for several months, and can do a washing in one-half the time with less soap, less water and less wood, than any other way I ever tried, and think no one who has given them a thorough trial would part with them for twice their cost, if they could not get more like them.

WASHING WINDOWS

When washing windows put a few drops of kerosene in the water, and see how much easier they will dry.

WASHING WOOLENS

Light summer woolens, which are too easily soiled, may be cleansed by finely powdered French chalk. The soiled parts should be thickly covered with the chalk, which should be allowed to remain for one or two days, and then removed with a camel's hair velvet brush. In most cases this treatment will cause the spots to disappear entirely.

WASHINGTON PIE

Two cups of sugar; one cup of butter; one cup of milk; three and one-half cups of flour; four eggs; two teaspoonfuls of cream tartar; one of saleratus.

WASHSTAND MATS

Serviceable little mats for the washstand may be made of bath toweling. After these mats have been cut to the size and shapes required, the edges are overcast and finished with a basket stitch in Shetland wool.

WATER

Remember it is more injurious to drink too little water than too much. Two quarts a day is little enough. It helps to carry off effete matter through the skin, kidneys and bowels.

WATER SPONGE CAKE

This is a small sponge cake: One egg, one-half cup of sugar, one-half teaspoon lemon juice, three tablespoons cold water, three-quarters cup of flour sifted with one teaspoon baking powder.

WATERMELON CAKE

White part: Two cups of white sugar, one cup of butter, one cup of sweet milk, three and one-half cups of flour, whites of eight eggs, two teaspoonfuls of cream of tartar, and one teaspoonful of soda dissolved in a little warm water.

Red part: One cup of red sugar, half a cup of butter, one-third of a cup of sweet milk, two cups of flour, whites of four eggs, one teaspoonful of cream of tartar, one-half teaspoonful of soda, one teacup of stoned raisins, one-half cup of blanched almonds.

Put the raisins in the red part to represent ripe seeds. Blanch the almonds by pouring boiling water on them, when the skins will easily slip off. Cut them in two and put them in the white part. Have a pan with a tube in the center, put the red part next to the tube and the white part around the outside. Very pretty and attractive.

WATERPROOF PAPER

Common paper may be converted into a substance resembling parchment by means of sulphuric acid. The acid should be of an exact strength, and mixed with half its weight of water. A sheet of paper placed in this solution becomes hard, tough and fibrous, yet its weight is not increased and it is far better for writing purposes than animal parchment.

WEED

And what is a weed? A plant whose virtues have not yet been discovered.

WEED DESTROYER

The best way to apply salt to paths to destroy weeds is as follows:

Dissolve the salt in water, one pound to one gallon, and apply the mixture with a watering-pot that has a spreading nose. This will keep weeds and worms away for two or three years. Put one pound to the square yard the first year; afterwards a weaker solution may be applied when required.

WELSH RAREBIT

Cut a pound of cheese in small pieces; put a piece of butter the size of an egg in a frying-pan and put in the cheese; when it has cooked five minutes add two beaten eggs, a spoonful of mustard and a little pepper; stir it up and pour over hot buttered toast. Serve hot.

WET BOOTS

Wet boots, after being pulled into shape, should be filled with dry oats, when they will dry very quickly, without losing their original shape. When the leather is dry, it should be rubbed with a soft cloth dipped in oil. The same oats may be dried and used several times.

WHEAT MEAL ROLLS

Pour boiling water on unbolted wheat meal, stirring rapidly with a strong spoon or stick. The dough should be scarcely stiff enough to retain its shape. Of this take portions about the size of a hen's egg, and roll it into a round form three or four inches in length; add plenty of dry flour to prevent sticking. Bake at once. The coating of flour also prevents the escape of air from the dough, as the sudden heat of baking expands it, thus making the rolls much lighter. Let bake in a very hot oven.

WHEEL-GREASE OR TAR REMOVAL

To remove wheel-grease or tar, rub the spots thoroughly with lard, then wash with soap and water. Cornmeal, rubbed into grease spots on a carpet, will cause them to disappear. I use the meal to clean straw hats, also, putting it on and scrubbing with a stiff brush. Mrs. K. M. Trivett

WHISK BROOM SPRINKLER

Try a clean and rather fine whisk broom for sprinkling clothes to iron, also for giving house plants a shower bath.

WHITE CAKE

One and one-half cups of sugar, one cup of sweet milk, two cups of flour; four tablespoonfuls of butter, one teaspoonful of cream of tartar, one-half teaspoonful of soda and the whites of three eggs.

WHITE CAKE

Two cups sugar, not quite one cup butter, one cup sweet milk, whites of four eggs, four cups flour, one teaspoonful yeast powder. Flavor with lemon or almond.

WHITE CAKE

One and one-half cups of sugar; one cup of milk; two teaspoons of cream tartar; one of soda; three eggs; beat the whites separate, sugar and yolks together.

WHITE CREAM CANDY

One pint of boiling water, two cups of granulated sugar. Boil all together for twenty minutes, adding two tablespoonfuls of cider vinegar when it is put over the fire. Try it on ice or snow; if not brittle enough boil longer. Let it cool in a buttered pan till in condition to pull; add vanilla, one or two teaspoonfuls. Pull very white, cut in sticks and keep in a cool place till the next day.

WHITE GEMS

Take one cupful of wheat flour, one cupful of milk, one egg and a little salt. Bake in a very hot oven in gem pans.

WHITE LACE REVIVED

White lace may be revived by breathing upon it and shaking it and flapping it. The use of irons turns lace yellow.

WHITE LAYER CAKE

Two cups powdered or fine granulated sugar, one-half cup of butter, the whites of four eggs, three cups of flour, three small teaspoons baking powder sifted with the flour. Beat the sugar and the butter to a cream, then stir in the milk and flour, a little at a time. Add the whites last. Never fails. It will make three thick layers, or four of medium thickness, and any filling can be used between them.

WHITE-MEAL PORRIDGE

Having boiled one quart of soft water, and mixed half a pound of meal in a little cold water, mix them together, and boil for fifteen minutes, stirring it occasionally. Pour it into basins, and let it stand for ten minutes. To be eaten with fruit, sugar or molasses, and bread.

WHITE MOUNTAIN CAKE

Two cups sugar, 2 eggs, 1 cup sweet milk, 3 ½ cups flour, ½ cup butter, 1 teaspoonful of soda, 2 teaspoons cream tarter and one teaspoonful lemon.

WHITE SAUCE FOR GAME

Boil an onion in a pint of milk till it is like a jelly; then strain, and pour into the boiling milk sifted bread crumbs enough to make it like thick cream when well beaten. Beat while boiling, and season with salt, black and Cayenne pepper and a little nutmeg.

WHITE SPOT REMOVAL ON FURNITURE

To remove white spots on furniture apply alcohol, it will restore the color at once.

WHITENING STRAW HATS

Scrape stick sulphur with a knife, mix the powder to a paste with water, plaster it thickly over the straw and place in the sun for several hours; brush off when dry.

WHITEWASH ━━━━━━━━━━━━━━━━━━━━━━━━━

A mason with over forty years' experience gives the following recipe for a valuable whitewash: Have a twelve or fifteen gallon kettle clean and dry; take eighteen pounds of quick lime, unslacked and fresh burnt, put it in the kettle and pour water on it and it will commence to slack immediately, but keep it covered with boiling water or it will burn; it will absorb water rapidly but keep putting in so fast that when the lime has done slacking the kettle will be full. Put in one and one-half pounds sulphate of zinc and one pound of alum, keep it stirred until well slacked, and it will be about the consistency of cream. It is then ready for use. It will mix up with any kind of paint, even oil paint; can be used with lamp black or yellow ochre or red lead for brick walls. It forms a perfect cement, so that water will not penetrate after it gets perfectly dry. Freezing will not scale it a particle.

WHOOPING-COUGH ━━━━━━━━━━━━━━━━━━━

If a little one is choking with cold or whooping cough, put two drops of kerosene oil on the tongue. We saved our little girl by so doing.

WINDOW CLEANING ━━━━━━━━━━━━━━━━━━

To keep my windows clean and bright I use a fine sand-soap, rubbing it over the glass with a damp cloth, allowing it to dry, then polishing with a soft, clean cloth.

WINE SAUCE ━━━━━━━━━━━━━━━━━━━━━━━━

Stir together to a cream equal quantities of fresh butter and powdered sugar. When quite light add part of a grated nutmeg or ground cinnamon, as you prefer, and a pint of perfectly boiling water, after which put in a gill of Madeira wine. The sauce is quite as good with the juice of a lemon and one orange mixed, as a substitute for the wine, but then it would not be wine sauce.

WINE STAINS

Wine stains may be removed from linen by rubbing it on both sides with yellow soap, then laying on a thick paste of starch and water. Rub in well and expose to the sun and air.

WINGS

Remember that wings of turkeys, geese and chickens should never be thrown away. Many people, especially in the country, keep them simply to brush off the stove or range, but there is nothing better to wash and clean the windows. Chamois or buckskin is very good, but wings are better and do not cost anything, and their use is an economy - utilizing that which would otherwise be thrown away. They are excellent to clean the stove or hearth, to dust the furniture, but best of all to wash windows, because the corners can be easily and perfectly cleaned with them, leaving no lint behind as when cloths are used. Use the wings also to put on paste when papering walls. There is nothing that does that kind of work better.

WORMS

Mrs. A. Pemberton, from the symptoms of your child, I should say that he is troubled by worms, and if you will try my remedy I feel sure you will be pleased with the effect: Give as many drops of turpentine as the child is years of age, on sugar, every third morning before eating, until you have given nine doses; then miss nine days and commence again. Do this at every recurrence.

WORMS - REMEDIES FOR CHILDREN BOTHERED WITH THEM

Take the leaves of sage powdered fine and mixed with a little honey - teaspoonful for a dose; or flour of sulphur mixed with honey is good for worms. Sweetened milk, with a little alum added to it, is good to turn worms.

WRINKLES

For wrinkles add a few drops of tincture of benzoin when washing the face, once a day.

WRINKLES

You who desire to regain your youthful appearance will do well to make the acquaintance of the simple, but valuable, prescription here given. To make an effective wrinkle remover, mix an ounce of powdered saxolite and a half-pint witch hazel. Bathe the face in the solution - immediately every wrinkle is affected. It acts wonderfully on sagging facial muscles, also, the lotion possessing remarkable astringent and tonic properties.

YANKEE BROWN BREAD

Take equal quantities of rye and corn meal, and mix with water, making dough that can be kneaded. Work with the hands until it loses its stickiness, and will readily cleave from the fingers. Let it stand several hours, or overnight, and bake in loaves, in covered dishes, in a moderate oven, from three to five hours, or it may be steamed three hours, and baked one. Coarsely ground meal is better than fine for this kind of bread.

YANKEE PLUM PUDDING

Take a tin pudding boiler that will shut all over tight with a cover. Butter it well. Put at the bottom some stoned raisins, and then a layer of baker's bread cut in slices, with a little butter or suet, alternately, until you nearly fill the tin. Take milk enough to fill your boiler (as they vary in size), and to every quart add three or four eggs, some nutmeg and salt, and sweeten with half sugar and molasses. Drop it into boiling water, and let it boil three or four hours, and it can be eaten with a comparatively clear conscience.

YEAST

Take six good sized potatoes; boil, pare and mash them fine; then add one-half cupful of white sugar, and one quart of boiling water; stir well; set away to cool. Then add one quart of cold water; one-half pint of good yeast; and set in warm place. It will rise and be ready for use in twelve hours.

YEAST

To one cup of grated potato pour one quart of boiling water. Add one-half cup sugar and one-half cup salt. Also, when cooled till a little more than milk warm, one cup of yeast. Put in a warm place to rise. Keep in a jug in the cellar.

YELLOWED LINEN

When linen has turned yellow, cut up a pound of fine white soap into a gallon of milk, and hang it over a fire in a wash kettle. When the soap has completely melted put in the linen and boil it half an hour, then take it out. Have ready a lather of soap and water; wash the linen in it, then rinse it through two cold waters, with a very little blue in the last.

CPSIA information can be obtained at www.ICGtesting.com
Printed in the USA
LVOW070440030212

266833LV00001B/2/P

9 781432 749200